Regis College Library
100 Wellesley Street West
Toronto, Ontario
Canada
M5S 2Z5
WITHDRAWN

DEEP CALLS TO DEEP

D1598350

More Praise for *Deep Calls to Deep*

"In a world often wracked by arguments and silencing, William Brown provides a valuable witness to those of us who treasure Scripture. Using the central metaphor of 'dialogue,' this fascinating study shows how all of the Bible interacts with the Psalms in a dialogical relationship. Brown invites us not only to listen in to that lively conversation but also to join in with our voices, no matter where we are. A necessary book for our time!"

—Roy L. Heller, professor of Old Testament, Perkins School of Theology, Southern Methodist University, Dallas, TX

"In this ethically and theologically relevant book, Brown paves a way for biblical interpretation that moves beyond the division and tribalism of the present day to transformative and restorative fellowship. *Deep Calls to Deep* illuminates not just the way we read the psalms but scripture, culture, and one another."

—Patricia Vesely, assistant professor of Hebrew Bible and Christian ethics, Memphis Theological Seminary, Memphis, TN

"In this moment of societal disruption, Brown warmly invites us to sit together and consider anew the glorious psalms of our faith. We are beckoned to see how these diverse poems create a conversation with other biblical texts, not for the sake of uniformity but for the sake of courageous dialogue."

—Tyler Mayfield, A. B. Rhodes Professor of Old Testament, Louisville Presbyterian Theological Seminary, Louisville, KY

"Brown's commitment to dialogical interpretation is just what the church needs in this unsettling and divisive time. The inner-biblical reading of the Psalms in conversation with the rest of the canon clarifies the dialogical nature of biblical revelation, and Brown provides a roadmap for our own self-critical engagement with others as a journey of 'fearless dialogue.'"

—Tom Dozeman, professor of Old Testament, United Theological Seminary, Dayton, OH

"The present moment is marked by disruptions that a surface reading of a psalm(s) in isolation cannot address. Readers of the Psalms need a 'deep reading' to dialogue with other texts inside the Psalter and other texts in the Hebrew Bible."

—Stephen Breck Reid, professor of Christian scriptures, Baylor University, Waco, TX

"In *Deep Calls to Deep* Bill Brown adroitly highlights the intricate interplay between the Psalms and the rest of the Bible. Brown then weaves from this dialogue an image of how we might conceive the authority of the Bible as a sacred dialogue among its readers."

—Jerome Creach, Robert C. Holland Professor of Old Testament, Pittsburgh Theological Seminary, Pittsburgh, PA

"Conversations change us. They can stir our emotions and convince us to act. They can give us comfort and deepen our understanding. In *Deep Calls to Deep*, Bill Brown shows us the unparalleled power of conversation within the Psalms, how the Psalter engages in a dialogue with itself, with the rest of Scripture, and, ultimately, with us. *Deep Calls to Deep* calls us together to a place where the Spirit is at work, into a community where God's word and human words intersect. This conversation shapes us into something new, into something more creative and more courageous than we were before."

—Joel M. LeMon, associate professor of Old Testament, Candler School of Theology, Emory University, Atlanta, GA

WILLIAM P. BROWN

Foreword by Tremper Longman III

DEEP CALLS TO DEEP

Regis College Library
100 Wellesley Street West
Toronto, Ontario
Canada
M5S 2Z5
WITHDRAWN

The Psalms in Dialogue amid Disruption

Abingdon Press
Nashvile

BS
1430.52
.B76
2021

DEEP CALLS TO DEEP:
THE PSALMS IN DIALOGUE AMID DISRUPTION

Copyright © 2021 by Abingdon Press

All rights reserved.

No part of this work may be reproduced or transmitted in any form or by any means, electronic or mechanical, including photocopying and recording, or by any information storage or retrieval system, except as may be expressly permitted by the 1976 Copyright Act , the 1998 Digital Millennium Copyright Act, or in writing from the publisher. Requests for permission should be addressed to Rights and Permissions, Abingdon Press, 810 12th Ave South, Nashville, TN 37203, or emailed to permissions@abingdonpress.com.

Library of Congress Control Number: 2021942068

ISBN: 9781501858956

Scripture quotations unless noted otherwise are translated by the author. All rights reserved.

Scripture quotations marked CEB are from the Common English Bible. Copyright © 2011 by the Common English Bible. All rights reserved. Used by permission. www.CommonEnglishBible.com.

Scripture quotations marked NRSV are taken from New Revised Standard Version Bible, copyright © 1989 National Council of the Churches of Christ in the United States of America. Used by permission. All rights reserved worldwide. http://nrsvbibles.org/

21 22 23 24 25 26 27 28 29 30—10 9 8 7 6 5 4 3 2 1
MANUFACTURED IN THE UNITED STATES OF AMERICA

CONTENTS

PART IV: REFLECTIONS

PERSONAL PREFACE

Deep Calls to Deep is about reading the Bible, and particularly the Psalms, dialogically in a time fraught with disruption and division. The writing of this book was driven by the conviction that one vital response to disruption is to reach out in dialogue across the landscape of division, if for no other reason than the Bible models the importance of doing so. The Bible is itself the canonical product of self-critical dialogue, of "deep calling to deep" (Ps 42:7[8]).

This book invites two kinds of readers: (1) those interested in practicing transformative dialogue to overcome polarizing division and foster moral growth, and (2) those who are intrigued with reading scripture dialogically. I do not presume that these two readers are one and the same, but perhaps they should be, ideally, or at least sharing a degree of interest in both areas. As one who teaches Bible in a seminary context, I am always looking for more effective ways to encourage dialogue among students and transform each class into a just community of inquiry. I am also looking for ways to engage scripture that are transformative. Both goals converge in this study.

As I look back on the direction of my scholarship, this book serves as something of a sequel to two very different books. One is my *Handbook to Old Testament Exegesis* (WJK), which explored the practice of exegesis as a dialogical encounter between text and interpreter, as well as between interpreters holding different perspectives. In that book, I cast exegesis as a way of facilitating the move "from text to table," from the biblical text in its various contexts to a round table that invites interpreters to engage each other in mutually edifying and challenging ways. The present study carries that theme of dialogue into the ancient scriptures themselves.

This book is also a sequel to my first foray into the Psalms, *Seeing the Psalms* (2002, WJK), in which I explored the Psalms for their iconic power in dialogue with the emerging field of iconography. In that book, my love of metaphor was unabashed. In this work, I explore another powerful dimension of the Psalms: their dialogical depth. This book could have been titled *Talking the Psalms*, as a complement to the earlier work. But it has turned out to be much more than that.

Abingdon Press originally invited me to write a book that explored the Psalter as the "little Bible," a study that would treat the Psalms as a gateway to the Hebrew Bible as a whole. I was intrigued. I had always appreciated Martin Luther's characterization of the Psalter (see chapter 1). However, over the last two years the focus broadened to include how the Psalms, the most diverse book of the Bible, engage the larger biblical corpus dialogically and how the psalms engage each other in the same manner. That manner of engagement, both externally and internally to the Psalms, I wanted to address in a way that extended beyond the standard academic forays into "inner-biblical exegesis" or "intertextuality." I wanted something broader that not only addressed linguistic and thematic issues but also treated larger theological and ethical matters, issues that would engage contemporary readers. "Dialogue" was key, inspired in part by the dire need for dialogue in American life today, disrupted as it is.

The result became a more ambitious project than originally conceived, and my thanks to Abingdon Press for their patience and openness to publishing a project that has significantly grown. Thanks also to the Issachar Fund, which not only generously funded a sabbatical to devote to this project but also helped shape the project in a groundbreaking way (see acknowledgments). The result turned out to be a journey of discovery. Given the vast inclusion of various themes addressed in the Psalter, I became more intimately familiar with parts of the Hebrew Bible I had for years avoided in my writing and teaching for lack of interest. Thanks to the Psalms, my range of interest in the Hebrew Bible has widened significantly. So also has my pedagogical range. Part of the project included teaching a class on the "dialogical diversity" of scripture and reaping insights gained from it, including how to teach such a class. I figured that teaching the Bible's dialogical diversity should best be done (surprise!) dialogically. It was a natural fit, and I am a wiser teacher for it (see chapter 12).

In the process of research, writing, and teaching, I was reminded of a comment from a senior colleague some years ago who asked me about how I was planning to structure my Old Testament exegesis handbook. I told him that I wanted to include more than the tried-and-true critical methods of biblical interpretation, such as gender and postcolonial criticism. His growling response was, "You're just going to stir up a hornet's nest," and he strongly advised me to limit myself to just the classical, "objective" methods.

This was the one piece of advice of his that I did not follow, but as predicted the book did stir things up a bit. The same may be said of this book. I could have safely narrowed the focus to how the Psalms "talk" to each other within the larger biblical corpus. But never satisfied with conducting scholarship for its own sake, I ventured into exploring how the Bible's dialogical diversity offers wisdom for such a time as this. Some might call it careless, others may deem it fearless, and others will no doubt simply shrug out of indifference. I defer to the reader for judgment. Regardless, my hope is that this book inspires "fearless dialogues," to borrow from Greg Ellison's well-known work (see chapter 1). As a self-identified white, cisgendered male, I have found it increasingly important to engage in dialogue with those who are different from me, to open my eyes to the "trouble [they've] seen" in trying to survive in a world of white supremacy.

I am blessed to work with colleagues at Columbia Theological Seminary who continue to help me see what they see, every day. The journey has been difficult, and the dialogues have been painful, but transformation is underway. It has taken courage on everyone's part. If the most common commandment in the Bible is to "not be afraid," then this study is biblical both in its subject matter and beyond its subject matter.[1]

1. As a young child coping with the disruption of a family move, I received an auditory vision while walking home from school one afternoon in a stretch of desert (near Tucson). A voice seemingly from out of nowhere asked me who I was and what I was doing. After I responded, the voice, which sounded female to me, told me to "not be afraid." I have taken that to heart ever since, considering it the voice of God's *ruach* (Hebrew for "spirit").

ACKNOWLEDGMENTS

Many have contributed to this project, more than I can name. First, I thank my educational institution Columbia Theological Seminary, including its Board, for granting me a year-long sabbatical leave to pursue this project. I thank my colleagues at CTS for "filling the gap" caused by my leave, which is never easy, but it is what we do for each other to encourage each other's development as scholars. Thus, I especially thank my Old Testament colleagues, Christine Roy Yoder and Brennan Breed, for covering my absence in the classroom.

Special thanks also goes to the Issachar Fund (https://www.issacharfund.org), which made possible my sabbatical leave through a generous grant and whose application process helped broaden this project for the larger Christian community. Because this project is meant to appeal to both self-identified liberals and conservatives in the theological and political spectrum, as well as those who disdain such labels (like myself), I consulted with well-known evangelical scholar Tremper Longman III, who agreed not only to review my work as it progressed but also to write the foreword, for which I am deeply grateful. I have long appreciated Longman's scholarship. His comments on the drafts of each chapter were most welcomed, sparing me from certain blunders and, I hope, widening the book's appeal across deep-seated theological divisions. This is not to say that Longman came to agree with everything I said and that I agreed with every comment of his. That was not the point. The point was that we learned from each other in our critical conversations, putting genuine dialogue into practice. Of course, whatever shortcomings this book has in the eyes of its readers, regardless of theological persuasion, they are mine and mine alone.

I am indebted to Abingdon Press for considering this project publish-worthy. Specifically, I want to thank David Teel, now the director of Laity and Leadership at Discipleship Ministries of The United Methodist Church, for having helped conceive the original idea several years ago. Thanks also to Paul Franklyn, associate publisher of Abingdon Press, for his diligence and thoughtful engagement in seeing the project through to its published form, as well as to Katherine Johnston, my production editor.

I also want to thank the members of the class I taught during my sabbatical research, "Breaking the Impasse: Dialogue, Diversity, and Transformation in the Old Testament" (Fall 2020), at CTS. It was a new venture for them as it was for me, both in content and in delivery, during a time of pandemic disruption. Their engagement with the Bible's diversity in many ways modeled the kind of dialogue I hope for in the church, and I learned much from them. Indeed, we all learned from each other. They may have seen themselves in the beginning as students, but they quickly became colleagues as we inquired together (see chapter 12).

Speaking of colleagues, I must express my gratitude to four Columbia faculty members beyond the Old Testament area. I give thanks to Raj Nadella, whose work with Mikhail Bakhtin on the Gospel of Luke greatly influenced me, and to Mitzi Smith, whose womanist wisdom in biblical interpretation and beyond continues to inform my work. Beyond the Bible area, I am grateful to ethicist Marcia Riggs, whose work over the years on "religious ethical mediation" (REM) has been an inspiration to me, and educator Christine Hong, who continues to perfect the art of dialogue within the decolonized classroom. I also want to express my gratitude to Mark Douglas, whose wisdom in all things ethical has helped make this project sharper than it otherwise would be. And to all my faculty and administrative colleagues at CTS, whose diversity makes teaching a joyous and broadening adventure, I give thanks. Finally, a special shout-out goes to Erica Durham, director of public services, and Mary Martha Riviere, circulation coordinator, of the John Bulow Campbell Library for their indispensable help during the pandemic.

Beyond my immediate colleagues, three notables in biblical scholarship have my undying gratitude: Carol Newsom, Walter Brueggemann, and Brent Strawn. All three have been indispensable dialogue partners throughout this project and beyond. Their encouragement, along with their formative scholarship, have greatly influenced me over the years.

Finally, I give thanks to my partner in life, Gail, for her support and patience during the pandemic crisis. We were fortunate to have the sabbatical fortuitously timed with the pandemic. Nevertheless, grief struck us in the death of family members and friends, as was the case for so many others. But we also discovered much joy and gratitude in our confinement. This project would never have been completed without Gail's steady encouragement and critical reviews during such an unprecedented time for our family, including our two daughters Ella and Hannah, who were able to follow their own vocational paths despite the pandemic.

I dedicate this book to two great mentors in biblical scholarship, both of whom passed away in 2020. The first class Patrick D. Miller taught at Princeton Theological Seminary was on the Psalms, and it was the last exegesis class I took before graduating in 1985. That class launched a "trajectory" (one of Pat's favorite words) that continues to define my scholarship and teaching. S. Dean McBride was one of my first teaching colleagues at Union Presbyterian Seminary, whose formidable scholarship, love of learning, and passion for teaching have been a constant source of inspiration. Pat and Dean, not coincidentally, were fast friends. I do not stand on their shoulders; I remain seated at their feet. From them, I have witnessed the depths of theological dialogue, of "deep calling to deep." To both I dedicate this work.

Patrick D. Miller Jr.
(1935–2020)

S. Dean McBride Jr.
(1937–2020)

In Memoriam

FOREWORD

While differing on its exact role and even scope, Christians of various ecclesial families (Catholic, Orthodox, mainline Protestant, and evangelical Protestant) regard the Bible as central to their faith and practice. The church throughout the centuries has proclaimed the Bible's essential place by acknowledging the Bible as canonical, as the standard of its faith and practice. That acknowledgment derives from the Bible's own testimony that it is the Word of God. Again, while differing on precisely how, most Christians turn to the Bible to hear the voice of God.

In *Deep Calls to Deep,* William Brown explores the dialogical nature of biblical revelation. He reminds us that the Bible is not a neat and tidy book, easily systematized or reduced to a series of straightforward propositions, but rather a collection of books in dialogue with each other. The Bible is a community of voices, not always saying the same thing in the same way, but rather offering differing perspectives that might at first strike us as wild and messy.

Brown brilliantly demonstrates the dialogical nature of scripture by moving through the various parts of the Old Testament (Torah, Prophets, Writings) to put them in dialogue with the book of Psalms. The Psalms themselves are a "little Bible" (so Martin Luther) or "an epitome of the whole of scriptures" (Athanasius), so Brown also explores the discussions that take place within that book itself. Indeed, Brown's exposition of psalms throughout the book is especially insightful, the result of his lifelong study.

Contrary to the Bible's dialogical nature, our first impulse is often to tame the biblical testimony through harmonization. That is typically done by coercing one of the voices to fit with the other in a way that silences one. Such a static reading of the Bible produces a flat interpretation. Brown's call for a "deep reading" ("a text's possible meaning in relation to other texts") along with a "close reading" of scripture leads us to a rich and lifegiving appreciation of scripture's role in our lives.

A deep reading of scripture that recognizes the Bible's dialogical nature encourages self-criticism and openness among its readers, a kind of interpretive humility, as well as cultivates a kind of wisdom that is sensitive to which voice of the dialogue might be most relevant for our present situation, both individually and as a community. A dialogical reading of scripture, I believe, should also bring us to prize listening to diverse interpretive voices as people different from us read scripture. Perhaps these fellow readers will attend to the part of the biblical dialogue that we might read over or disregard. Brown winsomely presents a "text to table" picture of interpretation, by which he means a table of discussion of diverse perspectives grounded in the diverse perspectives offered by scripture. In our present disruptive day, I hear his proposal with hopeful ears.

While Brown wisely limits his demonstration of the Bible's dialogical nature to that which exists between the various parts of the Old Testament and the Psalms, his study encourages attention to dialogue more broadly conceived. For example, my thoughts move to debates (that should be dialogues) within my own circles. These debates flow from different biblical testimonies that seem to make different, even contradictory points. Does God change his mind? Yes (Num 23:19; 1 Sam 15:29) or no (Jonah 3:10)? Are the children of sinners punished for the sin of their parents? Yes (Exod 34:7) or no (Jer 31:29-30; Ezek 18:2)? Is wisdom a gift of God (Prov 2:6) or something for which we strive (Prov 4:4-9)? For that matter, is salvation a gift of God or something that we work out with fear and trembling? Apparently, yes to both (Phil 2:12-13)!

As most who are familiar with these discussions know, such questions are usually resolved by choosing one side of the dialogue and explaining away the other. A more constructive dialogical approach to the Bible suggests that both sides should be held in tension. Perhaps both communicate important lessons to us. Perhaps one side of the equation will be particularly relevant for us or our community at a particular moment in our lives. A proper dialogical reading of scripture allows us to discuss and hold these at first apparently divergent passages in constructive tension.

I should point out that Brown is not saying the Bible is a collection that gives every voice a hearing. While inclusive, he rightly recognizes that it is not comprehensive. There are constraints on diversity. In terms of the Old Testament, Baʿal worshippers are not invited to the table. Those who systematically oppress the poor aren't invited either. The prophets don't open their arms to Baʿal worshippers or oppressors but rather first call them to repentance. There are limits too on who today can be invited and who should be called to repentance. I would suggest those who use the Bible in the interest of white supremacy or racist causes are not those we listen to with an open mind for their perspective but those whom we need to call to repentance before allowing them to the table.

Still even with these constraints Brown's study is particularly timely. As he points out, dialogue is especially critical during times of disruption, and by all accounts the world and the United States in particular are at a moment of division. Wracked by a global pandemic, we struggle over issues of justice when it comes to race and climate. Partisanship divides our political landscape.

Theology too has longstanding divides that continue today. For decades, for instance, mainline and evangelical churches have been in competition. Brown's work on the dialogical nature of biblical revelation gives ground to and should inspire a move from competition to discussion. That is why I, an evangelical biblical scholar, am so impressed and persuaded by this important book written by William Brown (a mainline biblical scholar). My hope and prayer is that many in all the ecclesial families will read this book with an open mind and heart as we all seek to hear the voice of God together.

Tremper Longman III
Distinguished Scholar and Professor Emeritus of Biblical Studies
Westmont College

ABBREVIATIONS

AB	Anchor Bible
AOTC	Abingdon Old Testament Commentary
AYB	Anchor Yale Bible
BCE	before the Common Era
BDB	Brown, Francis, S. R. Driver, and Charles A. Briggs. *The Brown-Driver-Briggs Hebrew and English Lexicon.* Peabody, MA: Hendrickson, 1996
BHS	*Biblia Hebraica Stuttgartensia.* Edited by Karl Elliger and William Rudolph. Stuttgart: Deutsche Bibelstiftung, 1983
BLS	Bible and Literature Series
BZAW	Beihefte zur Zeitschrift für die altestamentliche Wissenschaft
CBQ	Catholic Biblical Quarterly
CEB	Common English Bible
chap(s).	chapter(s)
Dtr	Deuteronomistic
DtrH	Deuteronomistic History
GKC	*Gesenius' Hebrew Grammar.* Edited by E. Kautzsch. Translated by A. E. Cowley. 2nd ed. Oxford, 1910
HALOT	Koehler, Ludwig, Walter Baumgartner, and Johann J. Stamm. *The Hebrew and Aramaic Lexicon of the Old Testament: Study Edition.* Edited and translated by M. E. J. Richardson. 2 vols. Leiden: Brill, 2001
HTR	*Harvard Theological Review*
IBC	Interpretation: A Bible Commentary for Teaching and Preaching

IBHS	Waltke, Bruce K., and Michael O'Connor. *An Introduction to Biblical Hebrew Syntax.* Eisenbrauns: Winona Lake, IN, 1990
IBT	Interpreting Biblical Texts
Int	*Interpretation: A Journal of Bible and Theology*
JBL	*Journal of Biblical Literature*
JET	*Jahrbuch für Evangelische Theologie*
JETS	*Journal of the Evangelical Theological Society*
JPS	Jewish Publication Society
JSOT	*Journal for the Study of the Old Testament*
JSOTSup	Journal for the Study of the Old Testament Supplement Series
KJV	King James Version
LHB/OTS	Library of Hebrew Bible/Old Testament Studies
LNTS	Library of New Testament Studies
LXX	Septuagint
MT	Masoretic Text
NASB	New American Standard Bible
NIV	New International Version
NJPS	*Tanakh: The Holy Scriptures; The New JPS Translation according to the Traditional Hebrew Text*
NRSV	New Revised Standard Version
NTL	New Testament Library
OBT	Overtures to Biblical Theology
OED III	*The Oxford English Dictionary, Volume III.* 2nd edition. Prepared by J. A. Simpson and E. S. C. Weiner. Oxford: Clarendon Press, 1991
OTL	Old Testament Library
RB	*Revue biblique*
SBLDS	Society of Biblical Literature Dissertation Series
SJSJ	Supplements to the Journal for the Study of Judaism
VT	*Vetus Testamentum*
VTSup	Supplements to Vetus Testamentum
WJK	Westminster John Knox Press
WUNT	Wissenschaftliche Untersuchungen zum Neuen Testamentum
ZAW	*Zeitschrift für die alttestamentliche Wissenschaft*

CHAPTER 1
INTRODUCTION: FROM DISRUPTION TO DIALOGUE

He could only fight with his words.

He was fighting for his life with his words,

and nobody would listen.

—Angela Harrelson[1]

In her book *No, You Shut Up,* political commentator Symone Sanders recounts an interview she had on CNN with Chris Cuomo in conversation with Ken Cuccinelli, the former attorney general of Virginia, about the white nationalist demonstrations in Charlottesville in August of 2017.

> The debate got heated, and we began talking over each other. Cuccinelli accused me of jumping from one thing to another; I replied I was being factual, and he was hedging to avoid the heart of the issue. . . . Cuccinelli tried to redirect the conversation. . . . By that point I was fuming. "And now someone's dead," I cut in. Cuccinelli did not like that. "Can I finish, Symone? Will you just shut up for a minute and let me finish?" "Pardon

1. The aunt of George Floyd, quoted in Molly Hennessy-Fiske, "Pain of Racism Nothing New to Floyd's Family," *Los Angeles Times* (June 4, 2020), at https://www.latimes.com/world-nation/story/2020-06-03/the-many-chapters-marked-by-racism-in-george-floyds-family-history.

> me, sir," I began, my voice getting louder. . . . "You don't tell me to shut up on national television." Cuomo agreed, and he said so. "Then how do you make them stop talking when they keep interrupting you?" Cuccinelli continued. "'Them'? 'They'?" I said. "I'm sitting right here!"[2]

So much for dialogue. The heated exchange offers a hard lesson on what to avoid in order to engage in genuine dialogue: "talking over" each other, accusation, interruption, changing the topic, and objectification, to name a few. Rather than about winning debates, Sanders's timely book is about hosting "constructive, critical conversations" that welcome divergent viewpoints for the sake of "innovation," "creativity," and "change."[3] The need for such dialogue, the kind that "reaches across the aisles" of division and counters the "othering" of others, is paramount for such a time as this. And how shall we describe this time in a word?

Many Faces of Disruption

"Disruption" comes to mind, manifest on so many levels: physical, political, social, environmental, economic, existential. Perhaps 2020 will be considered the year of the "perfect storm" of disruptions, which assumes, of course, that the subsequent years will not be quite as bad. Only time will tell. But for 2020, here are a few examples.

Pandemic

The disruption wrought by the novel coronavirus (COVID-19) killed multitudes, more so in America than in any other country, over five hundred thousand lives in the first twelve months of the pandemic. It crippled economies and exacerbated social misery in unprecedented measure within anyone's lifetime. The virus exposed social and economic inequities, particularly among communities of color, who have suffered greatly in the US due to lack of accessible healthcare and crushing poverty.

2. Symone D. Sanders, *No, You Shut Up: Speaking Truth to Power and Reclaiming America* (New York: HarperCollins, 2020), 2–3.

3. Sanders, *No, You Shut Up*, 222.

Responses to the virus lamentably widened deep political divisions in America, such as between those who adopted safety measures informed by science and those who regarded such measures as infringements on their individual rights, the latter reflecting a deadly mix of rugged individualism, personal liberty, and social entitlement. "Live Free or Die," the state motto of New Hampshire, took on a new twist in 2020: Live Free *and* Die. Live carelessly without regard for your health and that of others, live in disregard of science, and you are more likely to get sick and infect others. To mask or not to mask became a matter of identity politics. And science, which champions objectivity, became subjected to political bias in its interpretation in the public arena, a "biopartisan" issue.[4] What should have united Americans in the fight against such an insidious foe only sowed further division, with catastrophic results.

Environmental Catastrophes

The pandemic was only one example of environmental catastrophe that beset 2020.[5] The summer marked another unprecedented season of extreme disasters, from wildfires raging in the West to the devastating hurricanes in the Southeast. More acres were burned in one year than in any past year in recorded history, fueled by drought and near record-setting heat.[6] The year 2020 marked the most active Atlantic hurricane season in meteorological history, exhausting all alphabetically based names for tropical storms. For the second time ever, the Greek alphabet was deployed to name a seemingly unending series of storms. In response to these catastrophes, many Americans decided to move and establish homes elsewhere, resulting in what could be called the "great climate migration."[7] The often-referenced phrase *climate change* does not do justice to describing

4. This neologism was coined by Morgan Daly Dedyo in NextGen Voices, "Defining Events: 2020 in Hindsight," *Science* 371, no. 6524 (January 1, 2020): 22.

5. Most scientists are agreed that the novel coronavirus resulting in COVID-19 was likely the result of human encroachment upon wildlife.

6. Case in point: 130 degrees in Death Valley on August 16, 2020.

7. See the sobering assessment in Abraham Lustgarten, "The Great Climate Migration: Climate Change Will Force a New American Migration," *ProPublica* (September 15, 2020), at https://www.propublica.org/article/climate-change-will-force-a-new-american-migration.

the unfolding disaster that is affecting all life on the planet. Better is *climate disruption*—anthropogenic disturbance and disorder of the earth's circulatory atmosphere to the detriment of the entire biosphere.

White Supremacy and Racialized Hatred

Often referred to as "COVID-1619," there remains the unrelenting scourge of systemic racism, which continues to disrupt and degrade social life for non-whites in America, ranging from the steady stream of indignities suffered in the workplace ("microaggressions") to mass incarceration, from the lack of opportunities to develop intergenerational wealth to the now-publicized spasms of police brutality that have galvanized much of the nation.[8] Such are a few of the enduring legacies of African enslavement that began over four hundred years ago when at least twenty Africans were forcibly brought to Jamestown in August of 1619.[9] In the wake of recent killings of African Americans by the police and white vigilantes, renewed calls for racial justice erupted in nearly every urban center in America in the form of massive protests. In addition, the killings and beatings of Asian Americans and Pacific Islanders during the pandemic have also roiled the nation. If there are two mottos that best capture this year of racialized violence and hate crimes, they are, "I can't breathe" and "I'm not a virus."

Demographic Change

Americans of European descent are beginning to face the disruption of demographic change. According to the Census Bureau, 2013 was the

8. As of this writing, the killings include Ahmaud Arbery in the Brunswick area of Georgia, chased down and shot while jogging (2/23/2020); Breonna Taylor, killed by a hail of bullets from the police in Louisville under a "no-knock warrant" (3/13/2020); George Floyd, suffocated by a police officer's knee placed on his neck for nine minutes and twenty-nine seconds in Minneapolis (5/25/2020); Rayshard Brooks, shot twice in the back by a police officer while escaping arrest at a Wendy's restaurant in Atlanta (6/12/2020); and Andre Hill, shot by a police officer while he was visiting a family friend in Columbus, Ohio (12/22/2020).

9. However, enslaved (as well as some free) Africans were present in America much earlier, perhaps as early as Christopher Columbus in the late fifteenth century, but at least by 1526 with the Spanish occupation of Florida. See Crystal Ponti, "America's History of Slavery Began Long before Jamestown," *History* (August 26, 2019), at https://www.history.com/news/american-slavery-before-jamestown-1619.

first year that a majority of infants in the US under the age of one were non-white.[10] According to some projections, "non-Hispanic whites" will be in the minority by 2044, displaced by African Americans and those of "Hispanic origin."[11] Whites, who have been the dominant force in political life since America's birth, are now facing imminent minority status within the next twenty-three years. Such a tectonic social shift is considered by many whites to be a threat to their culturally entitled privileges, as demonstrated by the mounting backlash of resentment, hostility, and violence.[12] At the same time, such perceived loss of status is crippling the health of middle-aged white people.[13]

Partisan Polarization

Within the turbulent realm of politics, the explosion of partisan polarization in 2020 disrupted sound governance, particularly at the national level in response to the pandemic, and the presidential election, replete with false allegations of widespread election fraud. It all came to a head on January 6, 2021, when an angry mob, incited by President Donald J. Trump, besieged the United States Capitol, threatening the lives of members of Congress and delaying the certification process of the national election. On that day, democracy itself was disrupted.

In his investigative book *Why We're Polarized*, Ezra Klein documents how within the last fifty years the two main political parties in America

10. D'Vera Cohn, "It's Official: Minority Babies Are the Majority among the Nation's Infants, but Only Just," *Pew Research Center* (June 23, 2016), at https://www.pewresearch.org/fact-tank/2016/06/23/its-official-minority-babies-are-the-majority-among-the-nations-infants-but-only-just/.

11. See Noor Wazwaz, "It's Official: The U.S. Is Becoming a Minority-Majority Nation," *US News and World Report* (July 6, 2015), at http://www.usnews.com/news/articles/2015/07/06/its-official-the-us-is-becoming-a-minority-majority-nation.

12. Ezra Klein, "White Threat in a Browning America: How Demographic Change Is Fracturing Our Politics," *Vox* (July 30, 2018), at https://www.vox.com/policy-and-politics/2018/7/30/17505406/trump-obama-race-politics-immigration.

13. As discussed in Isabel Wilkerson, *Caste: The Origins of Our Discontents* (New York: Random House, 2020), 178–86. She draws from the work of Anne Case and Angus Deaton, "Rising Morbidity and Mortality in Midlife among White Non-Hispanic Americans in the 21st Century," *Proceedings of the National Academy of Sciences* 112, no. 49 (December 8, 2015): 15078–83.

"sorted" themselves to the point of being ideological opponents on most major issues.[14] As a result, policy debates frequently degenerated into ideological battles driven by identity politics.

> We are so locked into our political identities that there is virtually no candidate, no information, no condition, that can force us to change our minds. We will justify almost anything or anyone so long as it helps our side, and the result is a politics devoid of guardrails, standards, persuasion, or accountability.[15]

"What was once a positive-sum negotiation becomes a zero-sum war."[16] Or call it "pure political tribalism."[17] The ultimate, if not singular, point in politics now is to make the other side lose, and at all costs. Much of national politics in America can be characterized by "negative partisanship," driven "not by positive feelings toward the party you support but [by] negative feelings toward the party you oppose."[18] As a rule, "polarization begets polarization."[19] The proliferation of information sources, from cable channels to Twitter, has not helped. "Polarized media doesn't emphasize commonalities, it weaponizes differences; it doesn't focus on the best of the other side, it threatens you with the worst."[20] On hot-button issues, such as abortion and climate change, reasoning is often reduced to rationalizing or emotional venting, and receiving more information or facts seems to have little effect.[21] Partisan polarization fueled by increasing mutual distrust has turned American society into an arena of intractable moral conflict.

---

14. Ezra Klein, *Why We're Polarized* (New York: Avid Reader Press, 2020).

15. Klein, *Why We're Polarized*, xiv.

16. Klein, *Why We're Polarized*, xix.

17. Amy Chua, *Political Tribes: Group Instinct and the Fate of Nations* (New York: Penguin, 2018), 177.

18. Klein, *Why We're Polarized*, 9–10.

19. Klein, *Why We're Polarized*, 33.

20. Klein, *Why We're Polarized*, 149.

21. Klein, *Why We're Polarized*, 90–98.

The year 2020 (into 2021) illustrates well how genuine dialogue in American life is far too often replaced by rancorous division, empathy displaced by demonization. Ad hominem attacks are frequently the norm in political debates. Legitimate criticism and protest are deemed treasonous. Peaceful protesters are identified with looters and considered terrorists,[22] and domestic terrorists are considered patriots. The acrimony with which competing groups treat each other is symptomatic of deep-seated divisions sustained by misunderstanding, ignorance, distrust, bias, and outright lies. All in all, common ground no longer seems attainable, and the "common good" seems to be only an illusion.

As bad as it can be, polarization alone is not the problem, according to Klein. "In a multiparty system, polarization is sometimes required for our political disagreements to express themselves. The alternative to polarization often isn't consensus but suppression."[23] The real issue, at least politically, is how to keep functioning amid polarization in ways that can be beneficial to everyone.[24] Klein's solution is to work toward greater democratization of the American political system, all to achieve a more equitable "balancing" of political powers.[25] On the personal level, Klein proposes the practice of "identity mindfulness," the cultivation of self-critical awareness of one's own multiple identities, including an awareness of how they are *activated* in public discourse and *manipulated* by politicians and the media.[26] Klein also proposes practicing a "politics of place," in which more focus is directed toward local politics, where more personal interaction occurs and more immediate change is possible.[27]

Missing, however, among Klein's solutions is any attempt to retrieve a sense of the collective, as encapsulated in America's de facto motto (until

22. See Patrisse Khan-Cullors and Asha Bandele, *When They Call You a Terrorist: A Black Lives Matter Memoir* (New York: St. Martin's Press, 2018), esp. 3–8, 252–53.

23. Klein, *Why We're Polarized*, 249.

24. Klein, *Why We're Polarized*, 250.

25. For Klein, that includes doing away with the Electoral College and jettisoning the Senate filibuster. One could add to the list gerrymandering and voter suppression.

26. Klein, *Why We're Polarized*, 262–63.

27. Klein, *Why We're Polarized*, 264–66.

1956), *e pluribus unum* ("one out of many").[28] Amy Chua builds on this notion of unity out of diversity to counter the political tribalism that has balkanized national political life. America, she states, qualifies as a "super-group," a rarity among nations. Neither a triumphalist label nor an endorsement of American exceptionalism, a "super-group" is a distinctive kind of organization: one in which membership is open to individuals from all different backgrounds—ethnic, religious, racial, cultural. Even more fundamentally, a super-group does not require its members to shed or suppress their subgroup identities. On the contrary, it allows subgroup identities to thrive, even as individuals are bound together by a strong, overarching collective identity.[29]

For much of its history, America could not come close to such a status. Chua identifies the "civil rights revolution" as instrumental in moving the US toward "super-group" status, still more of an ideal than an achievement. Far from being a melting pot, a super-group is held together by a certain connectivity that complements rather than competes with its diversity. In America's case, that connectivity at the political level is the Constitution, its founding document,[30] itself subject to opposing judicial modes of interpretation.[31]

While the year 2020 was marked by unprecedented crises, its enumerated designation connotes "hindsight." How apt. Unprecedented in scale does not necessarily mean unexpected in context, including a rampaging novel coronavirus, police killings of Black men and women, environmental disasters, and the most tumultuous year of presidential governance in anyone's lifetime. "If we had only known . . .," "we" being those who refused to listen to the rumblings and warnings of the past, another mani-

28. The motto coupled with its converse (see below) draws from Heraclitus's tenth fragment, "The one out of all things, and all things out of the one" (*ek pantōn hen ex henos panta*).

29. Chua, *Political Tribes*, 12.

30. Chua, *Political Tribes*, 27–28.

31. Such as the originalist (i.e., textualist or intentionalist) and pragmatist positions. Sometimes this is cast in terms of viewing the US Constitution as either a "dead" or "living" document. For a nuanced discussion of the hermeneutical implications of originalism in biblical study, see Greg Carey, "Originalism in Bible and Law," *Church Anew* (October 15, 2020), at https://churchanew.org/blog/posts/greg-carey-originalism-in-bible-and-in-law.

festation of our intractable divisions. "We" should have known, and do so now by hindsight, of these reckonings long deferred.

Disruption and division fit hand in glove, one exacerbating the other like a positive feedback loop. The default response to disruption is to hunker down and circle the wagons, to find solace among like-minded folk while blaming others out of distrust and fear. By contrast, reaching out across our differences in a spirit of trust and collaboration seems to cut against the very grain of human nature. But that is patently not true: cooperation has been key to the evolutionary success of *Homo sapiens* ever since emerging three hundred thousand years ago.[32] For human beings, cooperation has proven to be of greater evolutionary value than competition. While the impulse to dehumanize those outside of one's in-group is strong, as tragically confirmed time and again, so also is the desire for inclusion and cooperation.[33]

This study of the Psalms proposes a modest agenda: to help cultivate inclusive, mutual dialogue within the church as a transforming witness to our collective life during this time of profound disruption and rancorous division. America's collective life, riven as it is, remains intact by the ideals of democracy, which "at its best . . . is full of contention and fluid disagreement but free of settled patterns of mutual disdain. Democracy depends on trustful talk with strangers."[34] Likewise, the health and mission of the church depends on "trustful talk" among Christians, on dialogue without disdain.

The Church: Trustful Strangers at the Table

Christians tend to mirror America's culture wars. Worse, the Christian Bible, the church's "founding document," is often deployed to fuel

32. The scientific literature on the evolutionary value of cooperation is vast, but a highly accessible account can be found in Brian Hare and Vanessa Woods, *Survival of the Friendliest: Understanding Our Origins and Rediscovering Our Common Humanity* (New York: Random House, 2020).

33. See Hare and Woods, *Survival of the Friendliest*, 150–85.

34. Danielle S. Allen, *Talking to Strangers: Anxieties of Citizenship since* Brown v. Board of Education (Chicago: The University of Chicago Press, 2004), xiii. In her work, Allen seeks to develop a "citizenship of political friendship" that is based on sacrifice.

division. James Calvin Davis identified in 2010 the "big four" issues that have divided Christians for many years: abortion, stem-cell research, euthanasia, and gay marriage.[35] One could add climate disruption and white supremacy. Over such issues, Christians have become strangers to each other, even within families.

Nevertheless, diverse and divided as they are, Christians profess their unity in Christ. Where, then, can such unity be found on the ground? Where *should* it be found? I propose at least one place of practice: the table of fellowship, where people of faith engage in good faith and in genuine dialogue across their ideological differences and cultural identities.[36] In addition to the church's unity in Christ, the biblical precedent is strong for striving toward such dialogue. Far from recounting God's curse against humanity, the "tower of Babel" story of Genesis 11:1-9 illustrates God's embrace of cultural diversity. As its continuation, the Pentecost story in Acts 2:1-13 demonstrates God's desire for the church to communicate the gospel across and within diverse cultures and communities, not at their expense but in their flourishing.[37] How can such communication take place for the sake of all cultures? Dialogically.

The need for Christians to engage in dialogue across political, cultural, racial, ideological, and theological divisions is dire. One would think that communities of faith could practice empathic ways of listening and self-searching dialogue leading to mutual understanding and even transformation. To do so, moreover, during this time of rancorous division and polarizing fear would be nothing short of prophetic—a clarion call to the world. But, alas, the fear of conflict and change, coupled with an

---

35. James Calvin Davis, *In Defense of Civility: How Religion Can Unite America on Seven Moral Issues That Divide Us* (Louisville: Westminster John Knox, 2010), 76. In a more recent work, Davis identifies "forbearance" or "bearing with one another" as a fundamental Christian virtue for dealing with conflict and division (*Forbearance: A Theological Ethic for a Disagreeable Church* [Grand Rapids: Eerdmans, 2017]).

36. The image is borrowed from the inclusive fellowship of "table community" practiced in the early Christian church, as modeled in Jesus's eating with others. See, e.g., János Bolyki, *Jesu Tischgemeinschaften*, WUNT 96 (Tübingen: Mohr Siebeck, 1998).

37. See Kathleen M. O'Connor, "Let All the Peoples Praise You: Biblical Studies and a Hermeneutics of Hunger," *CBQ* 72, no. 1 (2010): 1–14; Theodore Hiebert, *The Beginning of Difference: Discovering Identity in God's Diverse World* (Nashville: Abingdon, 2019).

unwillingness to engage in self-critical examination, continues to deter even faith communities from engaging in dialogue as the first step toward nurturing moral growth and transformation. Nevertheless, Christians have every good reason to engage in dialogue, and that reason comes first and foremost from the "Good Book."

The Bible

Many Christians are unaware that the Bible, inspired and foundational as it is, is itself an *e pluribus unum*, a work of theological and literary diversity. It is also, historically, a manifold response to monumental disruptions in the lives of communities, spanning centuries upon centuries of struggle, from military defeat and exile to occupation and imperial oppression.

Disruption and Diversity

Much of the Hebrew Bible was written in the wake of national disruption and trauma brought about particularly from the Babylonian invasion and destruction of Jerusalem (597–539 BCE).[38] The Northern Kingdom ("Israel") had earlier fallen to the Assyrian Empire (722 BCE), with a substantial portion of its population deported and new ethnic groups settled in the land,[39] resulting in complete cultural upheaval (2 Kgs 17:5-41). The Southern Kingdom ("Judah") survived for nearly a century and a half more before succumbing to the reigning superpower of the day, Babylon, under Nebuchadnezzar II (605–562 BCE), whose "captain of the

38. Trauma studies of the Bible are legion. For a sampling, see Elizabeth Boase and Christopher G. Frechette, ed., *The Bible through the Lens of Trauma,* Semeia Studies 86 (Atlanta: SBL Press, 2016); David M. Carr, *Holy Resilience: The Bible's Traumatic Origins* (New Haven, CT: Yale University Press, 2014); Kathleen M. O'Connor, *Jeremiah: Pain and Promise* (Minneapolis: Fortress, 2011), 19–27; O'Connor, *Lamentations and the Tears of the World* (Maryknoll, NY: Orbis, 2002); Daniel L. Smith-Christopher, *A Biblical Theology of Exile,* OBT (Minneapolis: Fortress, 2002). For a thorough historical analysis of the Babylonian exile, see Rainer Albertz, *Israel in Exile: The History and Literature of the Sixth Century B.C.E,* trans. David Green, Studies in Biblical Literature 3 (Atlanta: SBL Press, 2003), esp. 70–111.

39. 2 Kgs 17:24 refers to the peoples of "Babylon, Cuthah, Avva, Hammath, and Sepharvaim" being settled in the "cities of Samaria."

bodyguard," Nebuzaradan, burned Jerusalem's temple to the ground and destroyed its walls in 587 BCE (2 Kgs 25:8-10).

One historian's estimate is that up to 25 percent of the population of Judah was exiled to Babylonia via at least three waves of deportation.[40] The Deuteronomistic history claims that only the "poorest people of the land" were left (2 Kgs 24:14; 25:12), while 2 Chronicles insists that the entire surviving population was deported and the land lay "desolate" to enjoy its "sabbath rest" (2 Chron 36:20-21). While historians continue to debate the extent of Israel's collapse in the aftermath of Babylonian conquest, to say that many Israelite lives in the sixth century were "disrupted" would be an understatement. In response to such national trauma, an "almost frenzied literary production" took place, and in a host of genres.[41] Such production continued unabated beyond the exilic period, but often with a backward glance.

Social disruption in whatever form has a way of inspiring literary activity. The prolific Southern novelist Walker Percy was asked in 1962 why so many great writers have arisen from the American South. He answered with a mixture of shame and laughter, "Because we lost the war,"[42] which prompted another Southern writer Flannery O'Connor to write, "Dear Mr. Percy, I'm glad we lost the War."[43] One must also acknowledge many Black authors from the South and the North, from Toni Morrison and Maya Angelou to Ta-Nehisi Coates, who have confronted the horrific disruption of enslavement and its harrowing aftermaths, all wrought by the uniquely American caste system.[44]

Much of ancient Israel's literary activity codified in the Hebrew and Aramaic scriptures was driven by what one could call "pain seeking under-

40. Albertz, *Israel in Exile*, 88–89.

41. Albertz, *Israel in Exile*, 4.

42. See Allan Gurganus, "At Last, the South Loses Well," Opinion, *New York Times* (December 8, 1996) at https://www.nytimes.com/1996/12/08/opinion/at-last-the-south-loses-well.html.

43. Warren Cole Smith, "We're All 'Moviegoers' Now: Fifty Years Ago Walker Percy's *The Moviegoer* Launched an Unlikely Literary Career," *World Magazine* (July 14, 2012), at https://world.wng.org/2012/06/were_all_moviegoers_now.

44. See the encompassing analysis in Wilkerson, *Caste*.

standing." And such understanding was by no means uniform: national trauma generated a wide variety of responses, from the psalmic laments to historical retellings, from short stories and sapiential lessons to prophetic pronouncements. As the product in part of disruption's trauma, the Bible stands out for its literary diversity, including its conflicting viewpoints, all embedded in an overarching complexity forged from its divergent parts. Biblical scholar Seth Sanders observes that the Pentateuch is literarily unique in this regard, particularly in comparison to its ancient Mesopotamian counterparts. Genesis and Exodus, for example, are filled with incompatible yet parallel narratives that prove to be "glaringly inconsistent,"[45] resulting in an "incoherent interwoven source."[46] "The interweaving of parallel variants of the same event" without any attempt to harmonize is the Pentateuch's "most problematic and important feature."[47]

"Problematic"? Sanders does not use the term pejoratively, although I would have preferred "unprecedented." Put another way, the Pentateuch's "problematic" incoherence is its badge of honor. Sanders argues that such inconsistencies result in a biblical text that is "radically incoherent, yet still strangely readable."[48] Scripture's "strange" readability, I would add, is part of its appeal. What Sanders calls problematic is one of the Bible's most promising and powerful features for contemporary readers, as I hope to demonstrate. Sanders does find one value in the Bible's "incoherence": he claims that in light of the conflicting flood stories in Genesis 6–9 and the divergent creation accounts in Genesis 1–3, "comprehensiveness trumps cohesion."[49] The Pentateuchal authors and editors found great value in bringing together divergent accounts of common narrated events rather

45. Seth L. Sanders, "What If There Aren't Any Empirical Models for Pentateuchal Criticism?" in *Contextualizing Israel's Sacred Writings: Ancient Literacy, Orality, and Literary Production,* ed. Brian B. Schmidt, Ancient Israel and Its Literature 22 (Atlanta: SBL Press, 2015), 300. Drawing from Jeffrey Tigay's groundbreaking work, Sanders argues that the Gilgamesh Epic resembles the Genesis Flood Story in terms of its "sources" or "elements" but not in its "form" (282–83; for detailed comparison, see pp. 287–94).

46. Sanders, "What If There Aren't Any Empirical Models," 299.

47. Sanders, "What If There Aren't Any Empirical Models," 282.

48. Sanders, "What If There Aren't Any Empirical Models," 282.

49. Sanders, "What If There Aren't Any Empirical Models," 301.

than settling on one consistent story or seeking a harmonized unity. The same could be said of the four Gospel accounts in the New Testament, each one bearing its distinctive perspective(s). Our biblical editors and canonizers, in other words, recognized "the danger of a single story."[50]

However, to claim "comprehensiveness" as the single driving force behind the Bible's literary and theological diversity is open to question. I suspect that even as our ancient authors and editors masterfully wove together divergent perspectives, they also, at the same time, rejected other possible viewpoints, even alternative traditions. To be more cautious, I would propose "relative inclusiveness" rather than complete "comprehensiveness," recognizing that our biblical tradents rejected certain perspectives and traditions about God, such as YHWH having a female consort or arboreal cult object, which we know from archaeology was a widespread belief among Israelites.[51] The Bible embraces its theological diversity while also holding fast to certain nonnegotiable convictions regarding the character of Israel's God.[52] We do not know all the objectives and motivations that were at play in the production of scripture, but we do know that the Bible's composers were not slaves to consistency, as Sanders well points out. They excelled in preserving variant perspectives, accounts, and legal material, if only to a relative degree. The result is an expansive, eclectic sacred text, more an anthology than a book. The Bible is no echo chamber.

Dialogue

Why does the Bible preserve such a diversity of perspectives and traditions? In some cases, the Bible's canonical inclusiveness is strikingly

50. To borrow from the well-known Ted Talk given by Nigerian author Chimamanda Ngozi Adichie, *Ted Talk* (October 7, 2009) at https://www.youtube.com/watch?v=D9Ihs241zeg&t=47s.

51. See, e.g., the discussion in William G. Dever, *Did God Have a Wife? Archaeology and Folk Religion in Ancient Israel* (Grand Rapids: Eerdmans, 2005). See also chapter 6.

52. For an overview of the historical and theological complexities of ancient Israel's God within Israel's Canaanite context, see Mark S. Smith, *The Early History of God: Yahweh and Other Deities in Ancient Israel,* 2nd ed. (Grand Rapids: Eerdmans, 2002).

ironic: later traditions that were intended to replace earlier ones came to be bound together in fine codified fashion.[53] Even if "comprehensiveness" was a goal for the ancient editors of scripture, the question remains, why try to attain it? What purpose inspired such inclusivity? My guess is that *eliciting dialogue* was at least one critical aim,[54] if only from the simple fact that dialogue emerges when two or more differing perspectives are presented together without resolution or finalization. For ancient Israel, such dialogical diversity was, in part, a multifaceted way of understanding the disruptions it had suffered. With diversity as its "problematic" hallmark, the Bible itself could be called a "super-book."

The "Little Bible"

The same could be said of a particular corpus within the Bible: the book of Psalms, a "super-Psalter." While typically viewed as a book of ancient prayers and hymns, the Psalter's greatest hallmark is its theological and literary variety, providing some of the most dramatic examples of dialogical diversity set forth in scripture. The Psalter could easily have been less diverse and, hence, much shorter in length. Its 150 psalms (in MT; 151 in LXX or Greek Septuagint; 155 in the Syriac Bible) could have been more "cookie cutter" in its makeup, resulting in a much shorter Psalter. But no. The Psalter's diversity is characterized not only by its various genres but more so by its content, as we shall see.

Being so wide ranging in its theological scope and diversity, the Psalter was aptly called by Martin Luther as "a little Bible" (*eine kleine Biblia*). In his 1545 (1528) "Preface to the Psalter," Martin Luther gives his reasons:

> The Psalter ought to be a precious and beloved book, if for no other reason than this: it promises Christ's death and resurrection so clearly—and pictures his kingdom and the condition and nature of all Christendom—that it might well be called a little Bible. In it is comprehended most beautifully and briefly everything that is in the entire Bible . . . almost an entire

53. As, for example, with the Covenant Code and Deuteronomic Law. See chapter 6.

54. One could also include "compromise" in some cases. See, e.g., Walter Brueggemann, "Twin Themes for Ecumenical Singing: The Psalms," *Journal for Preachers* 43, no. 4 (2020): 3–10.

> summary of it, comprised in one little book. . . . It is really a fine enchiridion or handbook. In fact, I have a notion that the Holy Spirit wanted to take the trouble himself to compile a short Bible . . . so that anyone who could not read the whole Bible would here have anyway almost an entire summary of it, comprised in one little book. . . . There you will have a fine, bright, pure mirror that will show you what Christendom is. Indeed, you will find in it also yourself and the true *Gnothi seauton* ["know thyself"], as well as God . . . and all creatures.[55]

As a "Bible" in miniature, the Psalter covers much of the Bible's diversity, consisting of prayers, hymns, instruction, historiography, creation accounts, narrative, law, wisdom, and even love poetry (see Ps 45; cf. Song of Solomon). The Psalter addresses common themes and issues shared throughout the Hebrew scriptures while offering its own various perspectives.

In a time rife with polarizing fear and division, communities of faith can learn much from the uniquely dialogical nature of the ancient scriptures, particularly the Psalms. For contemporary readers, acknowledging and engaging the Bible's dialogical diversity could be a resource for cultivating a self-critical openness to dialogue with others, particularly those who are different. This study explores specifically the various ways the book of Psalms dialogues with itself and with the larger canonical corpus, while fostering a shared vision of life before the God who is considered above all else to be a God of "benevolence" or *ḥesed*, a God of unwavering concern for a people's well-being, a "tenacious solidarity."[56] By exploring how the Psalms "talk" to God and to each other, how they practice the art of dialogue, communities may find transformative ways of overcoming partisan polarization and fearful distrust to flourish together even amid disruption and division.

55. Martin Luther, "Preface to the Psalter" (1545 [1528]), in *Luther's Works Volume 35: Word and Sacrament*, ed. E. Theodore Bachmann (Philadelphia: Muhlenberg Press, 1960), 254–55.

56. Walter Brueggemann, "The Psalms: Tenacious Solidarity," in Walter Brueggemann, *Tenacious Solidarity: Biblical Provocations on Race, Religion, Climate, and the Economy*, ed. Davis Hankins (Minneapolis: Fortress, 2018), 354–55.

But a word of warning. The dialogues hosted by the Psalms are not for the faint of heart. They can be uncomfortable, particularly for polite or "civil"-minded Christians, which explains, for example, why the lament psalms are often overlooked in Christian worship.[57] But the present day calls for uncomfortable, fearless dialogues over issues that have been neglected or left simmering before exploding in the public arena. The Psalms are about being honest to God and honest with each other. They do not pull punches. Case in point: the "psalms of protest."[58]

Confronting God and Neighbor: Psalms as Protest

While typically viewed as a hymnbook, given its Jewish title *tĕhillîm* ("praises"), the Psalter has its fair share of protests, more commonly called "laments" or "complaints," an unfortunate label given its negative connotation in popular discourse. Complaints can be whiny. Protests are meant to be both disruptive and mobilizing in effecting worthwhile change. Protest turns grief into grievance.[59] Indeed, as Carleen Mandolfo points out, "nearly every lament [in the Psalter] can be characterized as a demand for justice," rather than as a plea for mercy.[60] Take, for example, Psalm 13, the model in miniature of the so-called lament psalm.

Psalm 13: How Long, How Long, *How Long?*

One of the shortest protests in the Psalter, Psalm 13 contains a rapid-fire succession of questions.

---

57. Perhaps until now. See Walter Brueggemann, "The Costly Loss of Lament," in Walter Brueggemann, *The Psalms and the Life of Faith*, ed. Patrick D. Miller (Minneapolis: Augsburg Fortress, 1995), 98–111.

58. Where the verse numbering differs between versions, the Christian versification is listed first, followed by the Jewish, set in brackets.

59. So also Carleen Mandolfo, *God in the Dock: Dialogic Tension in the Psalms of Lament*, *JSOT* 357 (London: Sheffield Academic Press, 2002), 1n.1.

60. Carleen Mandolfo, "Language of Lament in the Psalms," in *The Oxford Handbook of the Psalms*, ed. William P. Brown (New York: Oxford University Press, 2014), 122.

How long, YHWH, will you forget me? Forever?[61]
How long will you hide your face from me?
How often must I bear my own counsels,[62]
 agony in my heart? Daily?
How long must my enemy rise up against me? (13:1-2)

The speaker's complaint is punctuated by the repetition of four identical interrogatives: "How long/often . . . ?" (*'ad-'ānâ*). For the first and third questions, a rhetorical answer is given, making forcefully clear that such questions are asked not out of curiosity but out of outrage, out of protest. They are, in fact, accusations, as in the case of the identical interrogative in 62:3[4]: "How long will you assail someone?" Such accusatory interrogatives are common throughout psalmic discourse, although they have their variations in Hebrew: *'ad-mātay*[63] and *'ad-meh/mâ*.[64] Each one introduces a protest.

In Psalm 13, the protest covers three intersecting vectors of suffering: the theological, the psychological, and the social. The initial protest calls God to account for divine neglect, pointedly cast with two verbs: "forget" and "hide." The point is not that God has a feeble memory (although this could be sarcastically implied), but that God has willfully disregarded the speaker's plight. The speaker also complains of having to rely on his or her own "counsels," of resorting to self-deliberation rather than receiving God's counsel. Elsewhere in the Psalms, self-deliberations are held in situ-

61. Or "How long, YHWH? Will you forget me forever?" (so most translations). Although such syntax corresponds to the Masoretic accentuation, it is more likely that a syntactical division occurs at the end of the verb (and its object suffix). In other cases of the interrogative phrase *'ad-'ānâ*, the question typically extends through the first verb (e.g., Ps 62:3[4]; Hab 1:2). On the other hand, the word *nēṣaḥ* ("forever") at the end of the first line suggests a syntactical division, for to read the colon as one extended question makes little sense. The solution, thus, is to end the question with the verb and consider the following word *(nēṣaḥ)* as a rhetorical answer that packs its own accusatory punch.

62. So MT. Frequently suggested is the emendation of *'ēṣôt* to *'aṣṣābôt* ("pains") for better parallelism, but without textual support. Good sense can be made as the text stands in the MT.

63. Pss 6:3[4]; 74:10; 80:4[5]; 82:2; 90:13; 94:3; cf. Prov 1:22.

64. Pss 4:2[3]; 79:5; 89:46[47].

ations of isolation and hopelessness,[65] indicating that the speaker is at wits end, feeling cut off from God. Such is the speaker's "agony" (*yāgôn*).

Third, the speaker protests the "rising" enemy. The language implies outright attack; the enemy who "rises" is the enemy who assaults. In the span of four questions, the speaker covers the gamut of misery: divine neglect, social isolation, and persecution. But all is not lost: the speaker turns from complaint to demand, continuing the movement of protest.

> Look (and) answer me, YHWH, my God!
> Restore light to my eyes,
>   or else I will sleep the sleep of death,
>   and my enemy will say, "I have overcome him,"
>   and my foes will rejoice over my downfall.
> But as for me, I trust in your benevolence.
>   My heart shall rejoice in your salvation;
> I shall sing to YHWH,
>   when[66] he has done me good.[67] (13:4-6)

The two commands demand that YHWH take note and respond. YHWH's "answer" would break the traumatizing cycle of self-deliberations that plagues the speaker. It would secure protection from the enemy who seeks the speaker's demise. The speaker, moreover, prays for restored vision ("light") and, thus, renewal of life. Otherwise, death is the assured outcome, cast as perpetual sleep (cf. Jer 51:39, 57; Job 3:13).

The psalm assumes that YHWH values the speaker's life; hence, the loss of life would also be a loss for YHWH. In Psalm 6:5[6], the speaker points out that in death YHWH would lose the speaker's invocations: "For your invoked name is absent in death; in Sheol who can give you praise?" Moreover, the speaker's downfall would count as the enemy's triumph, and surely YHWH would not want that! Pointing out the prospect of

65. E.g., Pss 42:5[6], 11[12]; 62:5[6]. This is captured in dialogue between the speaker's *nepeš* (typically translated as "soul") and the speaking subject ("I").

66. Or "for" (*kî*). But see next note.

67. The poetic force of the perfect aspect of the verb *gml* might suggest enduring, "good-as-done" activity by God. But the syntax more likely suggests that the speaker's praise is contingent upon God's deliverance. See Ps 14:7.

death is the speaker's way of motivating YHWH to action. However, the most central reason for YHWH to act is the speaker's unwavering "trust in [YHWH's] benevolence" (*ḥesed*). Such trust constitutes the decisive motivating reason for God to act. It is God's *ḥesed* to which the speaker makes appeal. It is trust in God's "benevolence" that grounds the speaker's protest from the outset. For the speaker, there is no protest without trust.

The psalm ends with a contingent vow to praise, which parallels the ending of the following psalm "*when* YHWH restores the fortunes of his people, Jacob will rejoice and Israel will celebrate!" (14:7). For the speaker in Psalm 13, praise is promised only when justice is served. Salvation is yet to come, but when it does, the speaker stands ready to offer praise. Psalm 13, in short, illustrates well the psalmic move from protest to praise. Praise is contingent upon justice fulfilled. No justice, no praise!

Psalm 94: Calling Out God's Complicity

Cast as a protest against the wicked, Psalm 94 enlists YHWH as both witness to injustice and executor of justice.

> YHWH, God of vengeance,
> God of vengeance, shine forth![68]
> Rise up, judge of the earth!
> Pay back the arrogant with their just deserts!
> How long will the wicked, YHWH,
> how long will the wicked exult in triumph?
> They spew out impudence while speaking;
> all evildoers boast.
> Your people, YHWH, they crush;
> your heritage they violate.
> They kill the widow and the immigrant;
> they murder the orphan,
> saying, "YHWH does not see [it];
> the God of Jacob does not discern." (94:1-7)

68. Read *hôpîʿāh* (imv.) for MT *hôpiyaʿ* ("has shined forth") due to haplography. See Ps 80:2; cf. 50:2.

The speaker boldly demands justice from God ("Rise up!"//"Pay back!") while protesting the triumph of the unjust ("wicked"). As in Psalm 13, the repeated question "how long?" (*'ad-mātay*) is not a query for information, as if the speaker were asking for a specific time frame. Rather, the speaker calls out God's complicity with the wicked, because all that they do, from "crushing" to "killing," happens on God's watch. With God front and center in the speaker's protest, the accusatory question translates effectually to this: "How long" will *you* allow the wicked to act with impunity? Such is the psalm's way of arousing God to action, by calling God, the "judge of the earth," to account. In the Psalms, it is the speaker's right and privilege to pose such a question as a way of protesting divine negligence in establishing justice.[69] Psalm 94 calls out not only God but also the wicked for their murderous exploits against the most vulnerable in Israelite society (94:6): widows, immigrants, and orphans.[70] They are the special targets of the wicked, who are convinced that YHWH is blind to all that they do, giving them license to kill.

The speaker subsequently addresses the wicked and admonishes them for being clueless about YHWH's power of discernment.

> Pay attention, you idiots among the people!
>   You fools—when will you get wise?
> The one who planted the ear, does he not hear?
> The one who fashioned the eye, does he not see?
> The one who disciplines the nations, does he not rebuke?
> The one who teaches humanity knowledge, [does he not discern?][71]
> YHWH knows the thoughts of humankind,
>   that they are mere breath. (94:8-11)

The one who disciplines the nations is the one who discerns their thoughts. Discipline from God, moreover, should be welcomed, not despised. The psalm turns hopeful.

69. See also 13:1-2[2-3]; 35:17; 74:10; 79:5; 89:46[47]; 119:84.

70. See also 10:14, 18; 68:5[6]; 146:9.

71. In view of vv. 9-10a, this line is best considered elliptical. Emending the text is unnecessary.

How happy, YHWH, is the one whom you discipline,
and teach with your law,[72]
providing that person respite from disastrous days,
until a pit is dug for the wicked!
For YHWH will not forsake his people,
nor abandon his heritage.
For justice will return to the righteous one,[73]
and all who are upright in heart will follow it. (94:12-15)

After commending the individual who is receptive to YHWH's discipline and sounding a note of hope, the speaker offers both an invitation and a testimony. The former issues an open challenge for anyone to take a stand against the wicked, to not remain silent. The latter affirms YHWH's support, without which the speaker would have been as good as dead (in "silence").

Who will rise up for me against the wicked?
Who will stand for me against evildoers?
If YHWH had not been my help,
I would have promptly dwelt in silence.[74]
Whenever I think my foot is slipping,
your benevolence, YHWH, supports me.
Whenever my anxieties become too many,
your consolations soothe me. (94:16-19)

While YHWH's "benevolence" is the source of the speaker's comfort, YHWH is by no means off the hook. The speaker returns to protest mode by admonishing God for the questionable alliances God makes.

How could a throne of destruction be allied with you,
one who wreaks havoc through legal means?[75]

72. This translation of *tôrâ* (as opposed to "instruction") acknowledges the parallel reference to "statute" in v. 20b.

73. *BHS* proposes that *ṣedeq* ("righteousness") be read as *ṣādîq* ("righteous"), which could also be written defectively without any consonantal change.

74. That is, the abode of the dead. Cf. Ps 115:17.

75. Literally, "on [the basis of] a statute" (*ʾălê ḥōq*).

They mobilize against the life of the righteous,
    and condemn innocent blood. (94:20-21)

Taken literally, the expression "throne of destruction" (*kissēʾ hawwôt*) refers to a royal figure, suggesting that a king has taken the law into his own hands, violating the Deuteronomic prescription that no king is above the law (Deut 17:18-19). This king, however, twists the law perhaps by issuing executive orders that run counter to the norms of justice. The speaker asks rhetorically whether such a king could be "allied" with God, who is addressed directly in protest. Here, the questioned alliance is between God and a wicked ruler, a most unholy alliance that should have been precluded given what was earlier claimed about YHWH's justice (94:15, 17).

Psalm 94 concludes with a strong affirmation of faith and trust in YHWH as a "rock of refuge" (*ṣûr maḥseh*) and "stronghold" (*miśgāb*), root metaphors for safety and security (94:22). Protection for the speaker is matched by destruction of the wicked (94:23). The latter is a case of just deserts, of the exercise of violence by the wicked paid back in full, as in 94:2b. YHWH's justice, the psalm claims, is poetic justice. The psalm ends in affirmation of what was petitioned at the beginning, with protest serving as the means by which plea moves to hope.

Psalm 44: Israelite Lives Matter!

As one of the most anguished communal "laments" in the Psalter, Psalm 44 is a robust protest demanding action from God. Moving from communal to personal testimony, the psalm begins by affirming Israel's absolute trust in God, and with good warrant: God is given credit for liberating and settling Israel in the land.

O God, by our ears we have heard,
    our ancestors have recounted to us,
    the deeds you performed in their days, in days of yore.
You, by your hand, dispossessed the nations,
    but them you planted.
        You afflicted the peoples,
            but them you set free.

For not by their sword did they take possession of the land,
nor did their arm save them,
but rather your right hand, your arm,
and the light of your countenance,
for you delighted in them. (44:1-3[2-4])

You indeed are my King, O God,
who commands[76] victories for Jacob.
Through you we thrust away our foes;
by your name we have trampled our adversaries.
Indeed, I trust not in my bow;
my sword does not save me,
for it is you who saved us from our foes,
and you have put to shame those who hate us.
In God we glory always,
we give thanks to your name forever. *Selah* (44:4-8[5-9])

For achieving victory, the speaker proclaims trust not in weapons of war but in God the divine warrior. While the first half of the psalm concludes on a strong note of praise and thanksgiving for all that God has done to ensure Jacob's freedom and security, the second half rips God for all that God has done *against* God's people. The psalm's praise sets up the protest.

But alas you have spurned and debased us;
you do not go out with our armies.
You turn us back from the foe,
and our enemies plunder us.[77]
You hand us over as sheep for slaughter;
you have scattered us among the nations.
You sell your people short;
you have not increased their price.
You make us the butt of our neighbors,
the scorn and derision of those around us.
You make us a byword among the nations,

76. The verbal form in the MT (imperative) is likely the result of a haplography.

77. Read *lānû* for MT *lāmô* ("them"), consonant with certain Hebrew witnesses, as well as Peshitta and Targum.

a head-shaker[78] among the peoples.[79]
All day long my disgrace is before me;
and the shame of my face has covered me
at the sound of the taunting despiser,
at the sight of the enemy avenger. (44:9-16[10-17])

Such is the psalm's protest, signaled as countertestimony by the single particle *'ap* ("but alas"), which introduces a dismantling of all that was previously claimed about God and the people's success. Instead of God "delighting" (44:2b[3b]), God "debases" (44:8a[9a]). The evidence is clear: the people suffer from defeat, diaspora, dispossession, and disgrace, all because of God's unconscionable rejection of the people. God refuses to accompany the people onto the battlefield (cf. 1 Sam 4:3-4). As a result, enemies "plunder" and the people are slaughtered as "sheep" (Ps 44:10[11]; see also v. 21[22]). They are devalued in God's sight (44:11[12]), suffering disgrace as the laughingstock of the nations (44:12-13[13-14]). God has completely reversed course, and for no reason, as the next strophe drives home.

All this has come upon us, yet we have not forgotten you,
and we have not broken your covenant.
Our heart has not turned back,
nor has any of our steps strayed from your way.
Nevertheless,[80] you crushed us in the abode of the sea monster,[81]
covering us with deep darkness.
If we had forgotten the name of our God,
or spread our hands out to some strange deity,
would not God have found it out?
For he knows the secrets of the heart.
No, it is because of you that we are being slain everyday;
we are reckoned as slaughtered sleep. (44:17-22[18-23])

78. I.e., laughingstock.

79. Read *bal'ummîm* for MT *bal-'ummîm*, a mistake in the Codex Lenningradensis.

80. Adversative use of the *kî* particle (see also v. 23a).

81. Most commonly translated "jackals." However, several Hebrew manuscripts read *tannîn* ("sea monster"). Moreover, Ezek 29:3; 32:2 feature *tannîm*, identical in form, clearly denoting "sea monsters." Here, *tannîm* can be considered a by-form of *tannîn*.

The psalm turns toward defense, claiming unwavering faithfulness in the face of divine rejection: Israel has "not forgotten," "not broken" covenant, "not turned back," and "not strayed." The people have remained absolutely devoted to God, refusing to worship foreign deities. They have kept up their end of the covenant. The speaker even appeals to God's discerning knowledge of the heart's "secrets" to claim faithful integrity. That God knows Israel's faithfulness makes the shock of suffering at God's hands all the more grievous. The fault lies not with the slaughtered sheep but with the negligent Shepherd (44:21a[22a]).

Such is Israel's protest against God, one that demands decisive action while accusing God of being "asleep" through it all.

> Wake up! Why do you sleep, my Lord?
>   Awaken! Do not reject [us] forever!
> Why do you hide your face,
>   forgetting our affliction and oppression?
> Indeed, we sink down[82] into the dust;
>   our bodies cling to the ground.
> Arise, be of help to us!
>   Redeem us on account of your benevolence! (44:23-26[24-27])

The psalm's strategy is now clear: Israel's testimony of trust, the countertestimony of God's betrayal, and Israel's persistent faithfulness all build up to the pointed calls to action in the end: "wake up" (*ʿûrāh*) and "awaken" (*hāqîṣāh*) in 44:23[24], "arise" (*qûmāh*) and "redeem" (*pĕdēnû*) in 44:26[27]. God needs to get "woke," this God who is never supposed to "slumber" (see 121: 4). The first two commands implicate God as oblivious to the people's suffering.[83] "Arise," in fact, qualifies as the most frequent one-word imperative for divine intervention in the Psalms, let alone the Hebrew Bible.[84] The more specific command "redeem" or ransom (√*pdh*) operates within the cultic system of "buying out" individuals dedicated to

82. Given the parallel in the next line, the verb (*šyḥ* or *šwḥ*) suggests descending movement rather than dissolution.

83. See, e.g., Pss 35:23; 59:4[5], 5[6].

84. E.g., Pss 3:7[8]; 7:6[7]; 9:19[20]; 10:12; 17:13; 74:22; 82:8; 132:8.

God, such as the firstborn.[85] As applied to the community, the term connotes deliverance from oppressive conditions, such as Egyptian bondage (e.g., Deut 7:8; Mic 6:4), enemies (Ps 78:42), and sin (130:8). Nevertheless, the economic nuance of the term may be indicated in Psalm 44 in light of the earlier complaint of God devaluing the people (44:12[13]), suggesting that Israel's redemption would cost little on God's part. In between these framing commands lies one final protest, introduced by the accusatory question "Why?"—charging God with neglect ("forgetting"). The protest impresses upon God that the survival of a people is at stake.

Psalm 44 provides a dramatic example of psalmic protest directed to God. More than a complaint, this protest weds together complaint and command, lament and demand. Protest is a form of "telling truth to power" by naming and collectively confronting the atrocities suffered by a people and calling those in charge to account. The protest psalms give expression to "righteous anger," anger that is fully justified and works toward change.[86] Protest is also meant to be a show of force. As Walter Brueggemann points out, power is discursively redistributed through the performance of complaint (or "protest").[87] In psalmic protest, the speaker rhetorically assumes the "superior" position of confronting and motivating God to take corrective action, analogous to the rhetoric of rebuke one finds in the wisdom literature (see chapter 9). And because they are addressed primarily to God, psalmic protests are a confrontational form of prayer. The Psalms excel at prayerful protest, or "troubling" prayer, or arguing with God.[88] The "little Bible" proves to be the people's Bible, a book of theological reckoning from below.

85. E.g., Exod 13:13; Lev 27:27; Num 18:15-16.

86. See the discussion in Dan B. Allender and Tremper Longman III, *The Cry of the Soul: How Our Emotions Reveal Our Deepest Questions about God* (Colorado Springs, CO: NavPress, 2015), 45–57.

87. Brueggemann, "Costly Loss of Lament," 101–4. Brueggemann unpacks these implications with the help of object-relations theory in personality development.

88. See the in-depth analysis of other argumentative psalms (*Konfliktgespräche*) in Bernd Janowski, *Arguing with God: A Theological Anthropology of the Psalms* (Louisville, KY: Westminster John Knox, 2013), esp. 55–198, 322–45.

Psalms and Dialogue

For all their righteous anger directed toward God, for all their forceful demands, the protest psalms are grounded in a tenacious trust in God, in trust that God will take note and respond in kind. "In God we trust," one might say, is the underlying principle of psalmic discourse, for it is out of such trust that protests ring as much as praises sing.

The protest psalms constitute a critical part of a larger dialogue that unfolds throughout the Psalter between God and Israel. It is a complicated dialogue, facilitated by many voices, both individual and corporate, from differing levels of power, all directing their concerns to God in times of distress and disruption. As Brueggemann states regarding biblical faith viewed through the genre of "lament,"

> Most importantly, the laments show clearly that *biblical faith, as it faces life fully, is uncompromisingly and unembarrassedly dialogical.* Israel and Israelites in their hurt have to do with God, and God has to do with them. . . . Nowhere but with God does Israel vent its greatest doubt, its bitterest resentments, its deepest anger. . . . In the dialogue, Israel expects to understand what is happening and even to have it changed.[89]

"Nowhere but with God does Israel" convey its angriest protests, one could add. The dialogical nature of biblical faith, moreover, extends beyond psalmic protests. One can expand the dialogic framework to encompass much of the Psalter's generic spectrum: as lament and protest initiate dialogue with God, praise and thanksgiving conclude it, until the movement starts all over again. Such is what Patrick Miller identifies as the "heart of biblical prayer." It is a "movement" that hosts "a divine-human dialogue or conversation that identifies the very structure of faith as it is lived out in the words and lives of those who walk the pages of

89. Walter Brueggemann, "From Hurt to Joy, from Death to Life," in Walter Brueggemann, *The Psalms and the Life of Faith*, ed. Patrick D. Miller (Minneapolis: Fortress, 1995), 68. Italics original.

scripture."[90] It is a movement that, on the one hand, seeks help in times of distress and, on the other hand, strives for accountability. In between protest and praise we find in the Psalms various exchanges that call both the community and God to account. Psalmic dialogue leads to action for both parties: deliverance, redemption, justice, and forgiveness on God's part, and the promise to perform thanksgiving and praise as well as walk in God's ways of righteousness on the people's part. Psalmic dialogues are not idle conversations. To the contrary, they are "fearless dialogues" initiated in times of disruption.[91]

Psalms at the Table: Intrapsalmic Dialogue

The Psalms are not just dialogically engaged with God; they are also conversant with each other. Indeed, the Psalms provide some of the most dramatic examples of dialogue in diversity in the Bible. While addressing common themes and issues found throughout the Hebrew scriptures, the Psalter offers its own variety of perspectives from within, beginning, in fact, *within* certain individual psalms themselves.[92] Given their collected status, the psalms of the Psalter are also set up to "talk" to each other. Though each one being distinct, individual psalms are not meant to remain "socially isolated" but dialogically related, engaged in "animated conversations," as James Chatham describes: "One psalm will state a point, another will question it or speak from a different angle, and another will add an entirely new dimension, all feeding the hearer (you and me) with larger and richer perspectives."[93]

90. Patrick D. Miller, *They Cried to the Lord: The Form and Theology of Biblical Prayer* (Minneapolis: Fortress, 1994), 3. See also the discussion in Samuel E. Balentine, *Prayer in the Hebrew Bible: The Drama of Divine-Human Dialogue,* OBT (Minneapolis, MN: Augsburg Fortress, 1993), 261–64.

91. To borrow from Gregory C. Ellison II, *Fearless Dialogues: A New Movement for Justice* (Louisville, KY: Westminster John Knox, 2017). See below.

92. Carleen Mandolfo identifies thirteen psalms within which various "voices" are featured interacting with each other (Pss 4, 7, 9, 12, 25, 27, 28, 30–32, 55, 102, 130). See *God in the Dock*, 28–103.

93. James O. Chatham, *Psalm Conversations: Listening In as They Talk with One Another* (Collegeville, MN: Liturgical, 2018), vii.

In their collected arrangement, the psalms of the Psalter are given their seating assignments, as it were, at a common table to engage each other dialogically. In order to overhear their conversations, one would need to explore not only the psalms' *Sitze im Leben* ("settings in life") but also their *Sitze im Buch*, their literary settings. Moreover, to engage the Psalms dialogically readers would also need to explore their own settings in life, their *Sitze im Selbst.*

Psalmic dialogue, moreover, extends beyond the psalms themselves. The psalms of the Psalter also engage the larger biblical corpus, whereby the "little Bible" (à la Luther) addresses the (bigger) Bible. The Psalms and the larger biblical canon address common themes and issues, from divine action in creation and humanity's place in the world to the contours of justice, the nature of wisdom, and Israel's place among the nations. And, of course, there is David, the most complicated figure in the Bible and a central topic of concern in the Psalms and the historical books. The results of such dialogue, as we shall see, take us deeper into issues of human living and divine action, of justice and wisdom, of the lessons of the past and of hope for the future, than would be possible if we kept the Psalms simply to themselves and hermetically sealed from the rest of scripture. The canon does not allow such segregation.

A Hermeneutics of Dialogue

The beauty of a dialogical approach to the Bible is that it highlights differences in perspectives just as much as historical criticism does, while at the same time moving beyond the task of historical reconstruction. A dialogical approach to biblical interpretation need not depend on determining who said what first, that is, who is responding directly to whom, or whether there is a proximate historical relationship at all. For one thing, such determinations are never certain. Second, the focus here is more on identifying the issues at play, on articulating what is at stake in these dialogues theologically and ethically, than on historical reconstructions, which are helpful as far as they go but are not the end-all in the dialogical quest. A dialogical approach, in other words, embraces both the diachronic and the synchronic. Third, a dialogical approach avoids privileging one voice over another. Instead, it attunes the exegetical "ear" to listen attentively to every voice included (and muted) within the canonical text with the goal of understanding. A dialogue is not a win-or-lose debate. What then is it?

Dialogue is not just any conversation; it is the kind that operates out of "mutual respect," fostered by "listening and learning."[94] Dialogue accepts the "otherness" of others. The enemy of dialogue is prejudice, judgment made without knowledge.[95] Contrary to popular opinion, the *dia* in "dialogue" does not mean "two." Consonant with its etymological background, "dialogue" means "through" or "across" the "word" (Greek *dia* + *logos*). David Bohm compares the dynamics of dialogue to a "stream of meaning flowing among and through us and between us," out of which "may emerge some new understanding."[96]

Although a dialogue rests on shared meaning, without which no dialogue could take place, it does not necessarily seek common ground or resolution. Instead, it accepts conflict and tension for what it can teach those who engage in it, beginning with listening and proceeding toward mutual understanding.[97] Indeed, listening without the imposed goal of finding *common* ground can open the possibility of breaking *new* ground, of overcoming misunderstandings rooted in ignorance, on the one hand, and forging pathways toward possible transformation, on the other. Different does not mean defective, and genuine dialogue "across" (*dia*) differing perspectives holds the promise of transformation. At the very least, genuine dialogue begins to counter the debilitating "othering" of others. True dialogues are "fearless dialogues," dialogues grounded in

94. S. Wesley Ariarajah, "Creation of a 'Culture of Dialogue' in a Multicultural and Pluralist Society," in *Communication and Reconciliation: Challenges Facing the 21st Century*, ed. Philip Lee (Geneva: WCC Publications, 2001), 5.

95. Ariarajah, "Creation of a 'Culture of Dialogue,'" 6.

96. David Bohm, *On Dialogue* (London: Routledge Classics, 2004), 7. I am grateful to Marcia Riggs for this reference.

97. Lisa Schirsch and David Campt, *The Little Book of Dialogue for Difficult Subjects: A Practical, Hands-On Guide,* The Little Books of Justice and Peacebuilding (New York: Good Books, 2007), 5–8.

hospitality and honesty, as well as in the openness to change. Like the protest psalms, psalmic dialogues can be confrontative and challenging.

What does dialogue have to do with reading the Bible? Just about everything. Lamentably, we cannot go back in time to interview the biblical authors. We cannot directly engage these ancient voices, and we can only tentatively reconstruct their cultural and historical contexts. All we have are their words placed alongside the words of others spanning centuries of interpretive reception. Nevertheless, in these preserved and (re)interpreted words, the ancients speak in the living voice of scripture, calling out to be heard, speaking out together in manifold ways, all brought together into a canonical unity that preserves something of their diversity.

To hear and interpret the many voices of scripture in all their interrelated potential, I propose a "hermeneutics of dialogue" that requires a "deep reading," more than a "close reading," of biblical texts. While a close reading rightly involves careful attention to the rhetorical nuances of a particular text, a deep reading dives into the text's possible meanings *in relation to* other texts, to determine what makes a text "tick" *vis-à-vis* other texts. Deep reading engages differences not just within a text, such as reflected in its compositional layers or editorial reworkings, but also across (*dia*) texts. Deep reading is reading for meaningful differences within and among texts, treating themes, however common, as issues "fraught with background." Greater depth demands wider breadth. Deep reading attunes the exegetical ear to discern more clearly the different voices in and behind the texts, imagining them positioned on a level playing field, however wide that field may be, all reciprocally engaged with each other in dialogue. I call it "reading for reciprocity."

Within the domain of biblical scholarship, there is much precedent for a dialogical approach to biblical interpretation. A number of scholars have drawn from the groundbreaking literary work of Mikhail Bakhtin,[98]

98. Most notably Walter L. Reed, *Dialogues of the Word: The Bible as Literature according to Bakhtin* (New York: Oxford University Press, 1993); Carol A. Newsom, *The Book of Job: A Contest of Moral Imaginations* (New York: Oxford University Press, 2003); Barbara Green, *How Are the Mighty Fallen? A Dialogical Study of King Saul in 1 Samuel*, JSOTSup 365 (London: Sheffield Academic Press, 2003); Green, *Mikhail Bakhtin and Biblical Scholarship: An Introduction*, Semeia Studies 38 (Atlanta: SBL, 2000); and Raj Nadella, *Dialogue Not Dogma: Many Voices in the Gospel of Luke*, LNTS 413 (New York: Bloomsbury T&T Clark, 2011).

whose analysis of Russian novels helpfully distinguished between "polyphonic" and "monologic" novels. A "polyphonic" novel features a rich variety of different "voices," without any one of them dominating the literary landscape.[99] Certain characters in Dostoevsky's novels, for example, voice divergent viewpoints, each one treated more or less equally. With such a polyphony of voices at play, dialogue naturally emerges among these characters.[100] While the "monologic" novel can accommodate a limited variety of viewpoints, one perspective invariably wins out, subordinating all others. But with any polyphonic piece of literature, there is ample room for dialogue, for interaction between viewpoints. While "polyphony" indicates what *is* in the text, "dialogism" refers to what *transpires* in the text.[101]

There is no need to probe further, except to note that Bakhtin's work focused on the novel; hence, his work is not directly applicable to the Psalms. While certain psalms feature narrative, albeit in poetic form, such as the so-called historical psalms (78, 105, 106, 135, 136), the Psalter largely consists of liturgies cast in various genres. Nevertheless, Bakhtin's overall schema, simplified as it is in this all-too-brief discussion, remains useful. Although not a novel, the book of Psalms is undeniably polyphonic, indeed the most polyphonic of all biblical books, including Job, populated by its myriad voices addressing God as well as God addressing the community in various ways.

But as God and the community engage in dialogue, there is another level of discursive interaction among the psalms themselves, as noted above. The Psalms "talk" to one another due to their placement next to each other or, in some cases, away from each other while linked by shared language or common issues. Unlike in a novel, this level of dialogue among the psalms is entertained by the reader, who is invited to imagine the questions and issues that the psalms are addressing. That, in fact, is the work of

99. Particularly the novels of Dostoevsky, whom Bakhtin considered the "creator of the polyphonic novel" (Mikhail M. Bakhtin, *Problems of Dostoevsky's Poetics*, ed. and trans. Caryl Emerson, Theory and History of Literature 8 [Minneapolis: University of Minnesota Press, 1984], 7). Bakhtin considered *The Brothers Karamazov* as the most polyphonic of Dostoevsky's novels. See the helpful overview in Nadella, *Dialogue Not Dogma*, 8–26.

100. Nadella, *Dialogue Not Dogma*, 14.

101. Nadella, *Dialogue Not Dogma*, 23.

this study: to compare psalms of differing perspectives and to identify the questions and issues at stake in their interaction with each other and with biblical perspectives outside the Psalter. Here, "dialogism" refers to what these psalms provoke not "in the text" so much as in the act of reading, or performing, these psalms together.

I have learned over the years of teaching how powerful the tendency is among students to read for only harmony and agreement within and across biblical texts. Such readings are conflict aversive, which often results in settling for the lowest (and lamest) common theological denominator. Doing so invariably reduces the Bible's generative diversity into lazy generalizations. The alternative is to let scripture's diversity inspire engaging (and often troubling) dialogue. For some faith communities, achieving theological consistency, if not uniformity, in interpreting scripture is a goal of apologetics. Diversity of views in these groups is often viewed as a liability when it comes to biblical interpretation. In scholarship, by contrast, discerning divisions, fractures, and ruptures within and between texts is a staple of biblical research. A dialogical approach can help build a bridge across this chasm by finding and appreciating the Bible's diversity within its canonical unity, on the one hand, and shared meaning within its diversity, on the other. In a dialogical approach, *e pluribus unum* meets *ex uno plura*. Such, in fact, is the dialectic between Babel and Pentecost: out of one common language God brought forth many languages and cultures (Gen 11:1-9), and across many cultures and languages God's Spirit made possible communication of "God's deeds of power" (Acts 2:1-13). At Pentecost they asked, "What does this mean?" (2:12).

So what does this mean? It means changing the way we think about each other, to regard each other as partners rather than as opponents from the outset, as colleagues created in God's image (Gen 1:28), each "wonderfully and fearfully made" (Ps 139:14). It means overcoming implicit biases that invariably see "difference" as deviant rather than as opportunities for learning and growth. It means being present for the other, striving for mutual understanding and transformation. It means checking our privilege at the door, being open to changing long-held views, and practicing empathy. It means engaging hearts and minds, as well as being patient with oneself and with others. It means connecting with the struggles of others and taking action. It means living into a world that is to be filled with God's *shalom*: the wholeness that comes when justice and peace finally embrace (Ps 85:10[11]).[102]

Let the dialogues begin.

The Plan

This book features many biblical texts, psalmic and otherwise (whose translations are my own), because, to state the obvious, such texts are the voices of dialogue in the Bible. Paraphrases will not do. It is best to hear them in their "own" words as they engage each other.

By taking a cue from Martin Luther, the core of the book is structured according to the canonical divisions of the Hebrew Bible or *Tanakh* (i.e., Torah, Prophets, and Writings) to highlight how the Psalms engage dialogically with the rest of the canon. Within this schema, I address two interrelated areas of interest: (1) the Psalms' internal dialogues, and (2) the Psalms' external dialogues with other biblical corpora. The following provides an overview:

1. Within the first division of the Hebrew canon, "Torah" (Genesis–Deuteronomy), I explore the dialogues hosted by certain psalms that address issues of creation, Israel's origins (the ancestors, exodus, and the wilderness wanderings), and the nature of *tôrâ* in connection with Pentateuchal narrative and instruction.
2. In the second division, "Prophets" (Joshua–Malachi), I explore how the theme of justice is framed in the Psalms compared to certain prophetic perspectives. I also explore how kingship is (re) inscribed in the Psalms, with a particular focus on the character of David and his legacy.
3. Within the "Writings" (Psalms–2 Chronicles), I engage the Psalms in dialogue with the so-called Wisdom literature (Proverbs, Job, and Ecclesiastes), beginning with certain "wisdom psalms." Since the book of Psalms is itself such a dominant presence in the Writings, I also explore the Psalter's internal dialogues, beginning with

102. Or "shalom justice." See Clifton R. Clarke, "Shalom Justice," *Fuller Magazine* 9 (2017): 60–65.

> the so-called twin psalms, as well as more disparate psalms that are linked by shared language and common subjects of discourse. I conclude with how the book of Psalms begins by exploring the dialogical engagement between Psalms 1–2, and their role in orienting the Psalter as a whole.

Much is left out in this prolegomenon.[103] I highlight only those dialogical connections that seem particularly engaging (and manageable in one book). Others will see additional connections rife with dialogue. As for the dialogues that I find unfolding between the "little Bible" and the larger Bible, I first explore what the larger corpus has to say about a particular issue, noting the dialogues "already" underway, before listening in on how the Psalms engage dialogically. The result is a study that hears dialogue going on just about everywhere in the Bible, whether large or "little."

The penultimate chapter briefly explores the study's implications for biblical authority: How does the dialogical nature of scripture impact the contested issue of biblical authority? Finally, the book concludes on a personal note with reflections on teaching a course on the Bible's dialogical dynamics. The course was living proof that studying the Bible's diversity dialogically can generate new ways of engagement among readers who have come to appreciate the value of dialogue over zero-sum debate, transformation over triumph, and difference over division in this time of profound disruption.

103. For example, Psalm 83 features two events narrated in Judges: Israel's victories over Midian (Judg 6–8) and over Sisera and Jabin (Judg 4–5). But I have chosen not to discuss them, given their minimal treatment. Also, I do not explore the "conquest" in the Psalms as a separate theme (cf. Joshua), since it is sparsely referenced and often seamlessly connected with the wilderness accounts (see Pss 44:2-3[3-4]; 105:44-45; 106:34-35; 135:11-12; 136:21-22). Indeed, their minimal treatment in the Psalms may itself be a point of dialogue with the book of Joshua.

Part I

TORAH

CHAPTER 2
"IN THE BEGINNING": A PRIMORDIAL DIALOGUE

The dirt is our undeniable kin. Even geographical distance and the difference of strange tongues cannot thwart this truth—we are creatures bound together.

—Willie James Jennings[1]

How manifold are your works, YHWH!

—Psalm 104:24a

In the beginning, God created the heavens and the earth" (KJV). "In the beginning," the Bible initiates a dialogue, born from the union of two starkly different accounts of creation. In the first three chapters of Genesis, the Bible hosts its very first dialogue, one of truly cosmic proportions. One account is not meant to supplant the other; they are not competitors pummeling each other within the canonical boxing ring. Rather, they are set side by side as partners in dialogue over certain fundamental issues, such as God's purpose and humanity's place in creation. While Genesis 1:1–2:4a and 2:4b–3:24 (henceforth "Genesis 1" and "Genesis

1. Willie James Jennings, "Can White People Be Saved?," in *Can "White" People Be Saved?: Triangulating Race, Theology, and Mission*, ed. Love L. Sechrest, Johnny Ramírez-Johnson, Amos Yong (Missiological Engagements 12, Downers Grove, IL: IVP Academic, 2018), 30.

2–3") are only two of several creation accounts in the Bible,[2] they are the ones to initiate a dialogue that extends throughout the scriptures, enlisting many other partners, including the Psalms. We start with Genesis.

Cosmic King and Royal Humanity: Genesis 1

Genesis 1 is the most structured account of creation in scripture. With its methodically unfolding presentation, Genesis 1 reads like a dispassionate treatise. By its own measure, this account resembles more an itemized list of steps than a flowing narrative, more a report than a story.[3] It is as if God were "following a recipe" for creation.[4] But even in its literary austerity, the so-called Priestly account revels in the magisterial character of its primary actor, God, while at the same time describing in strikingly "naturalistic" ways how the world was created and ordered, from empty "chaos" to cosmic community. By issuing ten indirect commands, God acts as a cosmic king who enlists creation into being. Life, in particular, emerges from the creative agencies of the earth and the waters, each beckoned by God (1:11, 20, 24).

As the curtain rises to mark the beginning point of creation in Genesis, one "sees" only darkness and feels only water, a sort of primordial soup, empty of substance and lacking all form (1:2). Such was the primordial state of "formlessness and void" (*tōhû wābōhû*), a watery mishmash and nothing more. Neither Tiamat nor Leviathan, nor any other monster of the abyss, was lurking under the surface ready to rear its formidable head.[5] Far from threatening, primordial "chaos" in Genesis 1:2 was preg-

2. For a general overview of the creation accounts in the Bible, see William P. Brown, *The Seven Pillars of Creation: The Bible, Science, and the Ecology of Wonder* (New York: Oxford University Press, 2010).

3. S. Dean McBride Jr., "Divine Protocol: Genesis 1:1–2:3 as Prologue to the Pentateuch," in *God Who Creates: Essays in Honor of W. Sibley Towner*, ed. William P. Brown and S. Dean McBride Jr. (Grand Rapids: Eerdmans, 2000), 6.

4. Joshua Woodsmith, "Question 3" (Moodle Forum Post; November 20, 2020).

5. "Sea monsters" (*tannînim*) are, in fact, found later in the account (v. 21), but as "great" (*gĕdōlîm*) as they are, they are not a threat to creation, let alone to God. Indeed, they are part of God's "good" creation.

nant with possibility as God's "breath" (*rûaḥ*) was "hovering" (*mĕraḥepet*) over the dark waters, like a mother eagle over its nest (Deut 32:11).

In Genesis 1, creation turns out to be a thoroughly methodical affair. There is nothing particularly dramatic about it, except for God's first act of creation: the inbreaking or unleashing of light (1:3), which for modern readers is hard not to associate with the Big Bang, the primordial explosion of energy from which all matter derives. Otherwise, creation is conducted quite decently and in order. As every "day" follows the previous, so every step of creation builds on its predecessor. Creation, moreover, proceeds as a series of separations: light from darkness, day from night, the "waters above" from the "waters below," and land from the waters. For the final step, the last day is separated from all previous days, given its holy distinction. As the crown of creation, the seventh day signals creation's completion; it also gives final shape to the creative process and its outcome, as we shall see. In sum, creation is a graduated process of differentiation leading to a diversity of domains, on the one hand, and the diversity of life, on the other. The result is a self-sustaining cosmic ecosystem, all deemed "very good" (1:31).

What is so "good" about creation, repeated seven times (1:4, 10, 12, 18, 21, 25, 31)? That "God saw that" creation was "good" indicates God's approval of creation's worth. "Good," in fact, spans a range of meanings in Genesis 1. Completed as "good," creation is a bona fide cosmos, an ordered, harmonious, and beautiful whole, quite the opposite of chaos. "Goodness" also acknowledges the plenitude and diversity of life, both animal and botanical, as well as creation's providential capacities for sustaining life. A "good" creation is one that is stable, habitable, sustainable, and flourishing. Indeed, part of creation's goodness is that creation itself is creative (see 1:11, 20, 24).

Imago Templi

But there is more to this well-ordered "goodness" that points toward holiness. The Priestly account as a whole reflects a literary symmetry that unfolds within the first six days of creation.

Day "0" (1:1-2) (formless and empty)	
Day 1 (1:3-5) Light	**Day 4** (1:14-19) Lights
Day 2 (1:6-8) Sky Waters (below)	**Day 5** (1:20-23) Avian life Marine life
Day 3 (1:9-13) Land Vegetation	**Day 6** (1:24-31) Land life Human life Food
(form-full and filled) **Day 7** (2:1-3)	

According to their thematic correspondences, the first six days line up to form two parallel columns. Days 1–3 delineate the cosmic domains (i.e., sky, water, and land), which are then populated by various inhabitants of these domains (Days 4–6).[6] Vertically, the two columns address the two abject conditions of lack referenced in 1:2, formlessness and emptiness. The left column (Days 1–3) recounts the cosmos being *formed*, while the right column (Days 4–6) describes the cosmos being *filled*. Day 3, moreover, serves as the link by depicting the land as fully "vegetated," equipping the land to provide the means for sustaining animal life. Days 4–6 report the filling of these domains with their respective inhabitants, from the celestial spheres (1:14-18) to human beings (1:26-28). With the stars, sun, and moon set in the heavens and the various forms of life, each according to its "kind," filling the sky, land, and sea, creation proceeds

6. Relatedly, John H. Walton argues that God "establishes functions" during days 1–3 and "installs functionaries" on days 4–6 (*The Lost World of Genesis One: Ancient Cosmology and the Origins Debate* [Downers Grove, IL: InterVarsity, 2009], 54–71). However, I find "light," "land," and the oceans as more than merely "functions." They are generative, empowering domains.

from emptiness to fullness in the right column, just as it had proceeded from formlessness to form-fullness in the left.

That pattern commends itself not only by its symmetry but also by its architecture. The final day serves as the capstone for the entire structure, for it shares something of God's holiness. Without this conclusive seventh day, the creation pattern would lose a distinction that remains hidden to modern readers not acquainted with the ancient architecture of sacred space. Many temples of the ancient Near East, including the Solomonic temple, exhibited a threefold or tripartite structure, which can also be found in the literary symmetry of the Genesis text.[7]

The Solomonic temple described in 1 Kings 6, for example, consists of (1) an outer vestibule or portico, (2) the nave or main room, and (3) an inner sanctum or holy of holies:

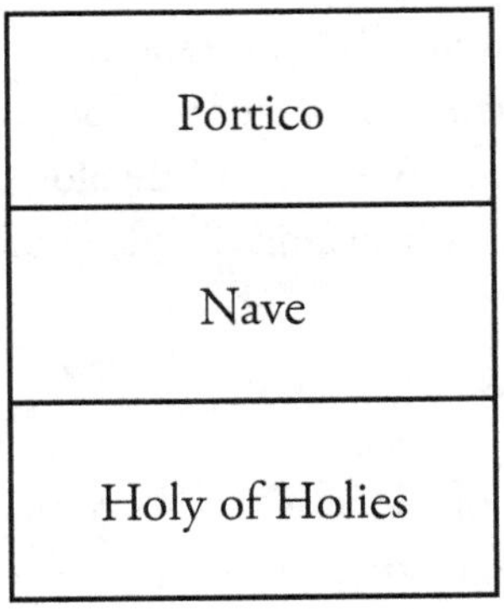

This threefold arrangement of sacred space corresponds to the way in which Genesis 1 recounts the various days of creation as they are distributed both chronologically and thematically. The first six days, by virtue of their correspondence, establish the architectural boundaries of sacred space, while the last day inhabits, as it were, the most holy space.

7. See Philip P. Jenson, *Graded Holiness: A Key to the Priestly Conception of the World*, JSOTSup 106 (Sheffield, UK: JSOT Press, 1992); and Michael B. Hundley, "Sacred Spaces, Objects, Offerings, and People in the Priestly Texts: A Reappraisal," *JBL* 132, no. 4 (2013): 749–67.

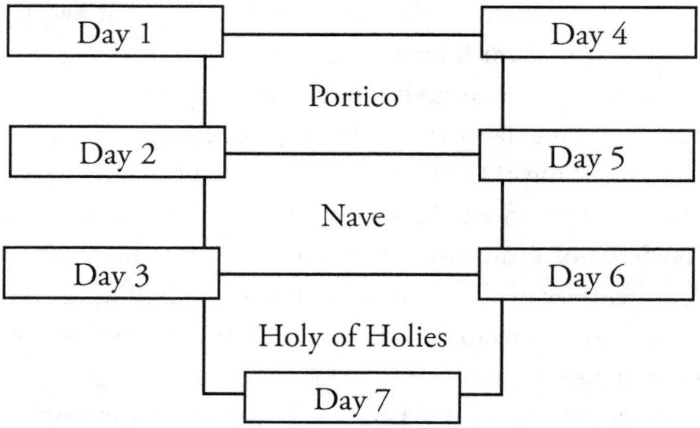

As creation unfolds "daily," it becomes constructed in the *imago templi*, in the model of a temple.[8] The correspondence is unmistakable: in the temple's holiest recess, its inner sanctum, God dwells, and on the holiest day of the week God rests.[9] The primary theological message of Genesis 1, thus, is that creation is God's cosmic temple,[10] the temple of life.

Imago Dei

The cosmic temple of Genesis 1 also reveals something significant about humanity's role and identity in the creation account. As a rule, temples throughout the ancient Near East contained an image of its resident deity. In Jerusalem, however, the physical representation of God was expressly forbidden, at least by the time of the exile (sixth century BCE), as one finds, for example, conveyed in a certain commandment of the Decalogue: "You shall not make for yourself an idol" (Exod 20:4; Deut 5:8). Because God was considered to be without form, the deity could not be represented (see Deut 4:12-18).

8. The cosmos construed as a temple is not unprecedented in biblical tradition. See, e.g., Isa 66:1-2, which criticizes those who are intent on rebuilding the temple by arguing that creation itself is God's sanctuary. See also Job 38:4-7.

9. See 1 Kgs 8:10-13; cf. Ps 132:8, 13-14.

10. For the ancient Near Eastern background, see Walton, *The Lost World*, 72–92.

However, Genesis 1 does not reject the language of divine "image" (*ṣelem*). Rather, it recasts it by identifying the *imago Dei* with human beings, created on the sixth day:

> Then God said, "Let us make humanity [*'ādām*] in our image [*ṣelem*],
> after our likeness [*dĕmût*]. . . ."
> So God created the human being [*hā'ādām*] in his image [*ṣelem*],
> in the image [*ṣelem*] of God he created them;
> male and female he created them. (1:26a, 27)

Human beings alone, according to the text, bear an iconic relation to the divine. The Hebrew term for "image," *ṣelem*, is elsewhere used for idols, such as the cult statues of other deities.[11] By virtue of their unique creation, human beings take on the status of near divinity. They bear a distinctly theophanic presence in creation. While God lacks a blatantly anthropomorphic profile in Genesis 1, human beings are unequivocally theomorphic by design. Made in God's "image," women and men reflect and refract God's presence in the world. The only appropriate "image of God," in other words, is one made of flesh, blood, and brain, not wood, stone, or gold.

While so much more could be said about the significance of humanity made in the "image of God," and on various levels,[12] it is clear that such language points foremost to humanity's elevated position vis-à-vis the rest of creation. Tremper Longman III puts it well: the "image of God" indicates "status" as opposed to "attribute," specifically a function-based status.[13] And what does such "status" entail? Exercising dominion. The language of Genesis 1 is admittedly harsh, particularly in the call to "subdue" the earth.

11. E.g., Num 33:52; 2 Kgs 11:18; 2 Chron 23:17; Ezek 7:20; Amos 5:20. For more detailed discussion of the semantic range of this term, see J. Richard Middleton, *The Liberating Image: The* Imago Dei *in Genesis 1* (Grand Rapids: Brazos, 2005), 45–46.

12. For a cursory overview, see Brown, *Seven Pillars of Creation*, 41–44. See also the possibilities laid out in Andreas Schüle, "Made in the 'Image of God': The Concepts of Divine Images in Gen 1–3," *ZAW* 117, no. 1 (2005): 5–7.

13. Tremper Longman III (personal communication).

God blessed them, and God said to them,
"Be fruitful and multiply,
and fill the earth and subdue it [*wĕkibšūhā*];
and have dominion over." (1:28)

Verse 1:28 has God charging humanity to *kabash* (the verb for "subdue") the earth! It sounds as bad as it means. Outside of Genesis, the verb can connote military conquest, as in Zechariah 9:15 and Numbers 32:29. In Jeremiah 34:11, *kābaš* refers to forced subjugation into slavery. It is difficult to soften its tone, even here in Genesis. Nevertheless, it would be an overstatement to claim that Genesis 1:28 in its larger context envisions the earth as something to be conquered, as if the earth were humanity's enemy. Creation is not chaos, warranting conquest either by God or by humanity. God had pronounced creation "good" six times before humanity arrived on the scene (1:4, 10, 12, 18, 21, 25). Nevertheless, reference to "subdue" carries the "dominion" motif into the setting of battle, and "dominion" affirms a hierarchy in which human beings assume supremacy.

What this passage meant to an ancient agrarian society does not call for outright war with creation. For the farmer who must toil painfully to turn rocky, hilly, and heavily forested land into arable fields, this passage spoke volumes. Backbreaking effort to make the land productive for human subsistence was no easy, peaceful matter. The land's rocky soil was resistant to plowing and thus had to be forced into productivity. The hills had to be terraced. This was how the passage was understood by our ancient agriculturalists, who were not only cultivators of the soil but experts in animal husbandry. The passage inscribes the farmer as a royal warrior in the cultivation of the soil and in the care of flocks and herds, all within a prescribed hierarchy of life.

Who is God? How good is creation? How and why did God create, and for what purpose? What is humanity's place in creation? All these issues are broached in Genesis 1, even if they are not fully answered. To be sure, there are many other layers and issues to explore in Genesis 1, but this will have to suffice for now. We can only scratch the surface of the cosmic temple and humanity's role in it. It is now time to scrape the garden soil in Genesis 2–3.

The Gardener and the Groundling: Genesis 2–3

In Genesis 2:4b–3:24, the God of the cosmos exchanges the royal scepter for a garden spade. The God from on high becomes the God on the ground, a down-and-dirty deity. Known as the Yahwist account for its prominent use of the divine name YHWH,[14] this second creation story is altogether different in tone, content, and scope from Genesis 1. Compared to the lofty liturgical cadences of its canonical predecessor, this account reads more like a simple story with a less than happy ending. Methodical progression gives way to narrative bumps and twists. While the Priestly account spans the breadth of the cosmos with systematic rigor, the Yahwist story, with its focus on a family, revels in messy drama.

The opening scene in Genesis 2 could not be more different: whereas the Priestly account begins with dark, watery "chaos," the Yahwist account opens with dry, barren terrain—a land of lack. Yet both scenes emphasize an initial setting of emptiness. In their canonical ordering, the reader exits, as it were, the glorious cosmic temple of Genesis 1 and enters "an inhospitable field of clay."[15] Here the "ground" (*'ădāmâ*) takes center stage, cast as a major character in the narrative. The grand cosmogony of Genesis 1 is followed by a soil-bound anthropogony in Genesis 2–3.

As the Priestly account follows a discernible pattern of presentation, so the Yahwist account bears its own narrative logic. But as a bona fide story, the structure is more dynamic and open ended. It unfolds in four scenes, each containing parallel elements (Gen 2:4b-17; 2:18-25; 3:1-7; 3:8-24). Each scene identifies a deficiency followed by God's response. The plot is driven by the fits and starts of ongoing creative activity, suggesting more an improvisation than a meticulously executed program, or if put to

14. Usually translated "Lord," beginning with the Greek Septuagint (*kyrios*) and found in most modern translations, this proper name for God in Hebrew is not pronounced by most Jewish readers. Hence, only the consonants are transliterated from the Hebrew in my translations.

15. Andreas Schüle, "Made in the 'Image of God,'" 15.

music, more like a jazz composition than a Bach fugue. The Yahwist tale is the story of God's responsiveness to certain free variables, particularly the serpent and humankind. In contrast to Genesis 1, creation according to the Yahwist is a series of "not-goods" made good, but with a tragic turn at the end.

The first recounted act of creation in Genesis 2 is not the creation of light out of darkness (1:3) but the fashioning of a human being out of the ground (2:7). The *ʾādām* is made not in the *imago Dei* but in the *imago terrae*, in the image of the earth. Humanity's identity is bound to the ground by a remarkable Hebrew wordplay: the *ʾādām* comes from the "dust" or topsoil of the *ʾădāmâ* ("ground"), which makes humanity a "groundling."[16] But humanity's tie to the land is more than an etymological accident; the *ʾādām*'s origin from the ground also reflects the *ʾādām*'s vocational identity to work or "serve the ground" (2:5, 15). Contrary to Genesis 1, the *ʾādām* is the first rather than the last of God's creatures to be fashioned. Yet this hominin of the humus remains a work in progress. For now, God places the deficient *ʾādām* in a garden, a horticultural feast for the eyes and the appetite (2:9). As "the divine farmer,"[17] God cultivates the soil and plants trees, as well as fingers clay. God's hands are dirty; such is required of God's organic work with the earth, in contrast to God's royal work in Genesis 1.

The theological shift from Genesis 1 to Genesis 2 could not be more dramatic. It is as if God's very royal self underwent an "extreme makeover." The king of the cosmos, the creator of the universe, becomes the king of the compost, grubbing about in the rich soil to plant a garden like a farmer and fashioning a human being from the moistened "dust" or clay like a sculptor. From a Mesopotamian perspective, this God of the garden, YHWH, might be seen as a good candidate for membership among the *lesser* gods (the "Igigi") of the Mesopotamian pantheon, who in one story rebel against their divine overlord, Enlil, because of the hard

16. Relatedly, the word "human" is etymologically related to the Latin *humus*. The Latin *humanus* literally means "earthling."

17. Theodore Hiebert, *The Yahwist's Landscape: Nature and Religion in Early Israel* (New York: Oxford University Press, 1996), 67.

work involved in building irrigation canals.[18] Not so in Eden. God works unbegrudgingly in the soil to cultivate a garden. YHWH has nothing against getting dirty.

Providing water for much of creation, Eden is no ordinary garden. Out of it flow four rivers to water the world: the Pishon, the Gihon, the Tigris, and the Euphrates. In fact, the etymological root of "Eden" has more to do with condition than with location; it designates a setting of delight and plenty (*ʿdn*), the sheer opposite of lack. The garden of "Plenty" is the garden of "Eden."[19] But Eden's garden is no pristine paradise of leisure: it must be tended. The human one is given the task to "serve" and "preserve" the garden and its soil (2:15).[20] The *ʾādām* is tied to the *ʾădāmâ* in service, as the *ʾădāmâ* yields to the *ʾādām* its productivity. Both are bound together in a relationship of reciprocity.

Unlike some ancient creation accounts, humans in Genesis 2 are not created to perform menial labor for the gods, who themselves loathe such toil. The God of Genesis 2 creates the *ʾādām* and bestows upon him the commission to preserve the garden. The garden exists for the "groundling" and the "groundling" for the garden. The *ʾādām* is given wide-ranging freedom with only one specific restriction: he is granted access to "every tree of the garden" except one, the "tree of the knowledge of good and bad" (2:16-17). Autonomous judgment, along with the freedom to act on it, is not in the groundling's cognitive tool kit just yet. Not everything in the garden is for the groundling's use, much less consumption.

For the first time in Genesis, God declares creation "not good" (2:18). While providing support for the *ʾādām*'s physical welfare, the garden is deemed deficient for his social well-being. The groundling lacks a companion, a corresponding other. As a remedy, God creates animals of

18. See the story of "Atrahasis," in Stephanie Dalley, *Myths from Mesopotamia: Creation, the Flood, Gilgamesh and Others*, World's Classics (Oxford: Oxford University Press, 1991), 9–38.

19. Cf. Gen 18:12; Ps 36:8; Neh 9:25; Jer 31:12; 51:34; Ezek 36:35; Joel 2:3.

20. Because the garden is already planted by YHWH, the *ʾādām* does not share in plowing and planting. Thus, his vocation *in* the garden is not the same as his work outside it. In the garden the *ʾādām* is to tend the trees, which are watered by irrigation. Outside the garden, however, the *ʾādām* must cultivate the ground itself, facing all the risks and rigors involved in dry land farming (Gen 2:5; 3:17-19; cf. Deut 11:11-12).

various species also "out of the ground" and brings them to the *'ādām* to be named. The groundling of the garden becomes the first taxonomist. By naming the animals, the primal human constructs a community. Although the *'ādām* shares a measure of identity with the animals, the groundling does not recognize any one of them as his match and mate; he sees nothing of his own "flesh" and "bone" in them (see v. 23). God's initial "experiment" has failed, but the results are not discarded. The animals are left to flourish along with the *'ādām*. The garden has become a community, but one that remains deficient for the *'ādām*.

God resorts to Plan B. God fashions another creature, but this time from the *'ādām*'s own flesh and bone, not from the dust of the ground. This new creation requires, however, a new lack: a part of the *'ādām* must be removed. This new being is no one-way derivation, however: from the creation of the woman (*'iššâ*), the *'ādām* becomes fully a "man" (*'îš*); the *'ādām* gains "his" gender. The narrative acknowledges that the man and the woman are mutually engendered and, at the same time, of common substance and form (flesh-and-bone structure [2:23]). By virtue of the woman's genesis, the groundling finds himself mutated, as it were, into a "man." With the creation of the woman, humanity is now "genderly" separated. In Genesis 1, separation played a key role in creation. In Genesis 2, the separation of flesh makes possible sexual differentiation and, in turn, sexual union. Call it "splitting the *'ādām*."

Through the creation of the woman, the groundling has become a man. In his transformation, nothing is subtracted. He remains a groundling, tied to the earth. Put paradoxically: through the act of "surgical" removal, the *'ādām gains* his manhood, with the woman bearing a functional and physical correspondence to this new man. His cry of joy celebrates their shared identity, which is more than biological.[21] The woman and the man are made in the image of each other, physically, socially, and covenantally.[22] Together, they form a community of correspondence,

21. See, e.g., Laban's acknowledgment of Jacob in Gen 29:14 and similar examples in Judg 9:2 and 2 Sam 5:1.

22. See Walter Brueggemann, "Of the Same Flesh and Bone [Gen 2,23a]," *CBQ* 32 (1970): 532–42.

enjoying mutual companionship and help. A new social world unfolds before them, but one that remains firmly grounded in the garden.

With the creation of the woman, the man now takes on a dual identity: he remains kin to the ground in his humanity as he has become kin to the woman in his gendered identity. As the ground is receptive to the *'ādām*'s labors, the *'ādām* receives its productivity. Analogously, the man and the woman are receptive to each other. No subordination pertains in the garden. The *'ādām*'s service to the garden is rooted in his kinship with the ground. Life in the garden is one of fruitful work, abundance, and intimate companionship. In the garden, there is no fear or shame, even before God. These are "lacks" that are meant to endure. But, alas, they do not.

The creation story of the garden in Genesis 2 leads to a crime-and-punishment story in Genesis 3, the details of which need not be recounted here. Suffice it to say that things do not turn out well. The primal couple's act of disobedience in partaking from the forbidden fruit to become "like God/gods" (3:5) compels God to expel them (3:11) to face the hardships of mortal life outside the garden, including the pain of labor, whether in bearing children or cultivating crops (3:16-19). Death, moreover, becomes a painful reality (v. 19). Outside the garden, humanity becomes fully human. Nevertheless, God does not abandon them.

Thus, a dialogue is born. Is humanity the lofty, nearly divine creature exercising unfettered dominion over creation? Or is humanity bound to the ground in identity, subject to delusions of divinity? Is it humanity's purpose to rule over creation or to serve it? Is God the cosmic king issuing royal commands for all creation? Or is God the divine farmer who gets dirty in the ground? From a Mesopotamian perspective, the question could be recast: Is Israel's God a "high god" or a "lesser god," an Enlil (or Marduk), or one of the lowly Igigi?

And then there is God's *modus operandi* in creation. Does God work out everything methodically and systematically? Or does God resort to alternate plans in the face of free variables, such as human behavior? Does God issue royal edicts, or does God ask questions (see 3:9; 4:9)? To launch a dialogue, one would have to first answer yes to all these questions and then explore their ramifications to make one's own informed judgment in light of one's own context.[23] But these may not be the only alternatives. Enter the Psalms.

Creation in the Psalms

The Psalms are replete with creation imagery, featuring some of the most evocative images of the natural world in all of the Hebrew Bible, whether it is the tree planted beside water channels in the very first psalm, or the "still waters" and "green pastures" of Psalm 23, or the "doe" longing for flowing streams in Psalm 42. Not surprisingly, then, the Psalms offer various visions of creation as a whole and humanity's place in it, continuing the dialogue that was initiated "in the beginning." We will focus on Psalms 8, 33, 65, 104, and 148, but not without occasional reference to other psalms. We begin with the two psalms that resemble Genesis 1 most closely.

Creatio ex iustitia: Psalm 33

Containing as many verses as there are consonants in the Hebrew alphabet, Psalm 33 is a praise hymn that highlights YHWH's benevolence, salvific power, and enduring counsel. The psalm's primary theme is divine strength, as demonstrated both in creation and in the political arena, evoking fear and awe among all inhabitants.

After an extended call to praise (33:1-3), the psalm launches into an account of creation that bears striking resemblance to Genesis 1.

> For upright is YHWH's word,
> and faithful is all his work.

23. From my own context as a white, middle-class member of the PC(USA) who feels the urgency of environmental justice and creation care, I consider the second creation account particularly relevant for recovering a sense of service to the land (and the sea and the air), while the first account underlines the gravity of our responsibility and the power of our ability to fulfill it. Call it a "dominion of service." The danger of stressing Genesis 1 at the expense of Genesis 2 is evident in our mounting environmental crises, as first noted by Lynn T. White Jr., "The Historical Roots of Our Ecological Crisis," *Science* 144 (March 10, 1967): 1203–7.

He loves righteousness and justice;
    the earth is filled with YHWH's benevolence.
By YHWH's word the heavens were made,
    and by the breath of his mouth all their celestial host.
He gathered the waters of the sea as in a bottle;[24]
    he put the watery depths in storerooms.
All the earth fears YHWH;
    all the inhabitants of the earth stand in awe of him.
For he spoke, and it came to be!
    He commanded, and there it stood! (33:4-9)

Psalm 33 gives praise-filled testimony to YHWH's magnificence and creative prowess. YHWH's "word" and "work" are united in divine integrity: YHWH is fundamentally "upright" (*yāšār*) and "faithful" (*be'ĕmûnâ*). The latter quality connotes a sense of trustworthy steadfastness, of being firmly grounded in past relational commitments.[25] YHWH, moreover, is committed unequivocally to "righteousness and justice" (*ṣĕdāqâ ûmišpāṭ*). The God of Psalm 33 is a normative God, not a deity who acts capriciously or unpredictably. Consequently, the earth is "filled" with God's "benevolence" (*ḥesed*) or unwavering care. How so? Because God created it so. Creation is itself testimony of YHWH's love for justice.

Like Genesis 1, Psalm 33 highlights creation by word. In Genesis, the divine word takes the form of a series of commandments, uttered ten times over six days (Gen 1:3-31). Psalm 33 also makes reference to divine "commandment" (33:9b), equivalent to God's "word" (*dābār*) and coordinated with God's "breath" (*rûaḥ*), similar to *rûaḥ* in Genesis 1:2. But the psalm adds something new to God's discursive way that is absent in Genesis 1. The divine "word" in Psalm 33 is deemed "upright" (33:4). The psalmist claims God's MO in creation as morally credible.

Creation begins in Psalm 33 with the fashioning of the celestial sphere, collapsing the distinction between primordial "light" and the "lights" in Genesis (1:3, 14-18). The celestial "host" (*ṣābā'*) comprises the stars, sun,

24. Read *kĕnōd* with LXX (*hōs askon*) for MT *kannēd* ("as a heap"), given the parallelism with "storehouses" (*'ōṣārôt*) in the second line.

25. See Hos 2:20; Prov 28:20; Deut 32:4; Pss 89:49[50]; 98:3.

and moon, as well as the lesser divine beings ("messengers" or angels) that populate the heavenly realm (cf. Job 1:6-12). The one divine deed that is prominently highlighted in the psalmic account is that of God "gathering" (*kōnēs*) the waters together as if into a "bottle." Such "gathering" marks the containment of chaos and the ordering of the world (see Gen 1:9-10; Ps 104:9; Prov 8:29). All in all, God's creation is infused with purpose: to render a creation that is secured for the flourishing of life. It is a morally benevolent purpose, one that is to be reciprocated by its inhabitants.

YHWH's cosmic accomplishments elicit "fear" and "awe" (√*yrh*, √*gwr*), a response that is "fitting" for all creation, just as much as praise to God is fitting for all God's people (33:1b). Indeed, the parallel is not one of contrast but of complementarity: fear and praise, awe and joy, are wedded together in this psalm. To praise YHWH who "loves justice and righteousness" is integral to "fearing" the God who created it all. The final verse of this section acclaims YHWH's power to create: YHWH speaks all creation into being, a testimony of YHWH's incomparable, sovereign power.[26]

Both Psalm 33 and Genesis 1 testify to God's creative prowess by word. But what Psalm 33 does that Genesis 1 does not do is identify God's motivating purposes in creating the cosmos. God's word is "upright" and "faithful," since it comes from a God who "loves righteousness and justice." No indication of such motivation is given in Genesis, as if the Priestly author wanted God to remain shrouded in mystery. There is, of course, nothing wrong with mystery, particularly when it comes to God and the cosmos; it is no deficiency of Genesis 1. Nevertheless, the psalmist found it paramount to give language to the divine motivating forces behind creation. It is not just God's sovereign power that is at stake in creation; it is also God's justice and righteousness, which play out in the rest of the psalm in the political sphere, as they do in the cosmic realm.

YHWH's "counsel" or word trumps the "counsel of the nations" (33:10-11). YHWH, the creator of all, hearts included, discerns all, hearts

26. Such psalmic testimony echoes the dramatic demonstration of Marduk's ascendancy to universal sovereignty in the Babylonian Epic of Creation, demonstrated by Marduk's destroying and re-creating a constellation, all by verbal command (*Enūma Elish* IV.25–26). But the psalm, by contrast, infuses YHWH's power with moral significance.

included. The psalm effortlessly makes the leap from YHWH's power to create to YHWH's power to discern all thoughts and deeds. Nothing is hidden from God's all-discerning gaze. A contrastive parallel unfolds: the psalm's creation account praises the seamless connection between divine word and deed as YHWH commands creation into being. Not so, however, with human beings: their plans of the heart may go unfulfilled, for YHWH has the power to override the might of kings and warriors. As creator of all, YHWH can be the frustrater of all, proving certain hopes to be vain or false.

In the psalmist's creation story, the seamless connection between divine word and deed is pressed into service to affirm YHWH's power to sever the connection between human scheme and deed, between nationalistic plans and military success. YHWH's plans are to fulfill YHWH's love of justice and benevolence for those who are faithful. In the end, as at the very beginning, the fulfillment of benevolence for a chosen people is itself an act of creation from the God who created all things, from the heavens to the watery abyss, including a people. Acting in benevolence within the political sphere is part of God's *creatio continua*, and acting by creating is acting with justice, uniting the cosmic and the political, the creational and the juridical, through YHWH's "upright" word. For the psalmist, creation does not end with creation, as one might gather from Genesis 1 with its final seventh day. In the psalm, creation never stops; it continues through God's benevolent and just word. Call it the "eighth day" and counting.

Fighting for Fertility: Psalm 65

Psalm 65 is a hymn of praise from start to finish, whose concluding focus suggests a harvest festival as its context, a year "crowned" with God's "goodness" (65:12a). It is easy to imagine the psalm as a communal expression of thanksgiving for a bountiful yield. The overall movement of the psalm, from sanctuary to creation, also makes a didactic point; the psalm serves as a reminder that the one who is responsible for the earth's fertility is the God of Zion. It is from Zion's sanctuary that God's blessing of fertility extends to all creation.

To you (even) silence is praise,[27] O God in Zion;
  to you vows are fulfilled,
    you who hear prayer.
  To you all life[28] comes.
When sinful matters overpower me,
  you yourself forgive our transgressions.
How happy is the one whom you choose and bring near (to you),
  who dwells in your courts.
We are satisfied with the goodness of your house,
  (with) the holiness of your temple. (65:1-4)

Psalm 65 locates the creator of all in Zion, the center of creation. Location or place is paramount. In Psalm 33, God is located in heaven, God's "royal dwelling place," looking down upon the nations (33:13-14). In Psalm 65, God is placed in Zion, God's dwelling place on earth. More contrastive is Genesis 1, in which *no* specific place is named for God, and for good reason: time is of paramount importance in the Priestly account. Indeed, it is out of time that a cosmic sanctuary is fashioned, a temple in time transcending all sense of locality. In fact, there is no center to creation in Genesis 1, as there is in Psalm 65. By comparison, Psalm 65 highlights the uniqueness of Genesis 1, the primacy of time over space, the temporal over the locational. Zion is to creation in Psalm 65 as Babylon is to creation in *Enūma elish* and as the sabbath day is to creation in Genesis 1.[29]

Psalm 65 also begins with a philosophical conundrum: even "silence" (*dumîyâ*) is considered praise by God. Throughout the Psalms, praise is typically expressed with words, whether sung or recited. Praise is meant to be loud and ringing (cf. Ps 42:4). But in Psalm 65, "silence" itself constitutes a form of praise to God in a sanctuary of silence. As God can "hear prayer" (65:2a), so God can hear silent praise. But how can silence, emptied of sound, be satiated with praise? The next strophe offers a clue.

27. *BHS* proposes *dōmîyâ* (Qal ptc 3fs from *dmh* I, "to be like, resemble") for MT *dumîyâ* ("silence, rest"), rendering "praise befits you" (so LXX). But MT makes perfect, if paradoxical, sense.

28. Hebrew *bāśār*, typically translated "flesh."

29. As the "home of the great gods" and "the center of religion," Babylon is the place where the gods can find rest whenever they want (*Enūma Elish* V.129).

With awesome deeds you answer us in righteousness,
O God of our salvation.
[You are] the trust of all the ends of the earth,
and the distant seas,[30]
who establishes the mountains with his strength,
girded with might,
who stills the roaring of the seas,
the roaring of their waves,
and the uproar of the peoples.
Even those who dwell on the margins stand in awe of your signs;
you make the gateways of the morning and evening shout for joy.
(65:5-8)

God is celebrated for "awesome deeds" in creation, specifically deeds that overcome chaos, beginning with the establishment of the mountains, which in ancient cosmology served as weight-bearing pillars that stabilized the earth and held aloft the celestial dome and the "waters above" (cf. Gen 1:6-7). The image of God "girded with might" highlights the warrior character of the deity who vanquishes chaos, specifically "stilling" (√*šbʿ*) or silencing the sea's "roaring" (*šĕʾôn*) and the people's "uproar" (*hămôn*). Chaos knows no boundary between nature and society. Political chaos is just as threatening to creation's integrity as cosmic chaos, represented by the unruly seas and their pounding waves (see Pss 74:13-14; 78:13).

As for the surging seas, the Psalms are not entirely in agreement about their status in creation. Two enthronement psalms, for example, regard the "roaring" of the seas as bona fide praise in response to God's sovereign rule (96:11; 98:7; cf. 93:3-4). But not in Psalm 65: the *silenced* seas are a sign of divine strength imposed upon creation and, at the same time, a form of praise to God, the silent sound of submission. The clue to how "silence" is a form of praise in verse 2 is now divulged: such praise-filled silence commemorates the silencing of chaos, both cosmic and political (v. 7). It is the "sound" of silenced sin, whose power is undercut by divine forgiveness (65:4). Such silence is received in awe by those on the

30. Perhaps read *yammîm* for MT *yam*, due to haplography, or the singular can be taken as a collective.

"margins" (*qĕṣôt*) and accompanied with joyful shouting by the "gateways," the geographical extremes where the sun rises and sets.

Silence is the pause of praise that gives way to the shouting of praise, and not just from a people. Even the meadows turn melodious and the valleys become vociferous in praise.

> You visit the earth, causing it to overflow,
> enriching it abundantly by God's channel, full of water.
> You prepare their grain, for so you have ordained it.[31]
> Drenching its furrows, leveling its ridges,
> with rain showers you soften it.
> You bless its growth.
> You crown the year with your goodness,
> your paths flow with fecundity.
> (Even) the desert pastures overflow,
> and the hills gird themselves with joy.
> The meadows clothe themselves with flocks,
> and the valleys deck themselves with grain.
> They shout for joy;
> indeed, they break out in song. (65:9-13)

The psalm's final strophe continues the theme of creation but with a particular focus on the land's fertility. Here, the divine warrior morphs into the divine farmer, as the suppression of chaos leads to creation's fructification. The move from victory to fecundity, moreover, hints of theophanic drama: God "visits" (√*pqd*) the earth with water. But God comes not in a lightning storm to gain victory over chaos but in "rain showers" to gain fertility, including "grain" (*dāgān*). As watery chaos was subdued to (re)establish order on earth, so now watery abundance is unleashed to bring forth "growth" on earth (v. 10b). From below, God's "channel" (*peleg*) waters the earth, and from above, showers soften the earth's "furrows" and "ridges." The result is not a flood but a farm (cf. Gen 7:11). The meadows and valleys break forth in "song," but they do so in ways that are silent to human ears. Their praise is their produce.

31. The same verb is used in both cola (√*kwn* in *Hiphil).*

The earth's fecundity extends even to the deserts and rocky hills, not just to the fertile valleys and meadows (65:12-13). Verse 12a serves as an effective summary: a bountiful harvest marks a year "crowned" with God's "goodness" (*ṭôbâ*), as much as the community is satisfied with the temple's "goodness" (65:4b). In Psalm 65, temple and creation are bound together, as they are in Genesis 1, but in a localized rather than temporal way. The temple's holy "goodness" reflects creation's fertile "goodness," and vice versa. Indeed, the temple's very existence signifies the defeat of chaos in ancient Near Eastern mythology: Marduk built his shrine only after Tiamat was slain. Ba'al built his temple after Mot was defeated. The silence of praise signifies the silencing of chaos. But from the psalmist's perspective, that is only one half of it. Such silencing also points to all creation in praise.

When compared to the two Genesis accounts of creation, one can discern how Psalm 65 integrates their "opposing" themes and corrects their perceived "deficiencies." The emphasis on temple, writ temporally and cosmically in Genesis 1, finds resonance in Psalm 65 with its identification of the creator as the God "in Zion" (65:1a). In the psalm, the "goodness" of the temple (65:4bα) parallels the fertile goodness of the land (65:11-13). In addition, explicit reference to the temple's "holiness" (65:4bβ) suggests a convergence that one finds elsewhere only in Genesis 1 with the sanctified seventh day (Gen 2:1-3). Psalm 65, however, does not discern the image of the temple applying to all of creation; the temple remains localized in Zion, as in Psalm 33. Nevertheless, a hint of the cosmic temple is registered where the psalm states, hyperbolically perhaps, that "all life comes to you" (65:2b), that is, to God "in Zion" (cf. Ps 84:3). The connection between temple and creation is strong: both are bountiful. But creation is not a replacement for the temple, as might be implied in Gen 1:1–2:3 (cf. Isa 66:1-2). In the psalm, creation and temple are paralleled, but one does not subsume the other.

In contrast to Genesis 1, Psalm 65 retrieves the image of God as the warrior who silences the forces of chaos, both cosmic and political. In Psalm 65, *Chaoskampf* ("chaos fight") matches *Schöpfermacht* ("creator might"). The creator's strength is demonstrated not only in the construction of the mountains (65:6a) but in the silencing of the seas (65:7). In the end, however, the divine warrior proves to be the divine farmer, as one finds in the garden story of Genesis 2. But lacking is any sense of divine "vulnerability" implied in Genesis 2–3. There is no improvisation on God's part in Psalm 65 as there is in Genesis 2. There is no strolling through the garden during the "evening breeze" and asking questions (Gen 3:8; 4:9). The God of Psalm 65 is all strength, "girded with might" (65:6b). The divine warrior in Psalm 65 is the warrior farmer, whose victory is testified to by the fructification of creation. Unsatisfied with the way God was depicted in Genesis 2–3, the psalmist resolved to rehabilitate God's image by infusing the farmer with all majesty and power. The resulting depiction: the divine warrior-farmer on the march, silencing seas, and unleashing streams, all for the enrichment of the land and the prosperity of a people. The divine farmer in Psalm 65 is no improviser but a royal warrior. It is as if the psalmist had found the link between the cosmic king in Genesis 1 and the immanent farmer in Genesis 2–3: God's militant might.

From Divine Majesty to Human Majesty: Psalm 8

As the first praise psalm in the Psalter, Psalm 8 finds direct kinship with Genesis 1, but with a very different agenda from what we find in Psalm 33.

> YHWH, our Lord, how majestic is your name throughout all the earth.
> You whose splendor above the heavens is recounted[32]

---

32. The text is corrupt; the Masoretic verbal form (Qal emphatic imperative from *ntn*) does not make sense. For a review of the proposals with a new solution, see Mark S. Smith, "Psalm 8:2b-3: New Proposals for Old Problems," *CBQ* 59 (1997): 637–41, who reconstructs an original phrase consisting of two first-person cohortatives, *'āšîrâ 'ētĕnâ*, from the roots *šyr* and *tny*, respectively, resulting in the following translation: "*I will sing / celebrate* your splendor over the heavens." For other suggestions, see *HALOT*, 1760–61. The simplest solution, which admittedly requires a redivision of verses, is to repoint the verb as a Pual perfect form of *tnh* (*tny*): *tunnâ* ("it is recounted/celebrated"). This may be reflected in LXX's use of the passive: "is exalted" (*epērthē* from *epairō*). In any case, the resulting redivision resolves the role of the "nursing infants": they are agents of expressive praise.

by the mouths of nursing children.[33]
You have established a strong refuge[34] on account of your foes;
you have utterly[35] vanquished the avenging enemy.[36] (Ps 8:1-2[2-3])

When I observe your heavens, the works of your fingers—
the moon and the stars that you have established—
"What are human beings that you call them to mind,
mortals that you care for them?" (Ps 8:3-4[4-5])

You have made them slightly less than[37] divine;[38]
with glory and grandeur you have crowned them.
You grant them dominion over the works of your hands;
you have put everything under their feet:
All sheep and cattle,
as well as the beasts of the field,
birds of the air and fish of the sea,
those that pass along the paths of the sea.
YHWH, our Lord, how majestic is your name throughout all the earth!
(Ps 8:5-9[6-10])

Psalm 8 is "bookended" by praise of YHWH's "majestic" and sovereign name. Within the bracketing refrain is a concentrically arranged prayer that proceeds from praise of God's glory to a claim of humanity's glory. While the psalm sets divine glory and human glory in mirror-like apposition (not opposition), it distinguishes them in terms of the different scales by which glory is measured: cosmic versus earthly. Lodged squarely

33. The appositional arrangement of *'ôlĕlîm wĕyōnĕqîm* (literally "infants and nurslings") constitutes a hendiadys.

34. The root of *'ōz* is better identified with *'wz* ("to take refuge"; cf. *mā'ôz*) rather from *'zz* ("to be strong").

35. The parallelism suggests that the masoretically pointed infinitive Hiphil construct was originally a finite form of the stem with a proclitic asseverative use of the *lamed*, as found often in Ugaritic (Smith, "Psalm 8:2b-3," 640).

36. The conjunction of *'ôyēb ûmitnaqqēm* constitutes a hendiadys.

37. From the verb *ḥsr*, "to lack."

38. Or "gods" (*'ĕlōhîm*), the members of the divine council (cf. Ps 82:1). LXX reads "angels."

in the center is the question regarding humanity's identity and place in creation (8:4[5]), serving as the psalm's pivot. Even here, a rhetorical link is established between the refrain extoling God's sovereignty and the central question of human identity: both begin with the particle *mâ*, which is used for exclamation in the bracketing refrains ("how!" in 8:1[2], 9[10]), but in the center used as an interrogative ("what?" in 8:4[5]).

But to get from divine majesty to human glory, the psalmist testifies to how YHWH's splendor "above the heavens" is recounted, namely through the mouths of nursing infants. How is that possible? The psalmist is not interested in translating baby babble. The answer lies in the next verse: YHWH has established a refuge that keeps even infants, the most vulnerable of human beings, safe and secure. They are free to express their praise in complete safety, as incoherent as such praise may sound. In God's refuge, all danger is banished, so that even the most helpless can render praise to God.

As the most well-known part of the psalm, the middle section (8:3-4[4-5]) pivots from YHWH's cosmic glory to humanity's earthly glory, introduced by a question that bears perennial significance: What is humanity amid the vastness of the cosmos? The speaker scans the night sky, observing the moon and the constellations, all creations of God's "fingers." No credence is given to their mythological background as deities. Nevertheless, the psalm's tone is distinctly unpolemical and, conversely, filled with awe.

It is in such awe that the speaker inquires of humanity's identity and place. The question posed is more than simply asking, "Who am I?" For the psalmist, the question of human identity cannot be asked apart from reference to God, posed as it is in the context of God's remembrance (*√zkr*) and active attention (*√pqd*). Of note, the question does not begin with "who?" (*mî*), but with "what?" (*mâ*), which could confer a sense of insignificance. More significantly, the interrogative echoes the refrain, thereby infusing the question with a sense of praise-filled wonder. The question, "What is humanity that you call them to mind?" could be rephrased with a touch of self-deprecation, "How is it that you would even consider calling tiny humanity to mind?" Why would God even bother with this creature? But God does, and therein lies the wonder.

In short, the psalmist's central question concerning humanity's identity and place in the universe carries a double significance: (1) a sense of humanity's insignificance before creation's cosmic splendor, and (2) a sense of awe and mystery that humanity remains the object of YHWH's caring attention. The former presses the latter. As for the reason behind the mystery of YHWH's mindfulness of humanity, the final section spells it out (8:5-8[6-9]).

The answer to why YHWH remains so attentive to humanity is because YHWH has created humanity for a particular role. Compared to the divine realm, the human realm is "slightly less" (√*ḥsr*) in terms of "glory" and "grandeur," indicating that the difference is only a matter of degree. When compared to the divine, a small deficiency turns out to be a great surfeit, a surplus of splendor. As God shares in "splendor" (*hôd*), so humanity shares in "grandeur" (*hādār*). It is no coincidence that "splendor" and "grandeur" are often paired as dual descriptors of divine majesty (e.g., Pss 21:5[6]; 45:3[4]; 96:6; 104:1). But in Psalm 8, the alliterative pair is split and consequently shared between God and humanity. "How great thou art" is complemented, in effect, by "how great we are." But humanity's greatness or "glory," the psalm makes clear, is a derived glory: it rests on God's glory in so far as humanity is created and endowed by God.

With such a statement, the pivot in Psalm 8 amounts to a whiplash, a rapid shift from a state of human insignificance to that of human glory. The occasion for such elevation is a shift in scale. Whereas God's glory is thoroughly cosmic, humanity's glory is localized on the earth. Moreover, humanity's "glory" is distinctly royal, the glory of dominion, whose exercise is found in ruling over the biological order, just as in Genesis 1:26-28. The list of animals proceeds outward from those closest to home (i.e., domesticated animals) to the wild and most far-reaching, including the creatures of the sea. But all are set "under [humanity's] feet," a vivid expression of royal subjugation (cf. Ps 18:38[39]; Lam 3:34). Humanity constitutes the holy human empire, whose subjects are the nonhuman animals. *Homo imperiosis* is the functional sign of humanity's "glory." But is the human empire given free reign?

With its final verse, the psalm closes the circle of glory with the refrain rendering praise once again to YHWH's "majestic name." Bracketing the psalm, the refrain represents the psalm's entry point and exit point. God's cosmic sovereignty is so manifest that it is recounted even by infants. Human dominion, however, is derivative. For all its testimony to human glory, the psalm reminds the reader whence such glory comes. As the refrain bounds the psalm as a self-contained unity, so divine sovereignty checks human sovereignty. The psalm-bracketing *inclusio* provides a critical theocentric emphasis for a psalm that celebrates anthropocentric glory. While the center of the psalm poses the question about human glory, the psalm's "bookends" answer the question regarding which glory (human or divine) is given the greatest weight. The answer is unequivocal.

Psalm 8 echoes Genesis 1:26-28 in its casting of humanity as dominant over all other creatures. Psalmically, human beings are made "slightly less than the divine" (8:5a). In Genesis, they are made "in the image of God" (1:27). In Genesis, they are to have "dominion over the fish of the sea, and over the birds of the air, and over the cattle, and over all the wild animals of the earth, and over every creeping thing that creeps upon the earth" (1:26b). In Psalm 8, "all sheep and cattle," wild animals, birds, and all sea life are placed "under" humanity's "feet" (8:6-8[7-9]). Whether in prose or poetry, both accounts apply the language of kingship to assert humanity's place in God's creation. The psalm, however, literarily brackets human dominion with divine dominion, making clear that the former is both derivative of the latter and bounded by it.

Can anything comparable be said about the Genesis account? Humanity, to be sure, is not self-made but derived as God's "image." While humanity is blessed and mandated to exercise such dominion, it also finds its royal power mitigated in at least two ways. God's final words in Genesis 1 make explicit that the produce of the land is given for both human and nonhuman animal life, with the only distinction that humans are given the plants "yielding seed" (for cultivation), whereas the nonhuman animals have "every green plant" (1:29-30). In addition, the Priestly account concludes climactically not with humanity's creation but with the establishment of the Sabbath, the holy day that is devoid of work. For human beings, the exercise of dominion stops on the seventh day (Exod 20:7-11). In Psalm 8, human dominion stops at divine sovereignty. The psalmist recasts the "image of God" language as something of a paradox: there is the contrast between divine and human glory, between the cosmic and the earthly, on the one hand, and there is the convergence of divine and human glory, on the other. The result is that humanity will always be "slightly" lacking in divinity while fully endowed with "glory."

Regardless of the different ways human agency is profiled, Genesis 1 and Psalm 8 promulgate a hierarchical view of humanity's dominant position over creation, of humanity's supremacy over all nonhuman animal life, a distinctly royal form of dominance. Such is not the only perspective of humanity's place in creation, however, in the Bible. As noted above, the garden story of Genesis 2 presents a radically different perspective in which the "original" archetypal human is commissioned to "serve" and "preserve" the ground (Gen 2:15), rather than to "subdue it" (1:28). Here, the *'ādām* is the servant of the soil. Nevertheless, God creates the animals for the *'ādām* to "name" and thereby define them relative to himself (2:19-20). Here, too, the animals find themselves subordinated to humanity. While Psalm 8 falls into the dominion camp next to Genesis 1, another psalm provides a powerful countermodel, while another recasts dominion in a way that forges a compromise, as we shall see, as the creation dialogues continue.

Homo sapiens in a *Terra sapiens:* Psalm 104[39]

A very different picture of creation is featured in Psalm 104, which celebrates creation's diversity and commends all of creation for YHWH's enjoyment, a poetic revelry of praise to YHWH as creator and provider. This cosmic liturgy proceeds from the meteorological to the zoological to the anthropological, all expressed doxologically.

39. This discussion builds on my earlier treatment of Psalm 104 in William P. Brown, *The Seven Pillars of Creation: The Bible, Science, and the Ecology of Wonder* (New York: Oxford University Press, 2010), 141–59.

Often noted is the parallel movement or structure featured in Genesis 1 and Psalm 104. It is so evident that one is tempted to delineate the psalm's structure in terms of the "days" of creation enumerated in Genesis: Day 1 = Psalm 104:1-2; Day 2 = 104:3-4; Day 3 = 104:5-9; Day 4 = 104:19-20; Day 5 = 104:12, 17, 25-26; Day 6 = 104:23. But as one can see, such paralleling works well only for the first three days, those days that establish the creational domains of light, heaven, and land (vs. sea). Thereafter, the psalmist veers away from the methodical progression of Genesis to revel in the wonder of creation's biodiversity. Creation in Psalm 104 is not simply a matter of the primordial past, as one might infer from Genesis 1. Rather, creation is ongoing in God's sustained provision and care for all creatures.

> All of them wait for you,
> to provide their food on time.
> You give to them, and they gather it up;
> you open your hand, and they are well filled.
> But when you hide your face, they are terrified;
> when you gather up their breath, they expire,
> returning to their dust.
> (But) when you send forth your breath, they are created,
> and you renew the face of the earth. (104:27-30)

Creation is as much a beginning point in the primordial past as it is the continuation of provision and renewal into the present.

As Genesis 1 testifies to how "goodness" is built into creation at every step in the process, so Psalm 104 acknowledges God's "wisdom" throughout creation.

> How many are your works, YHWH!
> With wisdom you have made them all.
> The earth is full of your creations! (104:24)

The psalmist exclaims God's wisdom in creation (cf. Prov 3:19-20), implying that the world itself is a *Terra sapiens*—a "wise world" of wondrous diversity, a world that hosts a staggering variety of animals: onagers, birds, cattle, cedars, storks, mountain goats, coneys, lions, and, yes, Leviathan—all attesting to God's wise handiwork.

By listing various animal species, the psalmist offers a rich sample of the vast panoply of life. As species are varied and numerous, so also are their habitats and niches, from towering trees and flowing wadis to mountainous crags and the deep dark sea. The psalm acknowledges that each species has its rightful habitat: the trees are for the birds (104:12, 17), the mountains are for the wild goats, the crags provide shelter for the "coneys" or rock hyrax (104:18), the lions have their dens (104:22), and Leviathan has its abyss (104:26).

As for human beings, they have their place but no dominant place in relation to the other creatures. While "cattle" are mentioned (104:14a), such reference is not given to highlight their use for human consumption. Instead, they are consumers of "grass" as much as human beings are cultivators of plants. In YHWH's cosmic mansion there are many dwelling places, each "fit" for each species. Humanity's place in creation is as legitimate as that of any other species, but it is not singled out as central or dominant within the psalm's expansive purview. Instead of assuming a dominant place in the "great chain of being," humanity in Psalm 104 is given a nonanthropocentric entry into what might be called the "great encyclopedia of being." Creation is not simply habitat for humanity; it is habitat for diversity.

Nevertheless, creation is more than a plethora of habitats; it is also the means of sustenance and provision for all life.

> [God] sends forth springs into the wadis;
>   between the mountains they flow,
>   giving drink to every wild animal,
>   breaking the onagers of their thirst. (104:10-11)

> Who waters the mountains from his lofty abodes;
>   from the fruit of your hands the earth is satisfied;
> Who makes the grass grow for cattle,
>   and plants for human cultivation

to bring forth food from the earth:
wine, which cheers the human heart,
oil,[40] which makes the face shine,
and bread, which sustains the human heart.
The trees of YHWH are well watered;
the cedars of Lebanon, which he planted.
There the birds build their nests;
the stork has its home in the fir trees. (Ps 104:13-17)

The psalmist lingers admiringly over the mighty cedars of Lebanon, whose timber was a prized commodity among the mighty empires of antiquity in the Fertile Crescent.[41] Armies from Mesopotamia would march westward, conquering cities and territories in their path, to get to the cedar forests near the Mediterranean seaboard, cut them down, and use the lumber for constructing their monumental palaces and temples. The psalmist, however, prizes these trees not for their lumber but for their majesty and their capacity to accommodate life. In God's creation, according to Psalm 104, even trees have standing.

Remarkably, for all its panoramic overview, the psalm does not directly mention human beings until 104:23, and only after the lions. As in Genesis 1, humanity is a literary latecomer, but it is not saved for last as the best of all creatures.

You bring on the darkness and it is night;
when every animal of the forest prowls.
The young lions roar for their prey;
seeking their food from God.
When the sun rises, they withdraw,
and to their dens they retire.
Humans go forth to their work,
to their labor until evening. (104:20-23)

40. The text is corrected in view of a likely dittography of the *mem*.

41. As attested in various royal annals of the ancient Near East, particularly Assyrian and Babylonian. Solomon, too, had cedar timber from Lebanon transported down the coast for building the temple in Jerusalem (1 Kgs 5:6-14).

If one did not know any better, one might think that the only difference between lions and humans is that the former take the "night shift," while humans take the "day shift" to earn their living. Humanity in Psalm 104 is merely one species among many, all coexisting together, each with its niche in creation and its rhythm for flourishing. Absent, however, is the language of dominance over creation; no animal is placed "under" humanity's "feet" in Psalm 104.

Another issue that Psalm 104 broaches is one that neither Genesis 1 nor Psalm 8 addresses explicitly, the matter of chaos. Enter Leviathan.

> There is the sea, both vast and wide.
> Therein are the sea creatures teeming[42] beyond count,
> living things both small and large.
> There go the ships,
> and Leviathan, with which you fashioned to play![43] (104:25-26)

As evidence of the creator's wisdom, the psalmist points to the vast teeming array of sea creatures. Curiously, the psalm also includes "ships" as part of the sea's domain (104:26a), modestly acknowledging humanity's cocreative role in God's creation (cf. Prov 30:19). More attention, however, is given to Leviathan, a distinctly divine creation (cf. Gen 1:21). Elsewhere in biblical tradition, Leviathan is a multiheaded sea dragon, a monster of mayhem, God's mortal enemy slated for destruction (see Ps 74:12-14; Isa 27:1). A terror-inspiring and detailed description of Leviathan is featured in Job 41, the only animal in the Bible that a whole chapter is devoted to describing. It is a creature clearly not for play but for combat, and its defeat is deemed an urgent necessity for creation's sake in certain biblical traditions.

But in Psalm 104, no hint of horror is to be found. No *Chaoskampf* rages here. Leviathan presents no threat to creation. The psalmist has

42. Literally, "creeping things" (*remeś*). Cf. Gen 1:21; Ps 69:35.

43. The syntax is ambiguous, given the possible antecedents for the suffixed preposition *bô*. Thus, the text could be translated "Leviathan, which you fashioned to play in it" (i.e., the sea; similarly NRSV, NIV, CEB). But this possibility is less likely in view of the syntactical proximity of "Leviathan" in the verse.

taken a symbol of monstrous chaos, a figure of abject terror, and turned it into an object of playful wonder. In the poet's hands, the monster of the deep is stripped of all the trappings of terror and becomes God's partner in play! So if Leviathan is not the purveyor of chaos, who or what is? The psalmist saves the answer until the end.

> May YHWH's glory endure forever!
>   May YHWH rejoice in his works!
> Who looks at the earth, and it trembles;
>   he touches the mountains, and they erupt in smoke.
> I will sing to YHWH as long as I have life;
>   I will sing praise to my God while I still live.
> May my poetic deliberation be pleasing to him;
>   I will rejoice in YHWH.
> Let sinners vanish from the earth,
>   and the wicked be no more.
> Bless YHWH, my whole being!
>   Hallelujah! (104:31-35)

Psalm 104 concludes with acclamations of YHWH's "glory" and "joy," cast injunctively ("may . . ."). YHWH's "glory" is to "endure" in and throughout the manifold character of creation. YHWH, moreover, is invited to "rejoice" in creation (104:31b), a rare request in the Psalms. Indeed, the entire psalm has been building up to this entreaty, revealing in the end its primary theological agenda: to provide credible cause for YHWH's joy. By so vividly describing creation's wise diversity and abundant flourishing, the psalm gives poetic reason for why YHWH's "joy to the world" should endure. Creation is something that God should not only be proud of but also find joy in. Complementing God's approbation of creation in Genesis 1, repeated seven times ("good"), is the psalm's culminating emphasis on divine joy.

But creation is not all perfectly harmonious: YHWH can also, with little effort, cause the earth to "tremble" (√*r'd*) and the mountains to "erupt in smoke" (√*'šn*). Such is the language of theophany. YHWH need only appear for a moment, and all creation convulses, signaling divine power over and against creation. It is to such power that the speaker appeals at the end of the psalm with an imprecation against "sinners" and the "wicked" (104:35a). The transition in this concluding passage from praise to imprecation and back again is jarring. The psalm's cosmic scope, which includes even the monstrous Leviathan within the orbit of God's providential (and playful) care, has no room for the wicked. By exhorting YHWH to destroy the wicked, the psalmist decisively transfers the chaos traditionally associated with mythically monstrous figures like Leviathan and places it squarely on human shoulders.

The "wicked," according to the psalm, pose a threat to creation's integrity. The purveyors of chaos in Psalm 104 are not mythically theriomorphic—monsters made in the image of animals—but monstrously human. Nevertheless, this one glitch in the created order—the threat of the wicked—does not displace the final burst of praise that concludes the psalm (104:35b). As a whole, Psalm 104 is a poetic reflection ("deliberation") on creation that the psalmist offers as praise and motivation for YHWH to rejoice. No mention is made of human dominion to be exercised over creation, contra Genesis 1 and Psalm 8. However, the absence of such language does not mean that humanity is to remain passive. To be sure, humanity's place in creation is neither dominant nor central in the psalm; *Homo sapiens* is simply one species featured among many. Nevertheless, there is a special, if not unique, role that human beings assume in such a flourishing creation (other than threatening creation as the "wicked" do). It is to do what the psalmist does, namely to do whatever it takes to sustain God's joy to the world so that the all the world can be sustained. In the psalmist's case, that means singing out the wonders of creation to YHWH and, by implication, preserving those wonders, all species of life, because that is precisely what gives God joy. It is the wise thing to do.

Psalms 8 and 104 are considered the two great creation psalms of the Psalter, but they could not be more different in their views on humanity's place and role in creation: dominant versus nondominant, supremacy versus coexistence. So how is one to adjudicate them? The question was not lost on the psalmists responsible for the Psalter as a whole. The issue of humanity's place in creation is addressed one more time toward the end of the book, and in a way that provides resolution, appropriately so within the arena of cosmic praise.

Psalm 148: The "Dominion" of Praise

Psalm 148 features a roll call of praise that enlists all of creation in descending order, from heaven to earth to human society.

> Hallelujah![44]
> Praise YHWH from the heavens!
> Praise him in the heights!
> Praise him, all his messengers!
> Praise him all his host.
> Praise him, sun and moon!
> Praise him, all you bright stars!
> Praise him, you highest heavens,
> including you waters that are above the heavens!
> Let them praise the name of YHWH,
> for he commanded and they were created;
> he established them forever and ever;
> he gave a decree that cannot pass away. (148:1-6)
>
> Praise YHWH from the earth,
> you sea monsters and all depths!
> Fire and hail, snow and thick smoke,[45]
> storm wind that fulfills his word!
> Mountains and all hills,
> fruit trees and all cedars!
> Wild animals and all cattle,
> creeping things and winged fowl! (Ps 148:7-10)
>
> Kings of the earth and all peoples,
> princes and all rulers of the earth!

44. Or "praise YH!" (*halĕlû yāh*).

45. The meaning is disputed. LXX, Vulgate, and Peshitta translate "frost," but the root *qṭr* suggests "smoke," or less likely "fog." See the chiastic parallel with "fire" (cf. Gen 19:28).

Young men and women alike,
  old and young together!
Let them praise the name of YHWH,
  for his name alone is exalted;
    his majesty is above earth and heaven.
He has raised a horn for his people,
  the praise for all his faithful,
    for the Israelites, the people that is close to him.
      Hallelujah! (148:11-14)

YHWH's claim on creation-wide praise stems from YHWH's status as the creator who commanded everything into being (148:5b-6). First, the heavenly realm, YHWH's "messengers" or angels and "host" are summoned, as well as the celestial beings and cosmic domains. Next in the roll call are creatures of the earth, from sea monsters to cattle, as well as mountainous domains. Finally, human beings, from kings to youths, men and women alike, are called upon to do the same. As for Israel, praise is warranted because YHWH has empowered the leadership ("horn") of the people, who remain "close" to their God (148:14).

As in Psalm 104, there is no position of dominance for humanity to assume, as if to say that the practice of praise, given its cosmic reach, levels the playing field (or better "praising field") for all God's creatures. Each creature has its rightful place in the choir. Praise seems to have erased all hint of hierarchy. One question to be asked is, What does it mean for "sea monsters" and "cattle" to give praise? For snow and smoke? How do they communicate praise? Like Psalm 19:1-4a[2-5a], Psalm 148 credits communicative power to even "nonliving" agents of creation. Nothing in creation is considered inanimate, and thus nothing lacks the ability to praise God. Everything, both living and nonliving, waits to be called upon to render praise.

Therein lies humanity's special role, a role that, admittedly, retains something of a hierarchy between humanity and all other creatures. However, it is not a hierarchy of dominance. A different kind of hierarchy is signaled in the opening "Hallelujah," a command to "praise Yah(weh)" that runs throughout the psalm until its final "Hallelujah." One need only ask who is issuing these commands of praise in the psalm. In ancient worship practice, it would have been the officiating priest in the temple commanding the congregation for responsive recitation, no doubt in song.

According to Psalm 148, humanity's powerfully prominent (but not dominant) role in creation is to call all creation to praise. While only God can call creation into being, humanity can call creation into praise, fulfilling God's purpose in creation. As we move from Psalm 8 (and Gen 1) to Psalm 148, human dominance over creation is replaced with human enabling of creation's praise. The language of subjugation, as found in Psalm 8, is transformed into liturgical leadership. If it is humanity's role to call nature to praise God, then it is also humanity's role to *make possible* creation's praise, that is, to establish a vital ecosystem of praise throughout the earth. The cosmic temple of Genesis 1 is in the psalmist's vision a temple of praise.

On the one hand, humanity in Psalm 148 is not merely one species among others in God's sight, as viewed in Psalm 104. On the other hand, humanity's role is not to dominate or subjugate creation, as implied in Psalm 8 and Genesis 1. Rather, according to Psalm 148, humanity's unique and powerful role is to enable all creation to render unhindered praise to God. What that looks like from the psalmist's perspective is open for dialogue.[46] But it is enough to note that these five psalms (Pss 8, 33, 65, 104, and 148) host a dialogue that broaches and perhaps resolves, albeit provisionally, the issue of humanity's rightful place and role in God's creation. Creation is not so much to be placed "under the feet" of humanity as to be called forth in praise by humanity. Humanity is the one creature that both summons and is summoned to praise. In the course of the Psalms, humanity moves from being a king over creation to being a priest for creation, ensuring that a creation fully praising is a creation fully flourishing.

As for God in the Psalms, the creator takes on various roles, from the most transcendent to the immanent. We find that the cosmic king is also the earthly farmer who does not begrudge getting dirty in the soil,

46. See the classic essay by Terence E. Fretheim, "Nature's Praise of God in the Psalms," *Ex Auditu* 3 (1987): 16–30.

providing for its fertility. God the creator must also be God the provider. In the Psalms, *creatio completa* (as in Genesis 1) turns *creatio continua* (as in Psalm 104). In the end, the provider of creation's needs is the recipient of creation's praise. Enabling creation's praise is also part of creation's continuing drama, a concluding act in the overarching movement from *creatio continua* to *creatio consummata*. And in the process, the psalmists do their level best to make sure that God remains pleased with creation, that God's "joy to the world" is sustained. God at least deserves that, and human beings can at least ensure that.

CHAPTER 3

THE ANCESTORS: ISRAEL'S STRANGE BEGINNINGS

Look to Abraham your father and to Sarah who bore you;

for he was but one when I called him,

but I blessed him and made him many.

—Isaiah 51:2

As the Bible traces humanity's origin to a primordial past (Gen 1–11), so it traces Israel's origin to an ancestral age, the age of Israel's patriarchs and matriarchs (Gen 12–50). And just as there are various perspectives held in the Bible regarding creation's origin, so there are divergent viewpoints regarding Israel's ancestors. Who were Israel's "ancestors,"[1] and why are they included in the larger narrative of Israel's formation as a people? How are the immigrant "ancestors" connected to Israel in the land and what sets them apart from Israel? What is their legacy for subsequent generations? These are all open questions for rich dialogue, particularly between Genesis and the Psalms.

Genesis 11–12 marks a dramatic pivot where the narrative shifts its attention from humanity in general to a single family, that of Abram and

1. Literally "fathers" (*'ābôt*).

Sarai, a vulnerable couple facing an unknown journey. Genesis recounts their migratory adventures from Mesopotamia, filled with travails and triumphs, as they sojourn across Canaan, extending into Philistia and even Egypt. Their stories are stories of small beginnings that together launch the formation of a people for the sake of worldwide blessing (e.g., Gen 12:3; 18:18; 22:18; 26:4).

The ancestral stories are set within a sweeping narrative that extends from Genesis to Joshua, from migration to land possession, from family story to national saga. Nevertheless, the ancestral community in Genesis is a world unto itself, set apart from Israel's constitution as a "congregation,"[2] a community led by Moses and governed by *tôrâ* (see chapter 6). As R. W. L. Moberly aptly notes, the ancestral narratives of Genesis form the "Old Testament of the Old Testament."[3] The Psalms, however, make no such distinction, as we will see. But first, we cover the narrative highlights of the "ancestral age."

The Ancestors in Genesis 12–50

By tracing four successive generations, this family history begins with a divine command, accompanied by an imperial promise:

> YHWH said to Abram:
>
> "Go forth, you, from your country, from your kindred, and from your father's house to the land that I will show you, so that I will make you into a great nation and bless you and make your name great!
>
> Be a blessing, so that I will bless those who bless you—whereas the one who belittles you I will curse[4]—and that by you all the families of the earth will gain a blessing!" (Gen 12:1-3)

2. The designation of Israel as a "congregation" (*'ēdâ*) is given for the first time in Exod 12:3 (see also 12:6, 47; 16:1; 35:4; 38:25).

3. R. W. L. Moberly, *The Old Testament of the Old Testament: Patriarchal Narratives and Mosaic Yahwism*, OBT (Minneapolis: Augsburg Fortress, 1992).

4. As Patrick D. Miller observes, the reference to curse constitutes an asymmetrically minor part of the blessing ("Syntax and Theology of Genesis 12:3a," *VT* 34, no. 4 [1984]: 472–76).

This new chapter begins with a disruptive divine command to sever family ties for a grand and global purpose: separation from one's family will lead to a blessing for all families. Such worldwide "blessing" is to be achieved by a splintered family becoming a "great nation," a promise given great prominence in Genesis[5] and finding fulfillment in a kingdom.[6]

The Connecting Thread of Blessing

"Blessing" pulses throughout this family's story, from one generation to the next. Abraham is blessed (14:19; 24:1); Sarah is blessed with a child (17:16); God is blessed (14:20); Ishmael is blessed (17:20); Isaac is blessed (25:11; 26:3, 12); blessing is fought over by Jacob and Esau (27:1-41); Jacob is blessed by God and, later, by a divine assailant (28:14; 32:29; 35:9-10); Laban is blessed through Jacob (30:27); Egypt is blessed through Joseph (39:5); Pharaoh is blessed by Jacob (47:7, 10); and Joseph is blessed by Jacob (48:15), along with his two sons (48:6, 20). Genesis concludes with Jacob blessing each of his sons, revealing their respective futures (49:3-28). The story of Israel's ancestors begins with a blessing and ends with many blessings, accompanying the journey of a small family toward a tribal commonwealth.

This thematic thread ties together the three discrete cycles of narrative,[7] similar to how the genealogical interludes turn Genesis 12–50 into a sweeping family history.[8] Abraham's blessing is passed on to successive generations, serving as Israel's divinely wrought DNA, from Abra(ha)m and Sarai/h to Isaac and Rebekah to Jacob and Rachel, Leah, Bilhah, and Zilpah, and finally to their twelve sons, including Joseph and his two sons, birthed by Asenath, an Egyptian (41:50). Blessing, according to Genesis,

5. E.g., Gen 18:18; 22:17-18; 26:3-4; 28:14.

6. See 2 Sam 7:9; 22:44; cf. 1 Kgs 4:34.

7. Abraham (Gen 12:1–25:11), Jacob (25:12–36:43), and Joseph (37:1–50:26). The figure of Isaac, featured mostly in Gen 25–26, is more of a transitional character who serves as a bridge between the first two cycles.

8. See the formulaic *tôlĕdôt* references ("these are the descendants of PN"), which serve to bind together genealogies, reports, and narratives in Genesis: 2:4a; 5:1; 6:9; 10:1; 11:10; 11:27; 25:12; 25:19; 36:1; 36:9; 37:2.

is baked into Israel's own identity. Indeed, Jacob's change of name to "Israel" during his wrestling match (32:26-29; cf. 35:9-12) highlights the identity-defining force of divine blessing. Blessing is Israel's primal calling to the nations as much as it is God's gift to Israel. The ancestral blessing is both a gift and a vocation. As Abram was commanded at the start, "Be a blessing!"

Compromise and Covenant

The ancestral stories in Genesis are full of twists and turns, failures and surprises, and through it all no ancestor proves to be morally stellar, although Abraham does demonstrate a radical obedience that is considered exemplary, despite its troubling ethical implications (Gen 22). Overall, "family values" are not the patriarchs' strong suit.[9] They are by and large morally compromised. Deceit, for example, is highlighted in the stories as a common practice among the patriarchs and occasional matriarch. Abram plots with Sarai before immigrating to Egypt to lie about their relationship (12:13, 19), repeated in 20:2, 5 in Gerar, where Isaac also commits deception later in 26:7, 9. This white lie, however, pales in comparison to the trickery practiced by Jacob (along with Rebekah) against brother Esau in stealing the firstborn blessing from father Isaac (27:35-36). In fact, supplanting through deception is reflective of Jacob's birth identity (25:26). But Jacob is not alone: he suffers deceit from his uncle Laban (29:26). Of course, Jacob gets even (30:31-43). The practice of deceit gets more serious in the next generation, which results in the wholesale slaughter of the men of Shechem (34:13-30). And Jacob, the quintessential underdog and trickster, is none too pleased—a bitter taste of his own medicine.

These stories from Genesis are all about a transgenerational family surviving as immigrants facing conflicts from without and within. Sometimes covenants are made to resolve or contain such conflicts (21:27, 32; 26:28; 31:44). But the one covenant extending over all is God's covenant with Abraham, established in two episodes (Gen 15 and 17). In the first,

9. See David Petersen, "Genesis and Family Values," *JBL* 124, no. 1 (2005): 5–23.

God's gift of the land is lifted up (15:18), preceded by the promise of progeny (15:5). In the second episode, progeny is singled out and Abram's name is changed to Abraham to reflect his new status as the "father of a multitude of nations" (17:4-5), followed by the promise of land (17:8), the sign of which is circumcision (17:10-14). These coextensive covenants are the formalized highpoints of God's twofold promise, sworn as an "oath" (26:3) to Abraham: (1) progeny as numerous as the "stars" in the sky,[10] the "sand" by the sea,[11] and the "dust of the earth,"[12] and (2) land,[13] whether of Canaan or of greater territory reflecting imperial extent (e.g., 15:18-21). The remarkable irony of the ancestral history is that the family of Israel's origin exists only as immigrants in the land. They are "aliens," whether on "their" land[14] or in other lands.[15]

Nevertheless, these stories testify to how such a family gained a foothold in the land promised to them. Abraham purchases a burial plot near Hebron "in the land of Canaan," namely the cave of Machpelah from Ephron the Hittite (23:4-20). There the ancestors are buried, including Sarah (23:19) and Abraham (25:9-10), Isaac and Rebekah (35:29; 49:31), Leah and Jacob (49:31; 50:13), but not Rachel, who was buried "on the way" to Bethlehem (35:19-20). Joseph is likewise buried in a plot purchased by Jacob in Shechem, "an inheritance of the descendants of Joseph" (Josh 24:32; see Gen 33:19). Burial plots serve as the deposits for future land possession.

Unorthodox Immigrants

These ancestral stories of migration and blessing are unique within the sweeping saga of Israel's formation as a people, and their ancestral

10. Gen 15:5; 22:17; 26:4.

11. Gen 22:17; 32:12.

12. Gen 13:16; 28:14.

13. E.g., Gen 12:7; 13:15, 17; 15:7, 18-19; 17:8; 24:7; 26:3; 28:4, 13; 35:12; 48:4; 50:24.

14. Gen 17:8; 19:9; 28:4; 37:1.

15. Gen 12:10; 15:13; 26:3; 47:4.

protagonists act in ways that are unprecedented within the larger biblical corpus. As Moberly observes, holiness is not a major concern of the ancestors as it is in Mosaic *tôrâ*, which prescribes an exclusive relationship to YHWH in a "sanctuary-centered relationship."[16] Instead, we find Abraham building altars in various locations to commemorate a theophany or to invoke YHWH's name, sometimes beside an "oak," accompanied by sacrifice.[17] So also Isaac and Jacob.[18] Jacob calls his altar *El-Elohe Israel* ("God, the God of Israel" [33:20]). Abraham plants a "tamarisk tree" to call on the "name of YHWH" (21:33). Such practices fly in the face of "orthodox" Deuteronomistic practice, which forbade sacred places established "under every green tree."[19]

It is no accident, then, that we never find Moses building altars and planting trees in his wanderings in the wilderness with the Israelites, not even at a water-streaming rock (cf. Exod 17:1-7; Num 20:1-13).[20] Put another way: nowhere is it said, "You shall love the immigrant as yourself, for you were immigrants *in the land of Canaan*, as your ancestors were," or "Remember that you were immigrants in *Canaan*." Such mandated remembrances always refer to immigrants or slaves in *Egypt*, not in Canaan.[21] For whatever reason, Israel's remembered *self*-identity ("remember that *you* were . . .") avoids referencing the patriarchs and matriarchs. Whenever the patriarchs are invoked as objects of remembrance, God is the one called upon to remember, not Israel, and it is done by way of contrast with the present generation, as when Moses prays to YHWH on Israel's behalf in the wilderness: "Remember your servants, Abraham, Isaac, and Jacob. Disregard the stubbornness of this people, their wickedness, and their sin" (Deut 9:27). The people's self-identity

16. Moberly, *The Old Testament of the Old Testament*, 103–4.

17. Gen 12:7, 8; 13:8; 22:9.

18. Gen 26:5; 33:20; 35:1, 3, 7; cf. 28:18.

19. That is, any place outside of Jerusalem's temple (Deut 12:1; 1 Kgs 14:23; 2 Kgs 16:4; 17:10; Jer 3:6; Ezek 6:13).

20. Whose location is named to commemorate Israel's resistance, not God's provision (Exod 17:7; Num 20:13).

21. Lev 19:34; cf. Exod 22:21; 23:9; Deut 5:15; 16:12; 24:18, 22.

is not the issue; it is their survival that is at stake, as in the wilderness, made possible by God's "remembrance" of Abraham. Moses appeals to God to "remember" in order to call God to action, not to call the people to a moral mandate. *Within* the Pentateuchal narrative, remembering the ancestors is deemed primarily God's business.[22] Nevertheless, *through* the Pentateuchal narrative the ancestors are preserved in collective memory for the community.

Another remarkable distinction between the patriarchal past and the Israelite present is this: the God worshipped by the ancestors[23] seems different from the God of Moses (aka YHWH). The God of the ancestors goes by various names: *El-roi*,[24] *El Shaddai*,[25] *Pachad Yitshaq*,[26] *Abir Ya'aqob*.[27] According to the Priestly narrative, God's official name, YHWH, was not given until the time of Moses.

> God also spoke to Moses and said to him, "I am *YHWH*. I appeared to Abraham, Isaac, and Jacob as *El Shaddai*, but I did not make myself known to them by my name *YHWH*. I also established my covenant with them, to give them the land of Canaan, the land in which they lived as immigrants."
>
> (Exod 6:2-4; cf. Exod 3:15)

Same deity, two different names, and as the narratives in Genesis attest, more names for God were operative in ancestral times. The division between Moses and the ancestors is not just a family matter; it is theological. While God's address to Moses seeks theological continuity across ancestral generations, it also admits to discontinuity. With a multitude

22. See, e.g., Exod 2:24; 32:13; Lev 26:42; Deut 9:27; cf. 1 Chron 16:15-18.

23. In scholarly circles, referred to as "the God of the Fathers." See Albrecht Alt's seminal essay, "The God of the Fathers," in his *Essays on Old Testament History and Religion*, trans. R. A. Wilson (Oxford: Blackwell, 1966 [1929]), 3–77.

24. "God who sees," the name given by Hagar (16:13).

25. Conventionally translated "God Almighty" (17:1; 35:11; 48:3).

26. "Fear of Isaac" (31:42; cf. 31:53).

27. Traditionally translated "Mighty One of Jacob" (Gen 49:24) but more literally "Bull of Jacob." See also Isa 49:26; 60:16; Ps 132:2, 5.

of identities, God in Genesis is given a wider "ecumenical" scope than in Exodus.[28] It's all in the name(s).

Why, then, are the patriarchs and matriarchs of Israel depicted so differently from Moses and the people Israel? Why highlight their flaws and failures in addition to their radical trust (particularly Abraham's)? Why admit to their "unorthodox" practices of worship and the different names they give to God? One would expect more harmony between the ancestral age narrated in Genesis and the Mosaic age recounted in Exodus through Deuteronomy, in which Israel came to be governed by *tôrâ*.[29] Abraham is no Moses, not even proleptically, and Moses is no Abraham *redivivus*.

One key may be found in the final verse of the Exodus passage cited above (6:4). The sweeping, composite narrative in Genesis repeatedly recognizes that the ancestors were immigrants in the land(s), not possessors of the land (Gen 23:4). The ancestral narratives acknowledge that the way of life for these immigrants, specifically the way of survival, was markedly different from that of a settled community. For Abraham and his wandering family, they had no land, except for their burial plots, an occasional well, and their sacred spots—no stretch of land to possess, only land that was promised. The possession of the land promised by covenant extends far beyond the ancestors' generations. The Genesis family story is not so much a "success story" as a survival story that demands living by one's wits and in tenacious trust and hope in God's promises, initiated by blessing and formalized by covenant.

Historically, there is much more at play. Even though Israel's "ancestors" embodied certain ways of living and worshipping that were starkly different from those of Israel in the land, their relevance would have been keenly felt by a people disrupted by exile and dispersed. One can imagine in the context of displacement how a people might have recounted the ways of their ancestors with renewed interest and appreciation as they too lived as immigrants, albeit forced. For a people without a land and a temple, without a capital and a king, the ways of the ancestors would have gained

28. See Moberly, *The Old Testament of the Old Testament*, 104.

29. The one glaring exception, which "proves the rule," is Gen 26:4-5. See below.

new significance. Israel's patriarchs and matriarchs were not simply relics of a distant past, but powerful examples of survival amid displacement. As such, Abraham and Moses represent competing narratives not only of Israel's origins but also of its future. So the dialogue continues from the "Old Testament of the Old Testament" to the "little Bible."

The Ancestors in the Psalms

As in the Genesis narratives, the "ancestors" (*'ăbôt*) in the Psalms bear a mixed legacy at best. On the one hand, they exemplify trust in the God who delivered them (Ps 22:4-5). On the other hand, they are condemned as stubborn and rebellious.[30] Nevertheless, they bear a privileged status in so far that they directly beheld God's "marvelous" and victorious deeds (44:1-3; 78:2-4, 12). In the Psalms, the "ancestors" extend beyond the patriarchs and matriarchs themselves to include the enslaved Israelites in Egypt, the freed Israelites of the exodus, and the wandering Israelites in the wilderness. There is little in the Psalms to distinguish theologically the ancestral immigrant family in Canaan from the wandering Israelites in the wilderness, as the Pentateuch does. But for the sake of dialogue, we will limit discussion to those psalms that specifically reference the "Canaanite" families of Abraham, Isaac, and Jacob, with a nod toward Joseph.

Psalm 105: Abraham's Gift of Covenant

Of the so-called historical psalms of the Psalter, only Psalm 105 attends to Israel's named ancestors, beginning with Abraham, the primary "patriarch." The other historical psalms either begin at the exodus event (Pss 78, 106, 135, 114) or bypass the "patriarchal" ancestors altogether, as in the case of Psalm 136, which leapfrogs from creation to the exodus with no patriarch or matriarch in sight. One wonders whether part of the reason for including Psalm 105 in the Psalter was to fill the yawning "patriarchal" gap. In any case, Abraham does have a starring role in the psalm.

30. Pss 78:8, 57; 79:8; 95:8-9; 106:6-7.

Remember the wonders [YHWH] has done,
his marvels, and the judgments he has declared,
O seed of Abraham,[31] his servant,
children of Jacob, his chosen ones!
He is YHWH, our God;
his judgments are [manifest] throughout all the earth.
He is forever mindful of his covenant,
the word that he has commanded for a thousand generations,
which he made with Abraham,
his oath [sworn] to Isaac.
He established it for Jacob as a statute,
an everlasting covenant for Israel,
saying, "I hereby give you the land of Canaan,
your inherited portion." (105:5-11)

The psalm opens with a corporate address, specifically a summons to praise. Who is addressed is designated the "seed of Abraham" and "children of Jacob"—grandfather and grandson, one and the same family. Here, communal identity is lodged in genealogical origin. But why Abraham in particular? This first section of the psalm answers that question. The story of Abraham marks the beginning of YHWH's history of "wonders" (*niplā'ôt*), "marvels" (*mōpĕtîm*), and "judgments" (*mišpāṭîm*), all bundled together. But it is the latter that figures decisively for Abraham and his descendants.

Abraham the Innocent and the Granting God

Beginning with Abraham, the ancestors are deemed the recipients of an "everlasting covenant" (*bĕrît 'ôlām*), a sworn "oath" (*šĕbû'â*), a "statute" or binding law (*ḥōq*). Such references all point to an unconditional grant of land by God, specifically the land of Canaan. YHWH's "statute" is divinely self-binding. Reference to an "everlasting covenant" parallels Genesis 17, in which God commits to make Abraham "the ancestor of

31. 1 Chron 16:13 reads *yiśrā'ēl*, claiming interchangeability between "Abraham" and "Israel."

a multitude of nations," resulting in his change of name (17:4-5), and to give him and his descendants the land (17:7-8). It comes not without an obligation on Abraham's part: the act of circumcision, to be kept perpetually as an "everlasting covenant in your flesh" (17:9-14). In Psalm 105, however, such covenant is unconditionally granted by God; circumcision is nowhere mentioned. It is an "everlasting covenant" rooted solely in God's fidelity, not carved into Abraham's flesh.

It is striking that the psalmist introduces the word "statute" (*ḥōq*) to apply to God's promise. The only place where the word is used in Genesis is in God's reminder to Isaac of the promise made to Abraham:

> I will make your progeny as numerous as the stars of heaven and will give all these lands to your progeny. Indeed, all the nations of the earth shall gain blessing for themselves through your offspring, because Abraham obeyed my voice and kept my charge, my commandments, my statutes (*ḥuqqôt*), and my laws. (Gen 26:4-5)

The passage reads as if Abraham had received his own legal corpus to follow! However, this is not explicated or even indicated elsewhere in Genesis. Instead, Abraham received from God only a smattering of oral directives, culminating in that command of all commands, the one to sacrifice his own son, Isaac (Gen 22:2; cf. 22:18). In Genesis 26, quoted above, Abraham is reviewed retrospectively as the exemplary representative of a community that has indeed received God's "commandments," "statutes," and "laws" (cf. Lev 26:46; Deut 4:44-45). Here, the figure of Abraham points proleptically to Israel as a fully constituted community, one governed by Mosaic *tôrâ*. Here, there is no categorical division between Abraham and Israel. Here in Genesis 26, Abraham turns orthodox by obeying God's codified instructions. But in Psalm 105, the legal language of "statute" as applied to Abraham does not require adherence except from God, specifically God's adherence to the covenantal commitment to give the land. Abraham need not do a thing.

So far in Psalm 105 no ancestral story is yet to be offered, only a divine declaration backed by a suspenseful buildup (105:11). But once the covenant is established, the story can proceed, and it starts disjunctively.

But when they were but few in number, a mere trifling;
they were immigrants in [the land],
wandering from nation to nation,
from one kingdom to another people,
He did not allow anyone to oppress them;
he rebuked kings for their sake.
"Do not mess with[32] my anointed ones!
Do not harm my prophets!" (105:12-15)

The irony is thick. While Abraham's family is given the land, they are unable to claim it, as promised. Instead, they live as meager immigrants in the land and wanderers outside of it. In the Genesis account, Egypt and Philistia are the two "nations" in which Abraham and Sarah sojourn, endangering themselves (Gen 12:10; 20:1). Nevertheless, God protects them from opportunistic kings. In Genesis, such protection comes to a head with the "ancestress in danger" stories, in which the patriarch gets himself and, more so, Sarah into trouble with his (half) lies regarding their relationship (Gen 12:10-29; 20:1-18).

Nothing of the sort is recognized in Psalm 105. Abraham and his family are entirely innocent and potentially victims not of their own making. God's "rebuke" of the kings in Genesis is illustrated by God's plague against Pharaoh and his household (12:17) and the affliction of infertility against Abimelech and his household (20:18). Curious is the reference to "prophets" (*nĕbîʾîm*) in Psalm 105:15b. The only ancestor deemed a "prophet" in Genesis is Abraham in 20:7, revealed in God's rebuke of Abimelech. In Psalm 105, however, the label includes all in the family, designating anyone who has an intercessory relationship with the divine and, as Joseph will demonstrate, the ability to see the future through God's word (see 105:19). Abraham's family is also described as "anointed" in the psalm, a designation usually reserved for kings[33] and priests.[34] Together, "prophets" and "anointed ones" constitute much of the political and reli-

32. Literally, "touch" (√*ngʿ*).

33. 1 Sam 2:35; Pss 2:2; 20:6[7]; 89:38[39], 51[52]; Isa 45:1.

34. Lev 4:3; 6:15; Num 3:3.

gious leadership of a constituted community. Applying such language to Abraham makes the ancestral family the seedbed of a nation. Psalm 105, in other words, turns Abraham into a people fully constituted by God. All they lack is the land.

> When he summoned famine on the land,
> and broke every staff of bread,
> he sent ahead of them a man
> who was sold as a slave, Joseph.
> They restrained his feet with fetters;
> his neck was put into an iron collar,
> until the time his word came to pass,
> [until] the word of YHWH proved him true.
> The king sent and set him free;
> as the ruler of peoples, he released him.
> He set him lord over his house,
> and ruler over all his possessions,
> to discipline[35] his princes according to his desire,
> and teach his elders. (105:16-22)

Of all the patriarchs in Psalm 105, the narrative weight falls on Joseph, who now takes center stage. He is "sent" by YHWH in the wake of famine to be "lord" over Pharaoh's house. In Genesis, the famine is not an issue until Joseph's dream in prison, about one third of the way into the narrative (Gen 41:27). But in the psalm, famine sets the stage for the Joseph story from the outset, as it does in Genesis 12 for Abram and Sarai and in Genesis 26 for Isaac and Rebekah.

God on a Mission

The Joseph episode in Psalm 105, moreover, is cast as God's mission, and how Joseph suffers for it! First, he is sold as a slave and is confined in prison until he is proven to be a true recipient of YHWH's word. The

35. Read with LXX, *lĕyassēr* from √*ysr* ("discipline, rebuke, teach"), which makes better parallel sense and requires minimal emendation. MT reads "to bind."

transition from enslavement to imprisonment is seamless in the psalm, whereas in Genesis it happens at the moment of false accusation (Gen 39:16-18). In Psalm 105, Joseph's rise to power is to "discipline" and "teach" those in leadership ("princes" and "elders"). In Genesis, his ascendancy is to save Egypt from famine (Gen 41:37-57). In both cases, Joseph the enslaved becomes Joseph the sage—the royal sage working on behalf of the king (see Gen 41:39). Such is his political mission, according to the psalm.

Joseph's divinely ordained mission, however, is to settle Jacob's family in Egypt.

> So Israel went into Egypt;
> Jacob became an immigrant in the land of Ham.
> He made his people exceedingly fruitful;
> he made them mightier than their foes,
> whose hearts he turned to hate his people,
> to deal deceitfully with his servants. (105:23-25)

Like Abraham before him, Jacob is an immigrant in Egypt. But now the ancestral family is no longer "few in number" but numerous and mighty, which provokes the hostility of the Egyptian regime, now turned "foe," all part of God's design. And so another mission is implemented: Moses is "sent," and a new chapter unfolds—the exodus (see chapter 4).

Throughout Psalm 105, every event is orchestrated by YHWH, from "sending" the ancestors to causing "famine." In the Genesis narratives, God's providential work is more subtle, evolving from cycle to cycle, from Abraham to Jacob to Joseph. Particularly in the Joseph story, God recedes into the background and the human characters take center stage, heightening the suspense and intrigue that come with such a shift in perspective. But in the climactic scene in Genesis when Joseph reveals himself to his brothers, he attributes all that has happened to God, not unlike the way Psalm 105 tells the story overall:

> Now, don't be upset and don't be angry with yourselves that you sold me here. Actually, ***God sent*** me before you to save lives. . . . ***God sent*** me before

> you to make sure you'd survive and to rescue your lives in this amazing way. You didn't ***send me here; it was God*** who made me a father to Pharaoh, master of his entire household, and ruler of the whole land of Egypt. (Gen 45:5, 7-8 CEB; italics added)

This is the only moment in the Joseph story in Genesis when God is acknowledged giving direction so decisively (cf. 43:23). Elsewhere, God (YHWH) is simply said to be "with" Joseph, enabling him to be "successful" and prosperous (39:2, 21, 23). Divine direction in Genesis is acknowledged not in the narrated course of events but only in Joseph's discourse, which attributes God's "sending" as responsible for the entire course of the story. It is as if the psalmist picked up on Joseph's self-revelatory moment in Genesis and used it to recast the entire sweep of the ancestral narratives. Or the reverse could be said: the narrator placed in Joseph's mouth the theological perspective of Psalm 105. In any case, Joseph is never the subject of action in Psalm 105. He is "sent," "sold," "restrained," "proved true," "set free," and "set lord" (105:16-21). His only active role is to "discipline" and "teach," a role given to him by Pharaoh (105:22). Overall, Joseph remains passive as God remains active.

In the psalmist's eyes, the stories of the patriarchs and matriarchs are all part of a well-orchestrated divine mission. For Joseph, as expressed in his own words in Genesis, God's mission is to "preserve life," specifically a "remnant" of "survivors" (Gen 45:4, 7). For the psalmist, God's mission for Joseph extends what began with Abraham and works its way through the exodus and wilderness wanderings, namely the mission to fulfill God's covenant made to Abraham, the "sacred promise" of the land (Ps 105:42). Featured at the beginning and at the end, Abraham nearly rounds out the psalm, but not entirely. In the end, the fulfillment of the land promise points to another, more ultimate purpose: to fulfill YHWH's "statutes" and "laws."

> He gave them the lands of nations;
> they inherited the wealth of the peoples,[36]
> so that they may keep his statutes,
> and observe his laws. (105:44-45)

36. Literally, "the labors of peoples," that is, the fruits of their labors.

Possession of land becomes the necessary condition for *tôrâ* observance. These parallel goals reflect the shift that takes place in the use of the term "statute" (*ḥōq*) in the psalm: it initially designated YHWH's own "statute" or sworn "oath," which promised the land for Abraham and his progeny (105:10). But in the end, it gives way to the communal "statutes" that Israel is to observe, the "statutes" of YHWH's *tôrâ* (105:45). Through the figure of Abraham, the psalmist charts the journey from God's unconditional "statute," which binds God to Israel, to Israel's obligatory "statutes," which bind Israel to God, with the land serving as the link.

The possession of the land proves not be an end in itself but rather the prerequisite for *tôrâ* observance, a necessary but not entirely sufficient condition, as time will prove. But in the meantime, the people of the "law" is also a people of the land. Land leads to law; one self-binding "statute" regarding the gift of the land leads to a corpus of "statutes" and "laws" to ensure full communal life in the land. According to Psalm 105, the story of the ancestors was characterized by God's promise, making possible an ancestral community to be constituted by God's *tôrâ*. As one might note in German, from *Gabe* ("gift") comes *Aufgabe* ("task"). The promise points to the prescription.

In both Genesis and the Psalms, the immigrant saga of the ancestors in Canaan is held in cherished memory. But in Genesis, the sweeping narrative is fraught with calamities countered by God's blessing. In the psalmic account, the language of blessing is entirely lacking. Perhaps the blessing motif was considered too deeply tied to the intrigues and scheming, the self-inflicted trouble and complicated predicaments, that characterized the ancestors' sojourns. In a poetic retelling, of course, a single psalm can only say so much; selectivity is key. For Psalm 105, ancestral history is singularly defined by God's covenantal promise and protection. The psalm overlooks the checkered reputations of the ancestors and treats them primarily as recipients of God's covenantal promise and instruments of God's mission to fulfill that promise. For the psalmist, the covenant is everything with the exception of God's *tôrâ*, which concludes the psalm (105:45) but is foreshadowed by God's covenantal "statute" (105:10). The ancestors' relative invisibility as active human agents in the psalm serves to highlight the covenant's commanding visibility. Their passivity highlights God's leadership in directing the course of Israel's affairs from beginning to end. But it is the end of God's salvific guidance of the ancestors in their sojourns that marks the beginning of Israel's adherence to *tôrâ* in the land, a covenantal promise fulfilled for covenantal obedience to be realized.

Abraham's International Reach

In another psalm that mentions Abraham, God's leadership as "king over the nations" compels the leaders of the world to gather and be conjoined with the "people of Abraham's God."

> God is king over the nations;
>   God is seated on his holy throne.
> The leaders of the peoples gather themselves
>   with the people[37] of Abraham's God.
> For the shields[38] of the earth belong to God,
>   [who is] greatly exalted. (Ps 47:9-10)

This expansive international vision coheres well with Genesis's ancestral "blessing" of "all the families/nations of the earth" through Abraham and his descendants (Gen 12:3; 26:4). Here Abraham, rather than Moses, remains Israel's "ecumenical" figure on behalf of the nations as he did in Genesis.

Conclusion

Psalm 105 and Genesis offer divergent portrayals of Israel's ancestors. Who were they? How are they both different from and similar to Israel in its collective self-perception? How do they figure in the history of Israel's

37. Read *ʿim ʿam* for MT *ʿam* ("people"), due to haplography. Or the preposition is simply assumed in the poetry.

38. LXX reads "mighty ones," and Peshitta features "empires," both perhaps reading *signê* ("rulers") instead of MT *māgnê* ("shields"), due to graphic confusion between the *mem* and *samek*. However, the MT's reference to "shields" can be taken metaphorically in reference to divine strength and protection, and thus can be applied to anyone holding military power serving in the role of protector (cf. Deut 33:29; Pss 3:3[4]; 7:10[11]; 18:2[3]; 28:7).

formation as a people constituted by God in the land? For reasons that we do not fully know, the Pentateuch highlights certain distinctions that set the ancestors apart from their "descendants," those who form the community of Israel. The ancestors embarked on a journey that began in disruption but was sustained by God's blessing and a promise of land and progeny. Their status as underdogs among the nations required certain survival skills, including duplicity and trickery. Although the ancestral ways were not Israel's ways in the land (i.e., the ways of Mosaic *tôrâ*), Abraham's legacy endured, particularly for Israel scattered among the nations. The "Old Testament of the Old Testament" became a "new" testament for a people displaced from their land.

While the Psalms overall characterize the "ancestors" indiscriminately by their stubbornness and disobedience, Psalm 105 insists that Abraham and his family are not among them, since they preceded the rebellious Israelites at the sea and in the wilderness (see chapter 5). Moreover, their "unorthodox" conduct is overlooked in the psalm. Instead, these particular "ancestors," from Abraham to Joseph, are deemed bona fide recipients of God's covenant, without which there would be no people. Psalm 105 identifies what is most important about them, and it is covenant over character, divine agency over human initiative, and God's gift of land over everything else except Israel's obedience to *tôrâ*, made possible by possession of the land (105:44-45). For all his peculiar ways, Abraham retrospectively gains full membership into the Israelite community in Psalm 105, and his price of admittance is the covenant (105:9-11), plus God's "remembrance" (105:42). In Abraham, Israel remembers itself as erstwhile immigrants, growing in number (cf. Isa 51:2). In Abraham, Israel remembers God's unconditional promise of progeny and land. In Abraham, Israel also reaches out to the nations surrounding the land (Ps 47:9-10).

CHAPTER 4
THE EXODUS: A PARTING OF PERSPECTIVES

I am YHWH your God who brought you out of the land of Egypt.

—Exodus 20:2

The Jewish philosopher and Holocaust refugee Emil Fackenheim (1916–2003) identified two "root experiences" that define Judaism: (1) God's "saving presence" and (2) God's "commanding presence."[1] In light of our discussion in chapter 2, one might also include God's "creative and sustaining presence." In any case, God's "commanding presence" has to do with the giving of *tôrâ* on Mount Sinai, while God's "saving presence" refers most fundamentally to the exodus, that paradigmatic event of deliverance, God's singularity of salvation for Israel. Yet there is nothing singular in how the Bible recounts the exodus event. Even the book of Exodus is dialogically charged with different versions, as we will see. But first, a review of the narrative buildup to the crossing of the sea, which takes us back to the beginning.

1. Emil L. Fackenheim, *God's Presence in History: Jewish Affirmations and Philosophical Reflections* (New York: Harper & Row, 1972), 14–16.

From Slavery to Seashore

The exodus begins with the family of Jacob (seventy total) having settled in Egypt, far from Canaan (Exod 1:1-7). They became "fruitful" and "exceedingly strong," "filling the land" (Exod 1:7). What a blessing for them (cf. Gen 1:26), but what a bane for the Egyptians! The new king on the throne, one "who did not know Joseph," observes an emerging shift in the land's demographic center of gravity due to this growing immigrant population. He devises a "wise" plan to "deal shrewdly with them" by enslaving them for certain building projects (Exod 1:10-11). But it turns out that the greater the oppression, the more they multiplied, much to the Egyptians' dismay (Exod 1:12). "Ruthless" enslavement is imposed, making Israelites lives "bitter with hard labor" (Exod 1:14). A new imperial scheme is devised, taking a genocidal turn. The midwives Shiphrah and Puah are conscripted by Pharaoh to kill the male babies of the Hebrews. But because they "feared God," they commit civil disobedience with a ruse that circumvents Pharaoh's infanticidal plans. But not to be thwarted, Pharaoh turns his plan into national policy.

The slaughter of the male children sets the stage for Moses, the central character (next to God) for the remainder of the book of Exodus and beyond. Because Moses is so heavily featured from here on out, the book of Exodus could be called the "Biography of Moses," a title applicable all the way to Deuteronomy. This child of Levite parentage, Moses emerges as a powerful, albeit liminal, figure, born a Hebrew yet raised in an Egyptian household. But it does not take long for Moses to be on Pharaoh's most wanted list, after having murdered an Egyptian taskmaster (Exod 2:11-12). Fleeing to Midian and marrying into the family of Midianite priest (Reuel/Jethro), Moses remains an "alien" or immigrant[2] until he is called back to Egypt, not by Pharaoh but by the God of Abraham, Isaac, and Jacob, whose "new" name is YHWH, but whose identity reaches back to the ancestral age (Exod 3:13-15; 6:2-3).

This God of the ancestors, now YHWH of the exodus, has a mission. God has "heard" the people's cry, "remembered" the covenant, and

2. Note his son's name "Gershom" (from *gēr*) in v. 22.

"understood" the gravity of their suffering (2:23-25). And so Moses is "sent" to "bring" the people "out of Egypt" (Exod 3:10). Such is the exodus in a nutshell: Israel being "brought out" of Egypt by both God and Moses (Exod 3:12; cf. 20:2). Such is the double agency that launches the exodus, the purpose of which is twofold: (1) to "bring them up out of [Egypt's] land to a good and broad land, a land full of milk and honey" (Exod 3:8a), and (2) to "worship God on this mountain" (Exod 3:12). The exodus has a double destination: a mountain to worship on and a land to live in. Why they are not one and the same is a good question (see chapter 5). But for now, back to Egypt.

It is little wonder that Moses objects, five times no less, to return to Egypt and free his people. In the course of his objections, Moses is empowered by God with signs of theophanic power to impress both Pharaoh and the Israelites. But resistance comes from both sides. Regarding the Israelites, "they would not listen to Moses because of their complete exhaustion and their hard labor" (Exod 6:9). As for Pharaoh's intransigence, God has a game plan:

> I know, however, that the king of Egypt will not let you go unless he is forced to do so. Thus, I will stretch out my hand and strike Egypt with all the wonders that I will perform among them. After that, he will let you go. (Exod 3:19-20)

In addition to anticipating Pharaoh's resistance, this divine pronouncement clarifies how God will have a "hand" in Israel's liberation. Egypt will be "wonderstruck" by God's power such that Pharaoh will have no choice but to release God's people. Those "wonders" (*niplāʾōt*) will be the ten "plagues." Pharaoh's resistance, God later clarifies, will be evidence of his "hardened" (stubborn) heart, brought on by both Pharaoh and God. Such is the double agency of imperial intransigence.[3]

The exodus marks not only Israel's freedom but also Israel's enrichment. The Israelites are not to go empty-handed: silver and gold jewelry, along with fine clothing, will be theirs simply for the asking.

3. Compare Exod 4:21; 7:3; 9:12; 10:1 (with God as the agent) and 8:15, 32; 9:34 (with Pharaoh as the agent). Perhaps to preserve the ambiguity, several references to the "hardening" of Pharaoh's "heart" are cast in the passive (e.g., 7:13, 14; 8:19; 9:35).

"And so you shall plunder the Egyptians" (Exod 3:22; cf. 12:36), or put alternatively, "defund" the oppressors. Or one could count this as the first case of "reparations" for the enslaved in the Bible (cf. Deut 15:13-15).[4] In any case, for the Egyptians, Israel's departure was a "good riddance" rich in gifts.

YHWH's instructions to Moses before he confronts Pharaoh anticipates the end of the plagues and the beginning of Israel's release:

> And YHWH said to Moses, "When you return to Egypt, see that you perform before Pharaoh all the marvels that I have put in your hand. Nevertheless, I will harden his heart, so that he will refuse to let the people go. Then you shall say to Pharaoh, 'Thus says YHWH: Israel is my firstborn son. I said to you, "Let my son go so that he may worship me." But you refused to let him go; now I will kill your firstborn son.'" (Exod 4:21-23)

The last plague, the straw that breaks Pharaoh's hardened heart, is the first one to be announced. This is the only time in Exodus that reference is made to Israel as God's "firstborn," casting the exodus event as an act of redemption (cf. Exod 13:13-15).

The rest of the Exodus narrative leading up to the encounter at the sea[5] is devoted to the plagues and Pharaoh's intransigence. As an agent in these "wonders," Moses is elevated to be "like God to Pharaoh" (Exod 7:1). Nevertheless, Pharaoh with his hardened heart stands his ground, giving God all the more reason to "multiply" such "signs and wonders" (Exod 7:3). The intended result: "The Egyptians shall know that I am YHWH" (Exod 7:5). Indeed, God later admits to Moses that Pharaoh's intransigence was an excuse for displaying such "wonders," blow by blow (Exod 11:9).

These ten "wonders" are listed below, along with their highlights. Given their order of presentation, a movement of increasing severity is evident that culminates in the death of the firstborn. This is matched, in turn, by

---

4. For further discussion on this point, see Tremper Longman III, *The Bible and the Ballot: Using Scripture in Political Decisions* (Grand Rapids: Eerdmans, 2020), 292–98.

5. Also referred to as the "Red Sea" or better "Reed Sea" (*yam sûp*; see Exod 10:19; 13:18; 15:4, 22; 23:31), but most often in Exodus it is simply referred to as "the sea" (see Exod 14 [16x]; 15 [8x]). The "red" in the "Red Sea" comes from the LXX translation (*eruthros*), whereas the Hebrew *sûp* refers to "reed."

a movement of escalating power on God's part, as demonstrated by the increasing inability of Pharaoh's magicians to replicate God's "wonders." Note also the various means by which the plagues are accomplished.

1. Water into blood (7:14-24). Moses strikes the Nile with his staff, and Aaron stretches his hand over all other bodies of water. The results are a fish die-off and undrinkable water (7:18). The magicians, however, are able to replicate this "wonder" (7:22).
2. Frogs (8:1-15[7:26–8:11]).[6] Aaron stretches out his hand to perform this wonder. The magicians do the same by their "secret knowledge" (8:7[3]).
3. Gnats (8:16-19[12-15]). Aaron strikes the "dust of the earth" with his staff. The magicians cannot replicate it and declare, "This is the finger of God" (8:19[15]).
4. Flies (8:20-32[16-28]). YHWH performs this plague directly, with a distinction made between the land of the Egyptians and the land of Goshen, where the Israelites live. Moses prays to YHWH to remove the flies, and YHWH does so.
5. Livestock disease (9:1-7). YHWH does so, with a distinction made between Israel's livestock, which is spared, and that of Egypt (9:4).
6. Boils (9:8-12). Moses and Aaron are instructed to throw soot into the air. The magicians are unable to "stand before Moses because of the boils" (9:11).
7. Hail and thunder (9:13-35). Moses stretches out his hand/staff toward heaven after fair warning is given, so that those who "feared YHWH's word," including Pharaoh's officials, could find shelter (v. 20). No hail falls in the "land of Goshen." YHWH declares through Moses to Pharaoh the following purpose: "to show you my power and to declare my name throughout all the earth" (9:16).

6. Jewish versification is given in brackets.

8. Locusts (10:1-20). Moses stretches out his hand/staff over the land. YHWH causes "an east wind" to bring the locusts. Moses prays to YHWH to remove the locusts, and YHWH reverses the wind.
9. Darkness (10:21-29). Moses stretches out his hand toward heaven. Darkness reigns for three days, all the while the Israelites "had light where they lived" (10:23b).
10. Death of the firstborn (11:1-9 [announcement]; 12:29-32 [fulfillment]). YHWH declares, "I will pass through the land of Egypt that night and . . . strike down every firstborn. . . . On all the gods of Egypt I will impose judgments: I am YHWH" (12:12). The Israelite households are spared: YHWH "will pass over that door and not allow the destroyer [*hammašḥît*] to enter" (v. 23). The Passover rites are instituted (12:1-27, 43-49), as well as the festival of unleavened bread (13:3-10) and consecration of the firstborn (13:11-16).

The final plague serves as the coup de grâce not only against the Egyptian regime but also against the "gods of Egypt" (Exod 12:12; see also Num 33:4). Each wonder/plague has its own means of implementation: sometimes Moses and Aaron are involved; other times only God. Each one is announced to Pharaoh by Moses. Each subsequent plague becomes a greater test of divine power, given how the magicians succeed in replicating only the first two "wonders" but are unable to do so with the third. By the sixth plague (boils), they cannot protect themselves.

With the climactic death of the firstborn, Pharaoh finally relents to let Israel go. And go they must, led by God, but not without being enriched with Egypt's plunder simply for the asking (Exod 12:35-36). God leads them in a "pillar of cloud by day" and a "pillar of fire by night" (Exod 13:21). But victory is not yet achieved. God leads the people in a "roundabout way" toward the sea "readied for battle" (13:18). Once at the seashore, the narrative splits in two, like the waters themselves, but not entirely apart. It happens at the most dramatic moment of deliverance. Here, the drama turns dialogical.

The Exodus in Exodus

In Exodus 14, two significant accounts of the exodus event are interwoven, the so-called Priestly and Yahwist versions (plus the *Elohist*). Tightly intertwined, these two narrative strands offer two divergent perspectives on what happened. The following is a comparative presentation of Exodus 14:5-30 (adapted from the NRSV).

Yahwist (+Elohist) Version	Priestly Version
5 When the king of Egypt was told that the people had fled, the minds of Pharaoh and his officials were changed toward the people, and they said, "What have we done, letting Israel leave our service?" 6 So he had his chariot made ready and took his army with him; 7 he took six hundred picked chariots and all the other chariots of Egypt, with officers over all of them.	
	8 YHWH hardened the heart of Pharaoh king of Egypt and he pursued the Israelites, who were going out boldly. 9 The Egyptians pursued them, all Pharaoh's horses and chariots, his chariot drivers and his army. They overtook them camped by the sea, by Pi-hahiroth, in front of Baal-zephon.
10 As Pharaoh drew near, the Israelites looked back, and there were the Egyptians advancing on them; and they were in great fear. . . .	10 . . . the Israelites cried out to YHWH.
11 They said to Moses, "Was it because there were no graves in Egypt that you have taken us away to die in the wilderness? What have you done to us, bringing us out of Egypt? 12 Is this not the very thing we told you in Egypt, 'Let us alone and let us serve the Egyptians'? For it would have been better for us to serve the Egyptians than to die in the wilderness."	

[13]But Moses said to the people, "Do not be afraid, stand firm, and see the deliverance that YHWH will accomplish for you today; for the Egyptians whom you see today you shall never see again. [14]YHWH will fight for you, and you have only to keep still."	
	[15]Then YHWH said to Moses, "Why do you cry out to me? Tell the Israelites to go forward. [16]But as for you, lift up your staff and stretch out your hand over the sea and divide it, that the Israelites may go into the sea on dry ground. [17]Then I will harden the hearts of the Egyptians so that they will go in after them; and so I will gain glory over Pharaoh and all his army, his chariots, and his chariot drivers. [18]And the Egyptians shall know that I am YHWH, when I have gained glory over Pharaoh, his chariots, and his chariot drivers."
[19]The angel of God who was going before the Israelite army moved and went behind them; and the pillar of cloud moved from in front of them and took its place behind them. [20]It came between the army of Egypt and the army of Israel. And so the cloud was there with the darkness, and it lit up the night; one did not come near the other all night. [21]. . .YHWH drove the sea back by a strong east wind all night and turned the sea into dry land. . . .	[21]Then Moses stretched out his hand over the sea, . . . and the waters were divided. [22]The Israelites went into the sea on dry ground, the waters forming a wall for them on their right and on their left. [23]The Egyptians pursued, and went into the sea after them, all of Pharaoh's horses, chariots, and chariot drivers.

[24]At the morning watch YHWH in the pillar of fire and cloud looked down upon the Egyptian army and threw the Egyptian army into panic. [25]He jammed their chariot wheels so that they turned with difficulty. The Egyptians said, "Let us flee from the Israelites, for YHWH is fighting for them against Egypt."	
[27]. . . at dawn the sea returned to its normal depth. As the Egyptians fled before it, YHWH tossed the Egyptians into the sea.	[26]Then YHWH said to Moses, "Stretch out your hand over the sea, so that the water may come back upon the Egyptians, upon their chariots and chariot drivers." [27]So Moses stretched out his hand over the sea. . . . [28]The waters returned and covered the chariots and the chariot drivers, the entire army of Pharaoh that had followed them into the sea; not one of them remained. [29]But the Israelites walked on dry ground through the sea, the waters forming a wall for them on their right and on their left.
[30]Thus YHWH saved Israel that day from the Egyptians; and Israel saw the Egyptians dead on the seashore. [31]Israel saw the great work that YHWH did against the Egyptians. So the people feared YHWH and believed in YHWH and in his servant Moses.	

The following issues receive differing treatments between the two versions: (1) the purpose of the exodus, (2) Pharaoh's agency and reason for pursuing the Israelites, (3) YHWH's role, (4) Moses's role, (5) Israel's agency, and (6) how the exodus happened.

In the non-Priestly or Yahwist (+Elohist) account, Pharaoh pursues the Israelites once he and his officials realize they have released their guaranteed labor pool. While their "minds" (*lēbāb*) are "changed" (14:5), Pharaoh and his officials retain a measure of agency (14:6-7). In the Priestly account, there is comparatively little agency accorded to Pharaoh: it is simply stated that his "heart" was "hardened" by YHWH (14:4, 8), as had been planned all along (cf. 4:21; 7:3). Pharaoh remains passive for the sake of fulfilling one single overriding purpose: for YHWH to "gain glory," the glory of victory over Pharaoh and his army, so that all the "Egyptians shall know that I am YHWH" (14:4, 17). YHWH's "glory" shows who is in charge over this oppressive empire. For the Yahwist, however, the reason for the exodus is not so internationally oriented: YHWH's defeat of the Egyptians is intended to elicit "fear" and "belief" among the Israelites themselves (14:31). Together, these interwoven accounts provide a twofold reason for the exodus, one external and the other internal.

The respective roles of YHWH and Moses are also differently conceived. In the Priestly version, YHWH instructs Moses to lift up his staff and stretch out his hand (14:16), which he dutifully does, to divide the sea (14:21a). The same action occurs when Moses is instructed to stretch out his hand for the waters to "return" (14:26-27a, 28). For the Yahwist, however, it is YHWH alone who does the heavy lifting by driving the sea back with a wind all night long, turning it into "dry land" (14:21). Moreover, YHWH "tosses" the Egyptian army into the sea once it returns (14:27b). In the Priestly source, YHWH directs the whole scene, orchestrating the two major players: Pharaoh with his "hardened heart" and Moses with his staff in hand.

The two accounts, moreover, envision the event of deliverance quite differently. The Priestly version sees a division of the waters "walled" up on both sides to let the Israelites pass through on "dry ground" (14:22, 29). But the Yahwist sees no dramatic parting of the waters. Instead, the sea is dried up by an east wind, chariot wheels get "jammed," and the Egyptians are cast into the sea once it is restored. In the meantime, all the Israelites need to do is "keep still" as YHWH "fights" for them (14:14). In the Yahwist's version, there is no passage through the sea!

Such differences, though complementary, prompt a dialogue regarding how God works, with or without Moses, and how victory is achieved. In the Priestly version, Moses plays a central role whose lifted hand and staff, as commanded by YHWH, are instrumental in bringing forth the miracle of deliverance. The division of the sea marks a culmination in Moses's "performance" of YHWH's "wonders," wonders that YHWH has "put in [Moses's] power," beginning with the miracle of the staff-turned snake (4:21; 7:9-10). In the Yahwist version, Moses has no agency in the "performance" of the deliverance. He serves merely as the people's motivational coach, assuring them of YHWH's mighty work on their behalf. With such contrasting versions, however, one can also find much complementarity: YHWH's "gaining glory" over the Egyptians adds further reason to Israel's "fear" and "belief" in the end. In both versions, YHWH's international fame meets national reverence.

As for Moses's role, which differs significantly between the two versions, the prophet and the deity are nonetheless closely associated in both accounts. In the Yahwist version, Moses becomes worthy of belief as much as YHWH (14:31). In the Priestly account, YHWH and Moses are veritable partners in executing the exodus with Moses taking orders directly from YHWH. However the exodus is performed, YHWH is victorious, Egypt is vanquished, and Israel is delivered. While the Priestly account describes Israel's physical passage through the sea, the Yahwist complements with an inward journey as the people "keep still," passing from doubt and disbelief to belief and reverence (14:11-12, 31). One version without the other would result in an impoverished narrative with no chance for dialogue about the role of divine and human agency, or about the purpose of the exodus and how it took place.

The Pathos of the Passage: Exodus 15

But another dialogue partner enters the fray, a most ancient one. In contrast to the narrative account(s) in the previous chapter, Exodus 15 casts the exodus event in the evocative power of poetry, amplified with a generous measure of mythos. This exodus account begins with a praise-filled summary, placed in both Moses's and Miriam's mouths. While Moses testifies in song (15:1), Miriam commands the song to be sung (15:21). Logically, the order should be reversed: Miriam commands, and Moses and the Israelites would respond in song. But instead we find

Miriam exerting her leadership by continuing or recapitulating Moses's song with accompaniment (i.e., hand drums) for the whole community to join in. Still, one overhears an internal biblical debate reflected in the curious order of presentation, perhaps a debate over the status of female leadership in worship. But that would be another story. Our focus is on how the exodus is cast poetically in Exodus 15.

> I will sing to YHWH,
> for he is highly exalted;
> horse and rider he has hurled into the sea. (Exod 15:1; cf. 15:21)

Praise reverberates from beginning to end, accompanied by a breathtaking retelling of the exodus story. It begins with identifying YHWH's role in the exodus event: "YHWH is a warrior" (15:3a).[7] No surprise, given the opening verse of the song and all that follows. The poet, in contrast to the previous narrative(s), does not tell the exodus story in linear fashion—more like in reverse order. YHWH meets "Pharaoh's chariots and his army" and "casts" (√*yrh*) them "into the sea" (v. 4), language similar to 14:27b ("toss" [√*nr*ʿ]). Pharaoh and his retinue are sunk like a "stone" (15:5b). Rightful praise, thus, is due YHWH's "right hand" in bringing about victory (15:6), and it is in victory that YHWH's "majesty" and "fury" converge (15:7).

After retelling Pharaoh's defeat, the poet steps back in time and describes the role of the waters: they "pile up" and "stand up in a heap" (*nēd*) at YHWH's blast of "breath" (*rûāḥ*; 15:8a). The deeps "stiffen up" (√*qp*ʾ) at YHWH's command (15:8b), all the while the "enemy" boasts of his confidence to "destroy" the Israelites by his own "hand" (15:9). But with another divine blast, the sea "covers them," and they "sink like lead into the titanic waters" (*mayim ʾaddîrîm*; 15:10). Victory over Egypt is proof positive of YHWH's incomparable status "among the gods" (15:11): majestic, holy, awesome, and "performing wonders" (*ʿōśēh peleʾ*). Such is the expressed purpose of the exodus in the hands of the poet: to demonstrate YHWH's incomparable Otherness in the divine and earthly realms. Such

7. Literally, "man of war" (*ʾîš milḥāmâ*).

marks the beginning of YHWH's deliverance of a people, a journey whose destination is YHWH's "holy abode" (15:13b), YHWH's "mountain" and "sanctuary" (15:17), where the people are to be "planted" (15:17a). The exodus, thus, is a journey of transplantation, and the people is YHWH's victory garden.

Exodus 15 offers another account of the exodus that highlights YHWH's victory over Pharaoh's military might without any intermediary (i.e., no Moses). YHWH single-handedly defeats the Egyptians, an entirely "hands"-on, "breath"-blasting affair. Pharaoh and his army are thrown into the sea, engulfed by the waters (15:5-6, 12). The song exuberantly celebrates YHWH's military might in battle, a dramatic expression of divine "benevolence" (15:13). As for Moses's role, he is neither partner nor player in the event. He simply bears witness in song.

The Exodus in the Psalms

Speaking of song, we plunge into the Psalms. Each narrative in Exodus, whether poetic or prosaic, shapes the exodus event in a certain way. The same can also be said of the psalmic accounts. There are at least seven accounts of the exodus in the Psalter, each one offering its particular perspective. The differences are striking: one psalm makes no reference to Egypt at all, three make no reference to Moses, and two even lack reference to the sea! We start with those psalms that are most similar to the account(s) given in Exodus 14 and 15.

Psalm 78: The Pathway of Freedom and Wrath

Proving that repetition is the best form of "teaching" (*tôrâ*), Psalm 78 is a broken record of God's entangled history with an intransigent people. The psalm recalls God's acts of "wonders" countermatched by Israel's acts of failure, from failure to obey to failure to remember. The psalm sets in sharpest of relief the senselessness of the people's disbelief and rebellion in the face of God's "glorious deeds." Also presented in alternating fashion are God's wrath and forbearance. God's history of salvation begins with the exodus (not with the patriarchs and matriarchs) and concludes with the rejection of Ephraim (78:67; cf. 78:9-10) and, conversely, the choice of Judah/Zion (78:68). Related to God's choice of Zion is David's election as Israel's "shepherd" (78:70-72). It all begins with the first and most "glorious" of "deeds."

> In the presence of their ancestors he worked wonders,
> in the land of Egypt, the field of Zoan,
> He split the sea and led them through;
> he dammed up the waters like a heap.
> He led them with a cloud by day;
> and all night with the light of fire.
> He split open rocks in the wilderness,
> and gave them drink abundantly as from the deep.
> And he brought forth streams out of the rock,
> and caused waters to flow down like rivers. (78:12-16)

Similar to the poetic account in Exodus 15, the sea is "split" (√*bqʿ*) and "dammed up" (√*nṣb*) "like a heap" (*nēd*; cf. Exod 15:8), through which God leads the "ancestors" (Ps 78:13). Without pause, the psalm quickly moves to the wilderness with the people led by God with a "cloud by day" and "fire" by night (78:14).[8] There in the wilderness God also "splits" (√*bqʿ*) rocks to provide drink and causes water to flow "like rivers" (78:14-16). With poetic compactness, the psalmist constructs a symmetry of divine action in the sea and in the wilderness: God "splits" both the sea and rocks (78:13, 15), as well as manipulates and directs the flow of water (78:13, 16). Such are God's "wonders."

But this is not the only place in the psalm where the exodus is recounted. Later Israel is described wandering in the wilderness marred by repeated rebellions, described in over twenty verses, all because they "did not remember [God's] hand, the day he delivered them from the foe" (78:42). This extended indictment provides occasion to rehearse (again) how God's "hand" had brought about the people's deliverance from Egypt, but with a different twist. Given that the exodus through the

8. Note that the psalm lacks reference to "pillar," as one finds in Exod 13:21; 14:24.

sea was described earlier, the focus is now on God's "signs" and "marvels," beginning with turning canals into blood and concluding with the death of the firstborn (78:51). In between unfolds a series of ecological disasters: flies, frogs, locusts, hail, and cattle disease, all attributed to God's "burning anger" (78:49-50).

> How often they rebelled against him in the wilderness,
> distressing him in the desert!
> Time and again they tested *El*,
> aggrieving the Holy One of Israel.
> They did not remember his hand,
> the day he delivered them from the foe.
> When he performed his signs in Egypt,
> his marvels in the field of Zoan.
> He turned their canals into blood;
> their streams became undrinkable.
> He sent flies against them to devour them,
> and frogs to devastate them.
> He gave their crops to the caterpillar,
> and their produce to the locust.
> He killed off their vines with hailstones,
> and their sycamores with frost.[9]
> He gave up their cattle to disease,[10]
> and their herds to plagues.
> He unleashed upon them his burning anger,
> fury, indignation, and distress,
> a dispatch[11] of evil messengers.
> He blazed a pathway for his wrath;
> he did not spare them from death,
> but gave their life up to disease.
> He struck down all the firstborn in Egypt;
> the first products of (their) potency in the tents of Ham. (78:40-51)

9. The meaning of this *hapax legomenon* is uncertain. See LXX and Vulgate.

10. Read *laddeber* for MT *labbārād* ("hail"). See v. 50b.

11. A rare noun based on the verbal root "send" (*šlḥ*).

A comparison with the Exodus version of the plague account reveals parallels and differences.

Exodus 7:14–12:32	Psalm 78:43-51
Nile turned into blood	Canals turned into blood
Frogs	Flies
Gnats	Frogs
Flies	Caterpillars/locusts
Livestock disease	Hailstones/Frost
Boils	Livestock diseases
Hailstorm	
Locusts	
Darkness	
Death of the firstborn	Death of the firstborn

For poetic and didactic reasons, the psalm's list of plagues lacks reference to "gnats," "boils," and "darkness," as one finds in the Exodus account. The list in the psalm is structured by poetically paralleled pairs: canals/streams (of blood), flies/frogs, caterpillar/locust, hailstones/frost, and cattle disease/plagues. In fact, the psalmist adds two other items not found in Exodus to achieve such poetic correspondences: "caterpillars" (paired with "frogs") and "frost" (paired with "hailstones"). Poetry rules in Psalm 78! Nevertheless, both series begin and end with the same plagues: water turned into blood and the death of the firstborn. Interrupting the list in Psalm 78, however, is a vivid depiction of God's "burning anger" highlighted with various synonyms of divine fury set against the Egyptians (78:49-50). This interlude prefaces the final and most devastating plague: the death of the firstborn, which has no paired plague "partner," only a synonymous expression (7:51). Overall, Psalm 78 offers with its one climactic exception a series of corresponding pairs of plagues, easily learned and memorized (see 78:1).

The psalm continues seamlessly with God leading the people in the wilderness "like sheep," safe and secure, "as the sea engulfed their enemies" (78:52-53). Here is one brief reference back to the exodus (cf. 78:13). The psalm observes that the people "were unafraid" (78:53a), in contrast to Exodus 14:10-12. The wilderness wanderings are skipped over (cf. 78:17-

31, 40-41), and the people are brought to the land, God's "holy territory," specifically the "mountain" won by God's "right hand" (78:54; cf. 78:68; Exod 15:17). In the Exodus account, one expressed reason for Pharaoh to let God's people go was to allow them to worship at the mountain, "Horeb" (aka Sinai).[12] In Psalm 78, however, Sinai is bypassed to make a beeline through the wilderness to Mount Zion. The same can be said in Exodus 15:17. In Psalm 78, this streamlined journey may be consonant with God's choice of Judah over Ephraim (78:10, 68-69). The psalmist has Zion displace Sinai. In so doing, the psalm turns the exodus into an indictment against northern Israel, because Ephraim forgot about this marvel of a deed (78:11).

Psalm 78 illustrates almost ad nauseum the people's failure to reciprocate God's compassionate forbearance. Israel resorts to rebellion time and again, with the result of distressing, testing, and aggrieving God, all because the people refused to "remember [God's] hand" at work in saving them (78:42a). In Psalm 78, the exodus serves to highlight the absurdity of the people's rebelliousness in the face of God's benevolence. The psalm highlights in particular the plagues, more so than the exodus itself, because they illustrate so vividly the severity of God's anger directed against the Egyptians (78:49-50), the same anger that is directed at the Israelites in the wilderness and at Ephraim. As much as the exodus through the sea marks the pathway for Israel's freedom and constitution as a community, so the plagues "blaze a pathway for [God's] wrath" against Egypt (78:50). Psalm 78 presents Israel at a crossroads of commitment. By learning from the past, subsequent generations are compelled to choose the path of freedom to "walk according to [God's] *tôrâ*" (78:10). Psalm 78 presents the exodus as an event of freedom *for* obedience as much as freedom *from* enslavement.

Psalm 105: An Exodus sans Sea

The exodus account in Psalm 105 begins with Joseph's facilitation of Jacob's move to become an "immigrant" (*gār*) in Egypt.

12. See Exod 3:1, 12; cf. 7:16; 12:31.

So Israel went into Egypt;
  Jacob became an immigrant in the land of Ham.
He made his people exceedingly fruitful;
  he made them mightier than their foes,
    whose hearts he turned to hate his people,
      to deal deceitfully with his servants. (105:23-25)

In contrast to the Exodus account, the psalm glosses over Israel's enslavement in Egypt. Their increase in number and strength elicits the hostility of their "foes" (i.e., the Egyptians) who feel compelled to "deal deceitfully" (√*nkl*) with God's "servants," perhaps a slightly more honest assessment than what we find in Pharaoh's own words in Exod 1:10 ("deal shrewdly" [√*ḥkm*]). In any case, it is all orchestrated by YHWH, from the people's proliferation to their enemies' hostility. It is YHWH who "turned" the "hearts" of "their foes" toward hatred. Even an expected political consequence is deemed divinely ordained.

But YHWH also provides a remedy: Moses and Aaron are "sent" (105:26), just like Joseph (105:17). Moses, YHWH's "servant," and Aaron, YHWH's "chosen," are noted for performing the "announcements" (*dĕbārîm*) of YHWH's "signs." Such "announcements" refer to the performance acts and pronouncements of what YHWH will do to the Egyptians. The "signs" are the plagues, ten total (105:28-36), the most significant being the first and the last.

He sent Moses his servant,
  and Aaron, whom he had chosen.
They performed among them announcements of[13] his signs,
  marvels in the land of Ham.
He sent darkness and made [everything] dark.
  But did they not defy his announcements?[14]
He turned their waters into blood
  and killed their fish.

13. Hebrew *dibrê*. The MT makes good sense as it stands.

14. Read *Ketib* as *dĕbārāyw*. The translation of the line is a crux: MT contains the negative particle *lō'*, which is absent in LXX and Peshitta, suggesting the Israelites, not the Egyptians, are subjects. To retain the MT, NJPS casts the clause as a negative question, which is adopted here.

He caused their land to teem[15] with frogs,
even in the bedrooms of their kings.
He spoke, and swarms of flies[16] came,
gnats throughout their whole country.
He turned their rain into hail,
with fiery flames[17] throughout their land.
He struck their vines and fig trees,
and shattered the trees of their country.
He spoke, and locusts came,
and grasshoppers[18] without number.
They consumed all the vegetation in the land,
and devoured the fruit of their soil.
He struck every firstborn in their land,
the first of their whole potency.[19] (105:26-36)

In comparison to Exodus, Psalm 105 presents a remarkably different order of the plagues in the psalm, even as the total number is identical.

Exodus 7:14–12:32	Psalm 105:28-36
Nile turned into blood	Darkness
Frogs	Water into blood (dead fish)
Gnats	Frogs
Flies	Flies
Livestock disease	Gnats
Boils	Hail
Hailstorm	Lightning
Locusts	Crop destruction/shattered trees
Darkness	Locusts/grasshoppers
Death of the firstborn	Death of the firstborn

15. Contra most translations, it is unlikely that the verb's subject is "land," given the disagreement in gender. More likely, the verb here, though in the Qal, functions transitively, as also in Gen 1:20, 21.

16. Hebrew *'ārōb*; cf. Exod 8:17-20, 25-27. It is uncertain whether insects in general are meant or a particular kind of insect.

17. I.e., lightning bolts.

18. Or wingless locusts.

19. For similar language, see Ps 78:51.

For whatever reason, darkness is listed first in the psalm, severed from its association with the death of the firstborn, as one finds in Exodus 10:21-23. Perhaps darkness signaled for the psalmist the regression of creation into chaos (Gen 1:2; Jer 4:23), followed by water turning into blood and the killing of fish (cf. Exod 6:18a, 21a). Such would be an appropriate beginning for a plague list, a beginning that signals the end of creation, no less. All that follows are, in fact, signs of nature's disruption of Egyptian hegemony, infiltrating even the king's bedrooms (105:30). Featured are plagues of frogs, flies, and gnats, followed by meteorological disruption (hail and lightning), leading to crop destruction and shattered trees, and concluding with the familiar plague of locusts (and grasshoppers) and the death of the firstborn. From darkness to death, YHWH disrupts creation to disrupt empire and bring forth Israel into freedom.

That freedom is accompanied by Israel's enrichment (105:37-38), in parallel with the account in Exodus, which also mentions "clothing" in addition to silver and gold (Exod 3:21-22; 11:2; 12:35). The people go forth enriched and empowered (105:37; cf. Isa 40:30).

> He brought them out with silver and gold,
>   and not one among their tribes fell faint.
> Egypt rejoiced when they left,
>   for dread of them[20] had fallen upon them.[21] (105:37-38)

Unique to Psalm 105 is that Israel's exodus is matched by Egypt's rejoicing. Lacking is any regret on the part of the Egyptians for having released the Israelites (cf. Exod 14:5), leading to a pursuit to the shores of the sea. But more striking is the lack of a sea! YHWH "brought them out" from Egypt, enriched, but not through the sea, or even near it. Why such a glaring omission? Of note is the psalm's emphasis on land throughout the psalm, first the "land of Canaan," given to the people of Abraham in covenant (105:10-11), the landless ancestors immigrating "in [the land]," wandering from nation to nation" (105:12-13). With "famine"

20. I.e., Israel.

21. I.e., the Egyptians.

in the land, the landless immigrate to "the land of Ham" (105:23). God's "signs" and "marvels in the land of Ham" disrupt the land in various ways (105:28a, 30a, 31b, 32b, 33b, 35b). The firstborn are killed "in their land" (105:36a).

The psalmist makes "land" a constant point to reference throughout the plagues. Psalm 105 is framed by immigrants wandering "from nation to nation," on the one hand, and receiving the "lands of the nations," fulfilling the Abrahamic covenant, on the other. With such a thoroughgoing emphasis on the land, the sea has apparently evaporated! In Exodus, the sea was a place of pursuit and mortal combat. Without it, there is no pursuit and there are no casualties. (Another reason for Egypt to rejoice!) In any case, the psalmist finds the episode at the sea to be inconsequential, or worse, a distraction from Israel's larger journey from land to land.

Psalm 106: Sin at the Sea and Salvation for God's Sake

Much like Psalm 78, Psalm 106 highlights Israel's intransigence before God, but it does so confessionally: "We have sinned with our ancestors, committing iniquity and acting wickedly" (106:6). Such iniquity is traced all the way back to the sea. Psalm 106, in fact, is the only psalm that highlights Israel's rebellion *at* the sea, not just thereafter in the wilderness (106:7b). But like Psalm 78, Psalm 106 identifies the root problem: the failure to remember the "abundance of [God's] benevolent acts" and understand God's "wonders" (106:7a). Although left undescribed in Psalm 106, such "wonders" include the plagues (cf. Pss 78:44-51; 105:28-36). Psalm 106 presupposes Psalm 105, its poetic partner, in this regard.

Psalm 106 also seems to take something out of the Yahwist's script in Exodus, namely the people's desire to return to Egypt even as they await their deliverance at the sea (Exod 14:11-12), an act of outright rebellion in the psalmist's eyes. But YHWH saves them anyway, and for a reason not identified in other accounts. The rationale for the exodus in Psalm 106 has to do foremost not with effecting Israel's freedom from bondage (Exod 3:7b), or with bringing the Israelites into a "land full of milk and honey"

(Exod 3:8a), or with having them obey *tôrâ* (Ps 105:45). No, Psalm 106 takes a theocentric turn to highlight YHWH's personal stake in seeing that the exodus succeeds.

> Our ancestors in Egypt could not fathom your wonders;
> they did not remember the abundance of your benevolent acts.
> They rebelled by the sea, at the Sea of Reeds.
> Yet he saved them for his name's sake,
> to make known his mighty power. (106:7-8)

Elsewhere in the Psalms, YHWH's "name" serves as a basis of appeal for deliverance, as in Psalm 79: "Help us, O God of our salvation, on account of your glorious name . . . for the sake of your name!" (79:9 [cf. 31:3; 109:21; 143:11]). But in Psalm 106, there is no prayer for deliverance, only rebellion. Nevertheless, YHWH saves a people, for YHWH's own sake.

The exodus according to Psalm 106 commences with the sea being "rebuked" and, consequently, "dried up" (106:9). YHWH goes "hands on" by directly leading the people "through the depths" as if they were walking in a "desert" (106:9b). Moses is nowhere to be seen at the sea, although he does appear later in the wilderness (106:16, 23, 32). The exodus according to Psalm 106 (and unlike Psalm 105) marks both the people's deliverance and their enemies' destruction, with the waters having "covered their foes" (106:10-11). The result is Israel's belief and praise (106:12), thereby increasing YHWH's renown (106:8). This faith-building conclusion to the exodus nicely parallels Exodus 14:31, but without reference to Moses.

The people's belief in the God of "wonders," however, does not last long: "they quickly forgot [YHWH's] works" (106:13), or as a later passage laments:

> They forgot the God who saved them,
> the one who had done great things in Egypt,
> wonders in the land of Ham,
> awesome deeds by the Reed Sea.

So he determined to destroy them—
had not Moses, his elect one,
stood in the breach before him,
to avert his wrath from destroying [them]. (106:21-23)

In his intercessory role, Moses saves the people from YHWH's wrath. Elsewhere, however, divine anger cannot be thwarted, as when YHWH delivers the people "into the hand of the nations" (106:40-42). Only near the end of the psalm do divine "compassion" and "benevolence" come to the fore (106:43-46; cf. v. 7b). YHWH is "remorseful" (√*nḥm*), fed up with "his" own anger at the people's relentless rebellion. Instead of bringing about deliverance simply for the sake of YHWH's renown, YHWH responds to the people's "loud cries," akin to Exodus 2:24; 3:7, and remembers the Abrahamic covenant "for their sake" (106:45a; cf. Exod 2:24), but only at the end of the psalm and in another context altogether, rather than at the beginning with the exodus.

In view of the psalm's beginning and ending, Psalm 106 seems to claim that if God cannot muster compassion enough to act salvifically for *the people's* sake, God can still act salvifically for *God's own* sake (106:8). In the Priestly account, YHWH proclaims that Israel's rescue at the sea will demonstrate *to the Egyptians* that "I am YHWH, when I have gained glory over Pharaoh, his chariots, and his chariot drivers" (Exod 14:8). In Psalm 106, YHWH's glory or "mighty power" is less concerned with Egypt and more concerned with YHWH's own renown and "name." Not coincidentally, it is YHWH's "name" that the petitioner appeals to at the end of the psalm:

Save us, YHWH our God!
Gather us from the nations,
to give thanks to your holy name
and to revel boldly in your praise! (106:47)

The speaker appeals to what motivated YHWH to bring about the exodus at the outset, in the face of Israel's intransigence: YHWH's "name" and renown. Salvation, according to Psalm 106, is first and foremost about the praiseworthy "name" of God. Compassion can come later.

Psalm 135: A Tempest of an Exodus

On a different but related note, Psalm 135 grounds the exodus event not in compassion, at least not immediately so, but in God's sovereign freedom. YHWH can do whatever YHWH pleases "in the heavens and on earth, in the seas and all depths" (135:3). YHWH's power knows no boundaries; it extends throughout all these regions, even into the depths. The freedom of God's power is manifest in the storm: dark clouds, lightning, rain, and wind, all whipped up and harnessed by YHWH (135:4). Such are the combustible ingredients of a theophany, all wrought by the divine warrior. The psalmist deploys them to introduce the "signs" and "wonders" YHWH inflicts upon Egypt. To "strike down" (√*nkh*) is the same verb used in Exodus 3:20, which refers to God "striking" Egypt with all God's "wonders" (*niplā'ôt*). The worst of it, the psalm highlights, is the death of the firstborn, the climactic plague that results in Israel's release, YHWH's "treasured possession" (135:4b; cf. Exod 19:5). With YHWH as the storm maker, Egypt is struck by a veritable tempest of catastrophes. And as YHWH "struck down the firstborn of Egypt," so YHWH "struck down many nations," killing kings (135:8, 10).

But where is the sea? The psalmist raises up a storm theophany, complete with rain and wind, but there is no sea to part for the people's passage. For this exodus, the psalmist highlights a variety of divine actions: "raise up," "make," "release," "send," and "strike." But nothing about "dividing" or even "leading." The point? Perhaps to set in sharpest relief the contrast between YHWH's power and the impotence of the nations' "idols" (135:15), which do not speak, see, hear, or breathe, and thus are incapable of any action (135:16-17). The contrast reveals itself between the inert, lifeless idols and the robust, creator God, who both fashions and destroys, raises up and strikes down.

Curiously, one verb that is so often used to describe God "bringing out" (√*yṣ'*) the Israelites from Egypt[22] is used here to refer to YHWH "bringing out" the wind from YHWH's "storehouses" (135:7b)—an "exodus" of wind, as it were. The poetic implication is that YHWH's storm is the meteorological counterpart to the people's exodus, all conducted in terrifying power. As YHWH "raises up" the clouds and "brings out" the wind, so YHWH raises up a people and brings them out of bondage. As YHWH fashions "lightnings" to strike the earth, so YHWH "strikes down" the firstborn and many nations and kings. The exodus in Psalm 135 is a terrifying tempest; a "god-awful" storm of theophanic proportions that puts all the gods of the nations to shame, lifeless idols that they are. The exodus in Psalm 135 is the storm without the sea, and Israel is its precipitation.

Psalm 136: Passing through the "Pieces"

The exodus in Psalm 136 is an example of God's "benevolence" (*ḥesed*) in action. Indeed, everything from creation to deliverance to providing "food to all flesh" involves the exercise of divine benevolence. The uniqueness of Psalm 136 lies in its ever-recurring, "everlasting" refrain, appearing in the second line of every verse: "for his benevolence is everlasting." According to the Psalms, "benevolence" is the most central, enduring quality of God's character, reflecting an unwavering, tenacious commitment to a people. It is this quality of God's character to which the psalmic petitioner most frequently appeals when seeking help. Here, in Psalm 136, "benevolence" shines in every divine act, each one equally wondrous. What the psalmist offers, thus, is a historical taxonomy of divine benevolence.

After a threefold summons to give thanks (136:1-3), the psalm recites God's "great wonders" (*niplāʾôt gĕdōlôt*), beginning with creation: the heavens, the earth ("upon the waters"), and the great lights (136:5-9). The language echoes Genesis 1:14-16 regarding the respective functions of the sun and the moon. The cosmos and its orderly flow of day and

22. There are too many examples to cite: e.g., Exod 13:3, 9, 14; 18:1; 20:2; Deut 1:27; Pss 105:11; 105:37, 43.

night are reflective of God's enduring "benevolence." Next comes the exodus, which has less to do with cosmic order and more to do with cosmic disruption. Instead of creating and ordering, God disrupts and destroys, "striking down" (√*nkḥ*) Egypt by killing their firstborn (136:10). As in Psalm 135, the story of the exodus in Psalm 136 begins with the death of the firstborn, and in the same manner (see 135:8). With creation as God's first benevolent act, God's second act makes clear that the Egyptian empire has no place in the order of creation. Whereas the sun and moon rule their respective domains, Egyptian rule is a cosmic glitch that requires destruction, all out of divine "benevolence." Egypt's destruction paves the way for Israel's release, "brought out" by God with a "mighty hand and outstretched arm" (vv. 11a, 12a). Here, the sea is "split into pieces" (√*grz*), like something dismembered, through which Israel is led (136:13a, 14a).

Similar language is found in Genesis 15, in which Abram is commanded to split up several animals, through which a "smoking fire pot and a flaming torch" pass, ratifying God's covenantal promise (Gen 15:10, 17). Whether the psalmist is deliberately making such an allusion is hard to say, since it hinges only on three shared words (*gĕzārîm*, *ʿbr*, and *tāwek*). However, it may not be coincidental that as God's promise to Abram in Genesis 15 culminates in the gift of the land (15:18), so the psalm's "historical" recitation comes to the same culmination (136:21-22). Perhaps the psalmist is making the subtlest of allusions to this covenantal promise; otherwise, the psalm skips over the ancestral stories entirely.

In any case, the recounting of Israel's passage through the sea takes on an aura of awe, as the sea is defeated and Israel is saved. Egypt's imperial power is broken with Pharaoh and his army "tossed" (√*nʿr*) into the sea, just as in Exodus 14:27. But not only is Egypt destroyed. As Egypt is "struck down" by God (Ps 136:10a), so also "great kings" (136:17a), mirroring 135:8, 10. As in Psalm 135, the emphasis falls on divine action disrupting imperial regimes. In Psalm 136, however, the exodus is given more explicit play as part of God's itinerary of "wonders" (136:4a). The splitting of the sea, the defeat of Pharaoh, and Israel's safe passage are all part of the unfolding drama of divine benevolence, which begins with creation and ends with creation, with God providing "food" for the living (136:25). As Psalm 105 frames the exodus and beyond with the covenantal promise given to Abraham, so Psalm 136 frames it all with creation in view, from beginning to end. In between, the exodus explodes with God's power to save a people by destroying an empire and splitting the sea. The sea has its own imperial power that requires destruction. Such destruction reflects the benevolence that motivated God to "remember" the people in their "lowly" condition (136:23). In short, the exodus in Psalm 136 is merely the first "strike" of God's benevolence, the same benevolence that wrought the universe.

Psalm 77: Changing Hands in the Exodus

Unique to Psalm 77 is the exodus cast as part of a lament. With outstretched "hand" (77:2), the speaker laments that the "right hand of the Most high has changed" (77:10) and asks whether God's "benevolence" has come to an end (77:9a). To both heighten and remedy the despair, the speaker resolves to ponder all God's "wondrous deeds of old" (77:12) but recalls only one, the exodus. In Psalm 77, the exodus event is deemed the paradigmatic event of God's salvific deeds, the wonder of all wonders.

Psalm 77 imbues the exodus event with a healthy dose of mythos: the watery depths are personified; they "see" God and "roil" (√*ḥyl*) and "reel" (√*rgz*) in response (77:17). And for good reason: God pulls no punches in assailing the waters with a blast of theophanic might in the form of a storm. Clouds explode with water, and lightning bolts strike like "arrows." God's thunderous "voice" comes out of the "whirling wheel," the wheel of a charging chariot (cf. Ezek 1:15-21). As the "depths reeled," so the earth "quivered and quaked" (77:19b). The divine warrior is on the march "through the sea" (77:20). God's route is paved by God's rout of the "mighty waters"—now cowering waters. The psalmist, moreover, adds a bit of mystery to the theophanic proceedings. God leaves no trace (77:20b); there is no trail of blood.

The speaker's awe over God's "undetectable" footprints concludes with an acknowledgment of Moses's and Aaron's role in leading the people (77:21). For all God's theophanic might in bringing about safe passage, the credit for leading the people goes to Moses and Aaron. Attention to the "right hand of the Most High" (77:11b), not to mention God's outstretched "arm" (77:16), concludes with the "hand of Moses and Aaron" (77:21). Psalm 77, in fact, is the only psalm that establishes a direct connection between Moses and the people's crossing of the sea. The closest Moses gets to the exodus elsewhere in the Psalms is in his "performance" of the plagues in Ps 105:26, while God gets all the glory for the crossing. God gets God's fair share of credit in Psalm 77 as well, but not to the exclusion of the pivotal role that Moses and Aaron play. It is striking that the psalm ends where it does, with the "hand of Moses and Aaron" leading the people rather than with further "wondrous deeds of old" in the wilderness. Instead, the psalm concludes with human agency (77:21).

Psalm 77 mysteriously conjoins divine and human agency in this most dramatic of salvific acts. The "hand" of salvation is one that is shared, both divine and human. While God's "footprints" are "undetectable" (*lōʾ nōdāʿû*), the human "hand" is readily discernible. The speaker earlier expressed concern about God's "right hand" having "changed" (77:11b), that it no longer wielded the power it did in the glory days of the exodus (cf. Exod 15:6a). In pondering an event of divine agency, the psalmist ends anticlimactically with human agency. God's agency has indeed changed, by changing "hands." Psalm 77 acknowledges human agency having a hand in divine agency, and what matters now is how human hands lead the way, as the speaker's hand remains "outstretched."

Psalm 114: Praise in the Fray of the Exodus and *Eisodus*

Of the seven notable psalms in the Psalter, Psalm 114 casts the exodus most mythically.

> When Israel went forth from Egypt,
>   the house of Jacob from a people of obscure speech,
> Judah was his sanctuary,
>   Israel his dominion.
> The sea saw and fled;
>   the Jordan retreated.

The mountains skipped like rams,
  the hills like lambs.
Why is it that you, O sea, fled?
  O Jordan, that you retreated?
  O mountains, that you skipped like rams?
  O hills, like lambs?
Tremble, O earth, before the presence of the Lord,
  before the presence of the God of Jacob,[23]
    who turned the rock into a pool of water,
      flint into a spring of water. (114:1-8)

As in Psalm 77, the sea is personified. It "saw and fled" before Israel's approach. In addition, the Jordan River "retreated," and the mountains and hills "skip" like rams and lambs. But the psalm takes the personification one step further; it directly addresses these elements of nature with taunting questions ("Why?"). The answer is, of course, God.

Whereas the sea in the psalm is the sea of the exodus, another body of water is also at play: the Jordan. By including this river as a target of God's theophanic might, the psalmist recalls not only Israel's exodus but also Israel's entrance into the promised land (Josh 3:15–4:18). In both cases, the waters part. In just two parallel lines, the psalmist combines the exodus and the *eisodus*, the exit from Egypt and the entrance into Canaan. Moreover, Israel's trek in between is tantamount to a victory march with God, whose overwhelming presence causes all creation to convulse (cf. Ps 29:6). The "mountains" and the "hills" represent the geographical challenges in the wilderness, as much as the waters are a challenge in the sea and the river. With such a thumbnail summation of divine agency, all of Israel's failings and challenges in the wilderness are effectively glossed over. The journey from sea to flowing river meets no resistance and offers no opportunity for rebellion.

In Psalm 114, God's victory march is Israel's march to the sea, through the sea, through the wilderness, and through the Jordan. God's presence is the people's presence on the move, and it begins with the exodus, carries over into the wilderness, where God turns the rock into a pool of water

23. Read *'ĕlōhê ya'ăqōb* for MT *'ĕlôah ya'ăqōb* ("God, O Jacob") due to haplography.

(114:8), and concludes with the "turning" of the Jordan, parallel to the fleeing sea. From exodus to *eisodus*, the journey is a singular trek of triumph, without the unnecessary detours of testing and failure. With God, it is all victorious.

The Exodus in Dialogue

The Psalms carry on their own conversations about the exodus, as they also do with the narrative accounts in the Pentateuch. Some mimic the "historical" narratives more than others. One could say that the range of presentation between prosaic narrative (Exod 14) and poetic mythos (Exod 15) is filled by the various psalmic accounts. The lengthier, more narrative-like psalms find greater affinity with Exodus 14, while the more mythic and shorter psalms gravitate toward Exodus 15. But to put them all on such a spectrum would be forced. Psalm 78, for example, integrates both ends of the spectrum. On the one hand, it covers many of the plagues. On the other, it describes the division of the sea in similar manner to Exodus 15 (cf. 78:13; Exod 15:8).

The accounts are as distinctive as they are interconnected, prompting dialogical reflection. The central questions they engage include the following: How is God's agency manifested? What motivates God to save Israel from Egypt and the waters? What is the role of human agency? Who is Israel, victim or rebel? Let's begin with God. Most psalms stress the exodus as a paradigmatic example of God's wondrous and mighty deeds. On the one hand, the exodus marks the culmination of God's plagues against Egypt; on the other hand, it marks the beginning of Israel's sojourn into the wilderness (see chapter 5). Either way, God is great in power, and the exodus proves it. But if one reads more deeply, differences emerge.

Psalms 77 and 135 describe God's exodus work as nothing short of a theophanic outburst. Both cast YHWH as the storm warrior on the march, akin to the language of Exodus 15:3. YHWH's "holy way" is demonstrated in YHWH's way "through the mighty waters" (15:13, 19). In Exodus 15, God's glorious "right hand" and billowing "breath" bring about deliverance (cf. Pss 77:10; 78:54; 136:12). In Psalm 135, God's primary activity is to "strike down," whether Egypt's firstborn or Canaanite kings (135:8, 10). Egypt is the enemy slated for destruction; it is even addressed directly (135:9). In Psalms 77 and 114, however, Egypt is absent; rather, the waters are the target of God's militant strength (77:16, 19; 114:3-5), which prompts the question how Egypt's imperial power mirrors the power of watery chaos. Are they one and the same? What is at stake for the psalmist in identifying Egypt as chaos itself? Is it to set in even starker relief the power of Israel's God as the divine warrior?

Other traditions offer a more "refined" or purposeful view of divine agency in the exodus. In the Priestly account, YHWH is more pedagogue than warrior, instructing Moses on exactly what to do in order to bring about safe passage for the people. For all its emphasis on God's theophanic might, Psalm 77 acknowledges the instrumental role of Moses (and Aaron) in the exodus and beyond. In other psalms, however, Moses figures nowhere. Most of the psalms count the exodus as the exemplar of God's deeds of wonder, a paradigmatic display of God's sovereign might.[24] But for some psalms, there is more. Psalm 105 locates the exodus as part of God's mission to bring the people to the land, as promised in the covenant with Abraham. God sends Joseph to the rescue for *Egypt's sake* as well as for Israel's, and then Moses and Aaron are sent to perform signs in order to bring about Israel's release from Egypt. Israel's exodus from Egypt is Egypt's relief and joy, and the waters play no role as God fulfills the "holy promise" of granting land for Israel (105:11, 42, 44). The poet of Psalm 105 takes pains to avoid any reference to the sea because of its association with Egypt's destruction. For whatever reason, the psalmist wants to preserve Egypt in the account, plagues notwithstanding. Egypt, after all, is the source of Israel's enrichment (105:37, 44b).

Psalms 78 and 106 together convey in equal measure God's power in performing "wonders" (78:4b; 106:22b) and God's wrath in punishing rebels, particularly Israel. Both psalms make the case that Israel warrants such punishment. Psalm 78 details the deity's double-sided wrath: anger against Egypt, as evidenced in the plagues (78:50; cf. 78:65-66), and anger against Israel, as evidenced in mounting fatalities (78:31, 33-34). Yet in

24. E.g., Pss 77:11, 14; 78:4; 105:5; 106:7, 22; 135:9; 136:4.

compassionate forbearance, God also spared Israel and "forgave their iniquity" (78:38). God's double-sided anger points to Israel as a double-sided community, one that is both spared and rejected by God. In the end, Judah wins God's favor while Ephraim does not. In the end, David is identified as God's "servant," while Moses is not.

Who is Israel in the exodus? For Psalm 105, Israel is the vulnerable bearer of God's promise, extending back to a vulnerable immigrant family favored covenantally by God and ultimately brought out "with joy" (105:43). In Psalm 136, Israel is the community that suffers from "debasement" (106:23a). At the other extreme, Israel in Psalms 78 and 106 is the consummate rebel, whose persistent disobedience leads invariably to punishment. Indeed, Egypt in Psalm 106 is not so much the problem as is Israel! The psalmist traces Israel's penchant for rebellion back to the sea, prior to release (106:7b; cf. Exod 14:11-12). God liberates a community whose relationship with God is perpetually conflictive, a community that, instead of being faithful, is full of flattery (106:43). Why does God even bother?

In Psalm 106, it is because God has a personal stake: God acts to preserve this people for the sake of God's own "name" (106:8a), to advance God's renown. In Psalm 136, it all comes down to God's everlasting "benevolence" (*ḥesed*). If God's benevolence made manifest at the exodus can be traced back to God's covenant with Abraham, according to Psalm 105, the question remains why God treated Abraham with benevolence. Why did God choose Abraham and Sarah in the beginning, promising them a land for their posterity? The Psalms provide no answer. Neither does Genesis. And so a mystery remains, the same mystery reflected in God's initiative to create a universe in the beginning, the cosmic mystery of benevolence (136:4-9).

CHAPTER 5

THE WILDERNESS: TEST, TRUST, AND INTRANSIGENCE

It is haunting work to recall the sins of our past.

—Austin Channing Brown[1]

The wilderness is often depicted in biblical tradition as a rugged landscape marred by distrust, complaint, and punishment. But the wilderness also proves to be a place of miraculous provision, divine forbearance, and tenacious trust. There is no "desert spirituality" to speak of in the wilderness. The wilderness was hardly considered a retreat for rest and reflection, let alone refuge. Rather, in Israel's collective memory, the wilderness was regarded as an arena of testing and conflict for both the people and God. It was the site of Israel's painful and failure-filled struggle to become a bona fide community. The wilderness was as formative as it was formidable, a truly liminal landscape, a place only for passing through, certainly not for settling down.

Indeed, the wilderness was for Israel something of a *rite* of passage, from chaos to community, from a people's freedom to their responsibility.

1. Austin Channing Brown, "Brené with Austin Channing Brown on I'm Still Here: Black Dignity in a World Made for Whiteness," Podcast with Brené Brown. Available at https://brenebrown.com/podcast/brene-with-austin-channing-brown-on-im-still-here-black-dignity-in-a-world-made-for-whiteness/.

In the wilderness, newly won freedom meets severe hardship, and the result is a cascade of crises and failures. Is God with us? Is it better to return to Egypt? Is Moses fit for leadership? Will God destroy us in anger? Such questions accompany Israel's journey at nearly every step, and prospects for a swift passage crumble in the face of rebellions and failures that push God's patience to the limit. Passage through the wilderness turns out to be nearly interminable, no thanks to the people's conduct. But forty years provide a lot of lessons. In the wilderness, wisdom is hard won. God gave the people secure passage through the mighty waters, but passage through the howling wilderness was far from safe. The passage from enslavement to freedom to covenantal community was apparently never meant to be easy.

Literarily and theologically, the wilderness stories featured in Exodus and Numbers are complex, particularly in the latter's case, in which narrative and instruction alternate like a swinging pendulum (see below). The Psalms, too, do not speak with one voice regarding how Israel fared in the wilderness. We will first review the highs and lows of the wilderness accounts in Exodus and Numbers, and then explore how the Psalms (re)shape the landscape of the wilderness and Israel's place in it. The differences between how the Psalms and the Pentateuchal narratives treat Israel's experience in the wilderness are dialogically charged in the way they address questions of divine agency, the role of Moses, and the nature of Israel's success and failures. What, in fact, was Israel's basic problem in the wilderness? What prevented God from simply giving up on Israel? What is to be learned from the wilderness? Let the dialogues begin.

Israel in the Wilderness in the Pentateuch

In the Pentateuch, the wilderness accounts are split into two swaths of narrative separated by Sinai (aka Horeb), the mountain of God associated with various collections of divinely authorized instruction (Exod 20:1–Num 10:10). There is, on the one hand, Israel's sojourn in the wilderness *before* Sinai (Exod 15:22–19:25), and there is, on the other, Israel's wandering in the wilderness *after* Sinai (Num 10:11–36:13), extending into Deuteronomy prior to crossing the Jordan. Despite their differences, both accounts are bound together by at least one connecting thread: Israel's obdurate desire to return to Egypt, manifest in the incessant complaints the people issue against Moses and God. Much like Pharaoh's "hardened heart," Israel in the wilderness is "stiff-necked."[2] But in the latter's case, God plays no role in the "stiffening."

As for God's role? Sometimes God is quick to anger, sometimes God proves to be forbearing. It depends on the context. As for Moses? Caught between the people's failures and God's wrath, Moses persists in his intermediary role to facilitate the move from God's fury to forbearance. The wilderness material is replete with highly charged, high-stakes dialogues between God and Moses in which Israel's fate hangs in the balance.

Forbearance amid the Murmuring: Exodus

Israel's trek from the sea to Sinai meets its first challenge with the people's need for drinkable water, given the water's "bitter" (*mar*) taste at Marah (15:23). An all-too-familiar exchange unfolds, repeated time and again throughout the wilderness sojourn. The people "complained [√*lwn*] against Moses," Moses "cried out" (*ṣʿq*) to YHWH, and YHWH provided a remedy. With provision fulfilled, YHWH establishes a "statute [*ḥōq*] and a ruling [*mišpāṭ*]" to "put them to the test" (15:25).

> If you listen carefully to the voice of YHWH your God and do what is right in his sight, heeding his commandments and keeping all his statutes, I will not bring upon you any of the diseases that I brought upon the Egyptians; for I am YHWH who heals you. (Exod 15:26)

Herein lies an additional function of the ten plagues directed against Egypt: they serve as chilling reminders of what God can also do to Israel in the case of rebellion—a big "stick" but without the "carrot." And so the stage is set not only for God to test Israel, but also for Israel to test God. To press the latter, the people's complaining continues unabated.

2. Exod 32:9; 33:3, 5; 34:9.

> The Israelites said to [Moses and Aaron], "If only we had died by YHWH's hand in the land of Egypt, when we sat by the cooking pots of meat and ate our fill of bread; for you have driven us out into this wilderness to kill this entire assembly with hunger." (Exod 16:3)

Lacking food, the people regard the wilderness as harsher and more threatening than their enslavement in Egypt and accuse Moses and Aaron with malevolent intent. Moses's first line of defense is to remind the people that their complaining is against YHWH, not against him (16:8). In the face of complaint, YHWH again responds with provision: meat in the evening and bread in the morning, the former in the form of quail and the latter as a "thin flaky substance, as thin as frost on the ground"—a mystery food that prompts the question, "What is it?" (*mān hû'*; 16:15), later called simply "manna" (*mān*). Such miraculous provision is meant to demonstrate two things (depending on the time of day): YHWH's "glory" in the morning (via manna) and knowledge of YHWH's deliverance (via quail) in the evening (16:6b-7).

Put more broadly, YHWH provides for a people so that "[they] shall know that I am YHWH your God" (16:12b). This theological objective shares a telling distinction with the one stated earlier about the Egyptians: "The Egyptians shall know that I am YHWH when I stretch out my hand against Egypt and bring the Israelites out from among them" (7:5). The critical difference is the additional reference "your God" in Israel's case. By releasing the Israelites from enslavement and providing for them in the wilderness, YHWH wants to demonstrate that YHWH is exclusively *their* God, neither the Egyptians' nor anyone else's. By being their God, YHWH expects something in return: obedience, which will be put to the test in the case of manna. YHWH instructs the people to gather only as much as needed every day and no more, not leaving any of it overnight (16:16-19). But they fail to do so, eliciting Moses's anger (16:20). Another test is proctored: to gather twice as much on the sixth day to cover the seventh day, since no manna will be available on the sabbath (16:22-26). Failure again (16:27).

As déjà vu, the people again complain over the lack of water, this time more vehemently by "arguing" (√*ryb*) with Moses and "testing" (√*nsh*)

YHWH (17:2). Camped at Rephidim, the Israelites charge Moses with the intent to kill them with thirst (17:3). Once again, Moses "cries out" to YHWH in fear for his life, and YHWH provides, this time instructing Moses to use his staff to strike "the rock at Horeb" to bring forth water (17:6). And it was so. "*Massah* and *Meribah*" ("Test and Quarrel") becomes the double-name of the place (17:7a). Meribah will be revisited post-Sinai, with even greater failure (Num 20:1-13). The people's testing of God comes down to one damning question: "Is YHWH among us or not?" (Exod 17:7b). For YHWH, the converse also applies: Is Israel my people or not? The testing goes both ways.

Life in the wilderness faces not only inner conflict but also external threat, beginning with the Amalekites (Exod 17:8-14), the first of many conflicts on the battlefield. In the meantime, Moses reunites with his father-in-law Jethro, who offers some sage advice. He first clarifies Moses's role as a teacher to the people, one who is to expound "the statutes [*haḥuqqîm*] and laws [*hattôrot*]" for their own good (17:20). As for adjudicating cases, Jethro proposes that Moses "represent the people before God" (17:19b) and choose "capable" judges (*'anšê-ḥayil*) to alleviate the burden of leadership on Moses (17:21). The wilderness proves to be a place not only of testing and failure but also of provision and learning, a social "experiment" in identity formation met with mixed success.

That experiment reaches its high point at Mount Sinai, where God imparts *tôrâ*, beginning with the Decalogue (20:2-17), followed by the Book of the Covenant (20:22–23:18) and detailed instructions for constructing the tabernacle (25:1–30:38). A narrative rift, however, occurs with the first of two paradigmatic acts of disobedience in the wilderness: the worship of the "golden calf" (Exod 32:2-35).[3] When Moses is away, the people play, and Aaron plays with fire. He fashions a calf made out of the gold contributed by the people and proclaims, "These are your gods, O Israel, who brought you up out of the land of Egypt!" (32:4b, 8b; cf. 1 Kgs 12:28). A more bracing slap in the (divine) face cannot be imagined, and YHWH is ready to give up on this people, imploring Moses to "leave

3. The other fundamental act of disobedience is the worship of Ba'al of Peor in Num 25:18.

me alone so that my fury will burn hot against them and I may devour them. Then I will make a great nation of you" (Exod 32:9). Moses declines the offer and instead implores YHWH to save face by pointing out that the Egyptians will only conclude from Israel's death in the desert that the exodus was motivated by "evil intent" (*rāʿâ*). Would YHWH prefer having "his" international reputation besmirched as a murderous or unsuccessful deity? Moses, moreover, reminds YHWH of the ancestral covenant that promised not only descendants but also land for Israel's inheritance (32:13). Moses beseeches a "change of mind" (*nḥm*) on YHWH's part, and he succeeds (32:12, 14).

The remainder of this potential break in relationship involves picking up the pieces. There is a violent purge as well as punishing plague (Exod 32:25-35). Nevertheless, YHWH promises to accompany the people by proxy; otherwise, YHWH's own presence would "consume" them "on the way" (33:2-3). But Moses presses for more, squeezing a promise out of YHWH to accompany the Israelites personally (33:14-17). The prophet further demands to see YHWH's "glory" as a way of confirming YHWH's favor (33:18). But YHWH has a self-revelatory limit and concedes to show Moses only YHWH's "goodness" (*ṭûb*), at most an indirect passing of divine glory with only YHWH's "backside" for Moses to see (33:19-23). Once a new set of tablets is cut, YHWH indeed passes "before" Moses, accompanied by the most central confession of divine character featured in the Hebrew Bible:

> YHWH passed before him, and proclaimed,
> "YHWH, YHWH, a God merciful and gracious,
> slow to anger, and abounding in benevolence and faithfulness,
> maintaining benevolence for the thousandth generation,
> forgiving iniquity and transgression and sin,
> yet by no means clearing the guilty,
> but visiting the iniquity of the parents upon the children
> and the children's children, to the third and the fourth
> generation." (Exod 34:6-7)

It is no coincidence that variant forms of this divine confession are scattered throughout the scriptures, including Psalms 86:5, 15; 103:8; 145:8. One quality of God that is consistently attested is God's "benevolence" or faithful love (*ḥesed*), the most central quality of divine character featured in the Psalms.[4] Moses's final prayer is for God to accompany this "stiff-necked people" and forgive them of their sin (34:9). Therein lies the theological tension that is lodged in the very heart of God: benevolent and forgiving forbearance, on the one hand, and punitive justice, on the other. As much as Moses is caught between a holy God and a sinful people, he is also caught between God's justice and forbearance.

Sanctuary Construction and Rebellion: From Exodus to Numbers

The struggle between divine wrath and forbearance continues with greater intensity once Israel departs from Sinai. But the Israelites also depart with a tangible sign of divine accompaniment: the tabernacle. While the various statutes, ordinances, and commandments given at Sinai apply to life in the promised land, there is another set of instructions that directly addresses Israel in the wilderness, namely the rules concerning the tabernacle and its construction. Related to the "tent of meeting," the tabernacle served as YHWH's formal and portable meeting place, YHWH's "sanctuary" (*miqdāš*), built so that YHWH would accompany them in their wanderings (25:8). Narratively, the tabernacle serves as the bridge between the wilderness and the promised land, between Sinai and Zion, between *tôrâ* and temple.

With its architectural "pattern" (*tabnît*) laid out (25:9), the tabernacle is not only a technological feat that facilitates God's holy presence with a sinful people, it is also a supremely artistic achievement, one that garners support from the entire community. In the tabernacle, holiness and beauty converge; divine transcendence becomes aesthetically immanent. The tabernacle is an act of creation inspired by the Spirit of God, no less (31:3; 35:31). Indeed, the instructions and construction of the

4. See Rolf A. Jacobson, "Christian Theology of the Psalms," in *The Oxford Handbook of the Psalms*, ed. William P. Brown (New York: Oxford University Press, 2014), 506–10.

tabernacle in Exodus loosely parallel the account of creation in Genesis 1:1–2:3. YHWH conveys a set of seven (!) instructions to Moses,[5] covering everything from the tabernacle's frame to its furnishings, including the ordination rituals for priests. "And it was so": the tabernacle is constructed exactly as commanded (Exod 39:32).

With the tabernacle completed, YHWH speaks from the "tent of meeting," imparting various priestly and ritual laws, all featured in Leviticus. Little by way of narrative unfolds until Numbers, when preparations are made for Israel's departure from Sinai. Consonant with its Jewish title *bammidbār* ("in the wilderness"), the book of Numbers chronicles the Israelites' itinerary from Sinai to Moab, beginning with preparations for departure from the mountain. The itinerary can be divided geographically into three parts: at Sinai (Num 1:1–10:10), from Sinai to Kadesh (10:11–20:13), and from Kadesh to "the plains of Moab" (20:14–36:13). A summary of the itinerary is given in Numbers 33. In addition to its geographical structure, one also notes an alternating movement between narrative and instruction.

1. Instruction: 1:1–10:10
   I. Narrative: 10:11–14:45

2. Instruction: 15
   II. Narrative: 16–17

3. Instruction: 18–19
   III. Narrative: 20–25

4. Instruction: 26:1–27:11
   IV. Narrative: 27:12-23

5. Instruction: 28–30
   V. Narrative: 31:1–33:49

6. Instruction: 33:50–36:13[6]

5. Exod 25:10–26:30; 26:31–30:10; 30:11-16, 17-21, 22-33, 34-38; 31:1-11, 12-17.

6. Thanks to Brennan Breed for a convenient outline of this structural feature of Numbers.

Such a pattern, unprecedented in the pre-Sinai wilderness narratives (Exod 15:22–18:27), testifies to the continuance of *tôrâ*-making even after Sinai/Horeb. While the Israelites continue to trudge through the wilderness, for forty years no less, so *tôrâ*, Israel's prescriptive corpus, continues to grow and evolve in the wilderness (see chapter 6).

As preparation for the journey ahead, a census is taken, as instructed by YHWH, and the Israelite camp is organized according to "ancestral houses" and tribes as if on a military expedition,[7] all surrounding the tabernacle with the Levites closest to the center, given their role in performing "service at the tabernacle" (2:17; 3:7). After nearly one year encamped at Sinai, the Israelites are ready to depart (10:11-12). With the tabernacle completed and a vast array of laws and instructions given, Israel departs from the mountain, moving forward in "stages," "company by company," with Judah leading the way, all in sync with the cloud's rhythm of movement. The contrast to the people's disarray when they first faced the wilderness is stark. Israel's departure from Sinai marks a promising new beginning; now Israel embarks fully equipped for the journey ahead.

Breakdown ensues, and it's déjà vu. The people fall back to complaining, and YHWH becomes angry, unleashing a consuming fire abated only by Moses's fearless intercession (11:1-3). Yet some, craving meat, desire to return to Egypt, with its plentiful fish and assorted vegetables. In the wilderness, there was only "manna to look at" (11:5-6). What was once a source of wonderment, as well as nourishment, manna is now greeted with disdain. "What is it?" or WTI (Exod 16:15), has become WTF! Once again, YHWH is angered (11:10), provoking another protest from Moses:

> Why have you treated your servant so horribly? Why have I not found favor in your eyes, for you have placed the burden of all these people on me? Am I the one who conceived all this people? Am I the one who gave birth to them, that you would say to me, "Carry them at your breast as a nurse carries a nursing child, to the land that you swore to their ancestors?" . . . I am not able to carry all this people on my own, for they are too heavy for

7. As Tremper Longman III notes, Moses's command, "Arise, YHWH, let your enemies scatter!" (Num 10:35a), given when the ark is set out, resembles a battle cry (personal communication).

> me. If you are going to treat me like this, then just kill me! If I have found favor in your eyes, do not let me see my misery. (Num 11:11-15)

Moses is no mother, and he makes that clear by charging YHWH with the maternal responsibility of carrying such a wayward people. If Moses did not conceive and give birth to this people, then who did? Moses reminds YHWH of "her" responsibility to exercise maternal care. And so YHWH conceives a plan: the burden of leadership is to be shared among seventy elders, who are to receive "some of the spirit that is on" Moses (11:17). As for the meat to be given to over six hundred thousand individuals, Moses has his doubts, to which YHWH responds derisively, "Is YHWH's hand too short?" (11:23). Is God's power too weak? YHWH proves otherwise, and with a vengeance: meat is given in abundance, along with a "very great plague" (11:33).

Observant readers may notice that YHWH's anger is not as easily assuaged as before, and it comes to an explosive head when the promised land is flatly rejected by the people after they assess the two conflicting spy reports. The majority report is favored; thus, the people "despise" what YHWH had promised across generations (14:31) by making plans to head back to Egypt (14:2-4). YHWH resolves to "disinherit them" and make Moses a "nation greater and mightier than they" (14:12). This is the second time that such an offer has been extended to Moses (see Exod 32:10). But Moses intercedes once again, appealing to how YHWH's reputation will suffer internationally. If Israel were to die in the desert, the "Egyptians will hear of it" (Num 14:13), and the nations would only conclude that "because YHWH was unable to bring this people into the land that he swore to give them, he slaughtered them in the wilderness" (14:16). Instead, Moses argues, "Let my lord's power be as great as you had declared" back at Sinai. Moses throws YHWH's own confession (see Exod 34:6-7) back at YHWH, now as a form of self-incrimination. YHWH's great power, Moses argues, is in line with YHWH's great "benevolence," a power manifest in divine forgiveness (Num 14:19-20). YHWH reaches a compromise that captures the tension within the great confession: "forgiving iniquity," on the one hand, and not "clearing the guilty," on the other.

Forgiveness, yes, but justice too: the present generation (with two exceptions) will not live long enough to "see the land" (14:20-22).

Upon hearing the news of their forty-year sojourn in the wilderness, the people try to take the "hill country" of the Amalekites and the Canaanites by force, only to be roundly defeated (14:39-45). Moses warned them not to, but they did so anyway (14:41-43). The irony could not be thicker: by rejecting the land promised by YHWH after receiving the spies' report, the people are prevented from possessing it. The irony could not be more tragic: the people gain their senses about taking the land only after they have rejected the land. Thus, there's no going to the land, just as there is no going back to Egypt. Forty years in the wilderness it is.

"Ten times" YHWH has been tested (14:22), and YHWH has had enough. But there are more trying moments to come. First, there are internal divisions: Aaron and Miriam protest against Moses because of his mixed marriage, an excuse to undermine Moses's authority and status as YHWH's favored spokesperson (12:1-15). YHWH intervenes by striking Miriam with leprosy. More conflict explodes when the Levite priest Korah and his company charge Moses and Aaron with exalting themselves and hoarding holiness (16:3). Moreover, Dathan and Abiram accuse Moses of "lording" his power by leading them astray from a land "full of milk and honey" (16:13). In the face of all these accusations, the narrator immodestly claims Moses as the most "humble" person "on the face of the earth" (12:3). A sure defense, perhaps, but it leads to no compromise. Moses doesn't give an inch.

The theological dispute does not go well for the protesters. It is resolved only with the earth swallowing them up and fire consuming those offering incense (16:31-35; but cf. 26:11). Case closed. As Moses was vindicated before Aaron and Miriam, so Aaron is vindicated before the community: all his detractors are annihilated. But not all conflict is eliminated: with a return to Meribah, quarreling erupts again, and with a surprising twist. The "congregation" gathers to charge Moses with bringing them to an uncultivable wasteland (20:5). YHWH instructs Moses to "take the staff" and "command the rock before their eyes to yield its water." But Moses deviates by using the staff to strike the rock twice after berating the people and highlighting his own and Aaron's agency: "Listen, you rebels, shall we bring water for you out of this rock?" (Num 20:10). Water does gush forth, but Moses is indicted for not "trusting" YHWH enough to demonstrate YHWH's "holiness" (Num 20:12). What the problem is remains obscure, but Moses apparently did not follow the prescribed protocol, and for that he is prevented from bringing the people into the land. Case closed.

Amid such failures, two successes are highlighted along the way, the defeats of kings Sihon of the Amorites and Og of Bashan (21:21-35). By refusing to give them passage, these two kings are killed and their respective territories are taken by the Israelites to be claimed as Transjordanian land for Israel's settlement in due time.[8] As for Edom, the Israelites had to turn away (20:14-21). As for Moab, King Balak hires a diviner to curse Israel. But YHWH has other plans, and Balaam blesses Israel four times, with ever increasing power (23:1–24:24).

But the pendulum swings back to one more brazen episode of apostasy, in addition to the "golden calf" incident: the Israelites intermarry with foreign women and become "yoked to Baʿal of Peor" (25:1-6). YHWH commands execution of all the leaders, and Moses orders a purge of all Baʿal worshippers. Meanwhile, an Israelite man flagrantly takes a Midianite woman to his family. The priest Phinehas, grandson of Aaron, kills them with a spear, stopping the spreading plague. Such shameless sin must evidently be met with violent zeal, and for such zeal, YHWH grants Phinehas a "covenant of peace," one of "perpetual priesthood" (25:13). The apostasy marks a pivotal point in the Numbers narrative; from here on out attention turns toward the new generation and their preparation for taking the land, formally marked by a census that signals the "rise of a new generation of hope" (26:1-65; cf. 1:1-47).[9]

As the trek continues stage by stage,[10] so *tôrâ* develops case by case. The daughters of Zelophehad bring their case before Moses regarding the inheritance of property in a family without sons. "The daughters of

8. See the near-disastrous conflict over Israel's settlement resolved in Num 32:1-42.

9. Dennis T. Olson, *Numbers: A Bible Commentary for Teaching and Preaching*, Interpretation (Louisville, KY: Westminster John Knox, 1996), 160.

10. See Exod 17:1; Num 12:10; 33:1-2.

Zelophehad are right," says YHWH (27:7); they are to receive their father's property. This "statute and ordinance" is given further refinement in 36:1-12. The passage through the wilderness, it turns out, is in part a journey of jurisprudence. Further regulations are developed regarding ritual offerings, vows made by women, military rules of conquest, land boundaries, designated cities for the Levites, cites of refuge, and rulings concerning murder and manslaughter (35:16-34). Such are the "commandments and the ordinances" commanded by YHWH "through Moses" on the plains of Moab (36:13). So concludes the book of Numbers and Israel's circuitous trek.

Perhaps the most striking feature of the two wilderness accounts is that despite so many shared elements between Exodus 15:22–18:27 and Numbers 10:11–36:13 there lies one categorical difference, a theological one. As Israel journeys from the sea to Sinai, YHWH responds to the people's complaint with gracious provision. Nowhere does YHWH follow through on executing judgment. In contrast, punishments plague the Israelites at almost every step from Sinai to Moab, accompanied by provision sometimes delivered with a vengeance. The complaints are the same in both legs of the wilderness journey, so also the desire to return to Egypt, but YHWH reacts in a decidedly different manner. The shift from provision and forbearance to provision and punishment revolves around Sinai, where *tôrâ* is given. With YHWH's instructions received at Sinai, YHWH now holds the people accountable, as if Sinai were Israel's bar mitzvah, marking the passage into responsible adulthood.

But as the second leg of the wilderness journey testifies, the people have not changed. They, in effect, refuse to grow up. In the Numbers account (post-Sinai), a new descriptor is applied to Israel: the people are deemed "rebellious" (√*mrh*).[11] The designation is never used for Israel in Exodus, even though they complain just as bitterly in Exodus as they do in Numbers.[12] After Sinai, the people's complaints are deemed rebellious, and they act rebellious against YHWH and Moses. The desire to return to

11. Num 14:9 (√*mrd*); 20:10 (√*mrh* and subsequent citations), 24; 27:14; Deut 1:26, 43; 9:7, 23-24; 31:27.

12. Exod 16:2, 7-8; 17:3; Num 11:1; 14:2, 27, 29, 36; 17:5, 10.

Egypt remains unabated, hence YHWH's decision to let the first generation, the generation that witnessed God's wonders in Egypt, pass away in the wilderness, with hopes now pinned on the second generation. Enter Deuteronomy.

Moses Idealized and the Nations Legitimized: Deuteronomy

In Deuteronomy, Israel's wanderings are over and done with, but the wilderness remains, and so Israel's formation continues. Moses addresses a new generation on the plains of Moab to prepare them for life in the land. While Deuteronomy is devoted primarily to revising *tôrâ* (see chapter 6), it opens with a review of the wilderness period, beginning with YHWH's command to set out on their journey from Horeb to the land for possession as sworn to Abraham, Isaac, and Jacob (Deut 1:6-8; cf. Exod 33:1-3).[13] Moses then reviews how bearing the burden of adjudicating so many disputes became alleviated by appointing "wise" and "discerning" leaders, complete with instructions on best practices, such as impartial judgment (Deut 1:9-18). Moses describes it as his own "plan," devised by him, which carries the assent of the people (v. 14), while in Exodus it is Jethro's plan that Moses implements (Exod 18:19-24). In Deuteronomy, Moses commands the tribes to elect their "leaders" (Deut 1:13), whereas in Exodus (pre-Sinai), Moses selects them himself (Exod 18:25). In a more distant version, YHWH commands Moses to pick seventy elders to help bear the burden of leadership by sharing some of Moses's prophetic spirit (Num 11:16-17). By comparison, Deuteronomy highlights Moses's initiative in leadership. He is a "one-man show." Even YHWH is pushed out of the picture, albeit momentarily.

13. For a review of the structure and theology of Deuteronomy 1–3, see Patrick D. Miller, "The Wilderness Journey in Deuteronomy: Style, Structure, and Theology in Deuteronomy 1–3," in *To Hear and Obey: Essays in Honor of Frederick Carlson Holmgren*, ed. Bradley J. Bergfalk and Paul E. Koptak (Chicago: Covenant Publications, 1997), 50–68 (reprinted in P. D. Miller, *Israelite Religion and Biblical Theology: Collected Essays*, JSOTSup 267 [Sheffield, UK: Sheffield Academic Press, 2000], 572–92).

Bypassing other events along the way, Moses in Deuteronomy reviews the account of spying on the land (1:22-33). In contrast to Numbers 13:1-33, the people in the Deuteronomic version hatch their own plan to send spies to Canaan, whereas in Numbers YHWH commands it (13:1-3). In Deuteronomy, there appears to be just one, albeit mixed, report, while in Numbers, there are distinctly two, a majority report and a minority report, with two sets of authors. In both cases, however, the people are united against taking the land. In Deuteronomy, Moses assures the people that YHWH "goes before you" and "will fight for you," just as in Egypt (1:30). Moreover, YHWH's provision in the wilderness demonstrates how YHWH "carried you, just as one carries a child" (1:31; cf. Num 11:12). In Numbers, such encouragement comes from Joshua (14:9). But to no avail.

In the face of imminent judgment, no intercessory report is given on how Moses convinced YHWH to refrain from destroying the people. YHWH decides without any prompting from Moses to prevent this "evil generation" from seeing the "good land" (1:34-36), including Moses (1:37). Instead of a separate incident of disobedience (cf. Num 20), Moses's punishment is linked with the people's punishment (Deut 1:37). Nevertheless, the outcome is the same. Their "little ones" will inherit the land (1:39), like the meek inheriting the earth (Ps 37:11). The Numbers version features a more elaborate verdict, filled with "dead bodies" littering the wilderness (14:29, 32). In both versions, Israel's response is remorseful, followed by a failed attempt to take the "hill country" (Deut 1:41-45; cf. Num 14:39-45). In the Deuteronomic version, it is the Amorites (instead of the Amalekites and Canaanites) whom they attack. The result: they are "chased" away as if they were attacked by "bees" (1:44; cf. Num 14:45). The failure of such a mission, as in Numbers, is a foregone conclusion.

In Deuteronomy, Moses identifies a lack of "trust in YHWH your God" as the fundamental reason for the people's failure in the wilderness (1:32). Such trust leads to obedience (9:23). Numbers, however, does not identify lack of "trust" as the people's core problem.[14] It is their

14. In Numbers, only Moses is noted for his lack of trust (20:12).

"rebellious" spirit (Num 14:9), which Deuteronomy also affirms,[15] and "disrespect" of YHWH that warrants divine punishment (Num 14:11; 16:30). Deuteronomy, however, identifies the central issue at stake: lack of trust as the root of rebellion.[16]

As for Israel's route through the desert, Deuteronomy and Numbers part company entirely. While Edom refuses to allow passage through its land in Numbers 20:18-21, the Israelites in Deuteronomy are able to pass through because "they will be afraid of you" (Deut 2:4). YHWH warns them not to engage in battle, for Edom's land was rightfully given to them, to Esau, by YHWH (2:3-6, 22). Instead, the Israelites are allowed to purchase food and water (2:7). In addition, as a historical aside, the Edomites are said to have dispossessed the former inhabitants of the land (the Horim) just as Israel will do in the land YHWH gives them (2:12). In Deuteronomy, Israel is not the only people privileged to occupy another people's land, made possible by divine ordination. Moreover, Deuteronomy explicitly refers to the Edomites, the "descendants of Esau," as Israel's "kin" (*aḥ*; Deut 23:7[8]).

The same goes for Moab, the "descendants of Lot" (2:9). YHWH forbids Israel from engaging the Moabites in battle, for Moab has also been given its land by YHWH, whose former inhabitants were the Emim/Rephaim (Deut 2:9-11). As for the Ammonites—also descendants of Lot—YHWH gave them their land by destroying the Zamzummim/Rephaim (2:19-21). And as a further aside, the text tells of the Caphtorim displacing the Avvim in order to take possession of the "vicinity of Gaza" (2:23). For all the violent takeovers of the land, YHWH's "colonializing care"[17] extends beyond Israel to include the Edomites, Moabites, and Ammonites, even the Caphtorim (cf. Amos 9:7). Their boundaries are to be respected as a way of acknowledging YHWH's international work. In

15. E.g., 1:26, 43; 9:7, 23-24.

16. See, also, Miller, "The Wilderness Journey," 61 (589).

17. I coin this phrase in full recognition of its damning irony: God's care in Deuteronomy apparently extends only to the conquering colonizers but not to the indigenous inhabitants.

Deuteronomy, Israel's God is shown to be providentially at work with nations other than Israel.[18]

Not so, however, regarding the lands of King Sihon and King Og, whose kingdoms are destined for defeat by YHWH and whose Transjordanian territories are given to Israel. Whereas Numbers gives comparatively minimal notice of their defeat, Deuteronomy turns the two events into a big deal. Similar to the Numbers version, King Sihon in Deuteronomy is offered the same arrangement that Edom was, namely peaceful passage and purchase of provisions. However, Sihon refuses, and so he is conquered, because YHWH had "hardened his spirit" (Deut 2:30), sounding all too familiar (cf. Exod 7:3). Israel's possession of this land of the Amorites comes with a concluding note of respect for the boundaries of the Ammonites (2:37). Numbers notes only that the "boundary of the Ammonites was strong." Either way, Israel did not encroach on the Ammonites (Num 21:24).

The same fate goes for King Og and his land: he attacked Israel on the road to Bashan (Deut 3:10). A curious sidebar is the description of Og's iron bed, approximately 13.5 × 6 feet, identifying him as one of the tall Rephaim, whose remnant is left in the land (3:11). Deuteronomy introduces an element of awe that is lacking in Numbers regarding Israel's conquered adversaries. All in all, these two conquered lands set a precedent and example of what will happen to the land of Canaan on the other side of the Jordan (3:21). Success is ensured because "it is YHWH your God who fights for you" (3:22).

Whereas Numbers gives a straightforward account of Israel's trek among the surrounding nations, Deuteronomy provides a more nuanced perspective, one filtered by a sensitivity toward international relations: Edom, Moab, and Ammon are given international legitimacy, because they, like Israel, received their land from YHWH. Israel's "right" to its land is paralleled by the "rights" of other peoples to their respective lands. In short, Deuteronomy offers a more diplomatic version of Israel's wilderness trek, and in so doing provides a broader perspective of YHWH's work

18. Miller, "The Wilderness Journey," 60 (586).

in the world. YHWH's providential care is not limited to one people; Israel is not the only game in town.

Wilderness in the Psalms

Much like the narratives in Exodus, Numbers, and Deuteronomy, two psalms in particular depict Israel's wilderness trek as marred by conflict and rebellion. Other psalms, however, recount the wilderness wanderings without reference to either apostasy or rebellion. We begin with those that are most similar to the Pentateuchal narratives.

Psalm 78: God's Struggle for Forbearance

As discussed earlier, Psalm 78 introduces itself as a "teaching" (*tôrâ*) of YHWH's "wonders" (78:4b) to be passed on to subsequent generations (78:1-4). The speaker is positioned between generations, between the "ancestors" and the "next generation" (78:5-6). Reference to the former recalls the infamous generation characterized as "obstinate and contentious" (78:8), which in the narratives is the generation destined to die in the wilderness (Num 14:14-20; Deut 1:34-40; 2:16). Psalm 78 is a "teaching" aimed at preventing a repeat of such failure. The psalm offers itself as the poetic counterpart to the book of Deuteronomy with its complementary aim of teaching *tôrâ*, but in this case a *tôrâ* focused more on God's "marvelous deeds" than on God's statutes and ordinances. The psalm weds together Israel's refusal "to walk according to [YHWH's] *tôrâ*" with Israel's forgetting YHWH's "wonders" (78:10-11).

Psalm 78 gets down to business by describing the exodus event with dramatic brevity: God "splits" the sea to allow for Israel's safe passage (78:13), matched by God "splitting rocks" in the wilderness to provide drink (78:15a). By dint of divine power, dry rock is transformed into watery depths (*tĕhōmôt*). The double use of the verb ("split") testifies to the versatility of God's power exercised in delivering Israel from various threats: bondage, on the one hand, and deprivation, on the other. God can work with water and rock with equal dexterity. In contrast to the accounts in Exodus 17:1-7 and Numbers 20:1-13, rock splitting in Psalm 78 is described without reference to Moses (or his staff). It is exclusively a matter of divine action. But then Israel's God is "their rock" and "redeemer" (78:35a). It takes the Rock to split a rock.

But things unravel after the flowing streams. As in the narrative texts, sin and rebellion accompany Israel's wilderness trek in Psalm 78. For the psalmist, the lack of water was not a matter of complaint but of legitimate need. The psalmist finds the need for water in the desert to be undeserving of condemnation. Wherever the rock splitting took place, it was not at *Meribah* ("Quarrel"). But food is another matter. Although the Israelites' need for food was not itself the problem, according to the psalm, it was the way in which their need was expressed, namely as a desire that signaled the people's lack of trust, as indicated in their faithless question: "Can God set a table in the wilderness?" (78:19). Such a question should have been precluded in view of God's miraculous provision of water. God is incensed, poised to punish, but does not. Instead, provision comes in the form of manna (78:24b-25a) and "winged creatures," a broad designation that extends beyond the specific reference to "quail" in Exodus 16:13 and Numbers 11:31-32.

As in Numbers 11, God punishes them as they satiate themselves, "killing the sturdiest among them" (Ps 78:31a), which Numbers describes as a "very great plague" (Num 11:33). This stand-alone account of provision and punishment in Psalm 78 sets in sharp relief the way in which Numbers combines the two stories: the craving of meat episode (Num 11:18-24a, 31-34) and the appointing of seventy elders to relieve Moses's burden of leadership (11:16-17, 24b-30). They are intertwined because Moses's earlier complaint was twofold: the burden of "carrying" an incessantly demanding people and the burden of being maltreated by a relentlessly angry deity (11:10-15). YHWH responds to both complaints with a composite answer. But in Psalm 78 there is no Moses burdened by God, just an overburdening people.

In view of God's wrathful punishment and Israel's audacious rebellions, Psalm 78 goes out of its way to highlight God's forbearance:

> But [YHWH], being compassionate,
> would forgive iniquity and refrain from destroying;
> he would often take back his anger and not arouse all his wrath.
> He would remember that they were mere flesh,
> breath that passes away, never to return. (Ps 78:38-39)

To forgive or not to forgive? That is one question. The other is this: *How* to forgive? The psalmist highlights YHWH's maternal compassion (*raḥûm*) as the root of divine forgiveness, suffused with pity on the people's frail condition. In Numbers, Moses appeals to YHWH's international standing among the nations. If Israel were to die in the desert, the "Egyptians will hear of it" (Num 14:13) and the nations would only conclude that YHWH was incapable of fulfilling the promise (14:16). Psalm 78, however, highlights an inner struggle on God's part, the struggle between compassionate forbearance and punishing wrath. In the Pentateuchal narratives, the struggle for forgiveness and forbearance is played out between God and Moses. But Moses is not around to facilitate the struggle in Psalm 78. Without Moses, from the perspective of Exodus and Numbers, God would have finished the people off in a fit of fury. With Moses, however, the people are spared, relatively speaking. In Psalm 78, however, the fight for forgiveness is God's struggle alone. Read in the light of Psalm 78, Moses in the Pentateuchal narrative serves as God's alter ego.

Psalm 106: Forgetting and Rejecting the God of Salvation

Like Psalm 78, Psalm 106 highlights Israel's repeated rebellions in the face of YHWH's prolific "wonders" (106:7). Unlike in Psalm 78, however, Moses plays a prominent role. First, Israel's rebellious character in Psalm 106 is demonstrated at the Sea of Reeds (106:7b). Rebellion in the psalm takes the form of "forgetting" God's "deeds" and "benevolent acts" and refusing to "wait for [YHWH's] counsel" (106:7, 13). The flipside of such intransigence is "craving in the wilderness," putting God to the "test" (106:14). The divine result is provision served with punishment (106:15; cf. Num 11:31-34). And that is only the beginning.

Psalm 106 recounts the Dathan and Abiram rebellion (minus Korah), claiming "jealousy" (*qn'*) over Moses's and Aaron's authority as the issue (106:16-18; cf. Num 16:1-40). Numbers highlights the theological issues at stake: Who qualifies to be holy? What are the rights and privileges of Levitical service? Who can exercise legitimate leadership over the community (Num 16:3, 9, 13)? The psalmist, however, is not interested in such matters. The incident serves merely as preface to something much more grievous: the golden calf apostasy (cf. Exod 32).

> They made a calf at Horeb,
>   and bowed down before a cast image.
> They exchanged [God's][19] glory
>   for the image of a bull, which eats grass.
> They forgot the God who saved them,
>   the one who had done great things in Egypt. (Ps 78:19-21)

Here, the psalmist identifies the root of the matter: by worshipping the image of an animal, the people "exchanged" God's "glory" for something domestically mundane, the wonder-working God who can devour the wicked with consuming fire exchanged for a grass-eating animal. A bad trade. The presenting issue is different in Exodus 32, where the crime lies in identifying "these gods" represented by the calf as agents of Israel's deliverance (32:4, 8). In both cases, theological amnesia reigns: "they forgot the God who saved them" (Ps 106:21a). God would be justified in "destroying" such a forgetful, rebellious people (106:23). But Moses intervenes, once again. In the Exodus account, Moses convinces YHWH that the Egyptians would conclude that YHWH's plan of deliverance was malicious from the outset (Exod 32:11-12). To clinch the deal, Moses reminds YHWH of the Abrahamic covenant (32:13). Moses convinces YHWH to "change" course or repent (√*nḥm*) from unwarranted punishment, and YHWH does (32:14).

The psalmist offers a different view of Moses's role, one that does not rely on speech.

---

19. MT "their," a theological correction for "his," i.e., God's. Another possibility is to take "glory" as a hypostasis for "God" to read "their glorious God" (see CEB).

So [God] would have determined to destroy them,
  had not Moses, his elect one,
    stood in the breach before him,
      to avert his wrath from destroying [them]. (Ps 106:23)

The metaphorical expression refers to someone who is willing to serve sacrificially as a barrier that averts or deflects disaster, in this case the disaster of divine wrath.[20] By "standing in the breach," Moses acts to save Israel from their God, the God whom they rejected and is now poised to destroy them. In Exodus, Moses convinces YHWH with words full of rhetorical ingenuity. In the psalm, Moses puts his body on the line, as it were. In both cases, Moses steps up to avert the people's annihilation.

Psalm 106 recounts Israel's rejection of the promised land but without the narrative engagement one finds in Numbers 13–14 or Deuteronomy 1:34-40. There is nothing about the spies or their divided report. Instead, the psalmist refers simply to the people's "despising" the "desirable land" and "grumbling in their tents" (Ps 106:24-25). Rejecting the land is tantamount to rejecting God's promise and disobeying God's "voice." God's response is a sworn oath to kill them in the wilderness and disperse their descendants among the nations (106:26). Such judgment overextends the judgment given in Numbers 14:20-24 by collapsing the judgment against the first generation with the judgment of exile.[21] But such a conflation coheres with the psalm's own rhetorical aim, given its plea-filled conclusion:

Save us, YHWH our God!
  Gather us from the nations,
    to give thanks to your holy name
      and to revel boldly in your praise! (Ps 106:47)

Death in the desert is tantamount to dispersion among the nations. Also significant in the psalmist's interpretation is the formality of YHWH's oath (106:26a), perhaps reflecting YHWH's oath in Numbers: "But as I

20. Cf. Ezek 22:30; 13:5; Job 16:14.

21. Cf. Deut 4:27; 28:64; 1 Kgs 14:15; Jer 9:16; Ezek 6:8.

live and as YHWH's glory fills the entire earth, none of the men who saw my glory . . . will see the land that I swore to their ancestors; none of those who despised me shall see it" (14:21-22). The irony is unmistakable: YHWH's sworn oath to punish the present generation contravenes YHWH's covenantal promise of land made to Abraham, Isaac, and Jacob.[22] One oath annuls a previous oath, for one generation at least. By correlating these two sworn promises, the psalmist deepens the gravity of punishment in the wilderness.

While none of the gory details are given, the infamous incident at Ba'al of Peor is recounted in the psalm with due praise given to Phinehas for his intercession. But the psalm adds one unparalleled detail: in addition to "joining themselves" to Ba'al, the wanderers also "consumed sacrifices [offered] to the dead" (106:28b), nowhere mentioned in the Numbers account (25:1-18). The background may be found in the *marzēaḥ* festival alluded to in Jeremiah 16:5-9 and Amos 6:4-7, reflecting a widespread West Semitic ritual involving lavish feasting that in some cases functioned in a funerary context.[23] The psalmist associates a forbidden funerary ritual with apostate Ba'al worship. With Phinehas saving the day, the psalmist confers righteousness on him with an expression found elsewhere only in association with Abram (Ps 106:31; cf. Gen 15:6): he is "reckoned" (*ḥšb*) "as righteousness" (*ṣĕdāqâ*).[24] In the Numbers account, Phinehas's legacy of righteousness is ensured through a "covenant of peace" (*bĕrît šālôm*; Num 25:12), further elucidated as a "covenant of perpetual priesthood" (*bĕrît kĕhunnat 'ôlām*; Num 25:13). Nothing about his priestly status is registered in the psalm; Phinehas's legacy parallels Abraham's. His righteousness is everlasting, across generations, just as Abraham's.

The last and final crime in the wilderness is the incident at "the waters of Meribah" (Exod 32:32-33), which draws primarily from Numbers 20:1-13 (rather than from Exod 17:1-7) with reference to Moses having "spoken rashly" (√*bṭ'*; Ps 106:33b). Numbers features a vivid account of

22. Cf. Pss 106:24b, 45; 105:8-11, 42.

23. For an overview, see Esteē Dvorjetski, "From Ugarit to Madaba: Philological and Historical Functions of the *marzēaḥ*," *Journal of Semitic Studies* 61, no. 1 (2016): 17–39.

24. The only grammatical difference is that the verbal rendering in the psalm is passive, whereas it is active (with God as subject) in Genesis.

such verbal rashness (Num 20:10b). Moses also acts rashly by striking the rock twice, not in accord with YHWH's command (20:11; cf. 20:8b). The psalmist, however, fashions a wordplay with another water-in-the-desert episode in connection with Moses's "embittered" (√*mrh*) spirit (Ps 106:33a). This other incident is the first one described in Exodus: after celebrating their freedom from Egypt, the Israelites encounter a place with no drinkable water called "Marah" (*mārâ*) known for its "bitter" (*mar*) water (Exod 15:23).

How ironic that at a place of *drinkable* water something becomes "bitter" (√*mrh*), namely Moses's own "spirit" (Ps 106:33a). It is with such a spirit that Moses spoke "rashly" (106:33b). Hence, "it went badly for Moses because of them" (106:32b), perhaps an indirect reference to Moses's punishment by God. It is clear that Moses's culpability is minimized. Nothing is said of Moses deviating from YHWH's command. Instead, the people are to blame: "they angered YHWH"; "they embittered [Moses's] spirit." One senses a veiled defense of Moses's innocence. In any case, Psalm 106 gives Moses his respectful due in the desert. And it is without Moses in the promised land that Israel sinks to new lows (106:34-39), provoking YHWH to give them "into the hand of the nations" (106:41). In short, Psalm 106 highlights Israel's repeated rebellions in the wilderness while exonerating Moses at nearly every step. He and Phinehas are cut from the same cloth. One "stood in the breach," while the other "stood up" and was "reckoned as righteous." Moses and Phinehas could have easily switched roles, except that Moses was the one who "spoke rashly." But that should not have been an impeachable offense, the psalmist seems to imply.

The Sanitized Psalms

Both Psalms 78 and 106 make no mention of military successes in the wilderness, specifically of conquering the kings Sihon and Og. However, Psalms 135–136 do and, in turn, make no mention of Israel's sins in the desert. This is not a coincidence.

Psalms 135–136: Benevolence All the Way Down

Psalm 135 tightens the relationship between the exodus and conquest in the wilderness by describing YHWH as the one who "struck down the firstborn of Egypt" as well as "struck down many nations" and "killed mighty kings," including Sihon and Og (135:8-11). As in Numbers 21:21-35 and Deuteronomy 3:8-17, their lands in the Transjordan become an Israelite "inheritance" (*naḥălâ*; Ps 135:12). The emphasis in Psalm 135 falls on God's power over the nations, much in contrast to their idols (135:15-18). In Psalm 136, given its omnipresent refrain, the emphasis falls on YHWH's "benevolence" as the driving force behind it all. It is by YHWH's "benevolence" that Israel is led "through the wilderness" (136:16a). It is by YHWH's "benevolence" that "famous kings" are killed (136:18a), including Sihon and Og (136:19-20).[25] But most notably, it is by YHWH's "benevolence" that no acknowledgment is given of Israel's rebellions in the wilderness, as if divine benevolence had wiped the slate clean for these wayward wanderers, even in their state of "degradation" (136:23). To be sure, reference to divine "benevolence" is not unprecedented in other historical psalms, as in Psalm 106 (see 106:7, 45), a psalm that does not hesitate to dive deep into Israel's sins in the wilderness. However, in Psalm 136 YHWH's overarching "benevolence" overrides and wipes away all incidents of Israel's complaining, rebelling, and apostate worship. Psalm 136 serves as historical testimony to the divine self-confession made on the summit of Sinai in Exodus 34:6-7a (see above). If divine "benevolence" is the ground for divine forgiveness, as claimed in YHWH's self-confession, then Psalm 136 is a historicized testimony of such forgiveness.

Psalm 105: A Journey of Joy

Like Psalm 136, Psalm 105 lacks all reference to Israel sinning in the desert, or anywhere else. The emphasis falls upon YHWH's salvific power and commitment to the covenant.

25. Except for the addition of the refrain, Ps 136 nearly repeats 135:10-12 in 136:17-22.

They asked[26] and he brought quail,
    and he satisfied them with the bread of heaven.
He opened the rock and out gushed water,
    flowing as a river through dry lands.
For he was mindful of his sacred promise,
    [to] Abraham his servant.
He brought his people out in joy,
    his chosen ones with peals of jubilation.
He gave them the lands of nations;
    they inherited the wealth of the peoples,
        so that they may keep his statutes,
            and observe his laws. (105:40-45)

Sustenance in the wilderness, according to Psalm 105, was simply there for the "asking" (√*š'l*), not for the complaining or craving (105:40). Such a polite people! Israel's wilderness trek is no trail of bitter tears but a journey of joy (105:43). The people were sent off by the Egyptians, who were happy to see them go enriched (105:38), and then they arrived "inheriting the wealth of the peoples" (105:44). Israel's journey was no wandering; it was a victory march from exodus to *eisodus*. In contrast to Psalms 135 and 136, Psalm 105 lacks the theological language of benevolence or compassion as the driving rationale behind this journey of joy. Instead, the psalmist's eyes are fixed resolutely on the covenant made to Abraham (105:6a, 7-10). The promise of the land sets the precedent and goal for all that happens from the ancestors to the inheritance. YHWH is a God of God's word, and this God is going to see Israel through no matter what. Period.

Psalm 95: A Bombshell Dropped in the Midst of Praise

Outside the so-called historical psalms, one psalm makes reference to the wilderness episode of "Massah and Meribah," and in a rather surprising way.

26. Read plural due to haplography and LXX et al.

Come, let us shout aloud to YHWH!
  Let us raise a joyful cry to the rock of our salvation!
Let us come before his face with thanksgiving!
  With songs let us raise a joyful shout to him!
For YHWH is a great God,
  a great king above all gods,
    in whose hands are the depths[27] of the earth,
      and to whom the heights of the mountains belong,
    to whom belongs the sea, which he [alone] has made,
      and the dry land, which his hands have formed.
Come, let us worship and bow down!
  Let us kneel before YHWH, our maker!
For he is our God, and we are the people of his pasture,
  the sheep of his hand. (95:1-7a)

If you would only heed his voice today!
"Do not harden your hearts as at Meribah,
  as in the day of Massah in the wilderness,
    when your ancestors put me to the test,
    when they tried me, even though they had beheld my works.
For forty years I detested [that] generation,
  for I realized, 'They are a people whose hearts are wayward;
    they do not acknowledge my ways.'
So[28] I swore in my anger,
  'They shall never enter my rest.'" (95:7b-11)

Psalm 95 begins with a corporate invitation to render joyful praise for YHWH's sovereign supremacy over the gods (95:3), creational power (95:4-5), and shepherding guidance (95:7a). But a warning disrupts such praise with an explosive oracular admonition, introduced by a plaintive speaker (95:7b). YHWH enjoins the community not to "harden" their

27. The word is a hapax legomenon. It is derived from the root *ḥqr*, meaning "investigate" or "explore"; hence, the form likely refers to a place of exploration (cf. the use of the cognate *ḥēqer* in Job 11:7; 38:16; Sir 42:16). LXX reads *merḥaqqê* ("ends, extremities"). Perhaps it is best to read as "depths" in parallel to "heights" in the second colon.

28. The subordinate clause, signaled by the *'ăšer*, is resultative.

"hearts" as at Meribah and Massah (95:8). Such was a time and place in which the ancestors "tested" YHWH, despite having witnessed YHWH's "works" (95:9). For forty years YHWH "detested" (√*qwṭ*) this generation in full awareness of their "wayward" hearts and their persistent refusal to acknowledge YHWH's "ways" (95:10). This historically based warning ends with a divine oath, "sworn . . . in anger," that the people "shall never enter" the land, YHWH's "rest" (95:11).[29] The psalmist echoes the familiar themes of test, anger, and judgment. In Numbers 14:22, God complains of having been tested "ten times" by this generation.[30] The contrast between the people "testing" YHWH and beholding YHWH's works highlights the absurdity of the people's conduct *coram Deo*, a not uncommon theme in the historical psalms.

One striking distinction, however, in the psalm's account of the wilderness story is the conflation of the Massah and Meribah episode (cf. Exod 17:1-7; Num 20:1-13) with YHWH's punishing response to the people's rejection of the land, resulting in a forty-year judgment against the wilderness generation (cf. Num 14:28-34). More significant is that the divine judgment recounted in Psalm 95 occurs at *the end* of forty years in the wilderness, not at the outset.[31] God proves to be more forbearing in Psalm 95 than in Numbers. In Numbers, the Israelites faced harsh punishment three times: in the quail episode (11:4-35), the spies's report (Num 13–14), and Korah's rebellion (16:1-35) with the subsequent plague in Numbers 17. In Psalm 95, YHWH withholds punishment until the end of Israel's forty years in the wilderness, as if extending the pre-Sinaitic sojourn, characterized by divine provision without punishment (Exod 15:22–18:27), to cover the forty-year sojourn until the end, when judgment is (finally) given.

No less striking is how the psalm contextualizes the wilderness journey, placing it as a divine disruption within the setting of praise, a bombshell dropped in the middle of worship, as it were. The first half of the psalm is filled with praise, concluding with the affirmation: "we are the people of his pasture" (95:7a; cf. 100:3). In 95:10, the "people" are

29. See also Gen 49:5; Deut 12:9; 1 Kgs 8:56; and Mic 2:10.

30. Cf. Ps 81:8, in which God "tests" the Israelites at the "waters of Meribah."

31. George W. Savran, "Contrasting Voices in Psalm 95," *RB* 110, no. 1 (2003): 25–26.

deemed "wayward" of heart because they refuse to acknowledge YHWH's "ways." The contrast could not be more stark, while the connection could not be more apparent. In Psalm 78, the metaphor of the sheep led by the shepherd serves to highlight God's guidance of Israel's journey all the way to God's "holy hill" (78:52-54). But according to Psalm 95, the journey led to failure.

Psalm 95 juxtaposes two contrasting ways regarding how the "people" respond to God: in praise and in rebellion. The mandate to give praise meets the testimony of historical failure. The divine admonition exposes the people's praise as a pious fraud, or at least what could be a pious fraud. The lesson? Praise must be morally accountable in order to be authentic, not unlike the judgment given in Amos 5:21-24. Genuine praise demands open, rather than "hardened," hearts—hearts receptive to YHWH's "ways." Otherwise, praise is a sham. Psalm 95 demonstrates how an episode of historic failure with resulting judgment can be deployed to critique and reform how a community is to worship. With such a warning, the psalmist places the praise-filled community in the sandals of the new generation who had to disassociate themselves from their forebearers (cf. Num 14:31-34; 32:13).

Failure in the wilderness presents a cautionary tale for success in worship made all the more pressing by the final word: "my rest" (*mĕnûḥātî*). In the wilderness context, the word refers to the land to which the people can no longer "come." "Rest" can also designate God's dwelling place, the sanctuary (Isa 66:1; Ps 132:8, 14). The psalm's first half summons the people to "come" and worship (95:1, 6). The psalm's ending prohibits the people of the past from "coming" to YHWH's "rest." The psalmist binds together land and sanctuary, with proper worship deemed their rightful entrance. "Hardened" and "wayward" hearts, in turn, prove to be the barriers of true worship.

Psalm 81: The Land of (Missed) Opportunity

Psalm 81 serves as an "historical" counterpoint to Psalm 95, featuring an extensive divine "decree" that recounts Israel's deliverance from Egypt, God's prohibition against worshipping foreign deities, and Israel's refusal to "walk in [God's] ways." In response, God laments Israel's stubbornness but at the same time keeps open the opportunity for provision.

> Rejoice aloud to God, our strength!
>   Shout for joy to the God of Jacob!
> Raise a song and strike the drum!
>   [Play] the sweet lyre with the harp!
> Blow the shofar on the new moon,
>   on the full moon for our feast day!
> For this is a statute for Israel,
>   a ruling of the God of Jacob.
> He established it as a decree on Joseph's account,
>   when he went throughout the land of Egypt,[32]
>   dealing with an unfamiliar language.[33]
> "I relieved his shoulder from the burden;
>   his hands were freed from the brick basket.
> In distress you called out and I rescued you;
>   I answered you under the cover of thunder.[34]
>   I tested you at the waters of Meribah." *Selah* (81:1-7[2-8])

Prefaced by a corporate call to praise, the psalm launches into a divine decree that recounts Israel's checkered history, beginning with Joseph's immigration in Egypt and the people's emigration from Egypt. God recounts liberating the people from enslavement: relief from the "burden" and freedom from the "brick basket," an image emblematic of enslavement. Switching to second-person address, God testifies to rescuing the people when called upon in such a crisis in the form of a storm theophany (81:7[8]). Jumping historically, God also refers to "testing" the people at Meribah, the site where the people complained about the lack of water.[35]

---

32. The syntax (*bĕṣēʾtô ʿal-ʾereṣ*) is curious but not unprecedented. Given the parallel in Gen 41:45 (cf. Zech 5:3), it assumes Joseph as the subject (not God, contra NIV, CEB) with reference to his rise to power in Egypt.

33. So LXX and Peshitta. MT, however, reads first person ("When I heard . . ."), which is likely the result of an inadvertent (?) harmonization of this line with the following verse.

34. Or "hidden place of thunder" (*bĕsēter rāʿām*), likely referring to a thundercloud.

35. Cf. Exod 17:7, in which it is the people who "test" God.

Throughout it all, God self-identifies as both liberator and tester, the perfect frame for the legislative decree.

> Listen, my people and I will warn you!
> O Israel, if you would only listen to me!
> There shall be no foreign god among you,
> and you shall not bow down to an alien deity.
> I am YHWH, your God,
> who brought you up from the land of Egypt.
> Open wide your mouth, and I will fill it up. (81:8-10[9-11])

YHWH's decree is a prohibition against worshipping foreign deities, as one finds also in the opening words of the Decalogue (Exod 20:2-3, 5a). Curiously, Psalm 81 reverses the order by stating the decree first, followed by YHWH's identification as liberator. The point? Perhaps to emphasize that "alien" deities offer neither freedom nor provision, only YHWH, who by serving as Israel's liberator and provider becomes Israel's "native" deity.

YHWH's decree is prefaced by a call to listen followed by a wish-filled lament ("If only" [*'im*]), to be elaborated further in 81:13[14]. The conditional particle suggests an oath formula, implying dire consequences for God if Israel does not "listen" (cf. 95:7b). The strophe concludes with a command for the people to be receptive to God's offer of provision, signaled by the wide-open "mouth." God is ready to provide, and the recipients' mouths should be open in order to receive rather than to complain. Moreover, their mouths should be directed to God for sustenance, not to another deity. Indeed, God's resolve to satisfy the open mouth constitutes the psalm's poignant conclusion (81:17b), but as experience will prove, it is a well-tested resolve.

> But my people did not listen to my voice;
> Israel was not inclined toward me.
> So I sent them off to [follow] their heart's stubbornness;
> they followed their own devices.
> O that my people would listen to me,
> that Israel would walk in my ways!

Then I would quickly subdue their enemies,
and turn my hand against their foes. (81:11-14[12-15])

The decree is followed by a lament or negative testimony of Israel's refusal to heed God's voice. By refusing to listen, Israel also refuses to depend upon God for their welfare. Consequently, God consigns the people to their own waywardness, their "stubbornness." The verb is telling: "send away" (√*šlḥ* in Piel) is the same form found in Genesis 3:21 when God expels the *'ādām* from the garden, a most forceful eviction. In Psalm 81, God testifies to having "expelled" the people to traverse the rugged terrain of their own intransigence, leaving them entirely to their own devices. Such language nimbly navigates the paradox of divine action and human freedom. While one could say that God *allowed* the people to follow the paths of their own destruction, the psalmist presents a more forceful role for God, while at the same time holding Israel accountable. Israel has hardened its own heart, but God has "sent them" there to do so.

Such decisive action reflects God's anguish over Israel's persistent recalcitrance. Verse 13[14] is expressed as a wish-filled, lament-laced conditional statement that builds on 81:8b[9b]. "O that my people would listen" complements "O Israel, if you would only listen." If Israel were to listen, then YHWH would fight against Israel's foes. But no.

Those who hate YHWH would cringe before him,
but their doom[36] will last forever.
But I would feed him[37] with the finest wheat,
and satisfy you with honey from the rock. (81:15-16[16-17])

Psalm 81 concludes with a divine pronouncement that distinguishes the fate of those who "hate YHWH" from those whom YHWH would lavishly feed. While the former would "cringe" (√*kḥš*) in feigned obedience, their doom remains sealed. But as for the latter, their fate is to flourish by

36. Literally "time [of disaster]."

37. Read *wā'ă'ăkîlēhû* for MT ("and he would feed him").

YHWH's lavish sustenance from the fertile land. Water from the rock at Meribah in the wilderness is now "honey from the rock," the Rock who is God.

Psalms 81 and 95 share much in common. Both recount Israel's intransigence in the wilderness. In fact, both feature a wish-filled lament that Israel would listen to God's voice (95:7b; 81:8b[9b], 13[14]). But they part ways regarding Israel's place before God. In Psalm 95, the wandering ancestors are "detested" by God for having tested God for forty years and are barred from ever entering YHWH's "rest," a done deal sealed with an oath that serves as a dire warning for subsequent generations.

Psalm 81 presents a more nuanced perspective, one that comes directly from God's anguished heart. First, it is God's very self that pronounces the wish-filled lament (81:8b[9b], 13[14]), not an unnamed speaker urgently warning the congregation (95:7b). More significantly, Psalm 81 lacks any reference to sworn judgment. What it lacks in formalized punishment, Psalm 81 makes up for in anguished admonition. On the other hand, Psalm 81 details what is required of Israel to sustain its relationship with God: to exclude all "foreign" deities in worship, as stipulated in the Decalogue. According to Psalm 81, this was Israel's failure in the wilderness; their complaining and craving were of little consequence by comparison. To the contrary, Psalm 81 depicts God as ever ready to fill their needs. All they had to do was "open wide [their] mouth" to YHWH and be fed. The wilderness was a missed opportunity. God would have been there to fill every need *if only* the people had worshipped the one who delivered them from Egypt.

But no. Instead, it is their "heart's stubbornness" that is their punishment. No need for a sworn oath or plague. Israel reaped what it sowed: stubbornness was their obstacle into the promised land. Nevertheless, Psalm 81 ends on a positive note: the promise of sustenance remains for the one whom God addresses at the end. The lavishness of divine provision carries the day. In the wilderness, it was water from the rock for the complaining Israelites. But for "you . . . honey from the rock." God's abundant provision is there for the taking; it simply requires exclusive acknowledgment of the one who "brought you up from the land of Egypt." In a contest among the gods, YHWH wins in the end by generosity.

Wilderness as a Place of Absence and Presence

Not only a place of rebellion, punishment, and missed opportunity, the wilderness takes on other nuances in the Psalms, particularly those psalms that do not recount Israel's wanderings in the wilderness. In these psalms, the wilderness is a place of both deprivation or unmet desire and divine encounter, even fulfillment.

Psalm 29: A Voice Shattering the Wilderness

In that most ancient of psalms, the wilderness provides the setting of YHWH's unrivaled power, manifest by YHWH's "voice."

YHWH's voice is over the waters;
 the God of glory thunders;
  YHWH is over the mighty waters.
YHWH's voice is power;
 YHWH's voice is majesty.[38]
YHWH's voice breaks cedars;
 yes, YHWH shatters the cedars of Lebanon.
He makes Lebanon skip about like a calf,[39]
 and Sirion[40] like a young wild ox.
YHWH's voice strikes with bolts of fire;
 YHWH's voice convulses the wilderness;
  yes, YHWH convulses the wilderness of Kadesh.
YHWH's voice causes deer to writhe in labor,[41]

38. In both lines, the preposition *bĕ* connotes identity (*essentiae*) or condition.

39. The Masoretic division reads, "He makes them skip about like a calf // Lebanon and Sirion like a young wild ox." The final *mem* of the verb is most likely enclitic.

40. The Sidonian name for Hermon.

41. So MT. Frequently proposed is a repointing of *'ayyālôt* to *'êlôt* (='*êlîm*), meaning "mighty tree," in parallel with the next line. However, this is unnecessary, given the verb's semantic double entendre in this verse and in the previous (√*ḥwl/yl*).

and hastens the mountain goats [to give birth],[42]
while in his temple everyone shouts, "Glory!"
YHWH sits enthroned upon the floodwaters;
YHWH sits enthroned as king forever.
May YHWH give strength to his people.
May YHWH bless his people with well being. (29:3-11)

The divine voice exhibits power that, on the one hand, "thunders" over the "mighty waters" (29:3) and, on the other hand, "convulses the wilderness of Kadesh" (29:8b), where it "shatters the cedars of Lebanon" (29:5b), "makes Lebanon skip about like a calf" (29:6a), and induces labor in wild animals (29:9). While the wilderness in Psalm 29, like the "mighty waters" (29:3), provides a foil for YHWH's unrivaled power, it is also a place that bursts forth with new life, also due to YHWH's power. The wilderness here is the arena of YHWH's wild and reckless glory, a place for YHWH to show off, both destructively and constructively, all to be observed from the temple (29:9b), as if it had been retroverted as the tabernacle, with its origin in the wilderness. Nevertheless, the temple also provides refuge from the violent storm: it is from the protected vantage point of such refuge that the worshippers can attribute the storm to YHWH's "glory." Notably, YHWH is not said to be enthroned in the temple but "upon the floodwaters" of chaos (29:10) and, by extension, upon the wilderness. The wilderness in Psalm 29 is far from God-forsaken; it is dramatically and destructively glorified.

Psalm 68: God's March from Sinai to Zion

The wilderness is a scene of divine theophany also in Psalm 68, a psalm of praise and petition.

O God, when you went forth before your people,
when you marched through the wasteland, *Selah*

42. The frequent proposal "strips the forests bare" draws from the common meaning of the verb *ḥśp* "strip" while positing an otherwise unattested feminine plural form of *ya'ar* (plural *yĕ'ārîm*). The Arabic cognate *ḥašafa* ("hurry") suggests a better parallel meaning. Of course, given the proximity of forms throughout v. 9, one cannot rule out a wordplay indicating both wildlife giving birth and trees being destroyed.

the earth shook; indeed, the heavens poured down
at the presence of God, the one from Sinai,[43]
at the presence of God, the God of Israel.
Abundant[44] rain you showered, O God;
when your inheritance languished, you restored it yourself.
Your community[45] settled in it;
in your goodness, O God, you provided for the impoverished.
(68:7-10[8-11])

The God of Israel, the "one from Sinai" (68:8[9]), marches through the "wasteland" or dry wilderness (*yĕšîmôn*), convulsing the earth with a downpour of rain. Psalm 68, in fact, is the only psalm in the Psalter to reference Sinai by name, and it does so to identify God's point of origin (68:8[9], 16[17]) as God marches from one mountain to another, from Sinai to Zion. Sinai in Psalm 68 exhibits no association with Moses. It is simply a mountain in the wilderness but with the notable distinction that it is *God's* mountain. This God of Sinai comes to be the God of Zion (68:15-17[16-18]). Moreover, God's theophany serves a salutary end: to restore God's languishing "inheritance" for the people's settlement (68:9-10[10-11]). Psalm 68 juxtaposes the watered "wasteland" and Israel's "inheritance" as the common grounds of God's restorative, theophanic power. Sinai serves as God's point of origin, and the wilderness serves as the victory path toward settling the people and establishing God's new home. But if God can leave Sinai for Zion, can Sinai ever leave God? Perhaps one should ask the "impoverished" (68:10b[11b]), or the orphaned and the widowed (68:5[6]), who are the featured recipients of God's care, elsewhere associated with justice in *tôrâ*.[46] Something of Sinai's ethos lives on in Zion's royal splendor, something from the wilderness.

---

43. For the same expression, see Judg 5:5. The demonstrative indicates origin or identity.

44. Literally, "free, generous" (*nĕdābôt*; cf. Exod 36:3-7).

45. Cf. the use of *ḥayyāh* in 2 Sam 23:13, referring to an organized group.

46. E.g., Exod 22:22; Deut 10:18; 16:11, 14; 15:11; 24:14-15.

Psalm 55: Wilderness as Refuge

For all the threats that the wilderness represents in the biblical traditions, prosaic and poetic, Psalm 55 stands out by identifying the wilderness as a place of refuge:

> My heart writhes within me,
>   for the terrors of death have befallen me.
> Fear and trembling beset me;
>   tremors have overwhelmed[47] me.
> I thought to myself, O that I had wings like a dove;
>   I would fly away and find rest.
> Yes, I would flee far away;
>   I would dwell in the wilderness. *Selah*
> I would hurry to this shelter of mine,
>   away from the rushing wind and storm. (55:4-8[5-9])

In nearly paradoxical fashion, the speaker wishes to flee into the wilderness for safety from the "rushing wind and storm" (55:8[9]). The stormy weather comes not from the wilderness but from within the speaker's own community! It is the "racket of the wicked" who harass the speaker (55:3[4]), as well as the betrayal of a former friend (55:12-13[13-14], 20[21]). Such turmoil at home prompts seeking refuge far and away, in the wilderness. Psalm 55 effectively reverses the wilderness-as-threat trope. Instead, the wilderness is a place of shelter from the "storm" of domestic chaos. Only in the wilderness can one find "rest" (55:5b[6b]). Such reversal is made possible by the parallel metaphorical shift from human victim to wild animal: the dove (55:6a[7a]; cf. 102:6). Such a shift in perspective "redeems" the wilderness as a bona fide place of refuge *from* danger. Historically, in fact, the wilderness was frequently a setting for flight from political persecution and war. Just ask David, to whom the psalm is attributed (see chapter 7).

47. Literally, "cover" (√*ksh*); cf. the same expression in Ezek 7:18; Ps 140:10.

Psalm 63: Desire in the Desert

In Exodus and Numbers, the wilderness is a place of deprivation that prompts craving and complaint for water and food. Relatedly, it is a place of misplaced desire, the desire to return to Egypt. In Psalm 63, however, the wilderness can be a place of desire for God.

> O God, my God, it is you I seek!
> My soul thirsts for you;
> My flesh grows faint[48] for you
> in a dry and wearied land, devoid of water. (63:1[2])

The thirst and fatigue felt by the psalmic speaker correspond metaphorically to a land that is "dry and wearied." The land's lack of water points to the speaker's felt lack of divine presence. Deprivation in the land is matched by God's absence. Where then is God to be found? It is in the sanctuary, where God is seen full of "power and glory" (63:2[3]), whereas the desert is devoid of divine presence even while it is filled with desire for God.

Psalm 42: Drowning in God's Presence

But what if access to the sanctuary is not possible? Enter Psalm 42. The first nine verses lay claim to God's worshipful presence in the wilderness.

> As a doe[49] longs[50] for ravines of water,
> so my soul longs for you, O God.
> My soul thirsts for God, the living God.
> When shall I come and see[51] the face of God?
> My tears have been my food day and night,

48. The verb is *hapax legomenon* whose Arabic cognate refers to paleness of face.

49. Read *'ayyelet* for MT *'ayyāl*, due to haplography and the gender of the following verb. Cf. Ps 22:1; Jer 14:5.

50. The verb *'rg* may also connote the sense of ascending or climbing up, given its Arabic and Ethiopic cognates. The same verb is used in v. 2b.

51. Read *wĕ'er'eh* (Qal) for MT *wĕ'ērā'eh* (Niphal), the latter being a theological correction.

while it is said[52] to me all day, "Where is your God?"
These things I shall remember as I "pour out" my soul within me:
How I passed through to the abode of the Mighty One,[53]
to the house of God,
with cries of joy and praise, a multitude making festival.
So why are you so downcast,[54] O my soul,
and so upset[55] inside me?
Hope in God; for I shall yet praise him,
my saving presence and my God.[56]
[Yet] my soul remains downcast within me.
That's why I remember you from the land of Jordan and Hermon,[57]
from Mount Mizar.[58]
Deep called[59] to deep at the noise of your cascades,
as all your breakers and your billows passed over me.
By day YHWH commands his benevolence,
and by night his song is with me, praise[60] to the God of my life.
(42:1-8[2-9])

The psalm opens with the famously evocative image of a doe in search of water, referring metaphorically to the speaker's yearning for God in the face of divine absence. The rare verb *'rg* is associated with the "cry" of a deer. The only other instance of the verb outside of Psalm 42 occurs in

52. See the parallel in v. 11b, which bears a plural suffix. Here, the suffix-less infinitive construct indicates an indefinite subject and thus can be translated passively.

53. The text is corrupt. Literally, it reads, "I passed over/through the throng" (from *sāk* [a hapax legomenon]); "I led them. . . ." The simplest reconstruction is to read *běsōk 'addīr* + enclitic *mem*, as reflected in the translation. For *sōk* as God's abode or refuge, see Pss 27:5; 76:4.

54. The verb is likely derived from *šwḥ* ("sink down").

55. Literally, "turbulent" or "clamorous" (*hmh*).

56. Read *yěšû'ōt pānay*, along with several Hebrew manuscripts and LXX and Peshitta. See v. 12; 43:5. MT also divides the verse incorrectly. The first word in v. 7 constitutes the end of v. 6, as attested in the versions.

57. "Hermon" here takes the form of a plural, suggesting the mountain range.

58. Geographically unknown but evidently within the Hermon mountain range. The term can also mean "few" or "little," perhaps designating a small mountain (range).

59. The participial form, given the context (i.e., memory), is best translated as past tense.

60. Read *těhillâ* for *těpillâ* ("prayer"), as evidenced in several Hebrew manuscripts.

Joel 1:20, which paints a scene of wild animals "crying" to God due to the drought-stricken, fire-ravaged land. Both Psalms 63 and 42 identify God as the object of deepest and most desperate longing in the context of the wilderness (cf. 84:3), comparable to the desire for water in the desert. In the place of water there are only tears to sustain the speaker.

To assuage the pain of God's absence, the speaker in Psalm 42 recalls two parallel memories of divine presence as poignant expressions of hope: the first is worship in the temple (42:4[5]); the second is "worship" in nature (42:6-7[7-8]). The speaker recalls the immersive experience of "joy and praise," the polyphony of "making festival" in the temple. Such recollection is followed by the psalm's refrain, in which the speaker chides his "soul" (*nepeš*) for being downcast and in turmoil, that is, for being depressed. Yet the self-admonition falls short: the speaker's "soul" remains downcast (42:6[7]).

Enter the next memory, one drawn not from the temple but from the headwaters of the Jordan. There, the speaker recalls the watery depths in discursive exchange (42:7[8]), comparable to the speaker's immersion in worship, a surround sound of thunderous discourse reflecting God's "benevolence" and praise (42:8[9]). The same expression of "billows" and "breakers" is found in Jonah 2:3[4], connoting danger and death by drowning. But in Psalm 42 the speaker survives, identifying the experience as a submersion in God's encompassing presence. God's "song" (*šîr*) is intoned in the call and response of the watery depths, liturgy performed under the surface. Submersion in water is likened to immersion in worship. Call it "deep praise."

Of all the psalms, Psalm 42 discerns most clearly God's presence in the wilderness. Having complained of the lack of water and, thus, of God's absence, the speaker recalls a place of feeling overwhelmed with water, submerged in God's presence—powerful, threatening, and uplifting. Psalm 42 testifies that there are two ways to die in the wilderness: by thirst and by drowning. At the headwaters of the Jordan River, the speaker imagines being "drowned" in praise before God's presence. All in all, the life of faith in the wilderness is one of extremes, from drought to deluge; it is where God can be encountered not only in the temple but also in the torrent.

Such memories for the psalmist point to another hope-filled encounter in the future (see 43:3-4). The wilderness is where memories come alive and where desire burns, whether to return to Egypt (so Exodus and Numbers) or to come into God's presence (so Psalm 42).

Conclusion

The wilderness in the Bible is a most polyvalent landscape: a place of danger and threat, of test and punishment, as well as a place of desire, formation, and provision. The psalmists took certain features of this variegated landscape of Israel's story for teaching, confession, prayer, and praise. On the one hand, Israel's trek through the wilderness served as a warning for future generations of what not to do: complain incessantly, nurture the desire for Egypt, worship Ba'al, forget God's wondrous deeds, defy Mosaic leadership, and despise the land given to them. On the other hand, the wilderness extends God's wondrous works of freedom to God's works of providential care amid severe deprivation. In the wilderness, the God of liberation becomes the God of provision, so also the God of judgment. As the ten plagues enacted God's judgment against Egypt, so various calamities are suffered by Israel in the wilderness as punishment.

Certain psalms present the wilderness experience with greater theocentric focus. Who gets the credit for leading Israel through the wilderness? The role of Moses and Aaron is minimized; conversely, God's agency is highlighted all the more. The impact of Moses's intercession in averting divine wrath is given only one nod in the Psalms (106:23), whereas in the narrative accounts Moses's mediation is far more pronounced; indeed, it is indispensable. The Psalms, unlike the Pentateuch, present no biography of Moses.

One critical issue addressed by both the narrative and the poetry is the reason behind Israel's failures in the wilderness. In the narratives, the reasons are varied yet interrelated: complaining,[61] rebelliousness,[62]

61. Exod 16:2, 7-8; 17:3; Num 11:1; 14:2, 27, 29, 36; 17:5, 10.

62. Num 14:9 (√*mrd*); 20:10 (√*mrh*), 24; 27:14; Deut 1:26, 43; 9:7, 23-24; 31:27.

obstinacy or stubbornness ("stiff-necked"),[63] sinfulness,[64] lack of trust,[65] and disbelief (Exod 17:7). The Psalms pick up particularly the language of rebellion,[66] even as Psalm 105:28 refers only to the Egyptians "rebelling." But what the Psalms add to the list is the people's failure to "remember" God's "deeds" and "wonders."[67] The language of remembering and forgetting on the people's part in the Pentateuchal narratives applies more to God's instructions[68] than to God's wonders, as one finds in the Psalms. As the height of irony, the people in Numbers declare how they "remember" the rich foods they had in Egypt (11:5). But for the historical psalms, the refusal to "remember" God's marvelous deeds lies at the core of Israel's failures in the wilderness, failures that the Psalms want future generations to remember. But Israel's saving grace in the wilderness is that God "remembered" the covenant (106:45) and "that they were mere flesh" (78:39). Israel's God is the God who remembers, both the Psalms and the Pentateuch agree.[69]

63. Exod 32:9; 33:3, 5; 34:9.

64. Num 16:26, 38; 21:7; 32:14, 23.

65. Deut 1:32; cf. Num 20:12.

66. Pss 78:8, 17, 40, 56; 106:7, 43.

67. Pss 78:7, 11, 42a; 106:7, 13; cf. 105:5.

68. Exod 20:8; Num 15:39, 40; cf. Exod 13:3.

69. Cf. Exod 2:24; 32:13; Lev 26:42.

CHAPTER 6
THE LIVING *TÔRÂ*: FOR THE LOVE OF "LAW"

The Lord*'s Instruction is perfect, reviving one's very being.*

—Psalm 19:7 (CEB)

Tôrâ in the Torah (i.e., Pentateuch) is introduced at a pivotal juncture in Israel's wilderness wanderings. *Tôrâ* in the Psalms is introduced at the Psalter's very threshold. Both are differently construed, resulting in a dialogue of truly biblical proportions, as we shall see. First, *tôrâ* in the Torah: three months after their deliverance, the Israelites arrive at a mountain (Exod 19:1-2), which proves to be not another waystation but a destination. As God had informed Moses earlier, this mountain is where the Israelites are to worship God "in the wilderness" (3:12; 7:16). But worship is only half of it. This mountain is also where God makes a public address. But first by way of preparation, a few divine words are shared with Moses to orient the people toward what they are about to encounter, contingent on their response:

> You have seen what I did to the Egyptians and how I lifted you up on eagles' wings to bring you to myself. So now, if you faithfully heed my voice and keep my covenant, you will be my treasured possession out of all the

peoples. Because[1] the whole earth is mine, you shall be for me a priestly kingdom and a holy nation. (Exod 19:4-6)

In these three verses, Israel is given a new mission, one that extends and transcends the ancestral goal of possessing the land as promised to Abraham (Gen 12:1-2, 7). It is the mission of becoming an exceptional people. God describes Israel's "flight" from Egyptian bondage not as fleeing but as flying, flight on "eagles' wings," in order to bring the people to God's very presence at a mountain.[2] Here, Israel is at a crossroads: God invites the Israelites to turn toward obedience, literally to "listen to" God's "voice" and "keep covenant," one that is yet to be made. The result is a singling out of Israel from all the peoples as God's "treasured possession" (*sĕgulâ*; cf. Ps 135:4). As such, Israel will become a special community among the peoples of the earth: a "priestly kingdom and a holy nation," the collective goal of covenantal *tôrâ*. Such is Israel's dual orientation: Israel is to be a "priestly kingdom" established *for* the world and a "holy nation" set apart *from* the world. Neither isolated from the world nor assimilated to it, Israel is granted a sacred status before God that makes possible its sacred responsibility for the world.

These three verses are more than introductory; they provide the hermeneutical key to an expansive collection of divine instructions that follows, all associated with the mountain, ranging from the Decalogic to the Deuteronomic, from the sacred to the societal.[3] Taken together, this sprawling corpus indicates the evolving growth of divine instruction, re-

1. The crux of the passage revolves around the function of the *kî* particle: is it causal or asseverative? Relatedly, does the clause conclude the previous line or introduce the new one? I opt for the causal reading and regard it as introducing the next clause in order to highlight Israel's mission to the world, which belongs to God.

2. The "eagle" or vulture (*nešer*) is known for its high nest in the "rocky crag" (Job 39:27-28).

3. Whether these collections were deemed legislative (i.e., as law) or consultative (guidance) cannot be resolved here. Suffice it to say, the picture is complex: "law" collections in the ancient Near East, including ancient Israel, seemed to be used primarily for instructional purposes, as sources of guidance to be consulted rather than as legally enforced regulations. Only later, either during the Persian or Hellenistic period, did Israelite "law" become "legal." See Michael LeFebvre, *Collections, Codes, and Torah: The Re-characterization of Israel's Written Law*, LHB/OTS 451 (New York: T&T Clark, 2016). Such a distinction in function, however, need not negate the fact that Israelite *tôrâ* is often cast as legislative.

flecting the monumental project of community building in the land. Assuming its primacy of place, the Decalogue opens the *tôrâ* collection at Sinai, whose importance is underlined as God's only public address to the community (Exod 20:2-17; Deut 5:4, 22-23). Its brevity ("ten words")[4] belies its wide range of coverage: from worship to neighborliness, with the sabbath commandment, the most extensive commandment, tucked somewhat in the middle (Exod 20:8-11). The people respond with fear and trembling and beseech Moses to speak on behalf of God from here on out (20:18-21).

Henceforth, *tôrâ* is mediated by Moses as it continues to unfold with the so-called Covenant Code (20:22–23:19), Israel's earliest law code.[5] This compilation addresses various matters, including the possession and release of slaves (21:1-11); capital and retributive punishment of violent acts (21:12-26);[6] movable property (i.e., ox and donkey [21:28-36]), restitution (22:1-14[21:37–22:13]), various social and sacred matters (22:16-31[15-30]), judicial issues (23:1-9), sabbatical year and sabbath (23:10-13), and annual festivals (23:14-19).

But *tôrâ* instruction at Sinai does not end there, even after ratification (24:1-11). Next come instructions for constructing the tabernacle and sacred paraphernalia (25:1–30:38 [fulfilled in 35:4–40:15]), sabbath law (31:12-17; 35:2-3), a renewed covenant that includes another set of "ten words" (34:10-28), instructions on offering sacrifice conjoined with various ethical and cultic norms (Lev 1–27),[7] duties of the Levites (Num 3:5-13), including the redemption of the firstborn (3:40-51), special duties of the Kohathites, Gershonites, and Merarites (4:1-33), miscellaneous laws for cleanliness, confession, alleged marital infidelity, the Nazirites, a priestly blessing, seven lamps (5:1–6:27; 8:1-4), consecration and

4. See Exod 34:28; Deut 4:13; 10:4.

5. Which finds resonance with, if not dependency on, Hammurabi's law code (ca. 1754 BCE). See David P. Wright, *Inventing God's Law: How the Covenant Code of the Bible Used and Revised the Laws of Hammurabi* (Oxford: Oxford University Press, 2009).

6. Which includes the famous *lex talionis* or "law of retaliation" ("eye for eye") in vv. 23–25.

7. The Holiness Code (Lev 17–26) stands out as a discrete collection regarding matters of moral purity.

duties of the Levites (8:5-26), instructions for inclusion in the Passover celebration (9:1-14), and instruction on the construction and use of two silver trumpets in war and worship (10:1-10). Whew!

The breadth of these collections put together is breathtaking, all associated with Israel's stay at Sinai. The mountain acts, as it were, like a powerful magnet, attracting much of Israel's prescriptive corpus. But its power of attraction is not total. After Israel's departure from Sinai, *tôrâ* continues to develop, as attested in Numbers, demonstrating that Israel's *tôrâ* is a living, evolving corpus, not law set in stone. What happens at Sinai, moreover, is not meant to stay at Sinai. On the plains of Moab, Moses in Deuteronomy extends *tôrâ* by revisiting Sinai (aka Horeb) and revising the divinely ordained instructions for a new generation.[8] Take, for example, a sample of comparable prescriptions from the Covenant Code (Exod 20:23–23:19) and Deuteronomy:[9]

Topic	Covenant Code Stipulations	Deuteronomic Stipulations
Altars	Multiple altars authorized (20:24)	Single altar (12:1-28)
Slavery	Male slaves released after six years; female slaves not released (21:1-11)	Male and female slaves released after six years; masters provide reparations on release (15:12-18)
Marriage/ adultery	A man who seduces a virgin either marries her or pays a fine equal to the bride price (22:16-17).	A man who seduces a virgin either marries her (without ever divorcing her) or pays a fixed fine (23:28-29).

8. Even the Decalogue is different in Deut 5:6-21 (cf. Exod 20:2-17). The Deuteronomic revisions of the Covenant Code, necessitated by the centralization of worship, are discussed in Bernard M. Levinson, *Deuteronomy and the Hermeneutics of Legal Innovation* (New York: Oxford University Press, 1997). Levinson states that it is a "major irony of literary history that Second Temple editors incorporated both the Covenant Code and the legal corpus of Deuteronomy into the Pentateuch. In so doing, they preserved Deuteronomy alongside the very text that it sought to replace and subvert" (Levinson, *Deuteronomy*, 153). Such "irony," I would add, was dialogically inspired.

9. Adapted and expanded from LeFebvre, *Collections, Codes, and Torah*, 69–70.

Carcass disposal	Animals that died naturally are to be thrown to the dogs (22:31).	Animals that died naturally may be sold to foreigners (14:21).
Festivals	Three feasts: Unleavened Bread, Harvest, and Ingathering (Passover conducted at home), to be celebrated by the males (23:14-17)	Three feasts: Passover/ Unleavened Bread (combined) Weeks, and Booths, to be celebrated at the central shrine by men, women, and children (16:1-17)
Sabbatical year	Land left fallow (23:10-11)	Debts released (15:1-11)
Returning neighbor's property	Ox and donkey (23:4-5)	Ox, sheep, donkey, cloak, or anything else lost by the neighbor. Provision is to be given for keeping neighbor's property until claimed.

Even the Decalogue has its distinct versions, as particularly evident in the Sabbath commandment. Distinctive language in the Exodus account is highlighted in bold; italics is used in Deuteronomy.

Exodus 20:8-11	Deuteronomy 5:12-15
Remember the sabbath day and keep it holy. Six days you shall labor and do all your work.	*Observe* the sabbath day and keep it holy, *as YHWH your God commanded you.* Six days you shall labor and do all your work.
But the seventh day is a sabbath to YHWH your God; you shall not do any work—you, your son or your daughter, your male or female slave, your livestock, or the immigrant in your towns.	But the seventh day is a sabbath to YHWH your God; you shall not do any work—you, your son or your daughter, or your male or female slave, *or your ox or your donkey,* or any of your livestock, or the immigrant in your towns, *so that your male and female slave may rest as well as you.*
For in six days YHWH made heaven and earth, the sea, and all that is in them, but rested the seventh day.	*Remember that you were a slave in the land of Egypt, and YHWH your God brought you out from there with a mighty hand and an outstretched arm.*
Therefore, YHWH **blessed the sabbath day and consecrated it.**	Therefore, YHWH your God commanded you to keep the sabbath day.

The main dialogical difference between the two Decalogues is found in their respective rationales, answering the question, Why keep the sabbath? The Exodus account grounds sabbath remembrance in the seventh day of creation (cf. Gen 2:1-3), whereas the Deuteronomic version highlights the story of release from Egypt (Exod 1–15). Consequently, Deuteronomy commands rest for the enslaved, not so in the Exodus version. Both point to divine initiative, whether in creating the heavens and the earth or in liberating the enslaved from Egypt. But both part ways in what they identify as the Sabbath's rationale: emulating God in creation or remembering enslavement in Egypt.

Such distinctions demonstrate *tôrâ* as dynamic and dialogical. *Tôrâ* in the Torah has its own journey. Call it *tôrâ* "on the road," and its journey begins at Sinai with the people's acceptance of their relationship with God (Exod 19:4-6). Nothing is said about what would happen if Israel were to decline. There is no "stick" that accompanies the "carrot"; God does not threaten punishment in the case of Israel's rejection. Instead, only reward is shared in the invitation, specifically the reward of a new identity for God's most "treasured possession," a special status accompanied by special responsibility. Israel agrees (19:8). So begins the journey of *tôrâ*.

So also begins a series of questions. What is the nature of *tôrâ*? What is its primary purpose? What does *tôrâ* do? How is *tôrâ* mediated, and by whom? How is it to be taught? Is *tôrâ* changeable? Who has authority to interpret *tôrâ*? While such questions are addressed by a variety of biblical traditions, our primary focus will be on Deuteronomy and the Psalms.[10]

Deuteronomy: Israel's Polity Pedagogically Cast

In the book of Deuteronomy, *tôrâ* is most often associated with a "book" (or scroll, *sēper*) written by Moses (Deut 31:26). Indeed, Deuteronomic *tôrâ* is the only biblical book that is cited elsewhere as a book in the Hebrew Bible (see 2 Kings 22). But the prescriptive body of *tôrâ* begins

10. Some of the groundwork has been laid by Patrick D. Miller, "Deuteronomy and the Psalms: Evoking a Biblical Conversation," *JBL* 118, no. 1 (1999): 3–18.

with two "tablets" written by God (Deut 4:13; 9:10). Beginning with the Decalogue (Deut 5:6-21), *tôrâ* consists of divinely authored instruction given to the community to follow for its own "good" (√*yṭb*; Deut 4:40). Such instruction, mediated by Moses, is considered fully codified and closed: it cannot be added to or subtracted from (Deut 4:2).

Tôrâ in Deuteronomy proves to be more than a law code that enumerates various cases along with their penalties, as one finds prominently in the Covenant Code in Exodus. Rather, there is a second-order quality to Deuteronomic *tôrâ* not found in case law. It may best be described as Israel's "polity" (*politeia*)[11] or "constitution," which the *Oxford English Dictionary* defines as "the system or body of fundamental principles according to which a nation, state, or body politic is constituted and governed. . . . It is more fundamental than any particular law, and [it] contains the principles with which all legislation must be in harmony" (*OED III*, 790). In addition to elucidating fundamental principles of Israel's communal life in the land, Deuteronomic *tôrâ* is replete with persuasive rhetoric intended to motivate its audience.

Taken together, the principles that constitute a nation's "constitution" invariably point to a particular vision for communal life. In the case of Deuteronomy, *tôrâ* sets forth a "divinely authorized social order that Israel must implement to secure its collective political existence as the people of God."[12] As part of that social order, Deuteronomic *tôrâ* explicates various political offices or roles (e.g., king, prophet, judge, priest). Nevertheless, *tôrâ* includes policies to be observed by "king and common citizen alike."[13] The king, too, is not above the law (Deut 17:18-20). There is, in other words, an egalitarian streak in Deuteronomic *tôrâ*. Moreover, such *tôrâ* exhibits Israel's unparalleled wisdom among the nations, reflecting "a god so near" (Deut 4:6-7). Broadly speaking, Deuteronomic *tôrâ* is both

11. S. Dean McBride Jr., "Polity of the Covenant People: The Book of Deuteronomy," *Interpretation* 41 (1987): 229–44. Reprinted in *Constituting the Community: Studies on the Polity of Ancient Israel in Honor of S. Dean McBride Jr.*, ed. John T. Strong and Steven S. Tuell (Winona Lake, IN: Eisenbrauns, 2005), 17–33. McBride draws from the Josephus's interpretation of Deuteronomy in *Antiquities*, especially 4.198.

12. McBride, "Polity," 233.

13. McBride, "Polity," 233.

instructional and aspirational: it commands the community's attention and motivates its obedience. It is hardly a playbook for punishment.

Structurally, Israel's constitutional polity comprises Deuteronomy 4:44–28:68, which begins with an editorial preface (4:44-49), followed by an expounding of the Horeb (Sinai) covenant (5:1–11:30), including a revised rehearsal of the Decalogue (5:6-21) and the Shema (6:4-9). The center of Deuteronomy is its prescriptive core in 11:31–26:15, which is followed by covenantal ratification (26:16–28:68). It can be outlined as follows:

A.	Prescriptive Core of Deuteronomy		11:31–26:15
	1.	Introduction	11:31–12:1
	2.	Single Sanctuary	12:2-28
	3.	Service to YHWH	12:29–17:13
	4.	Constitutional Powers and Offices	17:14–18:22
		a. King	17:14-20
		b. Levitical Priest	18:1-8
		c. Prophet	18:9-22
	5.	Juridical Principles and Precedents	19:1–25:19
	6.	Ritual Reaffirmations of Covenant Loyalty	26:1-15
B.	Ratification of the Covenant		26:16–28:68
	1.	Covenantal Oaths of YHWH and Israel	26:16-19
	2.	Directions for a Covenant Ceremony at Shechem	27:1-26
	3.	Covenantal Sanctions: Blessings and Curses	28:1-68

Deuteronomic *tôrâ* legislates matters in various domains of ancient Israel's political life: worship, priestly, royal, judicial, and prophetic, all as "statutes and ordinances" (4:45). In 12:29–17:13, *tôrâ* includes warnings against idolatry, dietary restrictions, regulations concerning tithes, sabbatical year stipulations, including freeing the enslaved with provisions, and instructions on holy festivals and the appointment of judges, as well as jurisprudential matters. In 19:1–25:19, one reads of the "cities of refuge," property boundaries, rules of warfare, homicide, right of the firstborn, rebellious children, sexual relations, marriage and divorce, ritual precepts, first fruits and tithes, and a host of other stipulations. Deuteronomy's sociopolitical order is broadly comprehensive, covering national, cultic, tribal, and familial matters of communal living. But it is not exhaustive. No *tôrâ* is.

Deuteronomic *tôrâ* enlists a variety of discursive forms: narrative, teaching, interpretive exposition, legislation (both apodictic and casuistic), cultic stipulations, royal restrictions, mandates for social justice, and poetry ("song"), all marshaled to build a cohesive social order founded upon faithful obedience to and reverence of YHWH.[14] Almost as a refrain throughout the book, Deuteronomy grounds its "constitution" in the holiness of its people, endowed by God:

> You are children of YHWH your God. You must not cut yourselves or shave your foreheads for the dead, for *you are a people holy* to YHWH your God; it is you whom YHWH chose out of all the peoples on earth to be his people, his treasured possession. (Deut 14:1-2)[15]

Deuteronomy grounds the prohibition against self-laceration in the fundamental principle of corporate holiness, established by YHWH's choice of Israel from "all the peoples on earth." The language recalls Exodus 19:4-6, in which Israel is to be established as "a priestly kingdom and a holy nation." Deuteronomy's view of corporate holiness, however, differs from that of Leviticus, setting up a point of dialogue regarding the nature of holiness in community. In Leviticus, holiness is more a mandated outcome than a condition established by God:

> Because I am YHWH your God, sanctify yourselves, and be holy, for I am holy. You shall not defile yourselves with any swarming creature that crawls on the ground. For I am YHWH who brought you up from the land of Egypt, to be your God; *you shall be holy, for I am holy.* (Deut 11:44-45)[16]

---

14. E.g., Deut 4:10; 6:2, 13, 34; 10:12, 20; 17:19; 31:12-13.

15. See also Deut 7:5-6; 14:21; 26:18-19; 28:9.

16. See also Lev 19:2; 20:7, 26.

Here, holiness is an outcome rather than a presupposition, as one finds in Deuteronomy. In Deuteronomy God makes possible Israel's holiness by choosing Israel; in Leviticus holiness is incumbent on the people themselves as demonstrated in practice. In Deuteronomy the people are to obey God *because* they are holy; in Leviticus they obey God *in order* to become holy. In Deuteronomy holiness is a gift given by God; in Leviticus it is commanded in imitation of God. The Psalms, as we shall see, have an entirely different take.

In Deuteronomy, *tôrâ* is not only to be obeyed but also to be taught (e.g., 14:23; 31:12).[17] Who is best to do that? Moses. Nearly the entire book of Deuteronomy is devoted to Moses engaged in reporting and teaching *tôrâ*; it is his pedagogical role, given by God.[18] With the exception of the Decalogue, God declares the "commandments," "statutes," and "ordinances" only to Moses, who then "teaches" them all to the people (Deut 5:31). Such is the chain of command: from divine legislation to Mosaic education. Such, also, are the two sides of the same Deuteronomically stamped "coin": legislation and education, policy making and polity teaching. The codified result is a book to be read every seven years at the Festival of Booths before the entire community (Deut 31:9-13).

Such is the ritual of teaching *tôrâ*, whose learning outcome is not only obedience but also reverence or "fear" of YHWH.

> Gather the people—men, women, children, and the immigrants residing in your cities—so that they may hear and learn to fear YHWH your God and to observe carefully all the words of this *tôrâ*, and so that their children, who have not known it, may hear and learn to fear YHWH your God, as

17. The verb *lmd* ("learn/teach") is deployed seventeen times throughout Deuteronomy (4:1, 5, 10 [2x], 14; 5:1, 31; 6:1; 11:19; 14:23; 17:19; 18:9; 20:18; 31:12, 13, 19, 22). The prominence of pedagogical language in Deuteronomy combined with legislative discourse has been a source of interpretive dispute. In contrast to McBride's position that Deuteronomy is essentially a "polity" (see above), Dennis Olson argues that Deuteronomy is best construed as a "catechesis" (*Deuteronomy and the Death of Moses: A Theological Reading*, OBT [Minneapolis: Fortress, 1994], 10). See the helpful synthesis in Patrick D. Miller, "Constitution or Instruction? The Purpose of Deuteronomy," in *Constituting the Community: Studies on the Polity of Ancient Israel in Honor of S. Dean McBride Jr.*, ed. John T. Strong and Steven S. Tuell (Winona Lake, IN: Eisenbrauns, 2005), 125–41.

18. Deut 4:1, 5, 14; 6:1; 32:2.

long as you live in the land that you are crossing over the Jordan to possess. (Deut 31:12-13)

Moses commands the Levites, who are tasked with carrying the ark of the covenant, to deposit the *tôrâ* beside the covenant chest as a "witness" (*ʿēd*) "against" the people because of their rebelliousness (31:26-27). Moses anticipates that the people will remain rebellious after his death, even more so. Thus, *tôrâ* serves to extend Moses's authority to subsequent generations; it is his lasting legacy. Moses concludes with calling "heaven and earth to witness against" the people (31:28). In sum, while YHWH is the author of *tôrâ*, Moses is the teacher of *tôrâ*. In Deuteronomy, YHWH's *tôrâ* is both legislative and instructional so that it can be followed most fully by the community, all under Moses's leadership and legacy.

Torah in the Psalms

The Psalms present a different take on *tôrâ*, perhaps even a different *tôrâ*. In any case, *tôrâ* in the Psalms is not a charter for establishing Israel's sociopolitical order. It is something more personal and intimate, while at the same time transcendent. We begin with the "Torah Psalms" (1, 19, 119), which were once regarded as the "problem children of the Psalter" in Psalms scholarship years ago.[19] Let's look at how they have grown up.

Psalm 1: Of Tree and *Tôrâ*

Given its primacy of place, Psalm 1 along with Psalm 2 provides an orienting introduction to the Psalter as a whole (see chapter 10). It sets in stone the dichotomy between the wicked and the righteous, a prominent theme that runs throughout the Psalms, pointing out in no uncertain terms whom God favors.[20] Psalm 1 also introduces an evocative image,

19. James Luther Mays, "The Place of the Torah Psalms in the Psalter," *JBL* 106, no. 1 (1987): 3.

20. See Jerome F. D. Creach, *The Destiny of the Righteous in the Psalms* (St. Louis: Chalice Press, 2008).

a tree flourishing beside flowing streams, imagery that, as we shall see, "branches out" into several other psalms.

> How happy is the one[21] who neither walks in the counsel of the wicked,
> nor stands in the pathway of sinners,
> nor sits in the seat of the insolent!
> Rather, in YHWH's *tôrâ* is his delight,
> he deliberates[22] on [YHWH's] *tôrâ* day and night.
> He is like a tree transplanted beside channels of water,
> yielding its fruit in due season,
> whose leaves do not wither.
> Everything that he does proves efficacious.
> Not so the wicked:
> they are like chaff,
> which the wind drives away.
> No wonder the wicked will not stand up in [the court of] justice,[23]
> neither will sinners in the assembly of the righteous.
> Surely, YHWH knows the pathway of the righteous,
> but the pathway of the wicked will perish. (1:1-6)

Whatever the range of meaning *tôrâ* has in Psalm 1, it is identified as an object of singular "delight" (*ḥēpeṣ*), the only instance in the Hebrew Bible in which *tôrâ* is specifically referenced as such.[24] In Deuteronomy, such "delight" applies to a man's desire for a woman, whether sexually or in the legal proceeding of marriage (Deut 21:14; 25:7-8; cf. Gen 34:19). But nowhere is the noun or cognate verb (√*ḥpṣ*) used in the Pentateuch in connection with *tôrâ*. While *tôrâ* in the Pentateuch is a matter of the

---

21. Literally, "the man" (*hāʾîš*).

22. The verb *hgh* in Hebrew often exhibits a discursively active sense in contrast to the typical translation "meditate" (so NRSV, NIV), which draws from the Latin Vulgate *meditabitur*, conveying silent reflection. See below.

23. Probably in the sense of "stand up in court." The poetic parallel in the verse ("assembly") suggests a judicial context.

24. Psalm 119 comes close with similar, even more intense, terminology, including that of "love" (see below).

people's obedience and learning, it is an object of "delight" and "deliberation" in Psalm 1.

For the righteous, YHWH's *tôrâ* takes the place of wicked "counsel," the "pathway of sinners," and the "seat of the insolent" (1:1). Put another way, one's object of "delight" determines how one "walks," "stands," and "sits" (particularly with whom), a desire that determines everything a person does (cf. Deut 6:7). By introducing the language of desire, Psalm 1 discerns something about *tôrâ* that is absent elsewhere in biblical tradition: *tôrâ* is not just something commanded and taught; it is not just a "witness" set against a people to be followed. No, *tôrâ* has its own irresistible appeal. *Tôrâ* is the ultimate desideratum.

As much as *tôrâ* is the object of delight, it is also the source and subject of "deliberation." Frequently translated as "meditate" (so NRSV, NIV, KJV), the verb *hgh* implies more than inward contemplation. Other instances of the verb indicate discursive activity of some sort, whose subject is frequently the "tongue" or "mouth."[25] Denoting recitation in some instances (see CEB ["recite"]), the verb can also indicate something more creative, as the nominal cognate of the verb (*higgāyôn*) and its synonym (*śîaḥ*) indicate.

> May the words of my mouth
> and the deliberation [*higgāyôn*] of my heart
> be acceptable before you,
> YHWH, my rock and my redeemer. (Ps 19:15)

> I will sing to YHWH as long as I have life;
> I will sing praise to my God while I still live.
> May my deliberation [*śîaḥ*] be pleasing to him;
> I will rejoice in YHWH. (Ps 104:33-34)

In both cases, the speaker's "deliberation" is reflected in the psalms themselves, the poetic product or performance offered to God. In this sense, the righteous one's engagement with *tôrâ* in 1:2 involves more than rote recitation or inward contemplation. Such "deliberation"

25. E.g., Pss 35:28; 37:30; 71:24; cf. 115:7.

involves discursive reflection, the kind of reflection that results in a psalm performed and offered to God.

What, then, is *tôrâ*, this supreme object of desire and source of deliberative reflection? Whatever it is, it bears divine, not human, attribution: it is YHWH's *tôrâ*, distinguished from, say, parental *tôrâ* in Proverbs.[26] Typically translated as "law," *tôrâ* in Psalm 1 and elsewhere in the Psalms is left unspecified. Compare Psalm 1:2-3 with its parallel in Joshua 1:8.

> This scroll of *tôrâ* shall not depart out of your mouth;
>   you shall ***deliberate*** [*wĕhāgîtā*] on it day and night,
>   so that you may be careful to act in accordance
>   with all that is written in it.
> For then you shall make your way ***prosperous*** [*taṣlîaḥ*],
>   and then you shall be successful [*taśkîl*]. (Josh 1:8)

> Rather, in YHWH's ***tôrâ*** is his delight;
>   he ***deliberates*** [*yehgeh*] on [YHWH's] *tôrâ* day and night.
> He is like a tree transplanted beside channels of water,
>   yielding its fruit in due season,
>   and whose leaves do not wither.
> Everything he does will ***prosper*** [*yaṣlîaḥ*]. (Ps 1:2-3)

In addition to the common reference to *tôrâ*, both passages share two critical verbs: "deliberate" (√*hgh*) and "prosper" (√*ṣlḥ* in Hiphil). Given that Psalm 1 is probably the later text, the psalmist likely adapted this Deuteronomistic charge to suit a certain agenda. In Joshua, the "scroll of *tôrâ*" is said to be a constant source of deliberation, something to always talk about ("mouth"). In Psalm 1, however, there is no "scroll" or book to speak of. Apart from the metaphorical image of the tree, the major difference between Joshua 1:8 and Psalm 1:2-3 is that the former defines *tôrâ* as

26. E.g., Prov 1:8; 3; 4:2; 7:2; 13:14. Not to be distinguished categorically, Deuteronomic *tôrâ* and parental *tôrâ* do overlap in content. See William P. Brown, "The Law and the Sages: A Reexamination of *Tôrâ* in the Book of Proverbs," in *Constituting the Community: Studies on the Polity of Ancient Israel in Honor of S. Dean McBride Jr*, ed. John T. Strong and Steven S. Tuell (Winona Lake, IN: Eisenbrauns, 2005), 251–80.

a "scroll" (*sēper*), written by Moses. Psalm 1, on the other hand, leaves *tôrâ* uncodified and undefined. The object of delight is not the "scroll of *tôrâ*" but simply "*tôrâ*." To be sure, *tôrâ* is considered formative for cultivating righteousness in Psalm 1:6, as also in Deuteronomy (6:25). However, the psalm eschews the language of obedience ("act in accordance") and codification ("scroll") while construing *tôrâ* as an object of both delight and deliberation and the righteous person as a flourishing tree (Ps 1:3).

Regarding trees, the other parallel to Psalm 1 is Jeremiah 17:7-8, which cultivates its own arboreal metaphor.

> Blessed [*bārûk*] is the one [*haggeber*] who trusts in YHWH,
> whose trust is YHWH.
> He shall be like a tree transplanted beside the waters,
> sending forth its roots by the stream.
> It shall not fear when heat comes, and its leaves will remain fresh;
> in the time of drought, it will not be stressed,
> and it does not cease from producing fruit. (Jer 17:7-8)

The one who trusts in YHWH is given elevated botanical status (in contrast to the "shrub" in the previous verse [Jer 17:6]), just like the righteous person in Psalm 1 (in contrast to "chaff" in the subsequent verse [Ps 1:4]). The comparison suggests that the psalmist regards engaging *tôrâ* as itself a way of cultivating righteousness as much as trusting in YHWH.

One key to knowing more about *tôrâ* in Psalm 1 is found in observing where "deliberative" attention (√*hgh*) is given elsewhere in the Psalter: specifically to God (63:7-8) and God's "works" (77:12-13) and "every deed" (143:5). Divine instruction in the Psalms is sometimes set in poetic correspondence to divine activity, as in Psalm 119.

> I shall ***deliberate*** [*'āśîḥāh*] on your precepts,
> and attend to all your pathways. (Ps 119:15)

> Make me understand the way of your precepts,
> so that I may ***deliberate*** [*wĕ'āśîḥāh*] on your wonders. (Ps 119: 27)

Psalm 119 includes YHWH's "precepts" (*piqqûdîm*) and "wonders" (*niplā'ōt*) as interchangeable objects of "deliberation." Indeed, divine word and deed find their convergence in the speaker's reflective deliberation.

In Psalm 1, *tôrâ* is the object not only of deliberation but also of "delight." A parallel is found in Psalm 111: "Great are YHWH's works, studied[27] by all who take delight in them" (111:2). Because YHWH's "works" are "great" (*gĕdōlîm*), they are worthy of "study" (√*drš*) and "delight" (√*ḥpṣ*). As in Psalm 1, "delight" indicates sustained devotion, whose object in Psalm 111 is YHWH's "works," whereas it is *tôrâ* in Psalm 1. Perhaps one deliberative outcome of such "study" as described in Psalm 111 is history telling, as one finds in the so-called historical psalms (Pss 78, 105, 106, 135, 136). In any case, a suggestive analogy is established between Psalms 1 and 111: "study" is to "deliberate" as YHWH's "works" are to YHWH's *tôrâ*. Such an analogy, in fact, finds common ground in the cultivation of righteousness.

What is *tôrâ* in Psalm 1? At the very least, it is more than a codified body of regulations to be heard and obeyed. As part of the Psalter's twofold introduction, Psalm 1 orients the reader of the Psalms by adapting language found elsewhere in the Psalms. Such is the case with the terms *tôrâ*, "deliberate," and "delight." Fully aware of God's "deeds" or "wonders" as objects of "deliberation" elsewhere in the Psalms, Psalm 1 redirects such "deliberation" toward *tôrâ*. As the object of "deliberation" and "delight," *tôrâ* either finds parity with God's "wonders" and "deeds" or, more likely, enfolds them as part of God's instruction. If the latter, then psalmic *tôrâ* weds together both divine word and deed.

The longest historical psalm in the Psalter, Psalm 78 gives confirmation. The widening of *tôrâ* is amply demonstrated in the psalm's opening verses.

A maśkîl *of Asaph.*
Give ear, my people, to my ***tôrâ***;
  incline your ear to the words of my mouth.
I will open my mouth with a proverb;

27. Verb *drš*, whose basic meaning is "seek." In various contexts, it can mean "care for" (e.g., Jer 30:14; Job 3:4), "study" (cf. Ezra 7:10), "inquire/investigate" (Deut 13:15; 17:4). The second sense seems most appropriate here.

I will declare enigmas[28] from of old,
which we have heard and known,
which our ancestors have told us.
We will not conceal [them] from their descendants,
declaring to the next generation
the praiseworthy deeds of YHWH and his might,
the wonders he has wrought. (Ps 78:1-4).

Despite its sapiential casting (see chapter 9), *tôrâ* in Psalm 78 refers first and foremost to YHWH's salvific deeds and Israel's history of failures. Also included in this "teaching" are references to Israel's "law," likewise indicated as *tôrâ* (78:5a, 10b), and "commandments" (78:7b). All of it, from YHWH's "praiseworthy deeds" to YHWH's "law," is subsumed under the psalmist's *tôrâ*.

Does this inclusive nature of *tôrâ* have a bearing on the Psalter as a whole in light of its fivefold division?[29] Contrary to widespread opinion, Psalm 1 identifies the Psalter not as *tôrâ*[30] but as *tôrâ*'s companion, a poetic, didactic, liturgical, musical complement to *tôrâ*.[31] With this one verse, Psalm 1 claims the Psalter as a response to divinely wrought *tôrâ*, the

28. Hebrew *ḥîdôt*. Cf. Prov 1:6; Ps 49:5.

29. Book 1 = Pss 1–41; Book 2 = Pss 42–72; Book 3 = Pss 73–89; Book 4 = Pss 90–106; Book 5 = Pss 107–150. Also of note are the numerous instances of divine discourse in the Psalms: Pss 2:7-9; 50:5-6, 7-15, 16-23; 75:2-5[3-6]; 81:6-14[7-15]; 82:2-4, 6-7; 89:19-37[20-38]; 110:1b, 4; 132:14-18.

30. Cf. Brevard S. Childs, *Introduction to the Old Testament as Scripture* (Philadelphia: Fortress, 1979), 513; Gerald H. Wilson, *The Editing of the Hebrew Psalter, SBLDS 76* (Chico, CA: Scholars Press, 1985), 206–7; James Luther Mays, *The Lord Reigns: A Theological Handbook to the Psalms* (Louisville, KY: Westminster John Knox, 1990), 121–22; Mays, *Psalms,* IBC (Louisville, KY: Westminster John Knox, 1994), 42. Rather, Psalm 1 marks the Psalter as a discursive response to divine instruction. For the scholarly debate, see David Willgren, *Like a Garden of Flowers: A Study of the Formation of the "Book" of Psalms* (Lund, Sweden: Lund University, 2016), 142–45. For further argumentation, see my "The Law and the Psalmists: Seeking *Tôrâ* among the Psalms," in *The Cambridge Companion to the Psalms,* ed. Joel LeMon and Brent Strawn (Cambridge: Cambridge University Press, forthcoming).

31. See the slightly different argument in Michael LeFebvre, "'On His Law He Meditates': What Is Psalm 1 Introducing?" *JSOT* 40, no. 4 (2016): 443, who identifies the "singing" of psalms with "meditating" on *tôrâ*. My argument is that such "deliberation" includes not only the performing but also composing of psalms, indeed, the whole Psalter, according to Psalm 1.

outcome of "deliberating" on *tôrâ*, the fruit of "delighting" in *tôrâ*. In light of the wide range of objects the verb √*hgh* has in the Psalter, *tôrâ* according to Psalm 1 enfolds the *magnalia Dei* into the *instructiones Dei*, a *tôrâ* that encompasses both narrative and law. As psalmic *tôrâ* testifies to both YHWH's deeds and prescriptive discourse, so the Psalter, according to its first psalm, becomes the deliberative and delight-filled response.

Of Torah, Trees, and Temple Streams

The delightful image of the tree and its location offers another clue to *tôrâ*'s identity in the Psalms, which is distinct from Deuteronomic *tôrâ*. The one who diligently engages YHWH's *tôrâ* is like a tree "transplanted" beside flowing "channels." The implied subject of the passive verb is YHWH, cast in the role of gardener, a not uncommon image in the Hebrew Bible (e.g., Gen 2:8; Exod 15:17; cf. Ps 80:8-11; 1 Chron 17:9). It is hard to say what kind of tree the psalmist has in mind (cf. Ezek 47:12). Regardless, the arboreal image conveys a multiple sense of flourishing, rootedness, and productivity, much in contrast to the image of chaff in the next verse (Ps 1:4).

As for the psalmic identity of *tôrâ*, reference to the "channels of water" (*palgê mayim*) offers another clue. The tree is planted not in the wilderness nourished by a natural spring or flowing wadi but beside *channeled* streams. The tree in Psalm 1 does not stand apart from its "built" environment, the temple complex, from which such water flows.[32] With "channels" flowing in the background, another more subtle association emerges that complements the link between the tree and the righteous individual. As much as the fruitful tree points to the righteous who delight in *tôrâ*, the soil and the flowing "channels" allude to *tôrâ* itself, the tree's source of sustenance. As trees "desire" flowing streams for their flourishing, so the righteous "delight" in *tôrâ* as their sustaining source of guidance. In Psalm

32. See 52:8[10]; 92:12-15[13-16]. For full discussion, see Jerome F. D. Creach, "Like a Tree Planted by the Temple Stream: The Portrait of the Righteous in Psalm 1:3," *CBQ* 61, no. 1 (1999): 34-46, who identifies telling parallels in Ezek 47:12; Pss 46:5; 65:10 and convincingly argues that the background imagery behind Ps 1:3 is that of a temple stream.

1, *tôrâ* and temple find a powerful convergence.[33] Perhaps the psalmist poetically pictures *tôrâ* "flowing" forth from the temple, issuing from Zion for all the righteous, comparable to the imperial vision espoused in Isaiah and Micah:

> For out of Zion shall go forth *tôrâ*,
>   and YHWH's word from Jerusalem. (Isa 2:3b [=Mic 4:2b])

In Isaiah and Micah, Zion is the home base and point of origin for *tôrâ*. For the psalmist, the temple is metaphorically cast as the headwaters of *tôrâ*, whose streams make glad the assembly of the righteous. To "delight" in *tôrâ* is to drink from its waters. To "deliberate" on *tôrâ* is to sink one's roots beside its nourishing streams. Two other psalms, not coincidentally, profile flourishing trees within the temple's precincts:

> As for me, I am like a verdant olive tree in the house of God;
>   I trust in God's benevolence forever and ever. (Ps 52:8[10])

> The righteous will sprout like the date palm,
>   [and] grow like a cedar in Lebanon.
> Those transplanted in the house of YHWH
>   will flourish in the courts of our God.
> They will bear fruit even in old age;
>   they will remain lush and fresh,
>   proclaiming, "YHWH is upright;
>   he is my rock, and there is no unrighteousness in him!"
> (Ps 92:12-15[13-16])

It is as if the tree, watered by temple streams in Psalm 1, is now transplanted within the very "house of YHWH." The arboreal passage of Psalm 92 in particular offers a striking parallel, employing the language of planting and fruitful production to refer to the (aged) righteous. The

33. Creach argues that *tôrâ* is meant to replace the temple, as one finds in later rabbinic literature ("Like a Tree," 44–46). David Willgren, on the other hand, offers a more positive assessment: "The verse brings torah and temple more closely together" (*Like a Garden of Flowers*, 147–48). The issue remains open.

unspecified tree in Psalm 1, moreover, takes on specific botanical forms in these other psalms: olive tree, date palm, cedar of Lebanon. The unidentified tree of Psalm 1 has diversified.

What remains distinctive of Psalm 1, however, is *tôrâ*'s association with the temple. While Psalm 1 does not necessarily replace or demote the temple in order to elevate the importance of *tôrâ* for the righteous, the psalm at least forges a pathway between the two. In Deuteronomic tradition, the book of the *tôrâ*, the *tôrâ* of Moses, is placed by the ark of the covenant, existing side by side (Deut 31:24, 26). In Deuteronomistic tradition, the book of the *tôrâ* finds itself concealed in the temple until discovered by the priests and taken to King Josiah for a reading that inspires an unprecedented reform, the result, one might say, of Josiah's own "deliberation" on *tôrâ* (2 Kgs 22:8-9). In Isaiah and Micah, *tôrâ* issues forth from Zion to all the nations, compelling them to come to "the mountain of YHWH" to be taught YHWH's "ways" (Isa 2:3; Mic 4:2). Each in its own way, such passages find a connection between temple and *tôrâ*, just as Aaron and Moses, the priest and the lawgiver, have their kinship in biblical tradition. Specifically in Psalm 1, *tôrâ* is poetically profiled as lifegiving streams issuing from the temple, sustaining the righteous in their righteousness. Suffice it to say: in Psalm 1 temple and *tôrâ* find their connection, a connection particularly relevant in times of exile and diaspora. But what kind of *tôrâ*? If psalmic *tôrâ* presupposes Deuteronomic *tôrâ*, then Psalm 1 "devotionalizes and personalizes" it.[34] But psalmic *tôrâ* also extends beyond Deuteronomic *tôrâ*, even correcting it.

Trees in the Temple?

As discussed above, while Psalm 1 singlehandedly attempts to align the Psalter with *tôrâ*, it does not identify the Psalter with *tôrâ*. *Tôrâ* in Psalm 1, as in Deuteronomy, is divinely authored; it is YHWH's *tôrâ*. Nevertheless, Psalm 1 distinguishes itself from Deuteronomic *tôrâ* by identifying a point of contention that may seem trivial at first glance but

34. Scott C. Jones, "Psalm 1 and the Hermeneutics of Torah," *Biblica* 97, no. 4 (2016): 538.

has all to do with its central arboreal image. Deuteronomy is adamant that trees and altars do not mix.

> You shall not plant for yourself an *'ăšērâ*, any tree,
> beside an altar of YHWH your God (Deut 16:21).

The prohibition can be taken in one of two ways: (1) one is not to plant an *'ăšērâ* or "any tree" next to the altar, or (2) one is not to plant "any tree" as an *'ăšērâ* next to the altar. Either way, an *'ăšērâ* cannot be "planted" in a sanctuary setting. Translated as "sacred pole" in the NRSV and CEB (cf. NAS), an *'ăšērâ* was a stylized tree serving as a cult object, perhaps reflecting a symbolic relationship to the goddess Asherah, but this is by no means certain. The nature of that relationship is complicated and remains a matter of debate.[35] What can be said is that iconographic depictions of an arboreal figure discovered in Palestine and elsewhere seem to symbolize fertility, and certain depictions of the goddess Asherah do the same.[36] The parallel suggests a connection. The Canaanite goddess Asherah (Athirat in Ugaritic) was the consort of the high god El and the mother of the gods. She was also a fixture in Israelite religion, much to the dismay of the Deuteronomist, the Chronicler, and the prophets.[37]

But Psalm 1 does something quite innovative. The psalmist employs an image forbidden in Deuteronomic *tôrâ* and transforms it into a profoundly generative metaphor: the tree that is admitted into the temple precincts, nourished by its streams, is none other than the righteous individual who delights in *tôrâ*. That person, moreover, is deemed "happy" or fortunate (*'ašrê*) at the very outset. Indeed, the implicit link between the fruitful "tree" and the *'ăšērâ* makes for an ingenious wordplay: *'ašrê-hā*[*'îš*] ("How happy is the [one]") is phonetically similar to *'ăšērâ*. In the consonantal form of Hebrew, the similarity is equally, if not more, striking:

אשרי ה[איש] *'ašrê-hā*[*'îš*]
אשירה *'ăšērâ*

35. For fuller discussion, see William P. Brown, *Seeing the Psalms: A Theology of Metaphor* (Louisville, KY: Westminster John Knox, 2002), 55–80.

36. Brown, *Seeing the Psalms, 62–64.*

37. See, e.g., Judg 3:7; 1 Kgs 18:19, 40; 2 Chron 24:18; Isa 17:8; 27:9; Jer 17:2; Mic 5:13[14].

The psalmist has taken the arboreal *ʾăšērâ*, a forbidden cult object, and turned it into an embodied metaphor. The tree is no longer an *ʾăšērâ* pole; it is the righteous individual, a flourishing "tree" rooted in *tôrâ*. The didactic poet has turned an image of apostasy into an icon of righteousness! This "tree" is not only permitted within the sphere of the holy, it is planted by YHWH as part of the temple garden. Pressed further, the righteous take on the attributes of Asherah, namely her productivity and intimate relationship with the high God. No wonder, then, the righteous find their "delight" *and* desire in YHWH's *tôrâ*.

Such an ingenious move is not unprecedented in biblical tradition. A comparable move is made in Genesis 1, in which humankind is said to be created in God's "image" (Gen 1:26, 27). The word for "image," *ṣelem*, typically refers to the illicit "image" of Baʿal (2 Kgs 11:18) or the cast metal "image" venerated by the Canaanites (Num 33:52). But in Genesis 1, the "image" of God is no lifeless statue representing the deity but human beings endowed with the responsibility of representing God on earth. Such is another creative wordplay that "redeems" the language of apostasy into something profoundly theological. One begins the story of creation, the creation of humanity within the cosmic temple. The other wordplay begins the journey of righteousness in the Psalms, righteousness rooted in *tôrâ*. That journey takes a creational route in Psalm 19.

Cosmic Torah: Psalm 19

Considered by C. S. Lewis to be "the greatest poem in the Psalter and one of the greatest lyrics in the world," Psalm 19 may also be the most creative "deliberation" on *tôrâ*.[38]

> The heavens are proclaiming the glory of God,
>   and the celestial dome[39] proclaims his handiwork.

38. Verse 2 in Hebrew versification, which adds a number to every verse because the superscription carries the first verse.

39. Or "firmament" (*rāqîʿa*; cf. Gen 1:6-8).

Day to day spews forth speech,
  and night to night dispenses knowledge.
There is no speech, nor are there words;
  their[40] voice cannot be heard.
Yet their "lines"[41] go forth throughout all the earth,
  so thus their "words"[42] to the end of the world.
For the sun, [God] has set a tent in the heavens,
  which goes forth like a bridegroom from his wedding canopy,
    rejoicing like a warrior running the path.
From one end of the heavens is its rising,
  and its completed circuit is at the other end.[43]
    Nothing is hidden from its heat.
YHWH's *tôrâ* is impeccable,
  restoring the self.
YHWH's decrees are sure,
  imparting wisdom to the simple.

---

40. The antecedent is most likely "day" and "night" rather than the "heavens." See Anja Klein, "Half Way between Psalm 119 and Ben Sira: Wisdom and Torah in Psalm 19," in *Wisdom and Torah: The Reception of 'Torah' in the Wisdom Literature of the Second Temple Period*, ed. Bernd U. Schipper and D. Andrew Teeter, SJSJ 163 (Boston: Brill, 2013), 139.

41. Collective sense. The meaning of *qawwām* is disputed. Poetic parallelism suggests that it refers to discourse. Often proposed is textual corruption of an original *qōlām* ("their voice," so LXX). However, the elision of the *lamed* is difficult to explain. The meaning of *qaw* is "measuring line," used for construction or demarcation (e.g., 1 Kgs 7:23; Job 38:5; Isa 44:13). Sense can be made by recognizing that the psalmist couches a visual image in the context of verbal discourse. In other words, the term likely refers to the divinely prescribed paths or circuits that the celestial bodies follow (e.g., the sun's "going forth" [*yōṣēʾ*], "rising" [*môṣāʾû*], and "path" [*ʾōrāḥ*] in vv. 5-6[6-7]). It is in their movement on prescribed pathways and their demarcation between day and night that "measure out" knowledge, as it were. See, similarly, Alan Cooper, "Creation, Philosophy and Spirituality: Aspects of Jewish Interpretation of Psalm 19," in *Pursuing the Text: Studies in Honor of Ben Zion Wacholder on the Occasion of His Seventieth Birthday*, ed. John Reeves and John Kampen, JSOTSup 184 (Sheffield, UK: Sheffield Academic Press, 1994), 21n18. For a slightly different interpretation that retains the sense of "measuring line," see Scott C. Jones, "Who Can Narrate El's Wonders? The Reception of Psalm 19 in Ben Sira and the Qumran Hodayot," in *Fromme und Frevler: Studien zu Psalmen und Weisheit. Festschrift für Hermann Spieckermann zum 70. Geburtstag*, ed. Corinna Körting und Reinhard Gregor Kratz (Tübingen: Mohr Siebeck, 2020), 32–33.

42. Such "words" signal nonverbal discourse.

43. Literally, "of them" (i.e., the heavens).

YHWH's precepts are upright,
  gladdening the heart.
YHWH's commandment is clear,
  giving light to the eyes.
The fear of YHWH is pure,
  enduring forever.
YHWH's rulings are true,
  altogether righteous.
They are more desirable than gold,
  more than abundant fine gold,
  sweeter than honey, even honey oozing from the honeycomb.
To be sure, your servant is enlightened[44] by them;
  in observing them there is great reward.
Who can discern [my] errors?
Clear me of any unknown sins![45]
  Even from insolent sins[46] deliver your servant!
Let them not gain mastery over me!
Then I will become entirely sound,[47]
  and innocent of great wrongdoing.
May the words of my mouth
  and the deliberation of my heart
    be acceptable before you,
    YHWH, my rock and my redeemer. (19:1-14[2-15])

44. The Hebrew verb √*zhr* carries the meaning of "warn, instruct" (e.g., Exod 18:20; Ezek 3:18, 21; 33:8-9), as well as "shine" (Dan 12:3; cf. the nominal form in Ezek 8:2). The above translation captures the double meaning of the verb in this context.

45. Literally, "hidden things" (*nistārôt*).

46. The Hebrew *zēdîm* can also be translated "the insolent," the more common meaning (e.g., Pss 86:14; 119:21, 51, 69, 78; Prov 21:24; Mal 3:15). However, the following petition (*'al-yimšĕlû-bî*) could allude to Gen 4:7, in which YHWH challenges Cain to resist "sin": "but you must master it" (*wĕ'attâ timšol-bô*). Whether an allusion or not, the psalmist's interior side is maintained in vv. 12a[13a] and 13[14], suggesting that sins are of utmost concern. If so, then v. 12[13] reflects a dual petition for God to purge the speaker of any faults unknowingly committed and to spare him of any willful, future offenses.

47. Hebrew *'êtām* from √*tmm*, "to be whole, complete." See v. 7a[8a].

The creative genius of Psalm 19 shines in the way the psalmist juxtaposes *tôrâ* and creation, resulting in a profound union of thematic contexts. Often regarded as two separate psalms stitched together, Psalm 19 establishes *tôrâ*'s cosmic conjunction, a connection lacking in Psalm 1. Some interpret the conjunction as a claim of *tôrâ*'s supersession of creation. But that seems not to be the point of Psalm 19. While creation depicted in the psalm does serve to enhance *tôrâ*'s efficacy, it is not at creation's expense or demotion, as if the second part of the psalm were a polemic of the first. No, creation and *tôrâ* are not competitors, as if God's glory were a limited commodity. In Psalm 19, divine glory is inexhaustibly shared by both creation and *tôrâ*.

The first half of Psalm 19 affirms that creation has its own modes of imparting glory. Creation engages in constant communication, day and night (cf. Ps 1:2b). Ancient Israel was not alone in sensing creation's communicative power. But what distinguishes Psalm 19 from, say, the vast observational data compiled by Babylonian astronomers is that the psalmist finds no predictive (i.e., astrological) value in the cosmos.[48] The cosmos is not divinatory, but it does communicate something divine: COSMOS spells GLORY. By way of illustration, the psalm showcases the sun, whose daily "path" is taken with vigor and joy, from east to west, the most visible display of creation's discourse of God's glory.

The psalm then shifts from the glory of creation to the efficacy of *tôrâ*, giving a far more detailed accounting of *tôrâ* than in Psalm 1. In *tôrâ*, the creator God (El) becomes Israel's personal God YHWH.[49] Like the cosmos populated by its celestial members, *tôrâ* has its host of "decrees" (*'ēdût*), "precepts" (*piqqûdîm*), "commandment(s)" (*miṣwâ*), and "rulings" (*mišpāṭîm*), all highlighting *tôrâ*'s prescriptive forms, not unlike the taxonomy of *tôrâ* given in Deuteronomy and expanded in Psalm 119 (see below).[50] In both Psalm 19 and Deuteronomy, *tôrâ* is a corpus of

48. See Francesca Rochberg, *The Heavenly Writing: Divination, Horoscopy, and Astronomy in Mesopotamian Culture* (Cambridge: Cambridge University Press, 2004).

49. See Benjamin D. Sommer, "Nature, Revelation, and Grace in Psalm 19: Towards a Theological Reading of Scripture," *HTR* 108, no. 3 (2015): 396–99.

50. Deuteronomy delineates the composite nature of *tôrâ* as "decrees" (*'ēdût*), "statutes" (*ḥuqqîm*), "rulings" (*mišpāṭîm*), and "commandments" (*miṣwôt*). See, e.g., 4:44-45; 5:1, 31.

various kinds of prescriptions, but in Psalm 19, each one is associated with a certain attribute and efficacy. Devoid of content, *tôrâ* in Psalm 19 carries great impact.

The attributes of *tôrâ* together form a collage of estimable qualities, both cultic and ethical, that are meant to be embodied. First and foremost, *tôrâ* is "impeccable" (*tĕmîmâ*), which can refer to a morally upstanding agent, such as Noah (Gen 6:6) or Abraham (17:1), or a people (Deut 18:13), or a follower of *tôrâ* (Ps 119:80; cf. 18:23[24]). It can also refer to a sacrifice offered to God that is devoid of defect (Exod 12:5; Lev 1:3; 9:2, 3; Ezek 43:22). YHWH's "decrees" are "sure" or reliable (*ne'ĕmānâ*), which can also apply to persons.[51] YHWH's "precepts" are "upright" (*yĕšārîm*), a term for moral conduct and character.[52] Indeed, a frequent expression found in the Psalms is the "upright in heart" (*yišrê lēb*).[53] YHWH's "commandment" is "clear" or clean (*bārâ*), a quality that also applies to the heart (Pss 24:4; 73:1) as well as to the individual as a whole (Job 11:4; Song 6:10). From a more ritual context, the quality "pure" (*ṭĕhôrâ*) is attributed to reverence or "fear" of YHWH in the psalm.[54] Finally, YHWH's "rulings" are deemed "righteous" (√*ṣdq*), a wide-ranging moral attribute.[55] This taxonomy of *tôrâ*'s attributes is no random selection; they have been carefully selected to cover the moral and the ritualistic, attributes that apply equally well to the individual and to the community. In the psalmist's eyes, *tôrâ* is not just a corpus of prescriptions to be read and followed; it is a carrier of commendable attributes that are meant to be embodied. *Tôrâ*, in short, presents the model of the human will.

But there is more: *tôrâ* not only reflects the full integrity of the human will; *tôrâ* sustains it. Accompanying *tôrâ*'s attributes are various efficacies or salutary effects that *tôrâ* imparts to the moral self: restoration, wisdom, joy, and light to the eyes. Taken together, such efficacies commend *tôrâ* as a source of wisdom and life, not unlike Wisdom herself as the "tree of life"

---

51. Num 12:7 (Moses); 1 Sam 2:35; Prov 25:13; Neh 9:8; 13:13; Ps 101:6; Prov 11:13.

52. E.g., Deut 12:25; Mic 7:2; Job 1:1; Pss 7:10[11]; 37:14, 37; Prov 20:11; 21:8.

53. E.g., Pss 7:10[11]; 11:2; 32:11; 36:10[11]; 97:11; cf. 125:4.

54. See also Lev 7:19; 10:10; Deut 12:15; Job 14:4.

55. Ps 143:2; Job 9:15, 20; 10:15; 15:14; 34:5; Isa 45:25.

(Prov 3:18). Indeed, *tôrâ*'s desirability parallels Wisdom's priceless value.[56] Such language intensifies the "delight" the righteous have in *tôrâ* (Ps 1:2). Now we know why *tôrâ* has such strong appeal: it is the singular source of vitality and wisdom.

In isolation, Psalm 19:7-10[8-11] highlights *tôrâ*'s incomparable value and power to shape and transform human character. But by way of juxtaposition with 19:1-6[2-7], *tôrâ*'s efficacy is underscored all the more. As the heavens communicate God's glory, so *tôrâ* imparts wisdom and gives life. *Tôrâ* too is a part of YHWH's "handiwork," a creation of God. By the juxtaposition of *tôrâ* and creation, *tôrâ* proves to be not so much a book or scroll as a world unto itself, and yet a world that is to be embodied, not simply obeyed as law. God is the author of the world of creation and the "world" of *tôrâ*, both imparting something of God's glory. Behold the sun, which "runs" its prescribed path with joy, filling the earth with its heat! Behold *tôrâ*, which enlightens and restores the self, gladdening the heart! The sun follows the path of *tôrâ*, so also the righteous, who conduct their lives with joy. The glory of God, in the end, is shown to be a human being fully alive and wise, fully righteous and vital.[57]

Psalm 19 concludes with petition for such attainment (19:11-14[12-15]). The speaker testifies to being "enlightened" by *tôrâ*'s prescriptions (19:11[12]) and prays to be "cleared" (√*nqh*) and "kept back" (√*ḥśk*) from sins, both witting and unwitting (19:12[13]). The purpose? To be morally "sound" or whole (*'êtām*), reflecting the "impeccable" integrity (*tĕmîmâ*) of *tôrâ* itself (19:7a[8a]). The link is unmistakable, both *tôrâ* and the purified speaker share in common the sense of moral completeness (√*tmm*). Through *tôrâ*'s efficacy and by YHWH's mercy, the speaker hopes to embody *tôrâ*'s integrity, receiving all its lifegiving benefits. Thus, *tôrâ* is as much a reflection of the human will in its full, righteous integrity as the human will is meant to be a reflection *tôrâ*'s "will," as it were, its core character and moral completeness. *Tôrâ*, it turns out, has its own moral agency for the sake of all human agents.

56. See Prov 3:13-15; 8:10, 19; 16:24; 24:13. For further comparison, see chapter 9.

57. The reader may recognize this extension of Irenaeus's often-quoted line, "The glory of God is a living human being" (*Gloria Dei est vivens homo* [in *Adversus Haereses*, 4.20]).

Torah and Temple Once Again

The breadth of *tôrâ*'s polyvalence in Psalm 19 even points to the temple, not so much by its content as by its location in the Psalter. As much as the tree's location beside flowing channels in Psalm 1 hints at *tôrâ*'s association with the temple, so the placement of Psalm 19 in literary context does something equally suggestive. The psalm is strategically positioned at the center of a concentric grouping or chiastic arrangement of psalms all arranged by genre.

A Psalm 15 (Entrance Liturgy)
 B Psalm 16 (Song of Trust)
  C Psalm 17 (Prayer for Help)
   D Psalm 18 (Royal Psalm)
    E Psalm 19
   D′ Psalms 20–21 (Royal Psalms)
  C′ Psalm 22 (Prayer for Help)
 B′ Psalm 23 (Song of Trust)
A′ Psalm 24 (Entrance Liturgy)

This cluster, moreover, is flanked by two "entrance" liturgies that lay out the requirements for ascending YHWH's "hill," Zion (15:1; 24:3), suggesting a topographical arrangement.

Psalm 19
Psalm 18 Psalms 20–21
Psalm 17 Psalm 22
Psalm 16 Psalm 23
Psalm 15 Psalm 24

Psalm 19 not only lies at the center of the chiasm; it also rests on its "summit." The concentric arrangement gives rise, not fortuitously, to a literary configuration shaped by ascent and descent when the psalms are read in sequential fashion, or by ascent from opposite directions if the psalms are read from their corresponding positions from "lowest" to "highest."

Given its primacy of place in this cluster, Psalm 19 serves to relativize the temple. Nowhere is Zion or the temple alluded to in Psalm 19, as in Psalm 1. Only a hint of what could be considered cultic is featured, as noted above. Whereas Psalms 15 and 24 elucidate the qualifications for gaining entrance into the temple, the portal into God's presence, Psalm 19 offers no such portal. One might expect a Zion psalm positioned at the center or summit of such an arrangement (e.g., Pss 46, 48). Instead, Psalm 19 shifts the focus from Zion, YHWH's "tent" (*'ōhel*; 15:1a), to the sun's "tent" (*'ōhel*; 19:5b) and to YHWH's *tôrâ* (19:8-10), which lies at the center of the psalm and thus at the center of the chiasm. In the case of Psalm 19, it appears that *tôrâ* replaces the temple, this *tôrâ* that even the cosmos complements. The temple is no longer the destination point of the "King of glory" (24:7-10). Rather, divine glory manifests itself throughout all creation and crowns every commandment and decree in YHWH's *tôrâ*.

A mystery may be solved regarding Psalm 19's uniqueness, albeit speculatively. The psalm's strategic placement in this cluster suggests that an earlier, more "coherent" form of Psalm 19 occupied this cluster, but it was disrupted to highlight *tôrâ*'s primacy over the temple. One can easily imagine Psalm 19 originally having two parts, as it does now,[58] but the original juxtaposition in the psalm was not between cosmos and *tôrâ*, but between cosmos and temple. That is to say, the second half of the psalm may very well have been devoted to detailing the efficacy of the temple in conjunction with creation. Such would have been a more conventional fit, given that the temple was considered a microcosm of creation,[59] or as we saw in Genesis 1, creation as a macrocosmic temple (see chapter 2). If the cosmos communicates God's glory, the temple communicates divine revelation, as in Psalm 73:13-17. It is there in the sanctuary where the speaker receives revelation of the demise of the wicked. Elsewhere in the Psalms, God's "glory" is said to abide in the temple, as Psalm 26 testifies (26:8; cf. 29:9;

58. Unless one counts vv. 11-14[12-15] as a third part, which I am reluctant to do given its interrelatedness to *tôrâ*.

59. See the discussion in Jon D. Levenson, *Creation and the Persistence of Evil: The Jewish Drama of Divine Omnipotence* (San Francisco: Harper & Row, 1988), 90–99.

102:16). Psalm 96, an enthronement psalm, locates YHWH's "glory" in YHWH's "courts," where the community praises YHWH by bringing an offering (96:8).

But not in Psalm 19, where *tôrâ* supersedes the temple, the localized space of God's glory. Now it is *tôrâ* that exhibits God's glory, in the form of life-giving righteousness. Temple revelations are no longer needed in view of the constancy of YHWH's revelation in word. So, yes, there is a demotion that takes place in Psalm 19 in view of *tôrâ*'s efficacy, but it is not that of creation. It is the temple. YHWH's *tôrâ*, in the end, is deemed a better fit for the "entrance" liturgies of Psalms 15 and 24, with their common emphasis on righteousness in all its ethical and cultic modalities (15:2-5; 24:3-4). *Tôrâ* imparts these very qualities and much more. The question is no longer about gaining entrance into the temple by virtue of these qualities but about "entering" *tôrâ* and embodying its qualities wherever one is. For a diasporic community, Psalm 19 asks the question, Which is more important, temple or *tôrâ*? The answer is clear.

Psalm 119: For the Love of "Law"

For all its cosmic breadth, *tôrâ* in Psalm 19 has its share of existential depth in Psalm 119. As the unrivaled "Psalm of the Law," Psalm 119 is not only the longest psalm in the Psalter, it is also the most impassioned psalm about *tôrâ*. The word *tôrâ* is repeated twenty-five times, a tenth of all the occurrences in the Old Testament.[60] Moreover, a host of synonyms and metonyms for *tôrâ* are attested. In the larger context of the Psalter, it could be said that Psalm 119 gives voice to the *tôrâ* lover of Psalm 1,[61] a voice that speaks uninterrupted for 176 verses, sustained by uncompromising zeal expressed with passionate words of petition, thanksgiving, and praise.

60. Karin Finsterbusch, "Yahweh's Torah and the Praying 'I' in Psalm 119," in *Wisdom and Torah: The Reception of 'Torah' in the Wisdom Literature of the Second Temple Period*, ed. Bernd U. Schipper and D. Andrew Teeter, SJSJ 163 (Boston: Brill, 2013), 119.

61. Hermann Spieckermann, "What Is the Place of Wisdom and Torah in the Psalter?," in *"When the Morning Stars Sang": Essays in Honor of Choong Leong Seow on the Occasion of His Sixty-Fifth Birthday*, ed. Scott C. Jones and Christine Roy Yoder, BZAW 500 (Boston: De Gruyter, 2018), 310.

Indeed, the speaker represents a composite of voices reflecting different stages in life, from youth to full maturity,[62] all united by a passion for *tôrâ*.

Speaking of passion, the verb "love" (*'hb*) occurs twelve times in the psalm, and it is not the only affective term employed by the psalmist. Take the following verses:

> How I ***love*** your *tôrâ*!
> It is my deliberation all day long! (119:97)
> Lead me on the path of your commandments,
> for I ***delight*** in it. (119:35)
> Therefore, I ***love*** your commandments
> more than gold, even pure gold. (119:127)
> I hate falsehood, indeed, I abhor it!
> It is your *tôrâ* ***that I love***. (119:163)
> I myself keep your decrees;
> I ***love them*** exceedingly. (119:167)
> I open wide my mouth, panting,
> ***for I long for*** your commandments. (119:131 [cf. 119:40])
> See how I ***love*** your precepts!
> Renew my life, YHWH, according to your benevolence! (119:159)
> Princes persecute me for no reason;
> my ***heart trembles*** at your word.[63] (119:161)
> My body trembles from fear of you;
> I am ***in awe*** of your rulings. (119:120)
> Were not your law my ***joy***,
> I would have perished in my affliction! (119:92 [cf. 119:77])
> I ***cling*** [*dābaqtî*] to your decrees, YHWH.
> Do not put me to shame! (119:31)

The speaker's desire for YHWH's *tôrâ* is so strong that his heart and body "tremble" and his mouth "pants." The speaker is "lovesick" over the "law" as much as he is struck in awe of its instruction. In short, the speaker

62. See Finsterbusch, "Yahweh's Torah," 119–35. Kent A. Reynolds, however, posits one, ideal student who reflects a "variety of situations and . . . emotions" (*Torah as Teacher: The Exemplary Torah Student in Psalm 119*, VTSup 137 (Boston: Brill, 2010], 58).

63. Read Qere.

is "law struck." The psalmist even uses a verb ("cling") that can connote sexual bonding elsewhere (119:31; cf. Gen 2:24). YHWH's "rulings" elicit a sense of *mysterium tremendum*, an awe-filled otherness about *tôrâ* that corresponds to YHWH's fearful presence (119:120). Language typically applied to God elsewhere is applied to *tôrâ* in Psalm 119, pressing *tôrâ*'s exaltation to the point of the speaker's undoing. The "delight" felt by the speaker in Psalm 1 is intensified to the point of all-consuming, self-destroying "zeal" (*qinʾâ*):

> My zeal destroys me,
> because my foes have forgotten your words.
> Your word is well-tested,[64]
> and your servant loves it. (119:139-140)

Like God's glorious deeds, *tôrâ* has its own share of "wonders": "Open my eyes so that I may behold the wonders of your *tôrâ*" (119:18). Such a claim is unique in the Hebrew Bible; it is the only instance in which the word for "wonders" (*niplāʾôt*) is applied to *tôrâ*, which otherwise refers to God's victorious deeds in history and marvelous works in creation.[65] What are the "wonders" of *tôrâ*? One wonders. Perhaps they are *tôrâ*'s prescriptive constituents, which Psalm 119 delineates as YHWH's "word" (*dābār*, *ʾimrâ*), "decrees" (*ʿēdōt*), "commandments" (*miṣwôt*), "rulings" or rules (*mišpāṭîm*), "statutes" (*ḥuqqîm*), "precepts" (*piqqudîm*), and "ways" (*dĕrākîm*).[66] On the other hand, *tôrâ*'s "wonders" may refer to its efficacies, which are addressed explicitly in Psalm 19, from wisdom to vitality and joy. In 119:27, YHWH's "precepts," when rightly understood, are the means to "deliberate" on YHWH's "wonders." Such "wonders," then,

64. Or "refined" (*ṣĕrûpâ).*

65. E.g., Exod 3:20; Jos 3:5; Jer 21:2; Pss 40:5[6]; 72:18; 78:4; 86:10; 98:1; 106:22; 136:4; 139:14; Job 5:9; 9:10; 42:3.

66. See the lexical analysis of each of these terms in Finsterbusch, "Yahweh's Torah," 125–27.

would include the *magnalia Dei* in history and creation. YHWH's words and deeds are, once again, subsumed under *tôrâ*.[67]

Still another dimension of *tôrâ*-related wonder is evident in this lengthiest of psalms, namely *tôrâ*'s cosmic scope and function.

> Forever, YHWH, does your word [*dābār*] stand firm in the heavens.
> Your faithfulness [*'ĕmûnâ*] extends from one generation to the next;
> you have established the earth, and it stands fast.
> On account of your rules [*mišpāṭîm*] do they[68] stand today;
> indeed, all things are your servants. (119:89-91)

In this passage, YHWH's "word" and "rules" have all to do with creation's integrity, from the "heavens" to the "earth." Jon Levenson describes *tôrâ* as "a kind of revealed natural law."[69] More specifically, YHWH's *tôrâ* is a cosmo-polity that ensures creation's stability and reflects YHWH's "faithfulness" across generations. Because of *tôrâ*, all creation "stands fast," while also standing at YHWH's behest. Creation's integrity is demonstrated in its "obedience," made possible by *tôrâ*. Such is the wonder of *tôrâ*.

> Your decrees are wonderful [*pĕlā'ôt*];
> therefore, I guard [√*nṣr*] them.
> The gateway[70] to your words radiates light,
> granting understanding to the simple. (119:129-130)

---

67. Cf. David Noel Freedman's expansive claim: "Everything else in Israelite religion—Temple, Covenant, Creation, Exodus, Messiah—is subsumed under *tôrâ*" (*Psalm 119: The Exaltation of Torah,* Biblical and Judaic Studies 6 [Winona Lake, IN: Eisenbrauns, 1999], 91–92).

68. That is, the "earth" and the "heavens."

69. See Jon D. Levenson, "The Sources of Torah: Psalm 19 and the Modes of Revelation," in *Ancient Israelite Religion*, ed. Patrick D. Miller, Paul D. Hanson, and S. Dean McBride (Minneapolis: Fortress, 1987), 569.

70. Meaning of *pētaḥ* is uncertain (as also in Hab 2:3). LXX reads "manifestation" (*dēlōsis*). If it is related to the more common *petaḥ*, the word is associated with "entrance/gateway" (see Symmachus *pylē*).

The wonder-filled nature of YHWH's "decrees" requires protection. The reference to "gateway" turns *tôrâ* into an edifice (a temple?), a structure that radiates "understanding" (cf. 19:6[7], 7-8[8-9]). *Tôrâ* proves to be pedagogically effulgent, at whose "gateway" the speaker stands guard to receive wisdom and guidance. To study *tôrâ* is to serve as *tôrâ*'s gatekeeper.

Regarding wisdom and guidance, the psalmist is adamant that *tôrâ* is didactically more effective than any human teacher or mediator:

> Indeed, your decrees are my joy;
> they are my counselors. (199:24)
> I have greater insight than all my teachers,
> for your decrees are my deliberation.
> I have more understanding than the elders,
> for I guard your precepts. (119:99-100)

The "insight" and "understanding" gained from YHWH's *tôrâ* exceeds even the wisdom of "teachers" and "elders." The psalmist boldly claims that there is greater wisdom in *tôrâ* than in the wisdom of the sages, precisely because *tôrâ*-based wisdom is gained without pedagogical mediation. YHWH's "decrees" are themselves "counselors" (119:24), and receiving *tôrâ*'s wisdom involves (once again) "guarding" YHWH's "precepts."

Nevertheless, there is a teacher above all others. The speaker repeatedly asks YHWH to fulfill the role of pedagogue.[71] Only divine mediation suits divine *tôrâ*. Such a claim not only critiques the sapiential pedagogy of Proverbs, in which parents are deemed teachers of *tôrâ*; it also strikes at the heart of the Pentateuch's presentation of *tôrâ*, in which Moses is exalted as the consummate teacher of the "law," as YHWH had commanded in Deuteronomy (5:30-31). In Psalm 119, YHWH alone "teaches," making *tôrâ* personally and directly accessible. Among the Torah Psalms, there is no mediating Moses, only YHWH and *tôrâ*.

Finally, Psalm 119 does something unprecedented in Deuteronomic thought. The psalmist correlates YHWH's *tôrâ* with salvation.

71. Verses 12b, 26b, 33a, 64b, 68b, 108b, 124b, 135b.

My whole being[72] ***languishes for*** your deliverance,
as ***I wait*** for your word.
My ***eyes fail*** for your word;
I say, "When will you comfort me?" (119:80-81)
My ***eyes fail*** for your salvation,
for your righteous word. (119:123)
I wait for your salvation, YHWH;
I fulfill your commandments. (119:166)

Both YHWH's "salvation" and YHWH's "word" are interrelated objects of the speaker's yearning. YHWH's "salvation" and "righteous word" are syntactically bound together in verse 123. Perhaps conceptually as well:

See how I ***long*** for your precepts!
Revive me in your righteousness! (119:40)
I ***long*** for your salvation, YHWH;
your law is my joy. (119:174)

The verb for "longing" (√*t'b*) serves double duty by embracing both YHWH's "precepts" and YHWH's "salvation," suggesting that they share much in common. Poetic juxtaposition may point toward conceptual coalescence. Certain references to YHWH's "word" in Psalm 119 could refer in isolation to an oracular promise or announcement of deliverance, as they would in psalms of petition (e.g., 12:6[7]; 18:30[31]; 77:8[9]). But in the poetic artistry of Psalm 119, YHWH's oracular "word" is bound up with YHWH's *tôrâ*, which is not only salutary (as in Ps 19) but also salvific. In other words, *tôrâ* itself takes on an aurora of the oracular in Psalm 119, given its unmediated divine source. *Tôrâ* in Psalm 119, moreover, proves to be not only salvific but also sapiential,[73] given its life-guiding efficacy, as one finds in Psalm 19. In Psalm 119, *tôrâ* is all-encompassing. The sum total of *tôrâ* proves to be far greater than its precepts.

72. Hebrew *napšî*.

73. For further discussion on this point, see Levenson, "Sources of Torah," 566–68.

Just how different *tôrâ* in the Torah Psalms and *tôrâ* in Deuteronomy are is well illustrated by a thought experiment conducted by student Katherine Johnson (see chapter 12):

> If I were an ancient Hebrew sitting down to the task of writing a long acrostic poem about the *tôrâ* of Yahweh, I can imagine myself trying to come up with statements about the law for each letter of the alphabet, asking myself, "Let's see, what starts with *mem*? Moses!" Or "What starts with *lamed*? Almost all of the Ten Commandments!" Clearly, Moses and written rules were not what came to mind to the psalmists as they meditated day and night on *tôrâ*.[74]

What did "come to mind" for the psalmists in their deliberative "meditations" was something much more exalted and existential than either a book or a mediator.

Moses in the Psalms

It is striking that Moses figures nowhere in the Torah psalms. Not one of them is attributed to him (cf. Ps 90), and there is no reference to him within them. Beyond these three psalms, Moses in the Psalter is known primarily in connection with the exodus and the wilderness narratives (see chapters 4 and 5). In Psalm 99, Moses and Aaron, along with Samuel, are referenced together as priests who "cried to YHWH" and were answered by YHWH, who "spoke to them in the pillar of cloud" (99:5-7a) and gave them "statutes" and "decrees" (99:7b). But Moses is not singled out as law recipient or lawgiver.[75] Psalm 103 refers vaguely to YHWH having "made known [YHWH's] ways" to Moses, the ways of justice, mercy, and benevolence, but nothing that is legislative (103:6-8). In the lengthy historical Psalm 105, Moses and Aaron are chosen to perform YHWH's "signs" and "miracles" in Egypt (105:26-27). At the psalm's conclusion, Israel's possession of the land makes possible observance of YHWH's "stat-

74. Katherine Johnson, "Weekly Reflection Paper 6: The Law and the Psalmists" (October 16, 2020).

75. The plural subject/object in v. 7 most likely refers to the people in general. It is also noteworthy that no mountain is referenced, only the "pillar of cloud."

utes" and "laws" (*tôrōt*; 105:43-45). But Moses is entirely absent. For all its historical detail, nothing is said in Psalm 106 of Moses imparting or teaching *tôrâ*. All in all, the Psalms avoid casting Moses in the role of lawgiver.[76] Why?

Moses's minimalized role in the Psalms is related to how the Psalms view *tôrâ* as unmediated divine instruction. The Psalms, moreover, refuse to tie *tôrâ* down to a specific corpus. Instead, *tôrâ* is transcendentally related to God, and as such is also related to creation. In Psalm 19, the cosmos complements *tôrâ* rather than the temple. *Tôrâ*'s reach embraces YHWH's salvific deeds. *Tôrâ* demands not only remembrance and obedience, as one finds in Deuteronomy; it also calls for passion, awe, deliberative reflection, and creativity, because *tôrâ* itself inspires such things, according to the Psalms.

Despite their contrasts, there are at least two themes that psalmic *tôrâ* and Deuteronomic *tôrâ* share dialogically: divine immanence and *tôrâ*'s accessibility. In Deuteronomy, obedience to the laws of *tôrâ* points to God's "nearness" to a people.

> For what other great nation has a god so near to it as YHWH our God is whenever we call to him? And what other great nation has statutes and ordinances so righteous as this entire law that I am setting before you today? (Deut 4:7-8)

Deuteronomy juxtaposes YHWH's accessibility through petition and *tôrâ*'s "righteousness" through its "statutes and ordinances." The Psalter does something similar: those psalms that acknowledge *tôrâ*'s efficacy are placed next to psalms of testimony and petition (Pss 18–20; 118–120). Moreover, Psalm 19, for all its poetic reflections on *tôrâ* and creation, is a prayer for deliverance (19:11-13[12-14]). The God who is "so near" to save is wedded to God's *tôrâ* that is so "righteous." So also God's "commandment":

> Surely, this commandment that I am commanding you today is ***not too hard for you or too far away***. It is not in heaven. . . . Neither is it beyond

76. The only psalm that is attributed to Moses, Ps 90, likewise overlooks his role as a lawgiver while emphasizing his role as intercessor (vv. 13-15). See chapter 10.

> the sea. . . . No, the ***word is very near to you***; it is in your mouth and in your heart for you to observe. (Deut 30:11-14)

Each in its own way, Psalms and Deuteronomy stress *tôrâ*'s accessibility. Moses in Deuteronomy is the messenger who teaches *tôrâ* to a new generation poised to cross the Jordan. His "scroll" is carried over into the promised land even as Moses himself must stay behind. The "scroll" of *tôrâ* is Moses's legacy; it is his literary surrogate for the people. In the Psalms, however, *tôrâ*'s accessibility requires no mediator, Mosaic or otherwise. Rather, *tôrâ* is built directly into the relationship between God and petitioner. By severing *tôrâ*'s ties with Moses, with the one person who is said to have spoken "face to face" with God (Exod 33:11), the Psalms have effectively "democratized" Moses and decentralized *tôrâ*, treating it as accessible to anyone who beseeches God. Deuteronomy's singularization of the sanctuary, limited to the "place" that YHWH will "choose" to "establish" YHWH's "name,"[77] corresponds to Moses, who embodies the centralization of *tôrâ*. Only through Mosaic codification is YHWH's *tôrâ* made accessible; only through Moses is *tôrâ* taught, so testifies Deuteronomy.

Not so in the Psalms: YHWH's *tôrâ* is immanently and directly accessible, comparable to the vision given of the new covenant in Jeremiah:

> But this is the covenant that I will make with the house of Israel after those days, says YHWH: I will place my law within them, and I will inscribe it on their hearts; and I will be their God, and they shall be my people. No longer shall they teach one another, or say to each other, "Know YHWH," for they shall all know me, from the least of them to the greatest, says YHWH; for I will forgive their iniquity and remember their sin no more. (Jer 31:33-34)

Likewise, the Torah Psalms aim to make *tôrâ* a matter of the "heart," the center of the human will and the seat of intelligence, both emotional and cognitive (see also Ps 37:31). Such, indeed, is the goal of "deliberating" on *tôrâ*: to take *tôrâ* to heart. But unlike Jeremiah's new covenant, no inscribing is required, figurative or otherwise, even on the part of God. Instead, it is teaching directly by YHWH:

---

77. E.g., 12:5, 11, 14, 18, 21, 28; 14:23-25; 16:2; 31:11.

Teach me, YHWH, the way of your statutes,
  and I shall keep to it until the end.
Give me understanding so that I may keep your law,
  and observe it with all [my] heart.
Lead me on the path of your commandments,
  for I delight in it. (119:33-35)
O how I love your law!
  It is my deliberation all day long!
Your commandment[78] makes me wiser than my enemies,
  for it is always mine.
I have greater insight than all my teachers,
  for your decrees are my deliberation. (119:97-99)

With Psalm 1 as its gateway and Psalm 119 as its "toranic" capstone, the Psalter bypasses Moses to appeal to the one and only teacher of *tôrâ*, YHWH. In so doing, every petitioner is permitted to stand in the place of Moses to receive YHWH's teachings.

Conclusion

The psalms of Torah (Pss 1, 19, 119) construe *tôrâ* differently from *tôrâ* featured in the Pentateuch. Psalmic *tôrâ* lacks Moses as its mediator, finding him unnecessary in the context of individual petition and personal vitality (Pss 19 and 119). While having its share of "decrees," "precepts," "commandment(s)," "rulings," and "statutes," psalmic *tôrâ* does not exhibit anything particularly "bookish." Nevertheless, there is one reference in the Psalms that comes close, creatively facilitating something of a dialogical convergence between Deuteronomic and psalmic *tôrâ*.

Then I said, "Here I am, entering into the written scroll,
  which is inscribed concerning me.
To do your will, my God, is what I delight;
  your *tôrâ* resides deep within my bowels." (Ps 40:7-8[8-9])

78. Read singular (*miṣwotkā*), along with one Hebrew manuscript and LXX, for the plural form in the MT, requiring only a slight consonantal change.

The "written scroll" (*mĕgillat sēper*) refers to a codified body of instruction, perhaps Deuteronomic in content (cf. Deut 28:58, 61; Josh 8:31). Unique, however, is the metaphorical language of "entering" the "scroll," like entering a temple.[79] For one poetic moment, written instruction is depicted as an edifice with an entrance for the one who "delights" in doing God's "will."[80] By entering the "scroll," God's *tôrâ* internalizes the speaker, as it were, who becomes "inscribed" or written into it. Conversely, by being internalized by the "scroll," the speaker internalizes *tôrâ*, which proceeds from book to "bowels" (cf. Ezek 3:1-3).

While the Torah Psalms presuppose codified instruction, given the plethora of prescriptive forms referenced particularly in Psalms 19 and 119, their concern extends beyond the statutes and ordinances that demand obedience. The aim of these psalms is to internalize *tôrâ* through "deliberation" and "delight" (Ps 1), through purgative prayer and redirected desire (Ps 19), through singular devotion ("love") and ardent petition (Ps 119). In all three psalms, divine *tôrâ* constitutes the object of deepest desire. Matched by these personal and affective dimensions, psalmic *tôrâ* also exhibits a measure of self-transcendence. In Psalm 19, the cosmos complements *tôrâ*, setting in relief its lifegiving efficacy. As the "heavens proclaim the glory of God," so *tôrâ* emanates the righteousness and vitality that comes from God. On a personal level, *tôrâ* illuminates the human self, exposing "unknown" or hidden "faults," from which the pray-er seeks deliverance. Indeed, *tôrâ* in Psalm 19 is YHWH's agent of moral revitalization; *tôrâ* makes one righteous and wise, vital and morally sound. In Psalm 119, *tôrâ* is the foundation of creation's order as much as it is the fundamental source of a person's integrity. The Psalms, in short, make *tôrâ* intensely personal and intimately efficacious, on the one hand, and gloriously cosmic and transcendent, on the other. In response to Deuteronomic narrative, the Psalms question the need for a mediator, a mountain, and a scroll for *tôrâ* to shape the self. *Tôrâ* can do quite fine on its own.

---

79. So Spieckermann, "What Is the Place of Wisdom and Torah," 307.

80. Without the necessity of sacrificial offerings, as stated in v. 6[7], the temple itself is rendered obsolete, but not authoritative instruction that leads to obedience (v. 8a[9a]).

So what is *tôrâ* according to the Psalms? Unlike the Pentateuch, the Torah Psalms do not provide legislative or instructional "precepts" or "statutes," etc., although they make ample reference to them. For all its length, Psalm 119 never expounds *tôrâ*, like Moses does in Deuteronomy. While Psalm 119 provides a taxonomy of *tôrâ*'s discursive forms, it does so devoid of content, suggesting that the Psalms provide a more open-ended view of *tôrâ*. Nothing, moreover, is said about punishment or "law and order" in psalmic *tôrâ*.[81] Far from punitive, psalmic *tôrâ* is restorative, indeed salvific, promoting well-being and fullness of life.

What actually constitutes psalmic *tôrâ*? The psalmists do not say. Rather, *tôrâ*'s life-giving efficacies are the focus. Their prominence in the Psalms, at the expense of prescriptive content, suggests that they may be more than efficacies. Perhaps they serve as criteria for what constitutes *tôrâ*. While presupposing *tôrâ* in the Torah in all its Mosaic variety, the psalmists crack open its codified shell to offer a more inclusive *tôrâ*, a *tôrâ* defined more by its efficacies and attributes than by its content. That is to say, the *tôrâ* of the Psalms may very well include divine instruction *of any kind* that would promote righteousness, convey wisdom, impart vitality and renewal, and elicit awe and wonder. The result is an open *tôrâ*, "God's teaching for life."[82]

There are, however, two things about psalmic *tôrâ* that are missing in comparison to Deuteronomic *tôrâ*: corporate holiness and a sociopolitical vision. It is striking that psalmic *tôrâ*, for all its efficacies and attributes, lacks the language of holiness—purity, yes, but not holiness (cf. Ps 19:7-9[8-10]). That is not to say that the psalmists were uninterested in matters of holiness. To the contrary. In the Psalms, holiness is attributed almost exclusively to the divine, including God's "name" and "sanctuary" or "hill," rather than to the people or to individuals.[83] In the Psalms, human holiness is almost an oxymoron; God alone embodies holiness. Whether in praise or protest, the psalmists highlight the disjunction between the

81. In modern political parlance, "law and order" has to do with enforcing security in the face of perceived threat or unrest with severe punishment in order to maintain the status quo.

82. Beat Weber, "Moses, David and the Psalms: The Psalter in the Horizon of the 'Canonical' Books," *Rivista Biblica* 68, no. 2 (2020): 192.

83. With only two exceptions: Pss 16:3; 34:9[10].

human and the divine. For Deuteronomy and Leviticus, the embodied expression of divine holiness, however defined, whether endowed or mandated, is necessary for a fully constituted people.

Relatedly, the parameters of *politeia* do not come into play in the Psalms. That is not to say that the psalmists were oblivious to matters of social justice (see chapter 8). But as for the Torah Psalms, establishing a just and holy social order is not their focus. What is critical to the psalmists is *tôrâ*'s personal efficacy, on the one hand, and transcendent appeal, on the other. Whether as the temple's replacement or extension, *tôrâ* in the Psalms continues the temple's "ministry" while not being limited to it. Nor is psalmic *tôrâ* limited to a "scroll" or book. Nor is it limited to "law." The "wonders" of YHWH's *tôrâ* include the "wonders" of YHWH's salvation.

If anything, *tôrâ* in the Psalms is divinely determined: it comes from God's mouth as an oracle as well as from God's deeds as in narrative. All in all, *tôrâ* in the Torah Psalms is expansive and, in principle, ever expanding. Whatever comes from the mouth of God or tells about God, whatever proves to be life-giving and wise, righteous and morally edifying, cleansing and convicting, qualifies as *tôrâ*. The Psalms offer an adaptative *tôrâ* for disruptive times and new circumstances, a living *tôrâ* that exceeds Moses's literary legacy, a self-transforming *tôrâ* shaped by continuing (re)interpretation and ongoing counsel. Psalmic *tôrâ* has no room for originalism. God is still teaching. God is still at work. *Tôrâ* is ever flowing. Such *tôrâ* would make the daughters of Zelophehad proud (Num 27:1-11).

Part II

PROPHETS

CHAPTER 7

THE DAVID DILEMMA: A LEGACY OF AMBIVALENCE

He was a liar, deceiver, and traitor.

That later tradition should have glorified and magnified him . . .

passes all understanding.

—J. M. P. Smith[1]

Who lives, who dies, who tells your story?

—*Hamilton: An American Musical*[2]

As Israel's most successful king, David was and continues to be a magnet of controversy. He is portrayed as victim and perpetrator, persecuted and opportunist, lamenter and schemer, forgiven and punished, hero and antihero. David is usurped, and he plays the usurper. While one might think only of the Bathsheba affair, David comes close to being implicated in various other crimes. Allegedly saved from bloodguilt, David remains a "man of blood" in the eyes of his detractors. It is no surprise that

1. J. M. P. Smith, "The Character of King David," *JBL* 52, no. 1 (1933): 11.

2. Composed by Lin-Manuel Miranda. For the original Broadway recording of this song, see https://www.youtube.com/watch?v=_gnypiKNaJE.

David is the Bible's most complex figure, an enigma,[3] even a dilemma, as we shall see. The debate over David's character in the Bible reflects something of the debate over kingship's legitimacy in Israel. The legacy of David's dynasty, moreover, addresses in conflicting ways how royal power is to be exercised and for what purpose.

The Psalms contribute to this lively discussion over David's legacy. This chapter does not aim to reconstruct a history of David's rise and reign.[4] Instead, the plan is to highlight various perspectives about David featured in DtrH, Chronicles, and the Psalms, as partners in dialogue about his legacy, including how he came to define the royal office. We begin with an overview of David in DtrH.

David in the Deuteronomistic History

As for David's story in the DtrH, scholars generally posit two literary sources conjoined together in "dovetailed" fashion. One recounts David's rise, extending from 1 Samuel 16:1 to 2 Samuel 5:3, and the other, the so-called Court History, narrates David's reign beginning with 2 Samuel 5:4 and extending to 1 Kings 1–2, with possible overlap in 2 Samuel 2:12–4:12.[5] Nevertheless, David's story is fraught with background that reaches back to the monarchy's conflicted beginnings, when Samuel's sons failed in their appointed roles as "judges over Israel" (1 Sam 8:2). They proved themselves corrupt by seeking "gain," taking bribes, and "perverting justice," prompting the elders to demand a king (8:5), as if a king were immune from such things. But YHWH enjoined Samuel to "listen to the voice of the people . . . for they have not rejected you; instead, they have rejected me from being king over them" (8:7).

3. Paul Borgman, in fact, considers David to be a figure of mystery (*David, Saul, and God: Rediscovering an Ancient Story* [New York: Oxford University Press, 2008], esp. 5, 15).

4. For a compelling historical reconstruction, see Steven L. McKenzie, *King David: A Biography* (New York: Oxford University Press, 2000). For a helpful comparative study of Davidic portraits in the Hebrew Bible, see Marti J. Steussy, *David: Biblical Portraits of Power, Studies on Personalities of the Old Testament* (Columbia: University of South Carolina Press, 1999).

5. See McKenzie, *King David*, 31–32.

So begins the most conflicted story in the Bible, driven by the pros and cons of having a king in Israel and determining who is right for the job. The story of kingship opens with YHWH's concession to allow the people to have their king, taken as a personal rejection rooted in the people's tendency to serve "other gods" (8:8). On the one hand, choosing a king is deemed an act of rebellion. On the other hand, it is permitted in light of its necessity in the face of enemy threat (see 10:1, 7). Samuel warns the people of the king's "ways" (8:11-17). He will "take," "take," "take"! From their "sons" and "daughters" to their best fields and cattle, the king will "take." And if things were not bad enough: they "shall be his slaves" (8:17b)—an echo of Egyptian bondage, but this time homegrown. But unlike back in Egypt, YHWH promises this time *not* to "answer" the people when they cry out, "because of [their] king" (1 Sam 8:18; cf. Exod 2:24-25; 3:9-10). Still, the people demand a king, so that they "may be like other nations" (1 Sam 8:20), the closest thing to a cardinal sin from the Deuteronomist's perspective.[6]

So Saul is chosen and anointed king (10:1). Signs of divine approbation include YHWH giving Saul "another heart" (8:9) and the "spirit of God possessing him" (10:10; see also 11:6). Nevertheless, divine disapproval is evident when YHWH upbraids the people for having "rejected your God, who saves you from all your calamities and your distresses" (10:18-19). Samuel is even more pointed in his farewell address: by choosing a king, the people have rejected their divine king, an act of great "wickedness" (12:12, 17).

The pros and cons of kingship are painfully embodied by Saul, who is chosen by YHWH and then rejected by YHWH, "two seemingly irreconcilable facts."[7] Moreover, there are three accounts of Saul's anointing: one private (1 Sam 9:1–10:16), one public (10:17-27a), and one marked by military victory (10:27b–11:15).[8] Saul is anointed by Samuel and confirmed with prophetic signs (10:1-16), yet he is also chosen by lot and

6. Cf. the mitigating stance in Deut 17:14-20, which allows for the appointment of a king "like all the nations" but does so in a way that prescribes a distinctive kind of reign.

7. V. Philips Long, *The Reign and Rejection of King Saul: A Case for Literary and Theological Coherence*, SBLDS 118 (Atlanta: Scholars Press, 1989), 1.

8. See Borgman's discussion of each account in *David, Saul, and God*, 18–23.

cannot be found because he is hiding among the baggage (10:17-24). Apparently, Saul does not want to be king any more than God wants Israel to have a king. On the positive side, Saul valiantly saves the people of Jabesh-gilead from the sadistic Ammonite king Nahash (10:27b–11:15), providing the occasion for this third anointing. On the negative side, Saul is rejected by Samuel because he prematurely offered a burnt offering prior to Samuel's appearance (13:1-14) and spared King Agag of the Amalekites in their defeat (15:1-9). Saul is flat-out rejected without the possibility of appeal (15:10-35).

Saul's character in the DtrH narrative turns poignantly tragic, a character both praised and vilified, eliciting both sympathy and disdain. As king, Saul does not impose any of the hardships Samuel foretold about having a king. Saul is not condemned for any policies of "taking" from the people; rather, he is rejected for cultic infractions, as if both Samuel and YHWH were looking for an excuse to remove Saul from the office of kingship. Nevertheless, Saul's misdeeds are a "symptom of a more deep-seated ill."[9] From the narrator's viewpoint, they point to Saul's refusal to obey YHWH's "commandment(s)" or "word" (10:13; 15:11, 26).[10] And there is another reason for Saul's rejection: David, "a man after [YHWH's] own heart," appointed to be "ruler over his people" (13:14). Saul's exit is necessitated by David's entrance; Saul's failures become the foils for David's success. Saul's insanity makes him unfit for office while also underlining David's sound character, who vows never to raise his hand against YHWH's anointed. One senses more than a faint whiff of royal propaganda; David's "spin doctors" are hard at work in (re)telling the tale of David at Saul's expense.[11] Even so, while Saul's character is deemed irredeemable, David's character remains complicated.

The contrast between Saul and David could not be greater. For one, David is anointed in a far different manner. Chosen among Jesse's eight

9. Long, *The Reign and Rejection of King Saul*, 167.

10. Borgman also identifies Saul's flaw with his "fearing" the people and obeying them (15:24), as well as attempting to manipulate God through ritual, tantamount to divination (v. 23). Saul is "fearfully insecure" in contrast to David (*David, Saul, and God*, 28–31, 72).

11. Even if they come a few centuries after the fact. For a concise appraisal of royal propaganda in DtrH, see McKenzie, *King David*, 25–46.

sons,[12] David is the youngest and, thus, the smallest, of the candidates for king, because YHWH "looks on the heart" and not "on outward appearance" (16:7). Saul, by contrast, was the tallest in the company (10:23). In his upcoming battle with Goliath, Saul notes that David is "just a boy" compared to warrior Goliath (17:33), who cannot handle the armor that is given him (17:38-40). Nevertheless, outward appearances count for something: David is said to be "ruddy" and "good-looking," with "beautiful eyes," as part of his youthful appearance (16:12). Elsewhere, David is noted as a "a strong man, a warrior, wise in speech, and a man of good physique"; moreover, "YHWH is with him" (16:18; cf. 10:7b). Is David a boy or a man, seasoned warrior or juvenile slingshot artist? Even with the contrasts between Saul and David drawn so sharply, David himself is a man of contrasts.

David is a "warrior" of a different order, a shepherd boy armed with five stones and a sling who refuses to carry a sword but uses Goliath's to finish him off (17:50-51). As such, David proves to be an antimilitaristic warrior, a living testimony of divine salvific power: "YHWH, who saved me from the paw of the lion and from the paw of the bear, will save me from the hand of this Philistine" (17:37; see also 17:45). David, in other words, embodies a tensive theological resolution: for this king to be truly a "man after [YHWH's] own heart" (13:14), David will have to be the human vessel of divine might. As Israel is to be like no other nation, so Israel's first dynastic king is to be unlike any other, one who showcases YHWH's strength on the battlefield through absolute dependence.

Yet David is no passive character on or off the battlefield. It is by his own initiative and ingenuity that David insinuates himself into Saul's favor as a chance worth taking against Goliath, much to the anger of David's oldest brother (17:28-30). David challenges Goliath to his face with the confidence of a victor (17:45-47). If YHWH "does not save by sword and spear," as David professes, then how does YHWH do it? By a boy with his five stones and a sling, by human "weakness" coupled with ingenuity and courage. David, the boy who would be king, is the miraculous instrument of God's salvation of a people.

12. So DtrH, but according to 1 Chron 2:15, seven sons.

David's election is met with Saul's rejection: such political polarity is a powder keg of conflict. In Saul's court, David has "success in all his undertakings," for YHWH is "with him" (18:14). His fame on the battlefield overshadows Saul's (18:7). As "YHWH's spirit came mightily upon David" from the day of his anointing, so YHWH's "spirit departed from Saul," only to be replaced by an "evil spirit" (16:13-14). In a possessed rage, Saul tries to kill David twice in the privacy of his palace (18:10-11; 19:9-10), while David spares Saul's life twice when Saul is in the most vulnerable of positions (24:1-22; 26:1-25). In each case, Saul relents from pursuing David and promises not to harm him again. Indeed, he acknowledges that David will be king and makes David swear not to "cut off [his] descendants after [him]" (24:20-21; but cf. 2 Sam 21:1-14). Nevertheless, no reconciliation is in the offing. The narrator gives a solemn assessment: "Saul was David's enemy ever after" (1 Sam 18:29).

While on the run, David nearly succumbs to becoming a "man of blood," as he is later accused of being (cf. 2 Sam 16:8). Like Robin Hood, David gathers together the distressed, the debtors, and the discontented, forming a ragtag band of armed supporters as they roam the countryside (1 Sam 22:2). With a rich property owner in Carmel named Nabal ("Fool"), a Calebite chieftain, David plays the extortionist (25:2-8). Nabal refuses David's offer of protection, and so David launches an assault that would have led to great slaughter if not for Abigail, Nabal's wife, who placates David with gifts of food and wine, thereby saving him from "bloodguilt" (25:26, 33). But Nabal dies anyway, apparently struck down by God (25:37-38), paving the way for David to "woo" Abigail and "make her his wife" (25:39). Mission accomplished: a politically advantageous marriage, one of several.[13] But how the narrator strains to clear David from criminal complicity! By divine intervention, and with Abigail's help, David is saved from "bloodguilt"—the first instance of what will prove to be a pattern of exoneration.

Case in point: David defects to the Philistines (1 Sam 27–29). The narrator claims it is David's means of escape from "the hand of Saul"

13. Immediately thereafter, it is said that David married "Ahinoam of Jezreel" (v. 43), whose identity is likely Saul's own wife (see 14:50), after Saul had given Michal to another (25:44). For discussion, see Steussy, *David*, 11–12.

(27:1). But more than asylum is in store for David: he is enlisted by King Achish of Gath to join him in his "fight against Israel" and is appointed as his "bodyguard for life" (28:1-2). Achish trusts David, thinking that he "has made himself abhorrent" to his own people (27:12). However, the narrator takes pains to point out that David makes himself a little less abhorrent by secretly engaging in raids against other enemies of Israel, including the Amalekites, while in residence in a village given to him by Achish (27:8-11). As a major battle against Israel approaches, with David and his troops bringing up the rear of the Philistine army, there is disagreement among the commanders about David joining them in battle with understandable suspicion. As a result, David is conveniently released from duty and sent back "home," where he avenges himself against the raiding Amalekites (29:11–30:20), whose spoil he distributes to the "elders of Judah" (29:26-31), proving his political savviness.

Meanwhile, Saul and his three sons, including Jonathan, are killed in battle on Mount Gilboa, far and away from David (31:1-6). Upon hearing the news, David mourns and intones a moving lamentation filled with praise for both Saul and Jonathan (2 Sam 1:19-27). In the throes of grief, David kills the messenger, conveniently an Amalekite, who presented Saul's crown to David and lied about killing Saul (2 Sam 1:6-10). David once again proves himself innocent of any complicity in Saul's demise.

A similar scenario plays out as the conflict mounts between the "house of Saul" and the "house of David" when Joab, David's general, kills Abner, commander of Saul's army, after Abner had pledged his support to David (3:12-13, 27). Once again, the concern over incurring bloodguilt is paramount, as indicated in David's response: "I and my kingdom are forever guiltless before YHWH for the blood of Abner son of Ner. May the guilt fall on the head of Joab, and on all his father's house" (3:28-29). But David does not punish Joab, who continues as David's military commander. Still, David mourns and fasts so that "all Israel" would understand that "the king had no part in the killing of Abner son of Ner" (3:36-37). If anything, David's grief is consistently strategic.

The pattern continues when Ishbaal, Saul's successor to the throne, is assassinated, and David kills the assassins who presented Ishbaal's head to David (4:11). Again, David is relieved of guilt. And after seven years and six months as king of Judah, David finally becomes "shepherd" over all Israel (5:2). After conquering Jerusalem and renaming it "the city of David" (5:9), David builds his "house" or palace and transports the "ark of the covenant" to the city with proper pomp, during which David "danced before YHWH with all his might," girded only with a linen ephod (5:14), much to Michal's felt shame (5:20). In response, David is happy to "make [himself] even more contemptible than this" (5:21), showing the lengths to which he honors YHWH to his own discredit, even with near-naked zeal. David offers well-being and burnt offerings "before YHWH," blessing the people "in the name of YHWH of hosts" and distributing food for all present (5:18), proving to be a most generous priest. Saul, it should be noted, was roundly condemned for having made the same offerings (1 Sam 13:8-14). Such is the apologetic work of the Deuteronomists.

The theological high point of the Davidic narrative is found in 2 Samuel 7, where YHWH makes a covenant with David. With the ark settled in its place, David wants to build a "house" for YHWH. The disparity between the king's cedar-lined "house" and YHWH's flapping "tent" is unbearable for David. But YHWH declines David's offer and instead offers to build a "house" for David, a "house" constructed not of cedar but of dynastic succession (7:11).[14] YHWH considers a permanent home unprecedented, given the history of YHWH's mobile presence with "all the people of Israel" (7:7-8). YHWH's expressed aim was to "plant" Israel in "their own place," a place of "rest from all . . . enemies," not to find YHWH's own place (2 Sam 7:10-11). The core of the covenant is found in YHWH's promise to establish David's kingdom through his son:

> He shall build a house for my name, and I will establish the throne of his kingdom forever. I will be a father to him, and he shall be a son to me. Whenever he does wrong, I will discipline him with a rod of men, with human blows. But my benevolence will never depart[15] from him, as I removed it from Saul, whom I removed from before you. Your house and

14. "YHWH will make you a house." Cf. 1 Chron 17:10b ("YHWH will build you a house"), referring to the temple.

15. So MT, contra LXX and Peshitta.

> your kingdom shall be made sure forever before me; your throne shall be established forever. (2 Sam 7:13-16)

David's son in question is Solomon, the temple builder, but all subsequent sons are included in YHWH's "benevolence" (*ḥesed*) or covenantal fidelity. For David, such "benevolence" is unconditional, and it translates into dynastic promise, a "benevolence" that overrides all wrongdoings committed by future kings. Punishment obtains, yes, but forbidden is the removal of YHWH's "benevolence," just as the love of a father to his son can never be removed. David and his sons, consequently, become part of YHWH's royal household, with the covenant serving as the family's theo-political DNA. David's prayerful response lifts up YHWH's incomparable status and the unique status of YHWH's people (7:18-29). As YHWH promised David to "make for [him] a great name" (7:9), so David acknowledges YHWH's great "name" (7:23, 26). The prayer expresses David's humble gratitude and YHWH's unrivaled greatness, the appropriate posture of a king before the King. As "YHWH of hosts is God over Israel," so "the house of [his] servant will be established before [YHWH]" (7:26). Both the covenant and the prayer forge an inviolable bond between YHWH's sovereign rule and the permanency of David's "house."

With "rest" achieved for David from all his enemies (2 Sam 7:1) and the dynasty firmly in place, trouble starts. David commits adultery as Joab and "all Israel" are sent out to battle at the "turn of the year" (11:1). Bad timing: David's stay at home suggests a hint of premeditation. What follows is not one but two crimes: the rape[16] of Bathsheba and the murder of her husband, Uriah the Hittite, the latter resulting from the former. The narrative is terse regarding the first crime. After spying Bathsheba

16. Interpretations of the encounter between David and Bathsheba range from a love story to Bathsheba's attempt to seduce David and manipulate him to gain access to the royal court. I simply note that the power differential between them cannot be overlooked, casting suspicion of any possibility of consent on Bathsheba's part. Moreover, Nathan's parable highlights forced violation (v. 4), and Amnon's rape of Tamar marks a fitting correspondence (13:1-19). See Suzanne Scholz, *Sacred Witness: Rape in the Hebrew Bible* (Minneapolis: Fortress, 2010), 99–102; Wilda C. Gafney, *Womanist Midrash: A Reintroduction to the Women of the Torah and the Throne* (Louisville, KY: Westminster John Knox, 2017), 214–15.

bathing from his rooftop,[17] "David sent messengers to get her, and she came to him, and he lay with her. . . . Then she returned to her house" (11:4). The contrast with David's wooing of the widowed Abigail is unmistakable. David on the run does not "take" Abigail on first encounter. But David on the throne takes Bathsheba at first sight. Moreover, David later plots to have Bathsheba become a widow in order to have her, whereas his hands appear clean when it comes to Abigail's widowed status (1 Sam 25:39). Nevertheless, Abigail's widowhood is desired by David as his vindication. Either way, David gets what he wants. The difference is that David gets Bathsheba by virtue of his royal privilege.

David's murder of Uriah, the second crime, is recounted in far greater detail than the rape (2 Sam 11:5-26). David tries to fix the timing of Bathsheba's pregnancy by giving Uriah the opportunity to have intercourse with her. When that plan failed, David has him killed in battle. Plan B works, and David, waiting dutifully after Bathsheba's period of mourning, "sent and brought her to his house, and she became his wife" (11:27a). Such was Bathsheba's abduction into marriage. The episode, however, concludes with a negative assessment: "The thing that David had done displeased YHWH" (11:27b). The line is finally drawn.

Enter Nathan, David's prophet. The encounter recounted in 2 Samuel 12 features a rhetorical masterpiece of "gotcha." As David sent his messengers to Bathsheba to abduct her, so YHWH "sends" Nathan to convict David. Nathan tells a parable that provokes David's anger to give judgment against the villain in the story, to which the prophet famously declares, "You are the man!" (12:7a). YHWH's judgment follows: by using the sword to kill Uriah and take his wife, David himself must suffer the sword, which "will never depart from [his] house" (12:10a). The verb "depart" (√*swr*) is the same verb deployed in the covenantal promise of YHWH's "benevolence" never "departing" from David's son(s) (7:15). Now David's kingdom abides in both "benevolence" and the sword. David's confessional response is as simple as it is effective: "I have sinned against YHWH" (12:13a). David repents, something that kings are not known to do, including Israel's kings. David's repentance sets himself

17. Not Bathsheba bathing on her roof, contrary to many artistic depictions.

apart from Saul, as it also does from most of his successors. He does not protest or act defensively, like Saul.[18] It is in this moment of confession that David's character is defined "before YHWH." David's confession prompts the prophet to declare, "Now YHWH has put away [√ *'br*] your sin; you shall not die" (12:13). Nevertheless, Bathsheba's firstborn shall die. The king who was given Saul's kingdom has grasped for even more and "despised YHWH's word" (12:8-9). The crime is summarized as follows: "You have struck down Uriah the Hittite with the sword and taken his wife to be your wife and killed him with the sword of the Ammonites" (12:9b). Marriage by murder.

David cannot be exonerated this time. He has proven himself to be a "man of blood," having escaped bloodguilt by the skin of his teeth until now, as if the narrator were saving David's guilt for this seminal moment.[19] Before Bathsheba, David was made of "Teflon," able to deflect all hints of criminality and complicity. Consequently, YHWH's covenant is tested, not by David's sons but by David himself, nearly to the point of dissolving his rule. Violence within David's family, beginning with that of rape, rips through his kingdom: Amnon rapes sister Tamar; Absalom avenges Tamar by murdering Amnon and then, in due time, usurps the throne, all the while David acts as an indulgent father at his own expense and that of the kingdom.[20] Absalom comes to steal "the hearts of the people" (15:6), and David is once again forced to take flight, but this time as a royal refugee rather than as a fleeing renegade. Nevertheless, David's heart yearns for his son Absalom, as he orders his army to "deal gently for my sake with the young man Absalom" (18:5). Earlier he had forgiven him for having murdered Amnon (14:38). David's love for Absalom is awkwardly excessive, politically speaking: upon hearing of Absalom's death, David mourns to the point of shaming his soldiers (19:3).

18. Borgman, *David, Saul, and God*, 209.

19. As is often noted, the Bathsheba episode is a late insertion in the narrative that serves as an indictment or warrant for the violent conflicts that transpire thereafter, culminating in Absalom's usurpation of the throne (see 2 Sam 12:11-12).

20. For this repeated pattern in biblical narrative, see Borgman, *David, Saul, and God*, 121–49.

When David left his city, Jerusalem, he was cursed as a "man of blood" by Shimei, a man from Saul's family (16:8). David accepted such abuse in hope that "YHWH will look on my distress,[21] such that YHWH will repay me with good for this cursing of me today" (16:12). Upon return, David shows mercy to Shimei and swears not to kill him. The "man of blood," in this case, avoids shedding blood. But not for long. Violence continues: a rebellion is suppressed in the north, prompted by the rallying cry, "We have no portion in David!" which includes all Israel minus Judah (20:1). Joab, David's own "man of blood," murders Amasa, who had served as Absalom's general in Jerusalem in place of Joab but threw his support to David once David returned (20:10). David avenges the Gibeonites by handing over seven of Saul's sons to be impaled (21:1-6), contrary to his sworn promise to Saul in 1 Samuel 24:21-22. The narrative apologetically lays the bloodguilt upon Saul (2 Sam 21:1). In the end, amid valiant victories, David sings a song of thanksgiving, crediting YHWH as his "rock" and salvation on the battlefield (2 Sam 22:2-51 = Ps 18). David's "last words" celebrate his just rule "in the fear of God," likened to the dawning of a new day, and the "everlasting covenant" that God established for David's dynastic "house" (2 Sam 23:1-7). Here, the covenant is not only about the perpetuation of the dynasty but about the ordering of a just and prosperous rule (23:5).

But David's story does not conclude with such a happy ending. The narrative continues with David conducting a census of "Israel and Judah," over Joab's objections (24:1). The count was to determine how many could "draw the sword" (24:9), demonstrating reliance more upon human strength in numbers than upon YHWH's might. After completing the census, David acknowledges his sin and prays that YHWH take away his guilt (24:10). David now says, in effect, "I am the man" who sinned—the self-scrutinizing counterpart to Nathan's "You are the man."[22] Nevertheless, punishment ensues, whose particular form rests entirely on David's choice: three years of famine, three months of pursuit by his enemies, or three days of pestilence. David chooses the one that he had not yet experienced:

---

21. Read *bĕʿonyî* for MT *baʿăwōnî* ("my iniquity").

22. Borgman, *David, Saul, and God*, 214.

pestilence, which breaks out killing seventy-thousand people but sparing Jerusalem (24:10-17). In response, David builds an altar on the threshing floor of Araunah the Jebusite in Jerusalem, where the destroying messenger of YHWH stands (24:16-17),[23] prompting David to confess, "I alone have sinned, and I alone have committed wickedness. But these sheep—what have they done [wrong]? Please, let your hand be against me and against my father's house" (24:17). In acknowledging his sin, David remains the mindful shepherd of his kingdom (24:24). That is his true calling, even if his character has not been fully receptive to it until now.

While David concludes his life in impotence (1 Kgs 1:1-4), the fight over his successor escalates.[24] In his dotage, David is convinced by Bathsheba and Nathan into naming Solomon king rather than Adonijah, the next in line to the throne (1 Kgs 1:5-31). Once he agrees, David rises to the occasion and takes charge by orchestrating Solomon's succession to the throne (5:32-35). When the dust settles, Solomon has secured the throne, and he receives advice from the erstwhile king. Narratively speaking, David's instructions to Solomon constitute his actual "last words," and they are not filled with oracular praise of his dynasty and God's faithful benevolence, as in 2 Samuel 23:2-7. Instead, they are more like mafia instructions. But first David, in fine Deuteronomistic fashion, impresses upon his son the importance of following "the law of Moses," the first time the phrase is used in the Davidic narrative (1 Kgs 2:3). By imparting such advice, David echoes YHWH's words to Joshua (Josh 1:6-9). David also casts the covenant conditionally: "If your heirs preserve their way by walking before me faithfully . . . there shall not fail you a successor on the throne of Israel" (1 Kgs 2:4). Nothing is said about God's benevolence. Solomon and his successors, in other words, have to "toe the line," or else.

But David's truly final words are instructions for Solomon to mete out vengeance. First, Joab is to be executed for having "retaliated in a time of peace for blood that had been shed in war" by murdering Abner and Amasa (1 Kgs 2:5-6). Second, Solomon is to ensure that Shimei, the

23. According to the Chronicler, David's altar is the site for the future temple (22:1).

24. As McKenzie notes, the focus of the apologetic account shifts from David to Solomon (*King David*, 176–80).

Saulide who cursed David during his departure from Jerusalem, be held accountable, even though David had promised not to kill him (2:8-9; cf. 2 Sam 19:23). "You are a wise man; you will know what to do," David instructs his son (2:9; cf. 2:6). David, the dying mafia don, instructs his heir on taking care of matters that he himself could not bring himself to do.[25] Solomon succeeds in fulfilling his father's wishes, faithful son and "wise" king that he is.

The DtrH portrait of David is complex, reflecting in part the complexities of kingship in Israel. David's own character is a mixture of humility and audacity, of ingenuity and initiative, on the one hand, and utter dependence and reliance upon YHWH, on the other. He is both commander and consoler in chief. His love for family verges on the indulgent, and his mourning over others, including his "enemy" Saul, is as intense as it is strategic. One primary concern of the Dtr narrator(s) is how to keep David's royal integrity intact during his rise to power and throughout his rule. His acts of kindness can easily be interpreted as politically driven, whether it is distributing the spoils of war to the elders of Judah (1 Sam 30:26-31), or mourning the deaths of Saul and Jonathan (2 Sam 1:11-17), or praising the people of Jabesh-gilead for burying Saul (2 Sam 2:5-6), or keeping a watchful eye on Mephibosheth/Meribbaal at the king's table (2 Sam 9:11), placing him effectively under palace arrest. David's respect for Saul as "YHWH's anointed" reflects his respect for the royal office that will be his.

On the other hand, David's escapes from incrimination are as narrow as they are myriad: the deaths of Nabal, Saul and Jonathan, Abner, and Ishbaal, as well as his defection to the Philistines. But there is a twofold crime that David cannot be excused from, which the DtrH considers to be the near-fatal crack in his rule. While David confesses only after getting caught (1 Sam 12:13), severe punishment ensues. The sword never departs from David's house (12:10). And David never departs from mourning, lamenting, and seeking forgiveness. From shepherd boy to royal shepherd, David is as penitent as he is perpetrator, both culpable and consecrated, guilty and innocent. David is a man of moral complexities reflecting in

25. Perhaps because David was actually complicit in the murders conducted by Joab throughout his reign. See McKenzie, *King David*, 117–22, 172.

part the complexities of kingdom building, and because of that he is a dilemma for posterity.

David Idealized in the Chronicler's History

David is not so complex in the Chronicler's selective rewriting of David's narrative in DtrH. Written at least a couple of centuries later (fourth century BCE), the Chronicler's history leaves out a host of inconvenient truths, such as David's crimes against Bathsheba and Uriah, as well as Absalom's nearly successful revolt. The Chronicler, moreover, omits most of the narrative of David's rise to power over Saul and much of Israel. Neither renegade nor refugee, David in 1 Chronicles has "all Israel" behind him from the very beginning.

As in DtrH, David in Chronicles is barred by God from building the temple (cf. 1 Chron 17:1-15). But the Chronicler offers a further reason: David's bloodshed on the battlefield, which renders him unfit to build the temple (22:8; 28:3). One recalls Shimei's curse of David as a "man of blood" in DtrH for having exterminated much of "the house of Saul" (2 Sam 16:8).[26] But such crimes in Shimei's eyes are overlooked by the Chronicler. Instead, David's bloodshed comes from his military ventures (18:1-13; 19:1-19; 20:1-8) and perhaps from the plague prompted by his census taking (21:1-17). Indeed, David's one misstep, according to the Chronicler, was conducting the census, incited by "Satan" (21:1; cf. 2 Sam 24:1), which led to many deaths but also to locating the site for the future temple (1 Chron 21:28–22:1). Otherwise, David had no need to ask forgiveness from God (1 Chron 21:17). Thus, the "man of blood" in DtrH (2 Sam 16:8) bears comparatively little bloodguilt in Chronicles. Overall, the Chronicler transfers the "blood" that Shimei identified as David's *morally* culpable violence into the *cultic* or ritual domain, specifically the blood of David's "great wars" (1 Chron 22:8).[27] God will have no bloody warrior build the temple. Only a "man of peace" can do the honors

26. Shimei is likely referring to the murder of Abner (1 Sam 3:22-30) and the assassination of Ishbaal (4:1-12), perhaps also the deaths of Saul and Jonathan on the battlefield (31:1-13). His curse, moreover, anticipates the execution of Saul's seven "sons" at Gibeon (21:1-14).

27. See Sara Japhet, *I and II Chronicles: A Commentary*, OTL (Louisville, KY: Westminster John Knox, 1993), 397.

(1 Chron 22:9). Nevertheless, the Chronicler finds a backdoor for David that allows him to put his handprint on the future temple.

Unlike DtrH, the Chronicler conjures an excuse for David to be involved with temple building: Solomon is deemed too "young and inexperienced" (*naʿar wārāk*) to do the job by himself (1 Chron 22:5; 29:1). So David comes to the rescue not only by providing Solomon with all the resources needed for temple construction but also by appointing all the personnel for its organization.[28] As David testifies to his son, "With great pains I have provided for YHWH's house" (22:14). Indeed. David's legacy turns out to be not just dynastic[29] but also sacral. In the Chronicler's hands, David becomes the founder and planner of the temple, stealing much of the limelight from Solomon. It makes sense for a new time and context when Israel, now the Persian province Yehud, no longer had a Davidic king. The Chronicler took pains to ensure that the community at least had a temple, a temple to claim as Davidic. Despite the loss of the monarchy, worship could continue, *thanks to David*.[30] With the restoration of the temple under Persian hegemony, something of David's legacy is also restored. The Davidic kingdom lives on in the temple. In the end, David died "a good old age, full of days" (1 Chron 29:28), quite different from the picture of David in his decrepitude in 1 Kings 1:1; 2:10. The transition of power in the Chronicler's account is peaceful, without any hint of artifice or conflict, all under David's guidance, the perfect end for a nearly perfect king.

In sum, the Chronicler's account of David is not so much a "cover up" as a reorientation. To be sure, 1 Chronicles presupposes awareness of the tangled web woven in David's rise to power and in the tragic court history as told in DtrH. The Chronicler knows that his readers know of David's misdeeds. Otherwise, he would have reached farther back in history to revise David's rise to power, rather than simply leave most of it behind. The Chronicler, rather, streamlines and embellishes the narrative with the heaviest of hands to focus only on the mostly positive aspects of the story

28. 1 Chron 23:1–24:31; 25:1-31; 26:1-19, 20-28.

29. Note the one major difference regarding God's covenant with David between 1 Sam 7:1-17 (esp. v. 14) and 1 Chron 17:1-15 (esp. vv. 13-14): there is no threat of punishment in the Chronicler's version.

30. See Steussy, *David*, 126.

so that David remains "strong and mighty," glorious king that he is. The Chronicler offers a counterproposal regarding David's legacy: for a people once disrupted by exile but now reconstituted in the land, it is better to focus on David's estimable qualities, particularly those that support David's status as kingdom builder and, more fundamentally, temple founder. The Chronicler renders David in "stained glass,"[31] and the people, in turn, become more of a congregation than a nation.[32] If David's legacy cannot be dynastic, it can at least be cultic, so reasons the Chronicler. The temple outweighs the throne.

The Deuteronomist's presentation of David and that of the Chronicler part ways because they address two different historical situations: Israel in exile and Israel back in the land. The Deuteronomist asks, Why did Israel have to suffer exile?, and answers by highlighting the sins of certain kings, from David's to Manasseh's (see 2 Kgs 23:26-27). The Chronicler responds to a people no longer in exile by highlighting David's estimable qualities and influence in building the temple, forging a new connection with the past. That both "historical" accounts are preserved provides the grounds for continued dialogue.

In the Psalms, the "David dilemma" is resolved differently; his portrayal is painted with different strokes. What do the psalmists overlook, emphasize, and add about David? What do they consider estimable about this complicated king? What are David's defining legacies for the worshipping community? In the hands of the psalmists David is a different David.

David in the Psalms

It would be an understatement to say that David figures significantly in the Psalms. While David is mentioned only twelve times *in* the Psalms, nearly half of the psalms in the Psalter are attributed to him in some fashion, typically with the ascription "of David" (*lĕdāwid*). Whereas the Hebrew Masoretic text attributes seventy-three psalms to David, the Septuagint (LXX) increases that by fourteen and adds the "extra" Davidic

31. Steussy applies the metaphor to all of Chronicles, in contrast to the more subtle, complex, and darker portrayal given in DtrH (*David*, 5, 99).

32. Steussy, *David*, 125.

Psalm 151,[33] which retells David's younger years leading to his triumph over Goliath. Over time, the entire book of Psalms came to be considered David's book, comparable to the Pentateuch "becoming" Moses's work. Noting the fivefold structure of the Psalms, the rabbis commented that "Moses gave the five books of Torah, and David gave the five books of Psalms."[34] As much as Moses was regarded as the prototype of the lawgiver, David came to be the prototypical psalmist.[35]

David *within* the Psalms

The vast majority of the psalms associated with David are protests and prayers for help, thus profiling David as the consummate petitioner. We begin with certain references to David *within* the psalms, where David is commonly referred to not as Israel's "king" but as God's "servant."[36]

Psalm 78: David as Consummate Servant and Israel's Consummation

The designation "servant" has a twofold nuance: service to God and leadership for the people, as described, for example, in the final strophe of Psalm 78.

> Instead, [YHWH] chose the tribe of Judah,
> the mountain of Zion, which he loves.
> He built his sanctuary like the high heavens,[37]
> like the earth, which he founded forever.

33. The one exception is Psalm 133, in which LXX does not bear Davidic attribution, suggesting an earlier Psalter composed of seventy-two psalms.

34. William G. Braude, *The Midrash on Psalms*, vol. 1, Yale Judaica Series 13 (New Haven, CT: Yale University Press, 1952), 3.2.

35. Norman K. Gottwald, *The Hebrew Bible: A Socio-literary Introduction* (Philadelphia: Fortress, 1985), 14.

36. Pss 78:70; 89:3[4], 20[21]; 132:10; 144:10. "Servant" also designates Abraham (105:6) and Moses (105:26), as well as the psalmic speaker (e.g., Pss 19:11[12], 13[14]; 31:16[17]; 69:17[18]; 116:16; 119:17; 143:12).

37. Read with *BHS kimrōmîm* for MT *kĕmô-rāmîm* ("like high things").

And he chose David, his servant, taking him from the sheepfolds.
He brought him from [tending] the nursing ewes,
to shepherd Jacob his people,
Israel his possession.
He shepherded them with a heart of integrity;[38]
and with the skill of his hands he led them. (78:68-72)

Consonant with YHWH's choice of Judah and Zion, David is chosen to lead the people as YHWH's "servant" and the people's "shepherd." The parallel between Zion and David is unmistakable: both are "chosen" by YHWH. As YHWH built "his sanctuary like the high heavens," so YHWH raised up "his servant" to royal status. Moreover, the temple is mentioned prior to David, a poetic reversal of order that highlights both as parallel tracks of God's work. Given its cosmic connection, the temple is attributed to YHWH's handiwork (78:69), not David's or Solomon's. David's agency is focused exclusively on "shepherding." This shepherd of the sheep is chosen to be a shepherd of the people (78:71-72; cf. Matt 4:18-19). Shepherding is what David does best, and what God does best is orchestrate it all.

In Psalm 78, shepherding takes on the sense of tender leadership, caring for the "nursing ewes" (78:71a), in contrast to how the boy David describes himself as a warrior shepherd in 1 Samuel 17:36, slaying lions and bears. In the psalm, David's leadership is focused internally on caring for the kingdom rather than on expanding it imperially. His integrity and skills represent an ideal combination for any ruler, both mercifully unproblematic in the psalmist's estimation.

As the consummate "servant shepherd," David also marks a consummation in Israel's history. The relationship between Israel and YHWH, characterized by Israel's disobedience and YHWH's forbearance, is finally resolved with the choice of David as Israel's new leader. Concluding the psalm, David also marks a new beginning in Israel's relationship with YHWH, filled with the hope of faithful obedience.

38. Literally, "with the integrity of his heart." Read *bĕtōm* for MT *kĕtōm* ("like integrity").

Psalm 89: From Divinely Promised Dynasty to Divinely Wrought Disaster

Two psalms in particular provide rich profiles of David but in strikingly different ways: Psalms 89 and 132. One provides a transcendent perspective; the other is more immanent in orientation. But both convey hardship on David's account. We begin with Psalm 89.

> Your benevolence, YHWH, I shall forever sing;
> from generation to generation I shall proclaim
> your faithfulness with my mouth.
> For you[39] have declared,
> "[My] benevolence is established forever in the heavens;[40]
> my faithfulness is fixed in them.
> I have made a covenant with my chosen one;
> I have sworn to David, my servant:
> I will establish your seed forever,
> and I will build up your throne from generation to generation."
> (89:1-4[2-5])

Psalm 89 features a song of YHWH's "benevolence" (*ḥesed*) and "faithfulness" (*'ĕmûnâ*), a pairing that reoccurs throughout the psalm culminating in YHWH's "covenant" with David (89:2[3], 28[29], 34[35], 39[40]). It is in covenant that YHWH's "benevolence" and "faithfulness" find their convergence. It is in covenant that David's "seed" and "throne" are established. David's uninterrupted line constitutes the kingdom's everlasting duration.

As the recipient of such covenant, David is deemed both YHWH's "chosen one" and "servant." From the people's perspective, David is their "shield" of protection, possessed by YHWH (89:18a[19b]). He is also deemed YHWH's crowned "warrior," especially chosen from his own people (89:19[20]) and "anointed" with YHWH's "holy oil" (89:20b[21b]). David's chosen status is evocatively depicted with parental imagery:

---

39. Read with LXX as second person for MT "I have declared."

40. Read *baššāmayim* ("in the heavens") for MT "heavens."

He will call to me: "You are my father,
my God, the rock of my salvation."
Indeed, I will make him firstborn,
highest[41] of the kings of the earth. (89:26-27[27-28])

Echoing the divine decree in Psalm 2:7, the psalmist gives YHWH's promise to the Davidic king a powerful familial twist. "Father" and "firstborn": such privileged-laden parental language enhances the king's status before God, surpassing all other kings on the earth.

As YHWH's "firstborn," the king reflects the power of his divine progenitor, as one can see in these comparable passages in Psalm 89.

9[10]You are the one who rules over the swelling of the sea; you are the one who stills the surging of its waves.	20[21]I have found David my servant; I anointed him with my holy oil.
10[11]It is you who crushed Rahab like a corpse; with your strong arm you scattered your enemies.	21[22]Thus, my hand will remain steadfast for him; indeed, my arm will empower him.
11[12]The heavens are yo urs, so also the earth; the world and its fullness—you founded them.	22[23]No enemy will ravage him, and no malevolent person will afflict him.
12[13]North and South—you created them; Tabor and Hermon joyously praise your name.	23[24]I will crush his foes before him, and will strike down those who hate him.
13[14]Your arm is [endowed] with strength; your hand is strong; your right hand is raised high.	24[25]My faithfulness and benevolence are with him; by my name his horn is exalted.
14[15]Righteousness and justice are the foundation of your throne; benevolence and faithfulness appear before you.	25[26]I set his hand on the sea, his right hand on the rivers.

On the left column, the speaker gives praise for YHWH's sovereign rule over the "swelling" sea and "surging" waves, recalling YHWH's victory over Rahab, a monster of chaos (89:10[11]; cf. Job 26:12). YHWH's power is anatomized with the image of the arm/hand (89:13[14]). Similarly, on the right column the earthly king is promised YHWH's hand/arm of strength (89:21[22]), such that even the king's hand is extended to

41. Or "the most high," the only instance in the Psalter in which *'elyôn* refers to the king.

the "sea" and "rivers" to exert cosmological control (89:25[26]). In both sections, "benevolence" and "faithfulness" are inseparably bound: they are, on the one hand, YHWH's central attributes "appearing" before YHWH (89:14b[15b]). On the other, they are promised to be "with" the king (89:24a[25a]). As YHWH "crushed" Rahab and "scattered" the enemies, so the king's "foes" will be crushed and struck down (89:23[24]). The king's rule reflects YHWH's rule.

The highlight of Psalm 89 is YHWH's covenant with David, a solemn unilateral promise founded on a gracious fidelity so strong that it supersedes any failure of obedience on the part of David's descendants (89:26-35[27-36]). In covenant, YHWH promises to establish David's "seed" and "throne" forever (89:29[30]; cf. 89:4[5]). YHWH's "benevolence" will never be removed; YHWH's "faithfulness" will never be betrayed (89:33[34]); YHWH's "covenant" will never be breached (89:34a[35a]). Punishment will be exacted, but YHWH's "benevolence will never be forsaken" (89:30-32[31-33]). Such covenantal promise is solemnly sworn by YHWH's own "holiness," no less (89:35[36]). Thus, David's "seed" and "throne" will endure forever, like the sun and the moon (89:36-37[37-38]).

So who is David so far in Psalm 89? Compared to DtrH, David in Psalm 89 is larger than life; he is self-transcendent in power. David is YHWH's "chosen one" and "servant," YHWH's anointed "warrior," the "horn" of the people and YHWH's "shield" (89:17-18[18-19]). David is YHWH's "firstborn," the preeminent recipient of a dynastic covenant that promises everlasting rule. YHWH's incomparability among the "godlings" (*bĕnê ʾēlîm*) is reflected in David's unrivaled status among the "kings of the earth" (89:27b[28b]). His sovereignty emulates YHWH's sovereignty. David is the very royal image of a very royal God. David is as everlasting as creation is everlasting, for David in Psalm 89 is no less than the divinely ordained dynasty of a nation. There is nothing problematic about David here. David's "self" is his everlasting rule.

But "everlasting" turns out to not last very long. From 89:38[39] to the bitter end, Psalm 89 takes a devastating turn, so also David's dynasty. The "chosen one" is now "rejected," the object of YHWH's scorn. YHWH has breached the covenant and, in so doing, turned against David. The psalm details blow by blow how YHWH has reneged on the promise of dynastic rule (89:38-45[39-46]) by rejecting David (89:38[39]), repudiating the covenant (89:39a[40a]), desecrating the crown (89:39b[40b]), destroying Jerusalem (89:40-41[41-42]), empowering David's enemies (89:42-43[43-44]), destroying his throne (89:44[45]), and bringing about defeat (89:45[46]). The speaker registers shock at YHWH's unwarranted anger directed against YHWH's own "anointed." David's "walls" and "strongholds" are breached and broken (89:40[41]). David, the destroyed dynasty, is also the ruined "city of David" (cf. 2 Sam 5:7, 9). With David's city destroyed and his crown desecrated, YHWH has profaned "his" own holiness (see 89:34a[35a], 38b[39b]). How could this be? YHWH promised to uphold the covenant forever; YHWH would never lie to David (89:34-35[35-36]).

Psalm 89:49a[50a] culminates with a final question: "Where are your benevolent acts of old?" recalling and countering the very first verse ("Your benevolence, YHWH, I shall forever sing"). Praise has turned to lament. While the "wonders" of YHWH's benevolence toward David are exuberantly recounted in praise (89:1-37[2-38]), they are now treated as artifacts of the past, buried in oblivion by YHWH's breach of covenant. Where are they now? The question is not asked out of curiosity; it is posed as a protest. The "benevolent acts" of the past were meant to continue into the present by virtue of David's dynastic legacy. The promise was for eternity, because such promises were sworn to David in "faithfulness" (89:49b[50b]).

The psalm ends with the "anointed" one complaining of the "abuses" he has suffered from "all the peoples' discords" and from the defiance of his enemies (89:50b[51b]). The first-person language at the psalm's conclusion reveals the speaker to be David himself. David's downfall was sudden, decisive, and, from start to finish, inconceivable. From YHWH's chosen one to the object of divine rejection, from anointed servant to suffering servant, from transcendent to "transient" (89:47[48]), David proves to be a character of extremes, a casualty of divine contradiction. David is at once a human being and a royal office, a dynasty for the ages and a representative of the human condition. As goes David, so goes the kingdom, so goes the city, so goes the people, so goes all humanity, sinking into ruin.

Nevertheless, there remains a power that the Davidic speaker holds. The latter half of Psalm 89 boldly testifies to the power of protest, of holding YHWH accountable for committing such an unconscionable miscarriage of justice. The favored recipient of YHWH's covenantal promise has every right to charge YHWH with covenantal malfeasance, and he exercises that right with all the audacity that it requires. Due to YHWH's failure of faithfulness, David's downfall from imperial power to undeserving victim marks David's rise in complaintive boldness. It is in his weakness that David musters the strength to call YHWH to account. It is such power, the power of protest, that far exceeds any portrait of David in DtrH. In Pentateuchal narrative, such power was demonstrated by Moses (cf. Exod 32:11-14; Num 11:11-15). But David was never so bold before YHWH, until he "ventured" into the Psalms.

Psalm 132: David's Restless Zeal

Whereas Psalm 89 is about one oath, Psalm 132 is a tale of two oaths: David's and YHWH's.

> Remember, YHWH, for David's sake
> all the hardship he endured.[42]
> How he swore to YHWH,
> vowing to the Mighty One of Jacob,
> "I will not enter the tent of my house,
> or go up to my bed,
> I will not give sleep[43] to my eyes,
> nor slumber to my eyelids,
> until I find a place for YHWH,
> an abode[44] for the Mighty One of Jacob." (132:1-5)

42. So MT, literally "his being afflicted."

43. Read *šēnāt* with the archaic feminine ending (absolute).

44. Or "tabernacle" (*miškānôt*).

The speaker calls upon YHWH to remember David (132:1) and to act accordingly in support of YHWH's "anointed" (132:10). YHWH is asked specifically to remember David's singular resolve to establish a dwelling place for YHWH, officially sworn and painfully fulfilled. The speaker reminds YHWH of the painful nature of David's oath-sworn commitment, his "hardship," specifically his sacrifice of sleep. Such deprivation illustrates the extent to which David is committed to establishing YHWH's place. The irony is that this place is itself a "resting place" (132:8, 14). David foregoes rest to establish YHWH's rest.

The psalm follows with an exhortation to make pilgrimage to YHWH's "abode" or "footstool" (132:6-7; see Ps 99:5). At the same time, YHWH is implored to "arise" (*qûmāh*) to the designated "resting place" (*mĕnûḥâ*), accompanied by the ark (v. 8) and a worshipping entourage (132:8-9). In DtrH, David is prohibited by God from building a dwelling place for God; the task is left for his son Solomon to fulfill (2 Sam 7:5-13). In the Chronicler's history, although likewise forbidden to build the temple (1 Chron 22:8), David locates the site for the temple's construction and provides all the resources needed for Solomon to follow through (22:1; 28:2, 11-19). As in the Chronicler's account, David in Psalm 132 establishes the place or location of YHWH's "abode" (132:5). The theme of "rest" resonates in all three accounts but in different ways. While Psalm 132 identifies YHWH's chosen place as YHWH's "resting place" (132:8, 14), DtrH makes no mention of divine "rest" under David. Once the ark is settled in its place, rest is established for the king, but not for God; the temple is yet to be built (2 Sam 7:1, 11; cf. 1 Kgs 5:4). The Chronicler, however, stresses the people's "rest," granted by YHWH, now that YHWH dwells in Jerusalem (1 Chron 23:25; cf. 1 Kgs 8:56). In the psalm, David's "rest," if one can call it that, is his royal empowerment (132:17-18).

In comparison to the DtrH, Psalm 132 replaces David's intent to *build* a house for YHWH (2 Sam 7:2-3) with David's resolve to *find* a place for YHWH. The former is foiled by God in the narrative accounts: it was not David's place to build a place for YHWH. In the psalm, even David's desire to do so is erased. Nevertheless, the psalm implies that by finding YHWH's "dwelling *place*" (*māqôm*/*miškānôt*), David laid the foundation for a permanent abode. Equally so, David prompted YHWH to make a covenantal promise, a divine oath sworn in response to David's oath (132:3-5), but with a different slant from the one given in Psalm 89.

> For the sake of David, your servant,
> do not turn away the face of your anointed.
> YHWH has sworn to David,
> a sure oath from which he will not turn back:
> "One from the fruit of your body
> I will set on your throne.
> If your sons keep my covenant
> and my testimonies, which I will teach them,
> then also their sons shall sit forevermore on your throne."
> For YHWH has chosen Zion;
> he desired it for his habitation:
> "This is my resting place forevermore;
> here I shall reside, for I have desired it." (132:10-14)

The oath begins with an appeal that YHWH, "for David's sake," not reject the "anointed" one, as if to rectify the reality of rejection conveyed in Psalm 89:38-45[39-46]. "For David's sake" points to YHWH's covenant with David. Explicated in 132:11b-12, the divine oath sets forth YHWH's commitment to ensure an uninterrupted rule for David, but with one condition: David's descendants must "keep" YHWH's "covenant" and "testimonies" in order to remain on the throne. Otherwise, violation of the covenant will result in an interruption of the royal lineage for subsequent generations.

The covenantal oath of Psalm 132 distinguishes itself from the unconditional promises given to David elsewhere. In Psalm 89, if YHWH's *tôrâ* is not kept, punishment will be meted out, but YHWH's "benevolence" (*ḥesed*) will remain steadfast, never to be "removed." So also in 2 Sam 7:14b-15. Psalm 132, however, qualifies YHWH's oath by omitting two things: the permanence of YHWH's "benevolence," on the one hand, and punishment, on the other. At the same time, the psalm identifies "covenant" with "stipulations" or divine decrees (*ʿēdōt*), which are to be obeyed, in contrast to Psalm 89, which distinguishes YHWH's "covenant" from YHWH's stipulations to be followed by the king (132:30-32[31-33]). Psalm 132, moreover, casts the covenantal formulation positively, even if conditionally: if David's descendants uphold the "covenant," YHWH will uphold David's lineage. The psalmist could have easily turned it negatively: "If your sons do *not* keep my covenant, then their sons shall *not* sit permanently on your throne." But the psalmist did not take the negative route, thereby carrying a greater sense of hope. In addition, the "throne" remains David's ("your throne"), with or without his sons.[45]

The psalm follows YHWH's oath for the dynasty with YHWH's choice of Zion as "habitation" (*môšāb*) and "resting place" (*mĕnûḥâ*; cf. 132:8b). What the people petitioned in 132:8 is now given divine declaration in 132:14. While divine residence and the Davidic dynasty are inseparably intertwined, it is YHWH's sanctuary "abode" that is given unconditional permanence, not the dynasty! Zion holds sway as YHWH's permanent dwelling place, no strings attached, even if the Davidic kingdom falls, conditioned as it is on the conduct of kings. Nevertheless, the psalm ends with the promise of a "horn to sprout up for David" (132:17), a symbol of royal power,[46] and a "lamp," a symbol of God's protective guidance.[47] Instead of the language of dynastic "house," as one finds in 2 Samuel 7, the psalmist chooses "horn" and "lamp" to illustrate YHWH's promise, perhaps particularly in times of disruption: while a "house" suggests uninterrupted succession, a "sprouting horn" evokes restoration, like a "shoot" from the "stump of Jesse" (Isa 11:1). The key to David's lasting power lies in one simple word: "there" (*šām*), referring to Zion (132:17). David's glory has its home in Zion, where YHWH is at home. As a "sprouting horn," David's dynasty has its roots in Zion. With YHWH at "rest" in Zion, so David also finds rest in Zion, his rest in power.

45. The closest parallel is found in 1 Kgs 2:4, where the covenant is also given its conditional spin.

46. Cf. Pss 89:17-18[18-19]; 92:10; 148:14.

47. Cf. 2 Sam 22:29; Ps 119:105.

Psalms 89 and 132 offer different but related profiles of David. Both stipulate YHWH's covenant with David but in divergent ways. Psalm 89 presents the covenant as unconditional, followed by the most disastrous of consequences. Psalm 132 casts it conditionally, but as positively as possible. One could say that as Psalm 89 queries what to do with an unconditional covenant broken by God, Psalm 132 answers by conditionalizing the covenant, to suggest that the fault lies not in YHWH's unfaithfulness but in the faithlessness of David's descendants. Such is the tack taken also in the DtrH, who attributes the demise of Judah to the unpardonable "provocations" of King Manasseh (2 Kgs 23:26-27). Did the Davidic covenant fail on the human end or on the divine end? That is the question, and it yields two very different answers.

As much as David is dynastically transcendent in Psalm 89, so he is singularly resolute, to the point of severe hardship in Psalm 132 (cf. 1 Chron 22:14). In both psalms, David turns out to be a suffering servant, but for very different reasons. In Psalm 89, David is the victim of a divine breach of covenant, forsaken and rejected. As if in response, Psalm 132:10 petitions YHWH not to reject David. Instead, David is the victim of his own zeal, afflicted and self-deprived, whose cause is fully warranted. In Psalm 89, David rises up to call YHWH to account and seek redress. In Psalm 132, David rises up to seek YHWH's rest and, thus, his own. But as we shall see throughout the myriad psalmic traditions, David never seems to find true rest. In most of the historicized psalms, we find David ever on the run, hiding and embattled.

David on the Run: The Historicized Psalms

We now look at those psalms that are associated with specific events in David's life, twelve of them total: Psalms 3, 18, 34, 51, 52, 54, 56, 57, 59, 60, 63, 142.[48] Here are their superscriptions.

48. I omit Ps 7, given its obscure superscription, which, moreover, does not reflect the syntax of the other historicized superscriptions. But see Vivian L. Johnson, *David in Distress: His Portrait through the Historical Psalms, LHB/OTS* 505 (New York: T&T Clark, 2009), 131–39.

Psalm 3 *A psalm of David, when he fled from his son Absalom.* (Cf. 2 Sam 15:1–19:43.)

Psalm 18 *To the music director. Of David, YHWH's servant, who spoke to YHWH the words of this song when YHWH delivered him from the hand of all his enemies, including from the hand of Saul.* (Cf. 2 Sam 22:1-51.)

Psalm 34 *Of David when he acted insane before Abimelech, who expelled him so that he left.* (Cf. 1 Sam 21:10-15[11-16].)

Psalm 51 *To the music leader. A psalm of David, when Nathan the prophet came to him after [David] had come to Bathsheba.* (Cf. 2 Sam 11–12.)

Psalm 52 *To the music leader. A* maśkîl *of David, when Doeg, the Edomite, came forward and informed Saul, saying to him, "David has gone to the house of Ahimelek."* (Cf. 1 Sam 22:6-23.)

Psalm 54 *To the music leader, with stringed instruments. A* maśkîl *of David, when the Ziphites came and said to Saul, "Is not David hiding himself among us?"* (Cf. 1 Sam 23:14-28; 26:1-25.)

Psalm 56 *For the music leader. According to "The Silent Dove [in] Distant Places." Of David, a* miktām, *when the Philistines seized him in Gath.* (Cf. 1 Sam 21:10-15[11-16]; 27:1-12 [?])

Psalm 57 *For the music leader. Do not destroy. Of David, a* miktām, *when he fled from Saul into the cave.* (Cf. 1 Sam 22:1-5; 24:1-22.)

Psalm 59 *For the music leader. Do not destroy. Of David, a* miktām. *On the occasion when Saul sent [men] to stake out the house in order to kill him.* (Cf. 1 Sam 19:11-17.)

Psalm 60 *For the music leader, according to "Lily." A testimony. A* miktām *of David. For instruction. When he engaged in fighting with Aram-Naharaim and Aram-Sobah, and when Joab returned and smote Edom in the Valley of Salt, twelve thousand [of them].* (Cf. 2 Sam 8:1-14; 10:6-19.)

Psalm 63 *A psalm of David when he was in the wilderness of Judah.* (Cf. 1 Sam 21–26.)

Psalm 142 *A* maśkîl *of David when he was in the cave. A prayer.* (Cf. 1 Sam 22:1-5; 24:1-25.)

Each of these psalms shares a temporal clause ("when"). They are not presented in chronological order. They begin with David as threatened king (Ps 3) and then proceed back in time to when he was pursued by Saul and surviving in the wilderness. Two of the psalms deal with his risky encounter with the Philistines. These psalms do not constitute a series by themselves; they are simply scattered reminiscences of David's life among the Psalms. Nevertheless, together they present a stunning profile of David as refugee and vulnerable king.

By focusing on the verbs in the superscriptions, we find David in distress: fleeing (3, 57), hiding (54, 142), acting insane (34), captured (56), surviving in the wilderness (63), and in one instance delivered from the heat of battle (18). These superscriptions describe David as one who is largely in pursuit by enemies, particularly by Saul (52, 54, 57, 59). Only in three instances do we find David engaged as king: fighting Arameans (60), facing the threat of usurpation (3), and raping Bathsheba (51), the latter two proving disastrous. In short, these historicized psalms "of David" are "woven out of incidents of trouble."[49] They profile David as "prayerful, pious, and penitent," in contrast to DtrH, which portrays David as a "consummate warrior, shrewd politician, talented musician, adulterer, and murderer."[50] Why such discrepancy? Is it more than a move toward associating biblical figures with pious prayer common in Second

49. James L. Mays, "The David of the Psalms," *Int* 40, no. 2 (1986): 152.

50. Johnson, *David in Distress*, 1.

Temple period literature?[51] How do these psalmic profiles engage with DtrH and the Chronicler? Space does not allow for a discussion of all the historicized psalms. We examine the most interesting.

Psalm 3: Trust Wins

A Psalm of David, when he fled from his son Absalom.

Psalm 3 is the first psalm in the Psalter to bear a superscription, and it is one that identifies the most vulnerable time in David's life as king: David is usurped from the throne by his own son, Absalom, forcing him and most of his officials to flee Jerusalem (2 Sam 15:1–19:43). According to DtrH, "all the Israelites" joined Absalom in the revolt, as well as Ahithophel, one of David's trusted counselors (16:15). A battle ensues but the tide ultimately turns in David's favor, and Absalom is killed (18:15).

The superscription not only contextualizes Psalm 3 but also introduces the subsequent collection of Davidic psalms (3–72). One might expect that at least one petitionary psalm would commemorate David's *via dolorosa* as the usurped king. Remarkable, however, is that it is the very first one, particularly following Psalm 2, an imperial psalm of vengeance against rebellious nations (see below). Psalm 3 not only identifies the speaker as David; it also identifies the nameless enemies as the king's internal foes, his conspirators, including one powerful betrayer, his son. The superscription construes the psalm as the plea of a royal refugee. Such is how David is introduced in the Psalms, in his greatest moment of royal need.

But Psalm 3 also reconstrues the Absalom episode and, particularly, David's character in it. David in Psalm 3 is shown to be utterly dependent upon YHWH. His trust in God is unwavering, even with the odds stacked against him.

YHWH, so many are my foes!
    So many are those who rise up against me!
So many are those who say about me,
    "There is no help for him in God"! *Selah*

51. So Johnson, *David in Distress*, 3-4, 141.

But you, YHWH, are a shield about me;
    [You are] my glory, the one who lifts up my head.
I cry aloud to YHWH,
    and he answers me from his holy hill. *Selah* (3:1-4[2-5])

The pronouncement made by David's enemies cuts to the heart of the conspiracy: David is bereft of divine support; thus, his doom is sealed. In DtrH, David entertained the possibility that God was not on his side when he decided to keep the ark in Jerusalem (2 Sam 15:24-26). The defection of Ahithophel, moreover, could have been the nail in David's coffin. But upon hearing the news of betrayal, David does not give up in despair but prays that YHWH "turn the counsel of Ahithophel into foolishness" (15:31). Another possible sign of divine abandonment is found in Shimei's curse (16:7-8), in which David is condemned as "a man of blood," with the usurpation regarded as divine vengeance on behalf of Saul's house. Divine abandonment has its reasons. But the psalm does not explore them as DtrH does. Psalm 3 simply states the conspirators' claim and proves it false by David's unwavering trust.

David's trust is that YHWH "answers [him] from his holy hill," Zion, even as Zion's temple is yet to be built. But no matter, the ark is there, and it remains there even as David is on the run. As much as the psalm is a cry for help, it is also a testimony of unwavering reliance on the sole source of deliverance.

I even lie down, sleep, and wake up,
    because YHWH upholds me.
I am not afraid of even tens of thousands[52] of people
    who are arrayed against me on all sides. (32:5-6[6-7])

To lie down and sleep without fear, including the fear of assassination, reflects absolute trust in God.[53] The psalm concludes with the stirring theological affirmation:

52. Hebrew *ribĕbôt*, a numerical designation that is not meant to be exact, hence its plural form.

53. Such safety, however, did not apply to Ishbaal (2 Sam 4:5-7).

Such salvation belongs to YHWH!
May your blessing be upon your people! (32:8[9]).

Psalm 3 lifts up David's life as stirring testimony that salvation does belong to YHWH. David's profile in Psalm 3 is that of a king on the run from internal threats who exhibits unflinching trust in God. David's trust trumps all fear and overcomes all threats. No ingenuity is needed.

Psalm 18: The Righteous Warrior Rewarded

Of David, YHWH's servant, who spoke to YHWH the words of this song when YHWH delivered him from the hand of all his enemies, including from the hand of Saul.

Paralleled with slight variation in 2 Samuel 22:1-51, Psalm 18 is a declarative praise or thanksgiving psalm that vividly recounts YHWH's deliverance of the king in the heat of battle. The Davidic character of this psalm is indicated not only in the superscription but also in the final verse. The identified occasion is David's persecution by "all his enemies," including Saul and extending throughout David's days as king. David's enemies ranged from northern Israelites and the Philistines, to his own son Absalom and trusted counselor Ahithophel.

According to the Chronicler, David shed too much blood to be allowed to build YHWH's temple (1 Chron 22:8; 28:3). Not coincidentally, Psalm 18 fits a king whose hands are filled with blood. The psalm's genetic twin in 2 Samuel 22 is positioned as David's penultimate words (cf. 23:1), a culminating psalm of thanksgiving whose superscription, as also here, suggests a vast span of time from Saul to David's final days as king. In both contexts, the reader/listener is invited to imagine David as a beleaguered king threatened on all sides, but who achieves victory and dominion with YHWH's help.

Like Psalm 3, Psalm 18 presents David as a model of trust, one who claims YHWH as the sole source of protection and deliverance. Distinctive of Psalm 18, however, is the staggering host of metaphors deployed at the outset to convey the speaker's solid trust in YHWH: crag, fortress, rock, shield, and horn of salvation (18:1[2]). Such trust is demonstrated in the speaker's first and only resort in crisis, to call upon YHWH (18:3[4], 6[7]), who responds "from his temple" (18:6b[7b]). Because such an anachronistic reference did not prevent the superscriptionist (and DtrH) from attributing the psalm to David, Psalm 18 (along with 2 Sam 22) invests David with a certain timeless quality. "David," in other words, includes his descendants (see 18:50[51]); he is the dynasty singularly embodied, establishing a royal paradigm of trust for every generation.

As for the manner of deliverance, Psalm 18 weds together in dramatic fashion divine and human agency. Divine agency is cast as a dramatic theophany (18:7-15[8-16]), and the speaker's agency is heightened as an empowered warrior (18:29[30], 32-45[33-46]). The reasons given for victory are, on the one hand, the king's "righteousness" (*ṣedeq*; 18:20-24[21-25]) and, on the other, God's "benevolence" (*ḥesed*; 18:50[51]). David testifies that he has never "wavered wickedly from" YHWH (18:21b[22b]). His reward and restoration from YHWH are due to his "righteousness" and the "purity of [his] hands" (18:20[21], 24[25]). David considers his own integrity unassailable. Such personal assessment cannot be sustained by the Dtr narrator. David did waver; his hands were impure; he committed iniquity. But not in Psalm 18. David's "righteousness" matches divine agency with human agency. Verse 40[41] says it most tersely: "As for my enemies, you put them to flight from me; as for my foes, I annihilated them." Such double agency continues as the speaker boasts of victory.

> They cried out, but there was no one to save them;
>   [they cried out] to YHWH, but he did not answer them.
> I pulverized them like dust before the wind;
>   I cast them out like mire in the streets.
> You delivered me from the people's conflicts;
>   you set me as head of the nations.
> People I have not known served me.
>   By mere report of me, they became obedient to me;
> Foreigners groveled[54] before me.

54. Perhaps read Niphal (*yikkāhăšû*; cf. Deut 33:29) instead of Piel, which most commonly means "deceive." But see Pss 66:3; 81:16. 2 Sam 22:45 reads Hithpael.

> Foreigners languished;
> they came quaking out of their strongholds. (18:41-45[42-46])

The end result is David's imperial dominion. The psalm began with David in distress on the battlefield, and it ends with David in dominion over the nations, from warrior David to royal David. Psalm 18, as also 2 Samuel 22, is David's lifelong psalm. It is also his psalm of self-professed integrity, integrity without iniquity, the proof of which, the psalm testifies, is found on the battlefield. But off the battlefield, as DtrH would readily remind us, David all too quickly jeopardizes his righteousness (2 Sam 11:1).

Psalm 34: The Insanity of Trust

[A psalm] of David when he acted insane[55] *before Abimelech, who expelled him so that he left.*

An acrostic psalm with an "extra" verse, Psalm 34 provides instruction in the ways of "fearing" God through praise, testimony, exhortation, and admonition. The superscription identifies a particular episode in David's life, whose narrative parallel is found in 1 Samuel 21:10-15[11-16], featuring the same expression "act insane" (21:13[14]). Out of fear for his life, David feigns madness before the Philistine king of Gath, Achish, by "scratching marks on the doors of the gate and letting his spittle run down his beard" (21:12[13]). Consequently, David was let go. Psalm 34, however, identifies the king as Abimelech (cf. Judg 9:1-57; cf. 2 Sam 11:21). There is no mention of an Abimelech elsewhere in the Bible who is contemporaneous with David, although the name does refer to a Philistine king in Genesis 20 and 26.

Regardless of the precise historical background, the question of why the superscriptionist would associate Psalm 34 with this particular incident in David's story is intriguing. One connection is that the word for "discernment" or "good sense" (*ṭaʿam*), which David altered (√*šnh*) to feign madness, is also found in its verbal cognate form in the imperative

55. Literally, "changed [*šnh* in Piel] his good sense/discernment" (*ṭaʿmô*).

in 34:8[9] (*ṭaʿămû*): "taste!" Call it a catchword-play. But regardless of the discrepancy in the foreign king's name, David's story in 1 Samuel is one of fear, ingenuity, and escape from danger. Imagining this psalm uttered by David in this context highlights the elements of relief and thanksgiving: YHWH has heard David's cry and delivered him once again from the clutches of the Philistines. Praise-filled thanksgiving is the result.

The psalm claims that the true way toward "refuge" is through petition and reverence, above and beyond human ingenuity, such as David's feigning madness. Like the warrior's prowess in combat or the king's army, human ingenuity and power only go so far and are often proven inconsequential. By crediting YHWH, rather than human cleverness, with his deliverance, David becomes an example of trust, indeed an exemplar of reverence. His testimony becomes a lesson for all: true deliverance comes from God. YHWH is David's "boast," not his cunning or even his righteousness (34:3), in contrast to Ps 18:20-24[21-25]. In Psalm 34, David is merely an "afflicted" person who cried out (34:6[7]). Yet he is identified as righteous in so far that he has been delivered by YHWH from his "afflictions," along with the "crushed in spirit" and "brokenhearted" (34:19[20]).

David's testimony, moreover, qualifies him as a teacher of reverence in the style of a sage (34:11-14[12-15]). Whereas David acted insane before the Philistine king, he imparts sound wisdom to his "children" (34:11[12]). And as for any guilt of his, it is rendered moot by YHWH's "refuge" (34:22[23]). In comparison to DtrH, the "crazy" David in Psalm 34 relies not on his wits but on his God to find a way out of a tight situation. In the hands of the psalmist, David becomes the poster child of trust at the expense of ingenuity.

Psalm 51: Caught for Confession; Sin as Condition

A psalm of David, when Nathan the prophet came to him after [David] had come to Bathsheba.

The superscription specifies the incident that sets the occasion for the psalm: Nathan's confrontation with David after his adultery with Bathsheba. The DtrH account is detailed in 2 Samuel 12:1-15, immediately following the incident that warranted the prophet's confrontation with David (11:1-27). The crime is summarized in the indictment: "You have struck down Uriah the Hittite with the sword and taken his wife to be your wife and killed him with the sword of the Ammonites" (12:9b). The first crime is not mentioned in the summary.

But adultery is very much indicated in the superscription of Psalm 51 (without mentioning Uriah's murder). Indeed, the superscription establishes a wordplay with the expression *bw' 'el* ("come to"). The first instance conveys Nathan's confrontation with David, the second with David's violation of Bathsheba, implying that God's judgment poetically fits David's crime. In 2 Samuel, David's response to Nathan is all too brief: "I have sinned against YHWH" (12:13a). But "David" in Psalm 51 wants to say so much more.

> Grant me mercy, O God, according to your benevolence;
> according to the abundance of your compassion,
> wipe away[56] my transgressions.
> Wash me thoroughly[57] of my iniquity;
> purify me of my sin.
> For I acknowledge my transgressions;
> my sin is ever before me.
> Against you, you alone, have I sinned;
> I have committed what is evil in your sight.
> For that reason, you are righteous when you render your verdict,
> irreproachable[58] whenever you pass judgment.
> Yes, I was born in guilt;
> my mother conceived me in sin.
> And yes, you desire truth in what is innermost;[59]
> and you make known to me wisdom in a secret place. (51:1-6[3-8])

56. The verb *mḥh* conveys two interrelated meanings: washing ("wipe clean") and annihilation ("wipe out").

57. Read Ketib (*harbēh*), taken adverbially, instead of Qere's imperative form (*hereb*).

58. Literally, "pure" or "clean" (√*zkh*).

59. The word *ṭuḥôt* is uncertain (see only Job 38:36 with a completely different meaning). The parallel in v. 8b suggests secrecy or hiddenness, literally "hidden places." The word likely functions as a circumlocution for internal organs. See *HALOT*, 373–74.

As in the narrative account, "David" in the psalm identifies God as the one who is singularly violated by sin. But the sin elucidated in the psalm is by no means singular: "transgressions"/"sins"/"iniquities" are all admitted, as well as iniquity so deep that the speaker acknowledges his guilt from birth (51:5[7]). Sin, here, is not so much tied to a particular crime as it is part and parcel of the human condition. As much as the psalm features a retrospective look over an entire life entrenched in sin, so it reflects a deeply introspective perspective regarding "truth," which reflects what is "innermost" of a person (51:6a[8a]), a place where wisdom is to be had (51:6b[8b]). Psalm 51 testifies to laying bare one's deepest truth; in David's case, it is the truth of his sin, which must be revealed so that it can be purged (51:7-13[9-15]). The speaker admits that his "transgressions" warrant rejection by God and the removal of God's "holy spirit" (51:11[13]), the same spirit that came upon David when he was anointed (1 Sam 16:13) and, in turn, departed from Saul (16:14). David in the psalm, moreover, pleads for deliverance from "bloodguilt" (51:14[16]), the guilt of committing murder[60]—perhaps an allusion to Uriah. David promises that with a "clean heart," he will teach other "transgressors" of God's ways so that they too will repent (51:13[15]). The speaker concludes with the claim that a "broken and crushed heart" is preferable to a burnt offering and that a "broken spirit" counts as "sacrifice" (51:16-17[18-19]).

The psalm concludes, however, with a corporate appeal for Zion's restoration and for sacrificial offerings (51:18-19[20-21]), countering the preceding sentiment. Psalm 51, it turns out, is itself dialogically engaged over the value of sacrifice. In the end, both David and Zion require repair and restoration. As in Psalm 132, David becomes "built into" Zion. David's appeal for deliverance from his transgressions culminates with an appeal for Zion's restoration from ruination. While this additional conclusion to the psalm legitimizes humble repentance as an appropriate "sacrifice," it does so only for the interim until Zion is restored along with its sacrificial system. The psalm's conclusion is historically anachronistic, yes, since the psalm now stretches from the time of David to the that of the

60. Cf. Isa 1:15; Hos 4:2; Mic 7:2.

exile. Consequently, David's sins are committed at Zion's expense; conversely, David's restoration is aligned with Zion's.

In sum, Psalm 51 serves to fill the gap between David's admission of sin and Nathan's pronouncement of (qualified) forgiveness. Perhaps the superscriptionist found the confession to be too brief and far too easy in DtrH. "David said to Nathan, 'I have sinned against YHWH.' Nathan said to David, 'Now YHWH has put away your sin; you shall not die'" (2 Sam 12:13). For the psalmist, it was necessary for David to wallow in guilt and seek mercy before receiving forgiveness. In so doing, David proves himself to be more contrite than he ever comes across in DtrH. The psalm also ensures that both of David's crimes are accounted for: the rape of Bathsheba and the "bloodguilt" of Uriah's murder. As David "had come to Bathsheba," so the "prophet came to" David. Is David about to be violated? Ironically, yes. David's premeditated world of self-deception is about to be dismantled, and YHWH demands a "broken spirit" and a "crushed heart" before the repair work can begin.

Psalm 54: Salvation over Cunning

A maśkîl *of David, when the Ziphites came and said to Saul, "Is not David hiding himself among us?"*

The superscription highlights another act of betrayal against David. The psalm itself petitions God for deliverance from enemies. Classified like its predecessor as a *maśkîl*, the psalm is given a narrative setting rooted in one or two episodes in David's flight from Saul (1 Sam 23:14-28; 26:1-25). The first tells of a close call for David on the run from Saul in the wilderness of Ziph, made all the more precarious by the betrayal of David's whereabouts by "some Ziphites" (1 Sam 23:19). David and his men are chased from the "wilderness of Ziph" to the "wilderness of Maon" with Saul and his army closing in on the "rock" where he stayed. David is saved only because Saul had to retreat due to an attack by the Philistines (vv. 24-28). How convenient.[61]

61. One could argue historically that David was actually colluding with the Philistines during this time to relieve Saul of his crown (see McKenzie, *King David*, 106–10).

In the second episode, the Ziphites again betray David's location (26:1), again prompting pursuit by Saul, along with "three thousand chosen men" (26:2). But this time David has the upper hand when he and Abishai stealthily infiltrate Saul's camp under the cover of darkness and gain opportunity to kill the king in his sleep. But David refuses to do so and steals Saul's spear and water jar, proving that he will not "raise [his] hand against YHWH's anointed" (26:11). The episode, like others, ostensibly demonstrates David's innocence before YHWH and Saul (see 26:18-20) while exposing Saul as a fool for having hunted a "partridge in the mountains" (26:20-25). The account concludes with Saul blessing his "son David" (26:25).

Psalm 54 is only loosely connected to either episode. No allusion, for example, is made to the "Rock of Escape" (1 Sam 23:28), a notable omission given the prevalent metaphor of "rock" to designate God throughout the Psalms.[62] Nevertheless, the conjured connection adds a dramatic pathos to the psalm's plea for deliverance (54:1-2[3-4]). The psalm, in turn, treats Saul and his armed men with contempt in light of the various pejoratives used to target them, including "arrogant" and "violent" (54:3[5]). The psalm, moreover, adds a theological layer: the speaker credits God/YHWH as his "helper" and sustainer (54:4[6]). The narrative accounts are not so explicit. In the first episode, David escapes only because Saul is forced to relent from his pursuit because of the Philistines (1 Sam 23:27-28). In the second episode, however, YHWH casts Saul and his soldiers into a "deep sleep" to make possible David's secret procurement of Saul's spear (26:12). Later, David issues an imprecation against those who have "stirred up" Saul against David (26:19). David's final words in the narrated episode sound strikingly psalmic: "As your life was precious today in my sight, so may my life be precious in YHWH's sight, and may he rescue me from all tribulation" (26:24). Here, David asserts his innocence while at the same time acknowledging his dependence on YHWH's salvific power.

In conjunction with the narrative, Psalm 54 spells out the imprecation that David uttered against his conspirators:

62. See, e.g., 18:2[3]; 19:14[15]; 28:1; 31:3[4]; 71:3; 89:26[27]; 144:1-2.

May evil return[63] upon my opponents.[64]
Annihilate them in your faithfulness! (Ps 54:5[6]; cf. 1 Sam 26:19)

The psalm ends on a promise of thanksgiving involving a "freewill sacrifice" (54:6[8]). Nowhere in DtrH do we find David doing that. The narrative simply says, "So David went his way" (1 Sam 26:25; cf. 26:19a). The psalmist, however, conjures a more appropriate conclusion: David formally gives thanks to God. Overall, the psalm highlights God's salvific power over David's "cunning," whereas the narrative holds both in balance (cf. 1 Sam 23:22).

Psalm 56: Exoneration by Victimization

Of David, a miktām, *when the Philistines seized him in Gath*

Psalm 56 is a petition to God for deliverance from a diverse array of enemies, from assailants to nations, while repeatedly expressing absolute trust in God's protection. The association with David in the superscription is made concrete with a narrative reference to his being taken ("seized") by the Philistines in Gath, recalling at least two instances of David's flight to Gath from Saul as narrated in DtrH. In 1 Samuel 21:10-15[11-16], David flees from Saul to Gath out of fear for his life and pretends to be insane before the Philistine king, Achish, so that he can exit freely (cf. the superscription of Ps 34). In 1 Samuel 27, David flees again to Gath and makes an arrangement with the king for temporary asylum in Ziklag but is also enlisted into the Philistine army, remaining there for at least a year and four months (27:7). David does this all on his own accord; nothing is said about David being "seized" by the Philistines, as claimed in the psalm's superscription. Rather, David goes to Gath to deal disingenuously with Achish, conniver that he is. In the psalm, however, David is simply a victim of the Philistines.

The speaker in Psalm 56 complains of oppression from unnamed assailants and conspirators while at the same time expressing absolute

63. Read with Ketib.

64. The term likely comes from the root *šwr*, "to be opposed" (*HALOT*, 1451).

trust in God. "What can mortal flesh do to me?," the speaker declares (56:4b[5b]). Distinctive of this psalm is the speaker's demand that his grievances be recorded in God's record or ledger (56:8[9]). In addition to identifying the speaker as David, the superscription equates the myriad enemies of the psalm, from "assailants" to "slanderers," with the Philistines, turning what may have been an internal (i.e., intra-Israelite) conflict original to the psalm's setting into an external threat. On the other hand, the reference to the "peoples" in 56:8b[9b] would fit the superscription, the "peoples" being the Philistines. DtrH adroitly navigates David's enlisting with the Philistines as a cunning way of seeking asylum from Saul while straining to keep him innocent of treason or complicity in Saul's death. In the psalm, David is "seized," forced against his will by the Philistines. The superscription, in other words, takes the easy road to exonerate David of any complicity with the Philistines, while DtrH takes the more difficult road to do the same by acknowledging David's ingenuity.

Psalm 59: From Victim to Vindication

Do not destroy. Of David, a miktām, *when Saul sent [men] to stake out the house in order to kill him.*

As in the previous psalms, the superscription embeds Psalm 59 in an episode of David's flight from Saul. Within DtrH, the superscription corresponds to 1 Samuel 19:11-17, in which David narrowly escapes Saul's clutches with the help of Michal, Saul's daughter. The narrative and the superscription exhibit nearly identical language: "Saul sent messengers to David's house to stake it out [*lĕšomrô*] and to kill him [*wĕlahămîtô*] in the morning" (1 Sam 19:11). Reading the psalm within the narrative underlines the desperation of David's pleas, as well as identifies the unnamed enemies with Saul and his "messengers," or better, assassins.

However, such a narrative "fit" is imperfect: the psalm, for example, identifies the speaker's enemies in part as the "nations" (59:5a[6a], 8b[9b]). On the other hand, likening the enemies to scavenging dogs is apt for enemies prowling at night (59:6[7], 14-15[15-16]). Indeed, the psalm's first petition fits particularly well: the "bloodthirsty" wait to ambush David at night when he leaves his house (59:2-4a[3-5a]). The speaker's insistence on David's innocence (59:3b-4a[4b-5a]) highlights his victimization in the face of Saul's madness (1 Sam 19:9-10). In addition, the reference to Saul's henchmen conducting a "stakeout" or keeping watch (√*šmr*) over David's house at night establishes an ironic link with the psalmic speaker's resolve to "watch for" (same verb!) God to deliver him (59:9[10]).

The danger the enemies pose in the psalm lies in their predatory, slanderous discourse: "swords" are "between their lips" (59:7[8] CEB); their "sin" is what comes out of "their mouths," full of "curses and lies" (59:12[13]). The speaker feels "staked out" by the words of his opponents. To identify the speaker as David, persecuted by Saul, is to acknowledge how dangerous slanderers are to the innocent. Slanderers are equivalent to Saul's henchmen. Moreover, nowhere in the psalm is the speaker seeking escape in the night. Rather, he seeks vindication at the expense of his enemies. He stands his ground in trust that his vindication is also God's vindication (59:13b[14b]). Psalm 59 turns an escape story under the cover of darkness into an occasion for vindication for all the world to know. Thus, David's successful escape from Saul, the first of many, is more than a down-to-the-wire moment of suspense; it is nothing less than an act of divine judgment on behalf of the rightful heir to the throne. David's escape by the skin of his teeth turns out to be a mighty sign of divine vindication.

Psalm 60: Loss amid Heroic Triumph

For the music leader, according to "Lily." A testimony. A miktām *of David. For instruction. When he engaged in fighting with Aram-Naharaim and Aram-Zobah, and when Joab returned and smote Edom in the Valley of Salt, twelve thousand [of them].*

Psalm 60 conjures a setting of both military (60:4b[6b]) and environmental threat (60:2[4]). The superscription labels the psalm as a "testimony" (*'ēdût*), referring to the divine decree featured in 60:6-9[8-11], aptly matched by the purpose clause "for instruction" or teaching (*lĕlammēd*).

The ascription to David is detailed with reference to David's battles against Aram-Naharaim (Gen 24:10; Judg 3:8) and Aram-Zobah, two regions in Syria, the latter recalling two episodes of successful military engagement with the "Arameans of Zobah" (2 Sam 8:1-8; 10:6-19). Also referenced is Joab's attack against Edom, resulting in twelve thousand casualties. DtrH and the Chronicler do not mention Joab, David's general, involved in a mass killing of Edomites, although he is mentioned in connection with the defeat of the "Arameans of Zobah" (2 Sam 10:7-14). In 2 Samuel 8:13, David killed eighteen thousand Edomites in the Valley of Salt, and in 1 Chronicles 18:12, Abishai is said to have killed the same number at the same location, bringing the Edomites under David's rule. Relatedly, Amaziah "killed ten thousand Edomites in the Valley of Salt and took Sela by storm" (2 Kgs 14:7). With all these engagements in play, the superscription contextualizes Psalm 60 as a time when David was proving himself as a successful military leader in the international arena, with YHWH giving " victory to David wherever he went" (2 Sam 8:6b, 14b), winning "a name for himself" (60:13b).

Thus, it is difficult to figure out why *this* psalm received such a superscription. Psalm 60 begins with little sense of triumph. Far from it, the psalm opens with a corporate cry of complaint that mirrors the individual complaint in 89:38[39].

> O God, you have spurned us, bursting forth upon us;
> you have been angry. Restore us!
> You have caused the land to quake, splitting it open.
> Repair its cracks, for it is tottering!
> You have caused your people to witness hardship;
> you have made us drink the wine of staggering. (60:1-3[3-5])

In the midst of victory, the psalm acknowledges great hardship and suffering, including an earthquake. In response to the people's plea for deliverance, God delivers an oracular address from God's "holy sanctuary," an oracle of victory in which the tribes themselves constitute God's army. With "Ephraim as [God's] helmet" and "Judah as [God's] scepter" (60:7[9]), so Moab, Edom, and Philistia will be defeated (60:8[10]). The oracle recalls David's success in war against three neighboring kingdoms. But the psalm does not end there: it concludes with a complaint of divine neglect on the battlefield:

> [But] have you not rejected us, O God?
> You, O God, do not go forth with our armies.
> Grant us aid against the foe![65]
> Human help proves worthless.
> [But] with God we shall prove heroic;[66]
> it is he who will tread upon our foes. (60:10-12[12-14])

"Human help" does not count; it is God who will bring about the defeat of Israel's enemies. The psalm's finality of trust recalls David's success on the battlefield as given by YHWH (2 Sam 8:6b, 14b). The psalm gives due credit, not to David but to God. Nevertheless, human agency is required, as the final verse makes clear: "with God we shall prove heroic," claiming in effect, "with God we shall prove Davidic"! As David was the royal embodiment of such heroism, heroism made possible by God, the psalm petitions God that Israel (Ephraim and Judah) emulate such heroism. By situating Psalm 60 at the height of David's military successes, the superscription recalls a time of heroism for a different kind of day, a day of disruption and distress. By recalling YHWH's victory through David, the superscription serves as motivation for God to deliver once again. As it was with David, so now it should be with Israel.

Psalm 63: A Piety of Thirst

A psalm of David when he was in the wilderness of Judah.

Psalm 63 evokes extreme contexts. It begins with a thirst for God in a desiccated landscape and then abruptly swings toward full satiation of God's presence in the sanctuary, as the psalm moves from lament to praise and finally to petition. The superscription attributes the psalm to

65. Or "from distress."

66. For the verbal construction √*ʿśh* + *ḥayil*, see 1 Sam 14:48; Ps 118:15; Prov 31:29.

David in connection to his travails in the Judean "wilderness" (1 Sam 21–26) evoking the episodes of David's flight to evade King Saul (e.g., 1 Sam 23:14; 24:2). To imagine Psalm 63 spoken by David is to experience David's personal piety *in extremis*, his yearning, thirsty self, ultimately satisfied with God's help. David's very identity is wrapped up in God. Historically, God's "sanctuary" cannot refer to the temple, built later by Solomon. Instead, it designates the tabernacle. But if one reads "David" as the dynasty, then such a prayer could be found on the lips of any royal descendant. In any case, David in Psalm 63 is shown to be one whose life is characterized by extremes. David knows the wilderness well, where he has sought escape and refuge. He knows the tabernacle well, having established it in Jerusalem. And he knows his enemies all too well, one in particular being his son. But whether in crisis or in triumph, David yearns for God and is ever grateful for God's "benevolence." David is painted as the thirsty and satiated self—thirsty for God alone and satisfied by God alone.

Psalm 142: Imprisoned in a Cave

A maśkîl *of David when he was in the cave. A prayer.*

Psalm 142 gives voice to one who is persecuted by powerful enemies and finds no way of escape. The speaker declares YHWH as his "refuge," as his source of freedom and protection, and counts on YHWH's power to release him from "prison." For such freedom, the speaker promises to offer thanks and anticipates his restoration in the community of the righteous.

The psalm is attributed to David in connection with a specific circumstance of distress, that of being trapped in a "cave" (*mĕʿārâ*), perhaps recalling 1 Samuel 24:1-25, in which "David and his men" hide in a "cave" from Saul and his soldiers. With both suspense and a dose of humor, the narrator recounts how David spared Saul while he was relieving himself in the very cave where David was hiding. The reference to *cave* in the narrative is given five times, stressing David's hidden position and Saul's vulnerable position when Saul is indisposed. David's encounter with Saul, however, is nowhere reflected in Psalm 142. Instead, the psalm reflects a

David who is in desperate straits, without "escape" (142:4b[5b]), trapped in a cave rather than finding refuge in it.

> With my voice I will cry out to YHWH;
> with my voice I will implore YHWH's favor.
> I will pour out before him my complaint;
> I will declare my distress before him.
> Even when my spirit within me is sapped, you know my way.
> But in the path that I walk, they have hidden a trap for me.
> Look to my right and see—
> there is no one to notice me!
> No escape remains[67] for me;
> There is no one who cares for me. (142:1-4[2-5])

Bereft of assistance where there is no exit, the speaker proclaims YHWH as his "refuge":

> I cry to you, YHWH!
> I declare, "You are my refuge,
> my portion in the land of the living."
> Attend to my cry, for I have been brought very low!
> Deliver me from my persecutors,
> for they are too powerful for me!
> Take me out of prison,
> so that I may give thanks to your name!
> [Then] the righteous will surround me,
> when[68] you deal well with me. (142:5-7[6-8])

In the eyes of the superscriptionist, the "prison" referenced in 142:7a[8a] refers metaphorically to David's "cave," not a place of refuge but a trap laid by his "persecutors" in pursuit. The "cave" is where David is cornered without any chance of escape. The cunning David is nowhere to

67. Literally, "perishes" (*'bd*).

68. The *kî* conjunction could be causal ("for"), as indicated in most translations, but a temporal nuance makes equally good sense. The speaker is anticipating deliverance. Cf. Ps 13:5b[6b].

be found in this psalm. Instead, this "David" is consumed with desperation, relying completely upon YHWH as his "refuge."

The superscriptionist suggests a striking, albeit subtle, intertextual link between Psalm 142 and 1 Samuel 24 with the shared use of the verb √*gml* ("deal with") in both passages. The narrative of the cave episode between David and Saul is resolved by Saul's testimony, "You are more righteous than I; for you have dealt well with me [*gĕmaltanî haṭṭôbâ*], while I have dealt wickedly [*gĕmaltîkā hārā'â*] with you" (1 Sam 24:17[18]). Not coincidentally, Psalm 142 concludes with the speaker's trust that YHWH, in due time, will "deal well with me" (*tigmōl 'ālay*; 142:7b[8b]). If the link is intentional, at least in the eyes of the superscriptionist, then Psalm 142 serves as commentary on the narrated incident in 1 Samuel 24. As David treated Saul graciously by sparing his life, so "David" in Psalm 142 anticipates that YHWH will do the same for him. Reading both texts together, one might conclude that David expects, even deserves, gracious treatment from YHWH because he has extended the same to his persecutor, Saul.

Conclusion

In summary, most of the psalms attributed to David "historically" feature him petitioning God for deliverance amid dire need. There is little in the way of David exercising sovereign rule among these psalms. David in distress rather than in dominion is most dominant among these psalms. In complaint, petition, and praise, David cedes his power to YHWH for deliverance, his source of refuge and forgiveness.

While the portrait of David is less ambiguous and more pious in the Psalms than how he is portrayed in DtrH, David is also given a more humanly vulnerable depiction, in contrast to the Chronicler. Moreover, the nearly exclusive focus on David in DtrH becomes decidedly theocentric in these psalms. Whereas God works behind the scenes in DtrH to bring about David's success, God is featured front and center in the Psalms. Such is to be expected from the genres of petition and thanksgiving in the Davidic psalms. Nevertheless, the genres serve from the psalmist's vantage point as windows into David's heart, yielding a glimpse of his personal thoughts, emotions, and desires, particularly in times of crisis. The only exception among the historicized Davidic psalms is Psalm 18, which paints a robust and righteous warrior working in tandem with the divine warrior to bring about victory on the battlefield. This exception, however, proves the rule: this is the one psalm that is incorporated into the DtrH account of David's military prowess. Otherwise, the David we find among the historicized psalms and beyond is primarily a figure in distress, overwhelmed by danger, thus seeking deliverance from God.

The (Ahistorical) Psalms "of David"

Such depictions of David in distress are carried over into other psalms associated with David by way of simple attribution but without historical superscriptions, as described above. The formulaic *lĕdāvid* (typically translated "of David") can designate a range of meanings, from "by David," in the sense of authorial attribution, to "for David," in the sense of dedication, to "regarding" David, all depending on the particular nuance of the preposition. To assume that all the psalms introduced with a superscription containing *lĕdāvid* are David's own words does not hold up in every case, as in Psalms 20 and 21, two psalms that are performed *for* the king in prayer and testimony; hence, they are "for David." Moreover, Psalm 72 is clearly not a psalm "by" Solomon, despite its superscription, but rather given "for" Solomon in light of the colophon in 72:20. Finally, the content of various psalms associated with David contradicts what we know from DtrH about David, particularly the not-infrequent reference to the temple.[69]

While the psalmic superscriptions were added much later to the psalms, these titles can be regarded as invitations to (re)imagine how certain psalms pertain to David in various ways, in some cases to imagine David's voice speaking or singing the psalm in question. Our purpose is not to prove anything historically but to explore how these psalms

69. E.g., 23:6; 27:4; 52:8; 69:9; 122:1. For fuller discussion, see Jerome F. D. Creach, *Discovering the Psalms: Content, Interpretation, Reception* (Grand Rapids: SPCK/Eerdmans, 2020), 48–53.

(re)shape David's profile, to discern how they wrestle dialogically over David's legacy for posterity.

David Humanized

The vast majority of psalms associated with David are cries for deliverance, whether from enemies, false accusations, or disease. Indeed, the final Davidic petition, which is Psalm 143, is notable for its particularly desperate tone, in which David is not so much YHWH's royal representative as he is simply YHWH's desperate "servant." Psalm 143 is the culmination of many Davidic psalms that portray David as ever vulnerable, ever seeking vindication and "refuge" under God's wings or shadow (e.g., Pss 5, 7, 17). Little is said, in turn, of David's royal majesty and power. Instead, David counts himself as "impoverished and deprived" (*'ānî wĕ'ebyôn*; 40:17[18]; 70:5; 86:1; 109:22). He is a mere "shadow," just like every mortal, an "immigrant like all [his] ancestors" (39:5-7, 13-14).

As much as David proclaims his absolute dependence upon God, he also pleads for forgiveness, not only in Psalm 51, but also in Psalms 6, 25, 32, 38, 41, and 143, while also inviting God to prove and test him for any wickedness within him (e.g., 26 and 139). The David of the Psalms is ever open to correction: "Let the righteous strike me, the faithful rebuke me" (141:5). And, in turn, he is ever willing to teach (31:23-24; 34:11-14; cf. 51:13[15]). An irony is evident in his admonition to "put no trust in extortion" (62:10), even as he has done exactly that in his dealings with Nabal (1 Sam 25:3-9). David in the Psalms is a man of integrity (Pss 14, 15, 53, 101) who is prone to iniquity (51) and bears the reproach and insults of many (69:7, 9b, 19-20).

As for the exercise of imperial power by David the king, Psalm 124 is abjectly modest:

If YHWH had not been for us
  —let Israel now say—
If YHWH had not been for us,
  when people rose up against us,
    then they would have swallowed us up alive,

as their anger was burning against us,
then the waters would have engulfed us,
the torrent would have swept over our throats,
then the raging[70] waters would have swept over our throats.
Blessed be YHWH,
who has not handed us over as prey for their teeth.
Like a bird, we have escaped from the fowlers snare.
The snare is broken, and we have escaped.
Our help is in the name of YHWH, maker of heaven and earth!
(Ps 124:1-8)

The analogy is clear: as David is the escape artist from his pursuers, so also David's "kingdom" from the "raging waters" of pursuing enemies. The contrast could not be greater with the so-called royal psalms, whose perspectives on kingship reign from above (see below). But David, as presented in "his" psalms, remains lowly:

A Song of Ascents. Of David.
O YHWH, my mind is not held high,
and my eyes are not raised up.
I do not traffic[71] among things too great
and wonderful for me.
Instead, I have calmed and quieted myself,
like a fully nursed child[72] upon its mother,
like the fully nursed child upon me—so I [am].
Wait, O Israel, for YHWH, from now and forevermore. (Ps 131:1-3)

Written possibly by a woman, the psalm commends a serene and intimate trust like that of a young child "fully nursed" with its mother, a trust that abjures dwelling on God's "great" and "wonderful" things.[73] The speaker self-identifies as both the child and the mother: the intimacy of

70. Or "insolent," a double entendre, from *zêdôn* (cf. √*zyd*).

71. Literally, "walk, go about" (*hlk* in Piel).

72. Or "weaned, sated."

73. Cf. Job 42:3; Prov 30:18. See Patrick D. Miller, *They Cried to the Lord: The Form and Theology of Biblical Prayer* (Minneapolis: Fortress, 1994), 239–43.

contented trust blurs the maternal boundary. With the addition of the superscription, such trust is attributed also to David, the same trust that undergirds David's petitions to God elsewhere in the Psalms (e.g., Pss 16, 22, 23, 25, 62). David the mighty warrior and king is here a serene and contented figure. What David lacks in imperial might in Psalm 131 he more than compensates for in tender trust. This is no David in distress but David in tranquility, at peace—a trusting king for a trusting people.

Psalm 145: Surrendering Kingship in Praise

To round out our discussion of the psalms of David, we turn to the final Davidic psalm in the Psalter. There is no specific episode in David's life to recall in this psalm. Nevertheless, Psalm 145 assumes a certain pride of place in the Psalter. Its superscription categorizes the psalm as "a praise of David," the only time the word "praise" (*tĕhillâ*) is used in a psalmic title. It applies well, since the psalm is replete with acclamatory affirmations of YHWH's royal majesty and inclusive care. The language of kingship is applied exclusively to God, as in the opening lines.

> I exalt you, my God, the King,
>   and I shall bless your name forever and ever.
> Every day I bless you,
>   and praise your name forever and ever.
> Great is YHWH and exceedingly praised;
>   his greatness is unfathomable. (145:1-3)

In fact, all attention in the psalm is directed to YHWH's everlasting kingdom and majesty.

> All your works give you thanks, YHWH,
>   and your faithful ones bless you.
> The glory of your kingdom they declare,
>   and your power they proclaim,
>   to make known to human beings his power,
>   and the majestic glory of his kingdom.

Your kingdom is an everlasting kingdom,
  and your dominion [endures] for all generations.
    YHWH is faithful in all his words,
      and dependably benevolent[74] in all his deeds.[75] (145:10-13)

YHWH's sovereign status trumps all claims to human kingship. The role of the "faithful ones" is to "bless" YHWH and proclaim YHWH's power, making known YHWH's royal might to all humanity. Nothing is said about earthly kingdoms. As for the character of the divine king and the nature of "his" rule, the psalm does not hold back in praise:

Merciful and compassionate is YHWH;
  slow to anger and great in benevolence.
YHWH is good to all;
  his tender compassion is over all his works.
YHWH supports all who fall,
  and raises up all who are bowed down.
The eyes of all look to you in hope,
  and you give to them their food in its season,
    opening your hand,
      and satisfying the desire of every living thing.
Righteous is YHWH in all his ways,
  and dependably benevolent in all his deeds.
YHWH is near to all who call on him,
  to all who call on him in sincerity.
He fulfills the desire of those who fear him;
  he hears their cry and saves them.
YHWH protects all who love him,
  but all the wicked he will destroy. (145:8-16)

Echoing YHWH's self-confession on Sinai (Exod 34:6), YHWH in the psalm is "slow to anger and great in benevolence" (Ps 145:9b). YHWH, moreover, exhibits "tender compassion" (*raḥămîm*), demonstrating maternal love to all "her" subjects. YHWH does not rule with a clinched

74. Hebrew *ḥāsîd*; i.e., one who practices *ḥesed*.

75. Hebrew *ne'ĕmān yhwh bĕkol-dĕbārāyw wĕḥāsîd bĕkol-ma'ăśāyw.* This *nun* strophe is lacking in the MT but is featured in one Hebrew manuscript, along with LXX and Peshitta.

fist but governs with an open "hand," providing for all (145:12, 16). YHWH responds to all who cry out in need (145:18-20a) but does not tolerate the wicked (145:20b).

Compare Psalm 145 with the following passage from Psalm 72, which describes the rule of the Davidic king:

> For he delivers the needy who cries out for help,
>   and the impoverished—the one who lacks a helper.
> He looks compassionately on the lowly and the deprived,
>   and saves the lives of the destitute.
> From oppression and violence he redeems their lives;
>   and their blood is precious in his eyes. (Ps 72:12-14)

Deliverance of the "impoverished" and compassion to the "lowly" are the king's job in Psalm 72. In Psalm 145, deliverance of the "bowed down" and compassion for all constitute YHWH's work. Both are royal callings, but near the end of the Psalter, it is clear who takes the reins of governance. Human kingship has faded into oblivion before YHWH's universal dominion. And who to facilitate the move is none other than David himself, YHWH's devoted "servant" (cf. Ps 144:10)! In this culminating psalm of praise and blessing, David effectively surrenders his kingship to YHWH's. In praise, David cedes his royal power to the royal God who has repeatedly saved and sustained him. Above all, David is YHWH's "servant." His portrayals in the Psalms find their dialogical nexus not only with DtrH and the Chronicler regarding his character but also with the so-called royal psalms regarding the issue of power.

Royal Power in the Royal Psalms

Although not a genre, the "royal psalms" are those psalms that place the king front and center in their focus. They include, at the very least, Psalms 2; 18; 20; 21; 45; 72; 89:1-37[2-38]; 110; 144. Several do not bear Davidic superscriptions, perhaps because they address issues that do not cohere with David's characterization features in most other psalms that are ascribed to him. By contrast, several of the royal psalms magnify royal power to imperial proportions.[76] But like so many psalms, even the royal psalms offer differing perspectives on how royal power is to be exercised. They are the products of centuries of experience under royal rule, both good and bad, as 1–2 Kings vividly testify.

Psalm 2: Imperial Sonship

Perhaps the greatest contrast between the Davidic psalms and the royal psalms is found in Psalm 2, which speaks of a king, chosen by YHWH as "son," dashing his enemies with an iron rod (2:9). Striking is the fact that this psalm is *not* attributed to David, even as the next psalm is. Psalm 2 likely draws from a coronation liturgy designed to inaugurate the rule of a new king set against the backdrop of international rebellion at the time of succession, a not uncommon phenomenon in ancient history. If one can imagine Psalm 2 as a dramatic production, then the curtain rises on a scene of political chaos and cacophony: nations are "ranting" and "raving" as the "kings of the earth" conspire against "YHWH and his anointed" (2:2). But have no fear: YHWH, enthroned in the heavens, "laughs" in derision at such chaos (2:4) and as remedy declares the king's installation on Zion (2:6). The king recounts YHWH's "decree":

> I will recount the decree that YHWH has declared to me:
> "My son you are;
>   today I hereby beget you.
> Ask of me to make the nations your possession,
>   and the ends of the earth your property.
> You will smash them with an iron rod;
>   like a potter's vessel you will shatter them in pieces." (2:7-9)

The parental language reflects that of the Davidic covenant, as expressed particularly in Psalm 89 and 2 Samuel 7. But here it is expressed more vividly, if not more literally: YHWH declares the king's sonship (2:7b). As YHWH's "son," the king is invited to call upon his "father"

76. I would identify them as a subset of the royal psalms by calling them "imperial psalms" (i.e., Pss 2; 45; 72; 89:1-37[2-38]; 110).

to take the nations as his "possession" (2:8). The psalm concludes with a warning to the kings:

> So now kings, wise up!
>   Be warned, you rulers of the earth!
> Serve YHWH with fear!
>   Rejoice with trembling!
> Kiss the son,[77] lest he become angry,
>   and you perish on the way,
>   for his wrath is quickly kindled. (2:10-12)

Psalm 2 "documents" the king's empowerment through the divine announcement of his sonship. The result is imperial dominion over the kings of the earth and, thus, over all the nations. Psalm 2 represents the apotheosis of royal ideology in the Hebrew scriptures. Such a psalm lacks David's imprimatur, perhaps because the Psalter's editors have in mind the David who emerges from below, not born from on high, the David who is ever caught in crises, ever seeking deliverance from God. Psalm 2 is not a psalm for the erstwhile shepherd boy or royal refugee (cf. Ps 3). By not associating David with Psalm 2, the editors seek to preserve at least at the outset David's uniquely vulnerable identity, protected from grand(iose) aspirations of imperial dominion, as one finds among the testimonies of ancient Near Eastern despots and certain royal psalms. The agenda of Psalm 2 is clear: the purpose of royal power in Zion is world dominion.

Psalms 72 and 101: The Two Sides of Just Rule

Psalms 72 and 101, the latter ascribed to David, register a different concern about royal power: both explicate the king's commitment to justice. Psalm 101 vividly depicts the king's zeal for integrity by first acknowledging YHWH's "benevolence" and "justice."

77. The MT features the Aramaic word for "son" (*bar*) rather than the Hebrew *ben*, indicating a particular rhetorical strategy of reaching out to the kings in their *lingua franca*.

I shall sing of benevolence and justice;
  to you, YHWH, I shall sing praises.
I shall study the way of integrity.
  When shall it come[78] to me?
I shall walk in the integrity of my heart
  within my own house.
I will not set my eyes on anything worthless;
  I denounce dealing in corruption;[79]
    it will not cling to me.
A perverted heart will be far from me;
  I am not cognizant of evil. (101:1-4)

The king declares his resolve to "clean house" by cultivating integrity and purging corruption, beginning with himself. Outwardly, his plan of action is to destroy the wicked, while favoring those who are "faithful" and walk in the "way of integrity" (101:5-8).

Psalm 72, meant "for Solomon," as indicated in the superscription, serves as the king's "job description," cast in the form of a petition. In addition to praying for the king's longevity, prosperous rule, and international acclaim—all the trappings of an imperial reign—the psalm requests that the king pay particular attention to the impoverished, granting them justice and salvation (72:2b, 4).

Give the king your judgments, O God,
  and your righteousness to the king's son.
May he judge your people with righteousness,
  and your poor with justice.
May the mountains yield shalom for the people,
  and the hills [do the same][80] with righteousness.
May he establish justice for the impoverished among the people,
  providing salvation for the children of the deprived
    and crushing the oppressor. (72:1-4)

78. Or "you come." The verb *bw'* can grammatically be either second-person masculine or third-person feminine. The translation reflects the latter, with "way" (*derek*) as the subject.

79. Literally, "deviations" (from *sēṭ*, related to √*śwṭ* ["deviate, turn away from"]).

80. Elliptically implied. The proposed transposition in *BHS* is unnecessary.

The superscription together with the colophon in 72:20 imagines Psalm 72 as advice given by David to his son Solomon. David's instructions to his "young and inexperienced" son, as the Chronicler describes Solomon (1 Chron 22:5; 29:1), are filled with injunctions concerning the disadvantaged, a far cry from David's instructions to his son in DtrH (1 Kgs 2:2-9)! The Solomonic superscription, moreover, highlights certain references within the body of the psalm, such as gold from Sheba (72:15a; cf. 10b; cf. 1 Kgs 10:1-13) and the proper exercise of judgment (72:2; cf. 1 Kgs 3:16-28). However, DtrH's account of Solomon's reign says nothing about the king's care for the impoverished or about him "crushing" the "oppressor." To the contrary, Solomon enslaved his subjects to undertake his monumental building programs, from the temple to the palace and various fortifications (1 Kgs 5:13; 9:15).

The message is clear of Psalm 72: royal power is to be exercised on behalf of the most vulnerable, whose welfare is the true measure of royal justice. The psalm recognizes that poverty is not a natural state. There is an agent of impoverishment, the "oppressor" (*ʿôšēq*), and the king is deemed responsible for "crushing" the oppressor in order to save the impoverished. Still, the king is not without his imperialism: the king's rule shall extend "from sea to sea" (72:8b) and throughout the desert (72:9). Kings as far as Tarshish and Sheba will offer tribute (72:10). Such imperialism, however, is matched by the king's responsibility for the disadvantaged.

> For he delivers the needy who cries out for help,
> and the impoverished—the one who lacks a helper.
> He looks compassionately on the lowly and the needy,
> and saves the lives of the destitute.
> From oppression and violence he redeems their lives;
> their blood is precious in his eyes. (72:12-14)

This central passage of the psalm breaks the series of jussive-oriented requests by stating unequivocally that the king does care for the impoverished and the underserved. Indeed, the king is not the last but the first resort for those who lack a "helper" (*ʿôzēr*). The king's job is to "deliver" and "save," by first regarding the destitute with "compassion" (√*ḥsh*). But the king does more than feel pity for the destitute; he saves them. That is his job.

Conclusion

Even the royal psalms offer differing portrayals of royal power. On the battlefield, the king is the conquering warrior, acting as YHWH's right hand and rod, exercising imperial dominion over the nations (Pss 2, 110). On the throne, the king exudes a magnetic majesty, a royal splendor that seduces and demands subordination, prompting "love at first might" (Ps 45). Nevertheless, the king's "glory" is entirely dependent on God's salvific power (21:5). Psalms 101 and 72, however, add a different dimension to the royal resume, namely the king's responsibility to establish justice, which is twofold: judgment against the wicked and justice for the disadvantaged. Psalm 72, in fact, paints a vividly eclectic picture of royal power, one that is as imperial as it is justice oriented.

Such language is scarce in DtrH, whether in relation to David or any subsequent king. DtrH is primarily interested in exclusive Yahwistic worship in a centralized location (Jerusalem). Hezekiah and Josiah are identified as the best kings within the Davidic lineage, but their credentials for YHWH's favor have more to do with establishing proper worship and destroying the high places than with delivering the impoverished from the hand of the oppressor. Bad kings, in turn, are condemned not for oppressing the weak but for worshipping other gods and practicing forms of forbidden worship. The only reference to the impoverished in DtrH comes at the end of the narrative when the most "impoverished" are left behind in the wake of Babylonian deportation (2 Kgs 24:14; 25:12). The emphasis on justice for the disadvantaged in Psalm 72 resonates more with the prophets than with DtrH (see chapter 8).

David Divested and Personalized

Nevertheless, the concern for justice in Psalm 72 also resonates with David in the Psalms, who as the imagined speaker of many psalms is repeatedly cast as "impoverished and deprived" (40:17[18]; 70:5; 86:1; 109:22). So now we come full circle: the imperial psalms set in sharp relief David's vulnerable status in most of "his" psalms, the David who is divested of power. In them, David counts himself among the persecuted and the destitute who cry out to God for help.

As the one imperial psalm that is ascribed to David, Psalm 110 reflects more the idealized Davidic dynasty than the individual (cf. Pss 2, 45, 89). But when the "dynasty" is taken out of "David," what is left is a person needful of God in times of distress. What is left is David's voice crying out to God. It is his cry for help that is most dominant in "his" psalms, not the pronouncement of dominion. In "his" psalms, David speaks little of his imperial privilege. At most, David self-identifies as the righteous warrior in the heat of battle either awaiting deliverance from God or giving thanks to God for victory (so Pss 18 and 144).

Most often, however, David casts himself as persecuted and deprived. Even as king, he was a refugee. Even as king, David confessed sin of the most egregious kind, seeking forgiveness. As the king who charged his son to establish justice for the most vulnerable, David did so with credibility, because he himself was needful. It is as if the psalmists were giving to every successor taking the throne the following charge: "Deliver the destitute who cry out for help! Look compassionately on the vulnerable! Do not forget that your 'father,' the founder of the dynasty, was himself impoverished and deprived."

And not just every king is implicated in these psalms. Every reciter of the Davidic psalms becomes dialogically engaged with the words "of David." The Davidic psalms provide repeated opportunity to identify with David. As the psalms were intended for widespread use in a variety of circumstances and settings, so the Davidic superscriptions remind readers that their distress, their oppression, their calamities, and their fears were shared by David, Israel's dynastic king. With these psalms, a bond is established by which the reader enters the intimate relationship that David himself had with God. By engaging such psalms, readers can relive David's challenges in ways that address their own concerns and lead them to trust in God, as exemplified by David himself. Or not. That is left for the reader to decide: to choose or to resist David's words. As for the former, one would need, moreover, to choose *which* David to accept, the imperial David, the "righteous" David, the divested David, the trusting David, the sinful David—a David for all seasons.

The Covenantal David

On a final note: among all the psalms related to David, we have identified three that feature covenantal promises made to the Davidic king, expressed in divergent ways, from the unconditional to the conditional (2, 89, 132). In these psalms, God is the agent of promise who ensures the continuation of the Davidic throne. Noteworthy is the fact that no prophet explicitly cites the Davidic covenant except one, and with a remarkable twist:

> Incline your ear, and come to me;
>   listen, so that you may live.
> I will make with you an everlasting covenant,
>   my faithful benevolence to David.
> See, I made him a witness to the peoples,
>   a leader and commander for the peoples. (Isa 55:3-4)

Reference to "everlasting covenant" (*bĕrît ʿôlām*) and "faithful benevolence" (*ḥăsādîm*) recalls the covenantal language of Psalms 89 and 132, as well as 2 Samuel 23:5. The key difference, however, lies in the plural object of address, "you" (*lākem*). In Isaiah, God promises to extend the Davidic covenant to the whole community. In the hands of the exilic prophet, "David" becomes "democratized." The entire community is now deemed the formal recipient of the Davidic covenant, a community disrupted by exile and divested of a Davidic king yet retains the Davidic covenant. In the words of the prophet, God's covenantal benevolence, once granted to David and his dynasty, is now granted to the people as a whole. God's "faithful benevolence," rooted in royal provenance, outlasts the kingdom. In their own way, the Davidic psalms also give assurance of such benevolence, for in them the cry of all who pray the psalms, seeking God's faithful, salvific love, is matched by the cry of the king, who does the same.

CHAPTER 8

ESTABLISHING JUSTICE: PROPHETIC AND PSALMIC

The fight for justice cannot be segregated

but must be integrated with the fight for life in all its forms.

—James Cone[1]

Think of "justice" in the Bible, and one naturally gravitates toward the prophets, such as Amos and his admonition made famous by Dr. Martin Luther King Jr., in his "Letter from a Birmingham Jail" (1963).

> Take away from me the noise of your songs;
> to the melody of your harps I will not listen.
> But let justice roll down like waters,
> and righteousness like an everflowing stream. (Amos 5:23-24, RSV)

The prophet prefers the sound of cascading justice over the melodious songs of meaningless praise. The sound of justice is likened to the rumbling roar of a torrent that never subsides. Is such justice destructive or restorative, disruptive or transformative? It depends on where one stands. In any case, prophetic justice disrupts the status quo. Justice requires change from top to bottom as it cascades "down." Or perhaps one thinks of the

1. "Whose Earth Is It Anyway?" *Cross Currents* 50 (Spring/Summer 2000): 36.

equally well-known passage from Micah, which has become something of a spiritual motto for many.

> What does the Lord require of you
> but to do justice,
> and to love kindness,
> and to walk humbly with your God? (Mic 6:8, NRSV)

Nevertheless, there are many other vivid references to justice among the prophets, from Elijah's protest against Ahab's murderous annexation of Naboth's vineyard (1 Kgs 21:19-26) to Isaiah's subversive Song of the Vineyard (Isa 5:1-7) to Ezekiel's divine shepherd feeding the sheep "with justice" (Ezek 34:15-16). The God of the prophets is unequivocally the God of justice who expects justice from the king (e.g., Isa 30:18; Jer 21:12) and, more broadly, from all those in power (e.g., Jer 22:15; 33:15).

Much of prophetic discourse bears witness to injustices suffered by the most vulnerable, cast frequently in the form of an indictment, as in Amos.

> Thus says YHWH: For three crimes of Israel, and for four,
> I will not revoke the punishment;
> *because they have sold the righteous for silver,*
> *and the destitute for a pair of sandals—*
> *they who trample the head of the impoverished into the dust of the earth,*
> *and push the afflicted out of the way.* (Amos 2:6-7b)

And the list goes on. The indictment (as italicized above) provides reasons for the announcement of judgment or punishment. Amos is particularly known for his condemnation of economic oppression.

> Hear this word, you cows of Bashan, who are on Mount Samaria, who oppress the impoverished, who crush the destitute, while saying to their husbands, "Bring us drinks!" (Amos 4:1)

These "cows" are not biologically bovine, but they are well sated. The prophet witnesses a direct correlation between their material wealth and the people's impoverishment. The same goes for luxury homes and fertile fields.

Therefore, because you exact taxes[2] from the impoverished,
and take from them levies of grain,
you have built houses of hewn stone,
but you will not live in them;
you have planted pleasant vineyards,
but you will not drink their wine.
For I know how many are your crimes,
and how great are your sins—
you who afflict the righteous, who accept bribes,
and push aside the destitute in the gate. (Amos 5:11-12)

Such judgment divests the rich of their wealth; wealth built on the backs of the "impoverished" (cf. Isa 5:8-10). For Amos, economic oppression is the polar opposite of a just society, and the misery it causes demands redress, warranting nothing less than divine judgment. But who are the victims? Amos identifies them with the "righteous" (*ṣādîq*; 2:6; 5:12), as well as with the "impoverished" (*dallîm*, *dal*; 4:1; 5:11) and "destitute" (*'ebyônîm*; 4:1; 5:12). This threefold identification of the oppressed is attested often in the Psalms, as we shall see.

Judgment is not the only genre in the prophet's tool kit for addressing injustice. Prophetic discourse is also filled with admonitions, as in the case of Isaiah, similar to Amos.

I hate your new moons and your festivals;
they have become a burden to me; I am tired of bearing them.
When you extend your hands [in prayer], I will hide my eyes from you.
Even when you offer many prayers, I will not listen.

2. A hapax legomenon with uncertain meaning (√*bšs*). It is plausible to identify the verb, via metathesis, with √*šbs*, whose Akkadian cognate means "exact corn tax" (*HALOT*, 165).

Your hands are filled with blood.
  Wash yourselves clean;
    remove your evil from my sight;
      cease to do evil, learn to do good.
Seek justice, lead the oppressed.[3]
  defend the orphan, plead for the widow. (Isa 1:14-17)

In place of festivals and communal prayers, Isaiah demands a moral purge that clears the way for justice, but justice not in any abstract sense. The prophet commands attention to the "oppressed" (*ḥāmûṣ*), the "orphan" (*yātôm*), and the "widow" (*'almānâ*). The last two designations, the most vulnerable in ancient Israelite society status-wise, are often paired together, serving as the barometers of justice in society.[4] But they are hardly ever alone: the "widow" and the "orphan" are often accompanied by others:

Thus says YHWH of hosts:
Administer true justice;
  extend benevolence and compassion to one another.
Do not oppress the widow, the orphan,
  the immigrant, or the impoverished;
  do not devise evil in your hearts against one another. (Zech 7:9-10)

The "immigrant" (*gēr*) and the "impoverished" (*'ānî*) join company with the "widow" and the "orphan," the company of the victimized. In Malachi, the "widow" and the "orphan" join ranks with the "hired workers," who depend entirely on wages for their welfare, as well as with the immigrant, who is landless.

Then I will draw near to you for judgment;
I will be swift to bear witness against the sorcerers,
  against the adulterers, against those who swear falsely,
  against those who oppress the hired workers in their wages,
    the widow and the orphan,

3. Read *ḥāmûṣ*, according to the versions.

4. See Isa 1:23; 9:17; 10:2; Jer 7:6; 22:3; 49:11; Ezek 22:7; Zech 7:9-10; cf. Jer 5:28.

against those who expel the immigrant,
and do not fear me, says YHWH of hosts. (Mal 3:5)

Here oppression is placed on the same par as adultery, false witness, and sorcery. Oppression takes its place within this list of judgments that could easily be recast as a list of prohibitions akin to the commandments of the Decalogue: "Thou shalt not commit adultery; thou shalt not oppress essential workers; thou shalt not cast out the immigrant," and so on.

As in the Psalms, the prophetic call for justice is given in the occasional lament:

YHWH, how long must I cry for help and you not listen?
[How long] must I call out "Violence!" and you do not deliver?
Why do you show me injustice
and make me look at trouble.
Destruction and violence are before me;
strife persists and conflict abounds.
No wonder the law is ineffective,
and justice is down for the count.
The wicked surround the righteous;
therefore, judgment comes forth compromised. (Hab 1:2-4)

The prophet complains of twisted justice that he is forced to witness, resulting in violent conflict and nullified law. For Habakkuk, the ultimate resolution to injustice is found in his concluding prayer, which seeks a theophanic intervention, described in detail in 3:2-15. Approaching from the south, YHWH shines forth "like the sun," with "pestilence" and "plague" at the vanguard (3:5). The earth is shaken, and the nations tremble (3:6). Mountains "writhe," and "torrents" "sweep by," while YHWH shoots arrows and throws the "flashing spear" (3:11). The nations are "trampled" (3:12). All of this takes place so that YHWH can "save" a people (3:13) and, in turn, crush the "head of the wicked" (3:14). A theophany, no less, is marshaled for the cause of justice. Justice requires God to show up because justice requires deliverance.

Another theophanic account that addresses Israel's injustice comes from Micah. The prophet addresses both the peoples and the earth to announce that YHWH will be a "witness against you" from the "holy temple" (1:2). The prophet continues:

> For lo, YHWH is coming out of his place,
> and will come down and tread upon the high places of the earth.
> Then the mountains will melt under him,
> and the valleys will split apart,
> like wax near the fire, like waters poured down a steep slope.
> All this is because of Jacob's transgression,
> and because of the sins of the house of Israel. (Mic 1:3-5a)

As in Habakkuk, YHWH's approach provokes cosmic travail (cf. Amos 5:24). The warrant is clear: Israel's sins. Both theophanic accounts (Hab 3:2-15 and Mic 1:3-5a) distinguish themselves from the theophany account described in Psalm 18:6-18[7-19]. Neither injustice nor transgression is the issue in Psalm 18; rather, it is deliverance on the battlefield. The Psalms and the Prophets testify that God can show up for very different reasons, judgment on the one hand, and deliverance on the other.

With this all-too-brief introduction of justice among the prophets, we jump into the Psalms with a few questions in mind: What are the marks of genuine justice? Who is most deserving of justice? What does justice look like for the oppressed and the wicked, as well as for the nations and creation? Who are the agents of justice? How inclusive is justice? Is justice punitive or restorative? Is it salvific or destructive?

Justice in the Psalms

While the prophets are known mostly for citing God in the form of divine address, the psalmists are not. Nevertheless, God does have ample opportunity to speak in the Psalms and does so in strikingly different ways.[5] In relation to prophetic discourse, the strongest oracular parallels in the Psalms are the divine "oracle against the nations" in Psalms 60 and 108 and the "covenant lawsuit" in Psalm 50. Most distinctive in the Psalms are God's command to "desist" in waging war in Psalm 46 and God's ordainment of human transience in Psalm 90. If anything, the Psalms feature a wide diversity of divine discourse, addressing a wide variety of topics. But, curiously, "justice" is not as prominent among them as compared to prophetic address (cf. only 12:6; 50:6; 75:2-5; 82:2-4). While the topic of justice is pronounced in the Psalms, it is lodged more in petition and protest than in divine address. But there are a few exceptions, the greatest being Psalm 82.

Psalm 82: The Ground of Being and the Grounds for Justice

Considered the most important passage in the Bible by at least one *New* Testament scholar,[6] Psalm 82 captures the theme of justice in the most dramatic way. One could call this psalm the Psalter's theological cornerstone of justice. Its distinctive literary setting offers a front-row seat to a heavenly courtroom proceeding in which God indicts and convicts the gods for their failure to establish justice on earth. The curtain rises revealing God addressing the divine assembly.

5. Divine discourse is featured in a total of eighteen psalms, including promises of salvation (Pss 12, 35, 68, 91), as well as divine judgments and admonitions set within various contexts: historical/national (60//108, 81, 95, 105), international (46), anthropological (75, 90), cultic (50), and the divine realm (82). In a special class are those that feature covenantal promises, both conditional and unconditional, made to David or the Davidic king (Pss 2, 89, 110, 132). See the overview in Herbert J. Levine, *Sing unto God a New Song: A Contemporary Reading of the Psalms* (Bloomington: Indiana University Press, 1995), 112–13. Levine counts, however, only sixteen psalms of divine discourse.

6. John Dominic Crossan, *The Birth of Christianity: Discovering What Happened in the Years Immediately after the Execution of Jesus* (San Francisco: HarperSanFrancisco, 1998), 575. See J. Clinton McCann, Jr., "The Single Most Important Text in the Entire Bible: Toward a Theology of the Psalms," in *Soundings in the Theology of the Psalms: Perspectives and Methods in Contemporary Scholarship*, ed. Rolf A. Jacobson (Minneapolis: Fortress, 2011), 63–75.

God takes his stand in the divine council;
amid the gods he renders judgment.
"How long will you judge unjustly,
showing bias toward the wicked? *Selah*
Give justice to the impoverished and the orphaned!
Maintain the rights of the afflicted and the destitute!
Rescue the impoverished and the deprived!
Deliver them from the hand of the wicked!" (82:1-4)

"God," the high God and judge of heaven and earth, renders judgment against the "gods." Comparable scenes such as 1 Kings 22:19-22 and Job 1:6; 2:1 refer to the "host of heaven" (*ṣĕbā' haššāmayim*) and "the sons of God" (*bĕnê hā'ĕlōhîm*), respectively. In Psalm 82, however, the "gods" and "God" share the same designation in Hebrew (*'ĕlōhîm*). But in 82:6, the "gods" are designated as "sons of the Most High" (*bĕnê 'elyôn*), confirming God's sovereign position.[7]

God, the Most High (*Elyon*), begins the proceedings with an accusatory question, "How long?" (*'ad-mātay*), an interrogative typically reserved for human protest against God.[8] Here, however, it is directed against the gods by God. Built into the question is the allegation of injustice, defined here as favoring the wicked, whose "hand" oppresses the "destitute" (82:4b). Whereas the "wicked" are referenced with only one common term (*rĕšā'îm*), attested twice (82:2, 4), the vulnerable are granted five descriptors: "impoverished" (*dal*, 2x), "orphaned" (*yātôm*), "afflicted" (*'ānî*), "destitute" (*raš*), and "deprived" (*'ebyôn*). In Psalm 82, injustice is revealed by its myriad casualties. Justice shows itself in deliverance from the "hand of the wicked." In a word, justice is salvation. But the gods have failed to establish justice: by not delivering the oppressed, they have demonstrated their partiality toward the wicked. In so doing, the gods have perverted justice without even knowing it.

7. For full discussion of the divine identities, see Peter Machinist, "How Gods Die, Biblically and Otherwise: A Problem of Cosmic Restructuring," in *Reconsidering the Concept of Revolutionary Monotheism*, ed. Beate Pongratz-Leisten (Winona Lake, IN: Eisenbrauns, 2011), 195–209.

8. E.g., Pss 6:4; 74:10; 80:5; 90:13; cf. Prov 1:22.

> But they do not know, nor do they understand;
> they wander about in darkness,
> [such that] all the earth's foundations are tottering.
> I had declared, "You are gods,
> sons of *Elyon*,[9] all of you.
> Nevertheless, you shall die as mortals;
> like any prince you will fall." (82:5-7)

The gods prove to be utterly clueless regarding matters of justice.[10] Lacking understanding, they wander aimlessly in the dark, their negligence threatening the earth's foundations. The connection between social justice and creation's integrity is not accidental. Foundational to God's just and sovereign reign is creation's stability.[11] Conversely, the failure to render justice is tantamount to an assault on creation (see Hos 4:1-3).

With the indictment formally submitted, God declares the verdict, first by identifying the defendants as "gods" (*'ĕlōhîm*; 82:6a; cf. 82:1b) in declarative, if not creational speech.[12] The divine designation, though generic, offers a stark reminder that as *'ĕlōhîm* ("gods") they are to do the work of *'Ĕlōhîm* ("God"). As "sons of *Elyon*," the gods serve at the behest of their sovereign progenitor. As "gods" they not only share in divinity, they also share in that which grounds divinity: the performance of justice. By failing to execute justice for the oppressed, the gods forfeit their divinity. They are dethroned from on high and, thus, rendered mortal, not because they have rebelled against the Most High in heaven but because they have neglected the cause of justice on earth.

9. Or "the Most High."

10. See the alternative reading of Brent A. Strawn, "The Poetics of Psalm 82: Three Critical Notes Along with a Plea for the Poetic," *RB* 121, no. 1 (2014): 26–31, who argues that it is the "impoverished," etc., who are rendered ignorant and aimless. While typically applied to human beings, such language evocatively serves to underline the absurdity of the gods' conduct, who are themselves condemned to mortality, anticipating the irony of such (poetic) justice.

11. Pss 93:1; 96:10; 104:5; 1 Chron 16:30; cf. Ps 46:6.

12. Strawn observes that such discourse is performative, as in Gen 1 ("Poetics of Psalm 82," 31–35).

In an earlier tradition adapted from Canaanite myth, *Elyon* ("Most High") is depicted as the high god who divides up the peoples, apportioning their territorial allotments, including Israel's. With each allotment there is an assigned deity.

> When *Elyon* apportioned the nations,
> dividing humankind,
> he established the boundaries of the peoples
> according to the number of the gods.[13]
> YHWH's own portion was his people,
> Jacob his inherited allotment. (Deut 32:8-9)

In this most ancient of passages, YHWH is profiled as one of the "gods" to receive a special inheritance from *Elyon*, namely Israel ("Jacob"). In its larger Canaanite context, the high god and the assigned god were two distinct deities. In its adaptation in the song of Moses in Deuteronomy (32:1-43), they came to be read as one and the same: two distinct epithets pointing to the same God, Israel's God, set within a polytheistic background.

Building on this heavenly scene of divine hierarchy, Psalm 82 collapses the divine distance by explicitly identifying Israel's "God" as *Elyon* and eliminating the "gods" in the name of justice, a decidedly monotheizing move. As princes die, so will the gods. By judicial proceeding, the elimination of the gods affords God *direct* sovereignty over all the earth. Divinity has now become a sovereign singularity. Such a move, remarkably, is not facilitated by violence or conquest: the God of Psalm 82 does not slay the gods on the battlefield, as one finds in Marduk's conquest over Tiamat and her retinue in *Enūma elish*. The "gods" of Psalm 82 pose no mortal threat to God. It is rather by divine judgment that they are eliminated. Justice demands the divestment of their divinity.

By drawing from an ancient depiction of divinity, one that populates the divine realm with high and low deities, Psalm 82 boldly claims the true nature of divinity. Genuine divinity is demonstrated in the practice of justice, not in raw power exercised willy-nilly. It is the *just* use of

13. Read *běnê 'ēl* (or *'ēlîm*), along with LXX and Qumran, instead of MT *běnê yiśrā'ēl* ("Israelites").

sovereign power that defines divinity, the kind of justice that is liberative and protective for the most vulnerable, who suffer from the "hand of the wicked" (82:4). Failure to establish justice is a failure to maintain divinity. "Godhood and injustice . . . *cannot* mix."[14] Such is the basis of appeal that concludes the psalm.

> Arise, O God! Judge the earth,
> for you hold all the nations in your possession. (82:8)

With all the nations in God's possession (cf. Deut 32:8-9), God's sovereign singularity demands sovereign responsibility on earth. The psalmist's stenography of the heavenly proceedings is followed by the community's plea for the God of justice to do the same on earth. The speaker beseeches God to do the same to all the nations as God had done to the gods. This "tail" end of the psalm turns out to "wag" the entire psalm: the courtroom scene now serves as precedent for the real and pressing issue at hand: justice on earth. What the gods have failed to do, God aspires to do, and the people expect God to do. In the heavenly court, God proved to be a champion of justice. Now justice must be completed on earth. Now the nations are to be held accountable. Like the gods, they have their responsibility to uphold justice. Now is the time for justice to take place "on earth as it is in heaven." Failure is not an option. Just ask the gods. But wait . . . they're dead! The responsibility of establishing justice now rests on God's shoulders, as well as humanity's. By reciting the psalm all the way to its petitionary conclusion, worshippers internalize the call to justice by calling upon God to establish justice.[15] God's divinity depends on it, so also Israel's integrity. Now the greater drama of justice is about to begin.

Psalm 75: Establishing Justice on God's Terms

Psalm 75 could be considered the (partial) fulfillment of the concluding petition in Psalm 82. It celebrates in declarative praise God's decrees

14. Strawn, "Poetics of Psalm 82," 37.

15. So Machinist, who argues that human beings become the gods' replacements in the establishment of justice ("How Gods Die," 235–36).

of justice issued against the wicked while vindicating the righteous. The psalm begins with a sovereign declaration from God, prefaced by the people's thanksgiving.

> We give thanks to you, O God; we give thanks!
> Your name is near; your marvelous deeds are recounted.
> "When I choose the right time,
> I will establish justice with equity.
> When the earth and all its inhabitants dissolve,
> it is I who will keep its pillars steady.
> I say to the boastful, 'Do not be boastful!'
> And to the wicked, 'Do not exalt your horn!'
> 'Do not exalt your horn on high,
> or speak arrogantly against the rock!'"[16] (75:1-5)

After a communal expression of thanksgiving, Psalm 75 issues a series of divine declarations. Although lacking a formal introduction, the first declaration makes clear who the speaker is: the divine judge who resolves to establish justice at the "right time" (*mô'ēd*). As if to answer the concluding petition of Psalm 82, God confirms that justice will be served, but only on God's own terms. Although not entirely solicitous to the people's demands, God will respond in "justice with equity" in due time, justice that is fair for all (cf. Isa 2:3-4).

As for the earth in judgment, God gives assurance that creation will remain intact even if the earth and its inhabitants "dissolve" away (*nĕmōgîm*; 75:4). The statement seems logically incoherent, given its hyperbolic description of creation in meltdown. If the earth dissolves away, what is the point of keeping its "pillars steady"? The language conjures the scene of a flood that appears to "dissolve" the land and its inhabitants by submerging everything in its path (cf. Gen 6:17; 7:17). But the "pillars," God declares, will be upheld; they are the high mountains that serve to hold aloft the firmament and keep the waters "above" at bay (Gen 1:6-7), preventing cosmic collapse (cf. Gen 7:11). So a catastrophe it is for the earth and its

16. Read *baṣṣûr* for MT *bĕṣawwā'r* ("with [arrogant] neck").

inhabitants, yet creation's structural integrity, its infrastructure, remains preserved.

The psalm, moreover, makes clear that it is not God who is doing the "dissolving." While cosmic chaos may happen on its own, the implication in the divine admonition is that the "boastful" and the "wicked" threaten creation's integrity (cf. Ps 104:35). The wicked wreak chaos by their "horn" (*qeren*), an image of violent power,[17] as conjured by the terrifying image of a goring ox (cf. Exod 21:28-32). God, in effect, warns the wicked against impaling others with their arrogant speech (v. 6). The destructive power of the wicked is regarded as cosmically disruptive and an offense against God. Even as the pillars remain firm while the world suffers a meltdown (cf. Gen 6:11, 13), so the divine "rock" remains resistant against the verbal onslaughts of the wicked.[18] A rock remains impervious; in fact, it can crush horns. As the "rock" of salvation (cf. Pss 89:26[27]; 95:1), the divine judge is set to "bring down" the wicked.

For not from the east or from the west,
  or from the south[19] [comes such] exaltation.[20]
For God is the one who judges;
  bringing down one while raising up another.
Indeed, there is a cup in YHWH's hand,
  with foaming wine, fully mixed with spice.
He will pour out from it.
Only[21] [down to] the dregs
  will all the wicked of the earth have to drain it,
    slurping it up. (75:7-9)

17. E.g., Jer 48:25; 1 Sam 2:10; 2 Sam 22:3; Ps 92:11.

18. For God as "rock," see, e.g., Pss 18:2[3], 31[32]; 19:14[15]; 31:2-3[3-4]; 62:2[3]; 95:1; 144:1.

19. Literally, "desert." Read *midbār* for MT *midbar.*

20. Read as Hiphil inf abs from √*rwm* ("rise up"), identical in form to "mountains" *(hārîm).*

21. Hebrew *'ak,* used in the restrictive sense.

The strophe elucidates the kind of justice God intends to establish, one that both "brings down" and "raises up" (75:8b). This is what "justice with equity" looks like (75:2b). While the objects of such opposing actions remain undefined at the moment, it is all sorted out at the end of the psalm: the wicked are brought down, and the righteous are raised up (75:11). As for the former, God has in store for them a special mixture of wine that will send them staggering (75:9). This is not "the cup of salvation" (Ps 116:13) but a cup of judgment (cf. Jer 25:15; 51:7; Lam 4:21)—a "cup of reeling" (Isa 51:17, 22).

By raising their glasses to drink down judgment, the wicked will no longer be able to exalt themselves, let alone raise their own "horns."

> But as for me, I will rejoice[22] forever;
>   I will sing to the God of Jacob.
> "All the horns of the wicked I will cut down,
>   but the horns of the righteous one will be lifted up." (75:9-10)

The psalm concludes with another divine decree (cf. 75:2), which effectively summarizes the earlier decree in 75:5-6 but adds reference to the "horns" of the righteous "lifted up" (cf. 75:5b, 8b). The contrasting juxtaposition between the "wicked" and the "righteous" has its precedent in the very first psalm (1:6). The wicked are destined to fall and perish, whereas the righteous will flourish. Such is the work of justice, which establishes an inverse relationship between the wicked and the righteous. While Psalm 75 does not fully answer the concluding plea of Psalm 82, it is a start—but only if the company of the "righteous" includes the "impoverished and the destitute" (82:3-4), which in fact is the case elsewhere in the Psalms, as we shall see.

Justice as Salvation

According to Psalm 82, divinely established justice translates into salvation for the oppressed, for God recognizes that their condition is not

22. Read *'āgîl* for MT *'aggîd* ("I will declare"), given the parallelism and likely graphic confusion.

a consequence of their actions (e.g., laziness) or a natural outcome of life not being fair. Impoverishment in God's eyes is nothing short of an abomination, a consequence of oppression. The misery of the oppressed is not of their own making but due to the "hand of the wicked" (82:4b). Deliverance is required.

Psalm 37: Justice for the Morally Profiled

At the very heart of God is a "love" for justice, which takes the form of solidarity with the victims of injustice at the expense of the wicked, the authors of injustice.

> For YHWH loves justice,
>   and he will not abandon his faithful.
> The unjust will be forever destroyed,[23]
>   and the progeny of the wicked will be cut off. (37:28; cf. 99:4)

YHWH's love for justice is not a self-evident claim. As Psalm 82 dramatically demonstrates, the gods were not known for being just or good or even wise. Not so with YHWH, Israel's God. YHWH's "love" for justice is definitive of who YHWH is, and it is equally determinative of the respective outcomes for the "faithful" and for the "unjust"/"wicked." Such justice is repeated in 37:32-33 with greater specificity.

> While the wicked profile the righteous,
>   seeking to kill them,
> YHWH will not abandon them to their power;
>   or let them be condemned when they are judged. (37:32-33)

YHWH will not abandon the righteous to the "power" (literally "hand") of the wicked, who seek to "profile" (√*ʿṣph*) and "kill" them. The first of these two verbs highlights the means by which the wicked target

23. A missing word (*ʿawwālîm*) is restored in light of the fact that the colon in MT begins not with an *ʿayin* but with a *lamed* (+*ʿayin*), suggesting a parablepsis, an omission by scribal oversight. MT reads "forever they are guarded," but LXX reads, additionally, "the lawless shall be persecuted," pointing to an original *ʿawwālîm lĕʿôlām nišmādû*.

the righteous, namely by watching them stealthily (cf. Ps 10:8). Although such language in isolation implies outright murder, the following verse suggests a more judicial means of killing: by execution. YHWH promises that the righteous will not be found guilty in a court of law. They will be proven innocent, a sign of divine support and vindication, indeed, a sign of "salvation" from YHWH, their "stronghold" and "refuge" (37:39-40). It is YHWH's mission to protect and deliver the righteous from the wicked, who relentlessly target them for death.

Psalm 12: In Need of a Witness

Psalm 12 features a divine declaration that combines deliverance and vindication for the sake of the "afflicted" and "deprived." As buildup, the speaker pleads to YHWH to counter those whose lips are "slippery" and whose tongue "boasts of great things" (12:3). Mouths of malice they are.

> Help, YHWH, for the faithful one is done for![24]
> The steadfast have disappeared[25] from the human race!
> They speak falsely to one another;
> with slippery lips [and] with a divided heart[26] they talk.
> May YHWH cut off all slippery lips,
> the tongue that boasts of great things,
> who say, "With our tongue we are invincible!
> Our lips are with us.
> So who can be lord over us?" (12:1-4[2-5])

This opening strophe concludes with a quotation from those who place their confidence in the sovereignty of their own tongue. The expression "our lips are with us" (12:4b[5b]) reflects an unusual use of the preposition (*'itānû*), perhaps a clever (and damning) play on the declaration,

24. Literally, "come to an end" (*gmr*).

25. So MT. The verb √*pss* is a hapax legomenon perhaps related to the Akkadian *pasâsu* ("do away, blot out") or more likely a by-form of the verb *'ps* (*HALOT*, 79, 949).

26. Literally, "with heart and heart," an idiom unattested elsewhere in biblical Hebrew, evidently meaning duplicity. In contrast, see Ps 86:11-12.

"YHWH is with us" (Num 14:9; cf. 2 Kgs 9:32). In other words, the wicked have replaced YHWH with their own lips! They worship their own words. Self-autonomy is self-sovereignty, the delusion of impunity. Such is the boast of the wicked.

It is amid such boastful words that YHWH's own words break in, disrupting such sovereign speech.

> "Because of the devastation of the afflicted
> and the groaning of the deprived,
> I will now arise," says YHWH.
> "I will appoint a witness[27] for their security."[28]
> The promises of YHWH are pure promises,
> [like] silver refined in an earthen furnace,
> purified seven times over.
> You, YHWH, will protect them;[29]
> you will deliver them[30] from this generation forever.
> The wicked roam around freely,
> all because worthless shit[31] is exalted by humanity. (12:5-8[6-9])

The wicked have had their say, so YHWH now has something to say. YHWH cites the exploited state of the impoverished as warrant for an intervention. When YHWH "arises," one expects YHWH to go out fighting like a warrior on the battlefield. Instead, YHWH rises up to appoint

---

27. MT: "for which they pant" (*pwh*). LXX reads "I will speak openly." Other versions reflect equal uncertainty, so also the various scholarly emendations (see *BHS*). However, the form *yāpîaḥ* is best taken as a verbal adjective functioning as a noun on the basis of the Ugaritic cognate *ypḥ* (so Dennis Pardee, "*ypḥ* 'Witness' in Hebrew and Ugaritic," *VT* 28 [1978]: 204–13). Moreover, the prepositional prefix *bĕ* functions as a *bet essentiae*. For etymology and syntactical analysis, see J. Gerald Janzen, "Another Look at Psalm XII 6," no. 2 *VT* 54 (2004): 157–64, who draws from Patrick D. Miller, "*Yāpîaḥ* in Psalm XII, 6," *VT* 28 (1978): 495–500.

28. Literally, "as salvation for him." The singular suffix is taken collectively (see v. 7b[8b]).

29. So MT, whose antecedents are the "afflicted" and "deprived" in v. 5[6].

30. So MT, the more difficult text. As in v. 6b[7b], the singular suffix is used collectively.

31. A hapax legomenon from the root *zll*, "to be worthless," contrasted with the value of YHWH's "pure promises."

a "witness" (*yāpîaḥ*), whose identity is unclear. But what is clear is that a "witness" gives verbal testimony—how fitting for a psalm filled with quoted discourse! God's "witness" will testify on behalf of the afflicted as counter-testimony to the wicked and as vindication for the "faithful." Such a witness will disrupt the deliberations of the wicked to oppress and eliminate the impoverished. With the tongue of God's "witness," the vulnerable, not the wicked, will prove "invincible" (cf. 12:4a[5a]). Each in its own way, Psalms 12, 37, and 82 equate justice with salvation. The shape of such salvation is explicated further.

Psalms 10 and 76: Freedom for the Afflicted

At the conclusion of Psalm 10 is a description of the God who empowers the "afflicted."

> You attend to the desire of the afflicted, YHWH;
> you strengthen their heart; you incline your ear,
> to establish justice for the orphan and the oppressed,
> so that no one from the land will ever again spread terror.[32]
> (10:17-18)

God's so-called preferential option for the poor, the psalmist claims, is not a matter of preference at all but one of justice, and it begins with God's "ear" inclined toward the "afflicted" (*'ănāwîm*) to fulfill their "desire," the desire for freedom from terror in the land. What does such freedom look like? Certain psalms elsewhere deploy a simple metaphor that vividly conjures the kind of freedom that results from divine deliverance: being set on a "broad" or wide-open place (*merḥāb*), the opposite of constriction or restriction (Pss 18:19[20]; 31:8[9]; 118:5). In a "broad place," security and freedom converge. Conversely, affliction, impoverishment, and deprivation are counted as conditions of constriction or oppression. In a "broad place" freedom has its home, the result of justice, which is the shape of salvation, as also in Psalm 76.

32. Literally, "cause to tremble." Here, "the land" refers to YHWH's "land" in v. 16.

You, yes you, are awesome.
  Who can stand before you once you are enraged?
From the heavens you pronounced judgment;
  the earth grew afraid and fell silent,
    when God arose for the cause of justice,
      to save all the afflicted of the earth. *Selah* (76:7-9)

God's "awesome" nature reflects God's impassioned justice for "all the afflicted" (v. 9b), justice driven by a righteous rage that is resolved in salvation (76:7b, 9b). In Psalm 76, salvation is the means of justice, and justice is salvation for the oppressed. Such justice, moreover, renders the "earth" fearfully silent. Why? Perhaps because the "earth" knows how disruptive God's justice can be in a world whose equilibrium is founded on its status quo (76:8b). It is against such a world that God pronounces judgment from heaven. But who on earth can establish such heavenly judgment? Psalm 72 offers an answer.

Psalm 72: The King as Savior of the Oppressed

God's salvific justice on earth is to be realized by the earthly king, as detailed in the royal job description in this *Psalm for Solomon*.

May he judge your people with righteousness,
  and your afflicted with justice.
May the mountains yield shalom for the people,
  and the hills [do the same] with righteousness.
May he establish justice for those who are impoverished,
  save the children who are deprived,
    and crush the oppressor. (72:2-4)

Such a passage could have easily been written with God in mind, but here it is the king, God's instrument of justice on earth. The king's justice is meant to yield peace and prosperity (*shalom*) for all the people, indeed, for the land. But for the impoverished, justice is nothing less than their salvation from the "oppressor," who is to be "crushed." Justice for the vulnerable requires the overthrow of the oppressor.

Greater detail is given in a subsequent strophe in this royal psalm, pressing the point that lives hang in the balance.

For he delivers the deprived, who cry out for help,
and the impoverished, who lack a helper.
He looks compassionately on the downtrodden and the deprived,
and saves the lives of the destitute.
From oppression and violence he redeems their lives;
and their blood is precious in his eyes. (72:12-14)

In God's stead, the king delivers those who are victims of "oppression and violence," the very conditions that keep them in their vulnerable status as "deprived" and "impoverished." In 72:4, salvation for the destitute targets "the oppressor" (*ʿôšēq*). In 72:14, however, the language shifts from the individual to something more abstract: "oppression" (*tôk*). Behind the "oppressor" stands a system of "oppression" and "violence" (*ḥāmās*; cf. Ps 55:11[12]; Hab 1:3). Redemption involves not only "crushing the oppressor" (Ps 72:4) but dismantling a system. While such language could easily pertain to Israel's God, it is applied by the psalmist to the king, whose responsibility is not only to maintain the kingdom's stability by defending its boundaries and exercising imperial control (see 72:8-11), but also to deliver the afflicted and save the impoverished. The kingdom depends on it. Such a king might even have Amos's endorsement.

The Righteous as the Afflicted: Psalms 140 and 34

Whether by the king or by God, justice translates as salvation for the vulnerable, which Psalm 140 describes as YHWH's championing of their "cause":

I know[33] that YHWH champions the cause of the afflicted,
justice for the deprived.
Surely, the righteous will give thanks to your name,
and the upright will dwell in your presence. (140:12-13[13-14])

33. Read *Qere*.

YHWH champions the "afflicted" (*ʿānî*) and the "deprived" (*ʾebyōnîm*), two designations of the socioeconomically exploited that are frequently paralleled or conjoined in the Psalms,[34] sometimes as a self-designation.[35] The speaker in Psalm 140 counts himself among them, as well as with the "righteous" (*ṣaddîqîm*). The association is not coincidental. In the Psalms, the "righteous" are often cast as the most vulnerable, as one finds in Psalm 34.

> The eyes of YHWH are [focused] on the righteous;
> his ears are [attuned] to their cry.
> YHWH's face is set against evildoers,
> to eradicate their renown from the land.
> When [the righteous][36] cry out, YHWH hears them,
> and delivers them from all their troubles.
> YHWH is near the brokenhearted,
> and saves the crushed in spirit.
> Although many are their afflictions,
> YHWH[37] delivers the righteous from them all.
> He preserves all their bones;
> not one of them will be broken.
> [Only] one misfortune[38] will kill the wicked;
> those who hate the righteous will be found guilty. (34:16-22)

The righteous are the ones who "cry out" to YHWH, who are "brokenhearted" and "crushed," and suffer many "afflictions." YHWH's salvation is for them. With YHWH's "eyes" and "ears" focused on the "righteous" (34:16), YHWH's "face," by contrast, "is set against" the wicked to eradicate all trace of them, including their remembrance. The resulting picture, pressed anthropomorphically, is physically impossible: how can God's "eyes" and "ears" be oriented favorably toward the righteous, while God's "face" is "set against" the wicked? God has a double visage. Such

34. E.g., Pss 12:6; 35:10; 72:12; 74:21; 86:1; 109:16, 22; cf. Prov 31:20.

35. E.g., 40:17[18]; 70:5[6]; 86:1; 109:22.

36. Understood and supplied by LXX.

37. So MT (cf. LXX).

38. Or "evil [deed]" (*rāʿâ*). The term is ambiguous. Cf. v. 20a.

are the limits of metaphor, particularly when applied to the divine. God's "face" in this case is metaphoric of God's resolve to "take care" of the wicked, and not in a good way (cf. Ps 51:9[10]), as God takes care of the vulnerable in a salvific way. The psalm paradoxically twists the theme of vulnerability: whereas the righteous suffer *many* "afflictions" or evil deeds (*rāʿôt*), from which they will be delivered, the wicked will suffer their demise by only one (34:22). It only takes one "misfortune" to take care of the wicked, perhaps one of their own making. Who, then, is the most vulnerable after all?

This disparity of misfortune between the righteous and the wicked points toward identifying the righteous with the most vulnerable in society, as noted elsewhere. Consequently, the notion of righteousness is recast in a way that defies conventional biblical wisdom, as one finds in Proverbs, in which the righteous are not identified with the oppressed (see chapter 9). In the Psalms, the focus is more prophetically oriented: justice in the Psalms is salvation for the most vulnerable, identified here as the "righteous." It is no coincidence, then, that many a psalmic petitioner self-identifies as "impoverished and deprived" (*ʿānî wĕʾebyôn*),[39] as oppressed and persecuted by the wicked, in order to elicit God's salvific care. In common to all these psalms is the claim that divine justice is liberative justice, that God's judgment is salvific. The salvation of the oppressed is "the salvation of the righteous" (37:39-40). It is to say that the cascading waters of justice in Amos will lift up the vulnerable and the violated while casting down the wicked and the oppressor, like the horse and its rider in the exodus (cf. Exod 15:1, 21).

Justice and Vindication

Another dimension of God's justice is righteousness, which for the oppressed takes on the sense not only of liberation but of vindication, as in Psalm 103:6, "YHWH works righteousness [*ṣĕdāqôt*], justice for all

39. See 40:17[18]; 70:5[6]; 86:1 (in reverse order); 109:22.

who are oppressed." Here, "righteousness" wrought by YHWH proves to be vindication for the oppressed.

Psalm 17: Vindication as Acquittal

Psalm 17 is an example of God's justice resulting in personal vindication. The speaker cries out desperately for "my justice," the kind that will clear the speaker of "wrongdoing."

A Prayer of David
Heed, YHWH, what is right;
  attend to my cry;
    Give ear to my prayer,
      [uttered] without deceitful lips.
From your face shall my justice come;
  may your eyes perceive what is fair.
You have tested my heart and assessed [me] at night;
  you have refined me, without finding any wrongdoing.[40]
    My mouth does not transgress.
As for the deeds of others,
  I have kept to the word of your lips;
[as for][41] the paths of the violent,[42]
  my steps hold to *your* paths;
    my feet have not slipped.[43]
I, for one, call upon you because you answer me, O God.
  [So] incline your ear to me! Hear my words!
Manifest your benevolence in wondrous ways,[44]
  you who by your right hand save those who take refuge
    from those who assail [them].

40. Read *zimmātî* for MT *zammōtî* ("I devise").

41. The *lamed* prefix at the beginning of the verse (*lip'ullôt*) is elliptically carried over.

42. Some find the meaning of the phrase ambiguous, suggesting that *pārîṣ* is etymologically related to Akkadian *parṣu* ("command"). But see Ezek 18:10; Isa 35:9.

43. This reading involves a redivision of the lines in order to achieve better poetic sense.

44. Read, along with Geniza manuscripts, *haplē'* for *hapleh* ("separate, set apart").

Keep me as the apple of [your] eye;
hide me in the shadow of your wings,
from the wicked who oppress me,
my mortal enemies, who surround me.
They have closed up their hearts with fat;[45]
their mouths speak arrogantly.
They track me down;[46] now they surround me![47]
They have set their sights to bend [me] to the ground. . . .
As for me, I will behold your face in righteousness;
when I awake I will be satisfied with your likeness.[48] (17:1-11, 15)

The speaker testifies to being "tested" and "assessed" by YHWH without finding any wrongdoing (17:3). Such language suggests the setting of false accusation. Alternatively, references to YHWH's "face" (17:2, 15) suggest the context of temple asylum, which may have included a ritual of probation, as some have argued. Regardless, the speaker yearns for an encounter with God that, in turn, confirms the speaker's innocence: YHWH's "face" is to be beheld "in righteousness," that is, in vindication in the face of predatory prosecution. Such is the shape of justice in Psalm 17.

Psalm 35: Vindication by Poetic Justice

Similarly, justice in Psalm 35 takes the form of deliverance from persecution into the "battlefield" of litigation.

Contend, YHWH, against those who contend against me!
Fight against those who fight against me!

45. Read *ḥēleb libbāmô* for MT *ḥelbāmô*, due to haplography (so BHS).
46. Read with one Hebrew manuscript ʾ*iššĕrûnî* for MT ʾ*aššurênî* ("our steps").
47. So Ketib (Qere reads "us").
48. The second line is elliptical.

Grasp shield and armor![49]
    Rise up with help for me!
        Brandish spear and battle-axe[50] against my pursuers!
Declare to me, "I am your salvation"! (35:1-3)

The opening lines of the psalm are punctuated with direct imperatives for God to wage battle against the speaker's opponents who "contend" (*ryb*) against him. YHWH takes on the role of divine warrior, fully equipped for war. On the surface, the imagery suggests military conflict, but likely points metaphorically to a legal "battle,"[51] given that the speaker complains against false accusations later in the psalm. YHWH is not just a contender but a combatant in the courtroom, specifically the city gate, where cases were decided, as the speaker's enemies act "without cause" (35:7b; see also 35:11-15).

For they have hidden their net against me for no reason;
    they have dug a pit for my life without cause.
Let disaster catch them unawares!
    Let the net that they hid ensnare them!
Into the pit[52] let them fall! (35:7-8)

The speaker desires that his persecutors be caught by their own means of persecution, their own "net" and "pit." Such means of entrapment should entrap his persecutors—a form of poetic justice: persecutors destined to fall by their own persecution.

49. The line identifies two kinds of shields, one small (*māgēn*) and one that covers most of the body (*ṣinnâ*).

50. Meaning uncertain. MT features *sĕgōr* ("close/shut up") seemingly in imperative form. However, a weapon comparable to "spear" is most probably meant. See *HALOT*, 743.

51. E.g., Isa 3:13; 50:8; 57:16; Jer 50:34; Hos 4:4; Ps 103:9; Job 40:2.

52. Read *bĕšûḥâ* for MT *bĕšôʾâ*.

Psalm 109: Vindication by Imprecation

A comparable complaint can be found in the opening lines of Psalm 109, which features the longest imprecation in the Psalter, but one directed against the speaker within the conjured setting of a criminal proceeding:

> O God of my praise,
> do not keep silent,
> For the mouths of the wicked and the deceitful open against me,
> speaking against me with lying tongues.
> They surround me with hateful words;
> they attack me for no reason.
> In return for my love, they make accusations against me,[53]
> but I am [their] prayer.[54]
> They inflict upon me evil for good,
> hatred in return for my love.
> "Appoint a criminal[55] against him,
> an accuser [*śāṭān*] to stand at his right hand.
> When he is judged, let him come out a criminal,[56]
> and let his prayer be reckoned as sin." (109:1-7)

The speaker's detractors want to haul him into court on trumped-up charges and convict him as a criminal. What follows is an invective issued against the speaker by his enemies, filled with accusations and curses (109:7-19), all beginning with the appointment of a *śāṭān*, or "accuser," to initiate this miscarriage of justice (109:6b), a criminal to criminalize the speaker. After quoting what his enemies have had to say, the speaker concludes with a final appeal.

---

53. Specifically, accuse falsely (√*śṭn*).

54. So MT.

55. More generally, "wicked man" (*rāšāʿ*). Its particular nuance is determined in the next verse.

56. I.e., found guilty. See v. 6a.

Help me, YHWH my God!
Save me according to your benevolence!
And may they know that this is [by] your hand,
that you, YHWH, have done it.
Let them curse, but you bless.
When they rise up, let them be put to shame,
and your servant rejoice.
Let my accusers be clothed with disgrace;
let them wrap themselves with their shame like a robe.
I will greatly give thanks to YHWH with my mouth,
and among the multitude I will praise him.
For he stands at the right hand of the deprived,
to save [him] from those who would condemn him. (109:26-31)

As befitting divine "benevolence," YHWH is expected to "save" the petitioner, an act that translates into the speaker's public vindication, to be acknowledged even by his enemies. The speaker, moreover, identifies the God of "benevolence" as the God of "blessing": by making such a claim, the speaker counters his enemies' imprecation at its very foundation. They can curse all they want, but it will prove ineffective, because YHWH is primarily a God of blessing. Nevertheless, the speaker issues his own imprecation, invoking the curse of "shame" (*kĕlimmâ*) and "disgrace" (*bōšet*) to be worn as clothing, just as his enemies had done against him but in much more elaborate fashion.

Having identified himself as "afflicted and deprived" (109:22a), the speaker claims YHWH as the champion of the "deprived" (*ʾebyôn*) and savior of the unjustly condemned. The "accuser" (*śāṭān*) that was appointed to "stand at [the speaker's] right hand" (109:6b) is displaced by the God who will stand at the right hand of the "deprived" (v. 31a), but with vindication rather than condemnation! Within the psalm's scope, the "deprived" and the unjustly "condemned" are one and the same, both in need of justice. Without YHWH as their champion, the speaker would not have a prayer, or an imprecation, to give.

Psalm 35: Waking Up the Silent God

In Psalm 35, the speaker appeals to YHWH first and foremost as a witness, as one who must not remain silent over the abuse he or she has suffered from enemies who "hate" without cause.

Do not let my treacherous enemies rejoice over me,
  those who hate me for no reason squint [their] eye![57]
For they do not speak peace.
  Rather, against those who [live] quietly in the land
    they devise deceptive words.[58]
They open wide their mouths against me,
  saying, "Aha, aha,[59] our eyes have seen [it]!"
But you have seen it [too], YHWH.
  Do not keep silent!
My Lord, do not be far from me! (35:19-22)

The speaker's recourse is to issue a "wake-up call."

Rouse yourself! Wake up to my just cause,
  my God and my Lord, to my case!
Vindicate me according to your righteousness, YHWH, my God!
  Do not let them rejoice over me!
Do not let them say in their heart, "Aha, [the object of] our appetite!"[60]
  Do not let them say, "We have swallowed him whole!"
Let those who rejoice together in my misfortune
  be disgraced and ashamed!
Let those who aggrandize themselves over me
  be clothed with shame and disgrace! (35:23-26)

Such desperate language implies that God has yet to bend the moral arc of the universe toward justice (to borrow from Martin Luther King

---

57. The expression is attested also in Prov 6:13; 10:10.

58. The poetic syntax requires a redivision of the verse, departing from Masoretic accentuation.

59. Hebrew *he'āḥ he'āḥ*, conveying both contempt and triumph. See, e.g., Ezek 25:3; 26:2; 36:2; Pss 40:16; 70:4.

60. Or "our desire" (*napšēnû*).

Jr.). But now is the time! The speaker seeks a judgment that vindicates him and, in turn, shames his enemies. Other psalms complain of "false witnesses" (27:12), "lying lips" (31:18), and a "deceitful tongue" (52:4). But the most famous psalmic defense against personal injustice is the poetically stirring Psalm 139.

Psalm 139: The Intimacy of Vindication

Psalm 139 is best known for its poetic power, soaring imagery, and surprising twists of language, all testifying to YHWH's discerning and intimate knowledge of the self, knowledge that will prove indispensable for the speaker's defense against her detractors.

YHWH, you have searched me and known [me].
  You know my sitting down and my rising up;
    you discern my inner purposes[61] from far away.
You determine[62] my going forth[63] and my lying down;
  you are thoroughly familiar with[64] all my ways.
When no word is on my tongue,
  still, YHWH, you know it completely.
Front and back you enclose me,[65]
  and lay your hand upon me.
Such knowledge is too wonderful for me,
  too high for me to grasp.
Where can I go from your spirit?
  Where can I flee from your presence?
If I ascend to the heavens, you are there.
  Or if I make my bed in Sheol, *viola*,[66] you are there!

---

61. Collective rendering of *rēʿa*, attested also in v. 17 but applied to YHWH.

62. Not in the sense of preordination but of careful observation.

63. Best taken as an infinitive construct rather than the noun "way/path."

64. The root *skn* in the Hiphil implies habitual practice (see *HALOT*, 755).

65. The verb *ṣwr* carries violent connotations of besiegement and barricade (e.g., Deut 20:21; 2 Sam 11:1; 2 Kgs 16:5; Isa 29:3; Dan 1:1; Song 8:9).

66. Hebrew *hinnekā*.

Were I to rise up with the wings of the dawn,
[and] settle on the far side of the sea,
even there your hand would lead me,
your right hand holding me fast.
If I say, "Alas,[67] the darkness will cover me,[68]
and the light will be night all around me."
Even the darkness would not become too dark for you;
the night would shine like the day;
[for] darkness is as light [to you].
Indeed, it was you who formed my kidneys;[69]
you wove me[70] in my mother's womb.
I praise you that I am fearsomely awesome![71]
Awesome are your works—
this I know very well.
My skeletal frame was not hidden from you,
as I was made in secret,
intricately woven[72] in the earth's recesses.
Your eyes beheld my shapeless form.[73]
On your scroll were written all of them—
[all] the days that were fashioned [for me]
when not one among them [had yet occurred].[74] (139:1-16)

---

67. Disjunctive use of the particle *ʾak* (cf. 2 Kgs 23:26).

68. Read *yĕśûkkēnî*, along with Symmachus and Jerome, for MT ("you bruised me"). See Exod 33:22.

69. The kidneys were considered the most secret, innermost organ of the human anatomy (see Jer 11:20; 20:2; Pss 7:10; 26:2), as well as the seat of moral conscience and self-knowledge (Ps 16:7; Prov 23:16; Jer 12:2). See Hans Walter Wolff, *Anthropology of the Old Testament,* trans. Margaret Kohl (Philadelphia: Fortress, 1974), 65–66, 96.

70. Cf. NRSV "knit me." However, the use of needles and yarn is not envisioned here.

71. The participle serves as an adverbial accusative of manner (*IBHS* 173; *GKC* §118q), meaning literally "in tremendous ways" (with indefinite feminine ending). LXX, Peshitta, and Targum evidently read *niplētā* ("you are wonderful"), in accordance with the following colon. Despite the plethora of textual witnesses, the MT represents the more difficult rendering.

72. Outside of this psalm, the verb (*rqm*) is exclusively found in relation to the multicolored, embroidered curtains of the tabernacle and priestly tunics (Exod 26:23; 27:16; 28:39; 35:35; 36:37; 38:18, 23; 39:29).

73. I.e., embryo. MT makes perfect sense (cf. LXX *akatergastos),* despite numerous proposals for emendation.

74. Literally, "when not one of them [yet]." Qere "corrects" the negative particle *lōʾ* to read *lô* ("to him belongs each one of them").

The speaker offers a stirring testimony of YHWH's intimate knowledge, which ranges from the speaker's daily routines to her very genesis, created "fearsomely awesome." The transcendent YHWH discerns from "far away" yet is so immanently present as to "enclose" and "weave" the self within the womb. YHWH is both intimately involved with the intricacies of the human self and omnipresent throughout creation, reaching as far as the farthest sea and Sheol.

But YHWH's knowledge of the speaker, vast and intimate that it is, is pressed to serve a particular purpose, and it is not to praise God. Rather, it is to exonerate the speaker.

> If only, O God, you would kill the wicked!
> [If only] violent men would turn away[75] from me,
> they who speak of you maliciously,
> who swear falsely[76] toward you![77]
> Do I not hate those who hate you, YHWH,
> and loathe those who loathe you?[78]
> I hate them with absolute[79] hatred;
> they have become my enemies.
> Search me, O God, and know my heart;
> test me and know my anxious thoughts.
> And see if there is any idolatrous[80] way in me,
> and lead me in the everlasting way. (139:19-24)

After such effusive praise of YHWH as creator, midwife, all-knowing, and omnipresent, the speaker's imprecation bursts upon the poetic scene with jarring effect. But so be it. The speaker turns toward YHWH's

75. Read *yāsûrû* for MT ("Turn away!").

76. MT *nāsu'* is an abbreviated form of *nāśĕ'û*. The language refers to the wrongful use of YHWH's name, literally "lifting the name to triviality" (see Exod 20:7; cf. Exod 23:1; Ps 15:3).

77. Read *'ādêkā,* along with multiple Hebrew manuscripts, for MT *'ārêkā* ("your foes").

78. Read *ûbĕmitqôṭĕṭêkā* for MT's textual error.

79. With the sense of "complete" (*taklît).*

80. The term can denote either agony or hardship (e.g., 1 Chron 4:9; Isa 14:3), or imply idolatry, the worship of false gods (Isa 48:5). See also the cognate *'āṣāb* ("idol" in Pss 106:38; 135:15). The latter makes better sense in context.

enemies, variously described as "wicked" and "violent," who "hate" YHWH. They are condemned for speaking "maliciously" and swearing falsely. By counting YHWH's enemies as her own, the speaker signals her allegiance to YHWH as one who honors YHWH in all her doings and turns away from violence. By doing so, the speaker strategically offers herself to YHWH as innocent of wrongdoing.

By way of confirmation of the speaker's innocence, the psalm ends where it began, but with a twist. While the psalm began with probing testimony of YHWH's search and discernment of the self, it ends with a plea to "search" and "know" (139:24), just as in the opening verses of Psalm 26:1-2. In both psalms, YHWH is invited to "test" the speaker's integrity. Curiously, however, such a plea comes at the end of Psalm 139, not at the beginning. Rhetorically, one would expect the reverse order: petition first and testimony to follow (as in Psalm 26). But no. With this rhetorical reversal, the ending of the psalm invites a return to the beginning, from plea back to testimony, as the psalm circles back on itself for repeated performance, to be done repeatedly until exoneration is fulfilled, or not. Psalm 139 is the Psalter's never-ending, ever-circling psalm.

Added at the end, however, is reference to the speaker's "anxious thoughts" (*śarʿapîm*) and the possibility of following "any idolatrous way" (see translation note). Is this one of the "inner purposes" or thoughts to which the speaker alludes at the beginning (139:2)? In any case, confidence in the beginning turns to anxiety in the "end." The final verse is telling, for it reveals that Psalm 139, for all its soaring poetry, serves as a strategic defense of the speaker's integrity in the face of false accusation. In the end, as anticipated in the beginning, YHWH is enlisted as witness to the speaker's innocence, both witness and judge. The psalm concludes with the speaker's plea to be led "in the everlasting way" (*derek ʿôlām*), in stark contrast to the "idolatrous way" (cf. Pss 115:3-8; 135:15-18).

Such is the shape of justice for the individual in the Psalms, offering both liberation and vindication, salvation from persecutors and a sure defense against false accusers. The Psalms give voice for those who otherwise would have no voice in the face of persecution and prosecution. What the prophets demand with divine discourse, the psalmists appeal to in prayer.

What the prophets point out to the king and to the people with God's indictments and judgments, the psalmists point out to God with their protests, pleas, and laments. In the Psalms, a more personalized view of injustice is in view. In them, we hear the voice of the victim. In the hands of the psalmist, "Thus says YHWH" becomes "YHWH, hear my cry!"

Justice for the Nations

Justice in the Psalms is not confined to the individual; it also applies internationally.

Psalm 9: The Problem with the Nations

The acrostic Psalm 9 (+10) parallels God's justice for the speaking individual with God's justice against the nations. The speaker expresses trust in YHWH for having "established [his] just cause" from the throne, and it is from the throne that the nations are judged.

> When my enemies turn and retreat,
>   they fall down and perish before you.
> For you have established my just cause;[81]
>   [for] you sit enthroned, judging rightly.
> You have rebuked the nations [and] destroyed the wicked;
>   you have erased their names forevermore.
> As for the enemy, they are finished—everlasting ruins!
>   You have plucked up [their] cities;
>   the very memory of them has perished. (9:3-6[4-7])

As objects of YHWH's punishing "rebuke," the nations are cast as the speaker's enemies, whose cities are "plucked up." The conjured scene is that of the king waging battle against the nations. But justice is more than simply victory on the battlefield:

> But YHWH sits enthroned forever;
>   he established his throne for the sake of justice.

81. As a word pair ("my justice and my cause"), the expression can be read as a hendiadys.

Indeed, it is he who judges the world rightly,
  who adjudicates the peoples with equity.
YHWH is a stronghold for the crushed;
  a stronghold in times of trouble.[82]
Those who know your name put their trust in you;
  for you do not abandon those who seek you, YHWH. (9:7-10[8-11])

Sing praises to YHWH who is enthroned on Zion!
  Declare his deeds among the peoples.
For the one who avenges[83] bloodshed remembers them;[84]
  he does not forget the cry of the afflicted. (9:11-12[12-13])

YHWH's enthronement has its cause: the establishment of justice. It is for the sake of justice that YHWH rules from on high, from "his throne."[85] As we have seen, Psalm 82 takes this identification one step further to claim that divinity itself rests on establishing justice for the most vulnerable (82:3-4). Justice in the divine realm, moreover, is translatable to the earthly realm, as attested in Psalm 72.

In Psalm 9, the "world" is judged "rightly" by YHWH. While justice is by definition impartial,[86] it is established on behalf of the oppressed. This is not a case of partiality but a matter of fairness. The impartiality of justice, according to the psalm, necessitates favor for the oppressed. The image of "stronghold" or fortress (*miśgāb*) denotes a place of impregnable defense amid threat and outright conflict.[87] Such specificity widens the scope of YHWH's beneficent justice. The beneficiary is not just the individual speaker, presumably of royal pedigree, but also the "crushed"

82. *HALOT* relates the noun to *baṣṣōreh* (149). *BHS* emends to *hăṣṣārâ* ("distresses"), which would be an easier reading. In any case, the term seems to suggest more broadly "trouble."

83. Literally "seeks" (*drš*), which is used in various ways in this composite psalm (see 9:10[11]; 10:4, 13, 15).

84. That is, the "afflicted" (see next line), not the "peoples" from the previous line.

85. See also Pss 89:14[15]; 97:2; 99:4.

86. See Lev 19:5; Deut 16:19; Ps 82:2.

87. See, e.g., Pss 46:7[8], 11[12]; 48:3[4].

(*dak*) and the "afflicted" (*ʿănāwîm*). They are the ones who know YHWH's "name," who trust in and "seek" YHWH (9:10[11], 13[14]).

As for the nations in Psalm 9, divine justice will always find a way but not necessarily through divine intervention.

> The nations have sunk into the pit they made;
> their feet are caught in the net they themselves hid.
> YHWH is known for[88] the justice he establishes:
> by the work of his hands, the wicked one is trapped.[89]
> Let the wicked return to Sheol;[90]
> so also all the nations that forget God. (9:16-17[17-18])

The psalmist declares that the nations have met their demise at their own hands. The metaphor of the pit is fitting, comparable to the wicked one who digs his pit only to fall into it (7:15[16]). As in Psalm 7, the psalmist also uses the image of the "net" (cf. Prov 1:17-18). Such is God's poetic justice: self-inflicted affliction. This applies both globally to the nations and individually to the wicked: conduct is destiny, particularly bad conduct. A trap set by the wicked is ultimately a trap set for the wicked. Nevertheless, verse 16b is wickedly ambiguous: is it by God's hands, or by the hands of the wicked, that the wicked meet their demise? The answer is yes: the poetic line allows for both interpretations. The case is comparable to Pharaoh's "hardened" heart, self-hardened or divinely hardened? Again, yes (cf. Exod 7:3, 13).

Such cases, the psalmist claims, are evidence of divine justice at work through human agency, a noninterventionist way of upholding justice, or a distinctly poetic form of justice, one could say. The world is created in such a way that actions carry their own consequences. Live by the pit,

88. The parallelism with the second line suggests an instrumental or causal relationship between the verb and *mišpāṭ*, rather than a separate clause. Cf. KJV.

89. The second line is ambiguous in terms of subject. The Masoretic pointing has God as the agent (the verb is pointed as a Qal participle from the verb *nqš*): "By the work of his hands [YHWH] strikes down the wicked." With slight repointing, the verb can be read as a Niphal from the verb *yqš*, as per LXX, Aquila, Peshitta, and Targum.

90. It is unclear whether the verse functions indicatively or injunctively.

die by the pit (repeat with "net," "sword," etc.). This is YHWH's justice: divine action fulfilled in human action. And for the nations that "forget God," Sheol is their destiny.

> No,[91] the destitute will not be forgotten forever,
> nor will the hope of the afflicted perish forevermore.
> Rise up, YHWH!
> Do not let mortals prevail!
> Let the nations be judged before you!
> Set a terror[92] for them,
> [so that] the nations may know they are only human! (9:18-20[19-21])

Psalm 9 ends with a direct appeal to God to get up and get going for the sake of justice. The complaint is that "mortals" and "nations" are gaining too much power, enough so as to "prevail." Divine judgment is called for. This psalm's conclusion sounds an anthropological note that human beings are not meant to gain power to lord over others, even the nations. They are not divine, but with their imperial designs in play, they seek to exceed their own mortal condition. The temptation is to see themselves as gods (see, e.g., Isa 10:5-19; Ezek 28:2-23). Thus, the nations need reminding of their finitude. The speaker calls for "terror" (*môrâ*) to beset them—"terror" with a pedagogical twist (see translation note), a knowing reminder or terrible lesson that even the greatest of empires, filled with imperial aspirations bordering on the divine, is ever poised to totter and fall. Justice for the nations in Psalm 9 begins with a stark reminder of their mortality, just like the "gods" in Psalm 82.

Psalms 2 and 110: The Nations in Defeat

Psalm 2, as we have seen, hews to an imperial vision of rulership that necessitates the vanquishing of the rebellious nations:

91. Emphatic use of *kî*.

92. Or "teacher." LXX translates "lawgiver" (*nomothetēn*), apparently reading *môreh* ("teacher") instead of *môrâ*, a variation of *môrāʾ*, as attested by several Hebrew manuscripts, Aquila, Theodotion, and Targum. The MT is the more difficult reading. In any case, in light of the governing verb, *šyt* ("set/appoint"), as well as the next line ("know"), a wordplay is created.

Why do the nations rant,
  and the peoples rave in vain?
[Why do] the kings of the earth take their stand,
  and potentates conspire together,
    against YHWH and his anointed? (2:1-2)

I will recount the decree that YHWH has declared to me:
"My son you are;
  today I hereby beget you.
Ask of me to make the nations your possession,
  and the ends of the earth your property.
You will smash them with an iron rod;
  like a potter's vessel you will shatter them in pieces." (2:7-9)

But all is not lost for the nations. The threat of complete destruction is a lesson to be learned as requisite of fearful submission:

So now kings, wise up![93]
  Be warned, you rulers of the earth!
Serve YHWH with fear!
  Rejoice with trembling!
Kiss the son lest he become angry,
  and you perish on the way,[94]
    for his wrath is quickly kindled. (2:10-12)

Although "justice" is not directly referenced in Psalm 2, it is assumed and made all the more explicit in Psalm 110, the imperial partner of Psalm 2.

Utterance of YHWH for my lord:
"Sit at my right hand,
  while I set your enemies as a stool for your feet."
YHWH will extend your mighty scepter from Zion.
  "Rule, then, in the midst of your enemies!" (110:1-2)

---

93. The verb *śkl* refers to the gaining of insight, used frequently in sapiential literature (e.g., Prov 1:3; 17:8; 21:16).

94. Or "[your] way perishes."

O Lord,[95] because[96] of your right hand,
  he will crush kings on the day of his wrath.
He will establish justice among the nations.
  Piling up corpses, he will crush heads[97] the world over. (110:5-6)

In Psalm 110, "justice" established "among the nations" is fulfilled through military conquest. The resulting picture is that of the nations serving as the king's footstool. Such is what justice looks like for the nations in these two blatantly imperial psalms. Not so in other psalms.

Psalm 79: Warrant for Judgment against the Nations

The treatment of the nations in the Psalms covers a range of variety. On the one end of the juridical spectrum, the nations are condemned for their rebellious uproar (2:1; 46:6), destined to suffer God's "vengeance" (149:7) and discipline (94:10), with their "counsels" nullified (33:10). God holds all them in derision (2:4; 59:8), deserving of divine anger poured out in full measure (79:6). Divine wrath against the nations is not unjustified, according to certain psalms. Psalm 79 is particularly vivid:

O God, the nations have encroached upon your inheritance;
  they have defiled your holy temple;
    they have turned Jerusalem into a heap of ruins.
They have given the bodies of your servants
  as food for the birds of the air,
  the flesh of your faithful to the wild animals of the earth.
They have poured out their blood like water,
  all around Jerusalem with no one to bury [them].
We have become a taunt to our neighbors,
  mockery and derision to those around us. (79:1-4)

How long, YHWH will you remain angry? Forever?
  [How long] will your zealous wrath burn like fire?

95. Reference to YHWH, as indicated in many Geniza manuscripts (cf. v. 1a).

96. A causal use of the preposition *'al* is preferable over the locative use, as indicated by the preposition *lamed* in v. 1a (see, e.g., Gen 20:3; Prov 28:21; Pss 39:12; 50:8; Jer 15:15).

97. Collective force.

Pour out your wrath upon the nations,
who refuse to acknowledge you.
and upon the kingdoms,
which do not call upon your name.
For they[98] have devoured Jacob,
and desolated his abode. (79:5-7)

The psalm recalls the horror of Babylonian conquest, resulting in wholesale destruction of both the temple and the city, not to mention the slaughter of YHWH's "servants" (for gory detail, see 74:3-8). As the nations have mercilessly "poured out" the blood of the faithful, littering the land with corpses, so the psalm implores YHWH to "pour out . . . wrath upon the nations." While the nations do not invoke God's "name," Israel does, as demonstrated in the plaintive cry, "How long, YHWH?" The nations refuse to acknowledge God, as demonstrated in their wanton destruction of "Jacob" and "his abode," which is "devoured" and "desolated" by the nations. Thus, the final petition in the psalm:

Why should the nations say, "Where is their God?"
Let the vengeance for the outpoured blood of your servants
be known among the nations before our very eyes!
Let the groaning of the prisoner come before you!
With your powerful arm spare[99] those condemned to die![100]
Pay back to our neighbors sevenfold, into their very bosom,
the insults with which they insulted you, Lord! (79:10-12)

The "poured out" wrath of God is called for because of the "outpoured blood" of God's "servants." Case closed.

Psalm 106: The "Snares" of the Nations and God's Right to Judge

There are other reasons why the nations get such a bad rap in the Psalms. From a psalmic perspective consonant with DtrH, the nations

98. Read *'ākĕlû* for MT *'ākal* ("he devoured").

99. The verb in its Masoretic form is derived from *ytr* ("leave over").

100. Literally, "children of death" (*bĕnê tĕmûtâ).*

were driven out of the land so that Israel could be "planted" (44:2; cf. 78:17). Such was Israel's "conquest" of the land. And yet, in the end, it is Israel that is "scattered . . . among the nations" in punishment (44:11). Psalm 106 is most vivid:

> They associated with the nations,
> learning their ways,
> serving their idols,
> which became a snare to them.
> They sacrificed their sons and their daughters to demons,[101]
> They poured out innocent blood,
> the blood of their sons and their daughters,
> which they sacrificed to the idols of Canaan,
> and the land was defiled by blood.
> They made themselves unclean by their works,
> and they prostituted themselves by their deeds.
> So YHWH's anger burned against his people,
> and he abhorred his own heritage.
> So he handed them over to the power of the nations;
> and their foes ruled over them.
> Their enemies oppressed them;
> they were subjected to their power. (106:35-42)

Serving as a "snare," the nations pose both a temptation and a curse: the temptation to assimilate and the curse of abandoning God's ways. One abhorrent practice of the nations is their "pouring out" of "innocent blood," sacrificing even their own children. The ironic atrocity, as another psalm testifies, is that the nations do the same against Israel.[102]

But does Israel's God have a right to judge the nations as God judges Israel? Again, the ancient portrayal of YHWH among the gods given in "the song of Moses" in Deuteronomy suggests only a limited right of jurisdiction (Deut 32:7-9). While Israel has only YHWH as its god, the other nations have their deities, each one "apportioned" by the Most High (106:8). The "fixed boundaries of the peoples" apply equally to the fixed

101. Hebrew *šēdîm*; see also Deut 32:17.

102. See discussion of Ps 137 in chapter 10.

jurisdictions of the gods. But as discussed above, things could not be more different in Psalm 82, in which God sentences the gods to death for their failure to establish justice on earth. The psalm's concluding verse provides a clear case for the international scope of God's judgment: "Arise, O God! Judge the earth, for you hold all the nations in your possession" (82:8). Because all the nations belong to God, apportioned by God, God has every right to "judge" them.

But how is it that the nations belong to God? Psalm 86 provides an answer:

> There is none like you among the gods, my Lord,
> nor anything like your works.
> All the nations, which you have made, will come,
> and bow down before you, my Lord,
> and give glory to your name.
> For you are great, working wonders;
> you are God, you alone. (86:8-10)

God's incomparable status "among the gods" is measured by the boundless extent of God's unrivaled sovereignty. God "made" all the nations (86:9a). Divine sovereignty is rooted ultimately (and primordially) in creation. God owns what God has made, and what God has made includes the nations. Or as Jeremiah would say, God is the "potter" of the nations (Jer 18–19). And as potter God can turn the nations into potsherds (Ps 2:9).

Psalm 67: The Nations in Thanksgiving

On the other end of the juridical spectrum, certain psalms consider the nations as bona fide recipients of God's blessing and, thus, vehicles of praise and thanksgiving. Psalm 67, for example, features a petition for blessing and a testimony of praise that embraces the nations.

> May God grant us grace and bless us;
> may he shine his face on us, *Selah*

so that your way be made known throughout the earth,
[so that] your salvation [be made known] among all the nations.
Let the peoples give you thanks, O God;
let the peoples give you thanks, all of them.
Let the nations be glad and shout with joy,
for you judge the peoples equitably,
and guide the nations on the earth. *Selah*
Let the peoples give you thanks, O God;
let the peoples give you thanks, all of them.
The earth has yielded its produce.
God, our God, does bless us![103]
May God [continue to] bless us,
so that all the ends of the earth will revere him. (67:1-7)

Psalm 67 opens with an indirect petition that God's way of blessing be made known "among all the nations." While such blessing is petitioned specifically for Israel ("us"), the nations are to give thankful acknowledgement of God's salvific "way." They are to know that the God of justice is also the God of blessing. Punitive judgment is not pronounced against the nations, but justice is (67:3-4), for which the nations are exhorted to give thanks, and for good reason: God's justice and guidance are given in their behalf, not at their expense. God's salutary ways are not limited to Israel but extended to all the nations, to adjudicate and "guide" (√*nḥh*) them, as God once guided the Israelites in the wilderness.[104] God's dealing with Israel serves as a sign of how God will deal with the nations: with equity and guidance. In return, the nations are to acknowledge the God of justice in the form of thanksgiving for the earth's abundant yield of produce. Such reverence is driven not by fear but by gratitude.

Psalm 117: The Nations Overcome by Benevolence

While God's judgment of the nations is deemed justified, its particular form is not settled in the Psalms, for justice can be either negative or positive, punitive or restorative, or something in between. Punishing

103. Or "may God bless us." The verb can be taken as indicative or jussive.

104. E.g., Exod 13:21; Ps 78:14; Neh 9:12.

judgment against the nations is, admittedly, more prevalent in the Psalms, but that is precisely what makes any positive formulation stand out, as we have seen in Psalm 67. Psalm 117 stands out even more, and not just for its brevity. From the standpoint of certain psalms, it does the theological unthinkable.

> Praise YHWH, all you nations!
> Acclaim him,[105] all you peoples![106]
> For his benevolence has prevailed mightily[107] over us;[108]
> YHWH's faithfulness endures forever.
> Praise YH![109] (117:1-2)

The psalm opens with a punctuated call to praise, directed not to Israel but to the "nations." Whereas the nations elsewhere in the Psalms are often considered enemies, this psalm treats them as partners in praise.

The parallelism of the first verse seems so straightforward as to be considered synonymous. However, there is a marked linguistic difference between the two poetic cola. While 117:1a is written in conventional Hebrew, 117:1b is Aramaic-like (see translation notes). The shift is no accident: an international call to the nations requires an international form of address. Aramaic became the *lingua franca* of the ancient Near East beginning with the Assyrian conquest of Damascus (732 BCE) and was spread throughout the empire. The Aramaic script came to be widely used in all the provinces of the Assyrian, Babylonian, and Persian empires, as

---

105. The verb *šbḥ* is an Aramaic loanword (Aramaic: Dan 2:23; 4:31, 34; 5:4, 23; Hebrew: Ps 63:4; 14:4; Eccl 4:2) and corresponds to the more common term for praise *hll* (cf. 147:12).

106. The MT features an Aramaism (cf. *ʿummâ* in Dan 3:4, 7, 31; 5:19; Ezra 4:10). Some correct it to the Hebrew *lĕʾummîm* ("peoples") or *hāʿammîm* ("peoples"), but neither is necessary.

107. The root *gbr* connotes force or might, frequently with military connotations (e.g., 2 Sam 7:24; 11:24; Ps 65:4). But cf. Gen 7:18-19 regarding the waters of the flood having "swelled."

108. The line could be translated as "For his benevolence has prevailed *against* us" (√*gbr* + *ʿal;* cf. 2 Sam 11:23; Gen 49:26). Ps 103:11 nicely parallels 117:2. See discussion.

109. Hebrew *halĕlû-yāh* ("Hallelujah").

well as in Egypt. That Psalm 117 contains two Aramaic loanwords in its appeal to the nations indicates a genuine invitation of international scope.

But what is the invitation about? Verse 2 concerns what is most central about YHWH's character vis-à-vis Israel: YHWH's "benevolence" or faithful love (*ḥesed*). In certain contexts, *ḥesed* is explicitly covenantal, indicating fidelity, both human and divine. In broader contexts, such as here, *ḥesed* denotes God's abiding, steadfast quality of care in the face of human need, a quality to which any petitioner can appeal in prayer for God to act.[110] "Benevolence," along with "compassion," has been "from of old" (Ps 25:6). The psalm's twofold formulation of divine character may very well draw from YHWH's self-profession on Sinai (Exod 34:6-7). There, YHWH declares to be "abounding in benevolence and faithfulness" (117:6). Distinctive, however, is the choice of predicate used in Psalm 117. Instead of the common qualification of "great" or "abounding" (*rab*) to modify "benevolence," the psalmist deploys the more forceful *gābar* ("be mighty"), which can designate everything from "swelling" floodwaters (Gen 7:18-19) to military victory ("prevail," e.g., Exod 17:11; 2 Sam 11:23). It is a verb of force, in this case a verb of victory. As observed in the translation notes, one possible translation for 117:2a is "For his benevolence has prevailed *against* us," as if "us" were God's enemy! While this makes little sense, this peculiar, if not ironic, use of the verb underlines the militant power of divine "benevolence," particularly in situations of distress.

In the case of Psalm 117, however, the "prevailing" power of God's *ḥesed* is directed not against but "over us." Who is behind the "us"? Israel *and* the nations. Otherwise, the call to worship that launches this inclusive song of praise would lose its force. Psalm 117 is an invitation to the nations, after all, and every call to praise has a reason. For the nations to give praise, they too must experience the same "benevolence" and "faithfulness" that Israel has experienced from YHWH. For the nations to be partners in praise, they too must be beneficiaries of God's benevolence. For all its brevity, Psalm 117 conveys an expansive vision of praise, a far cry from the nations vilified in other psalms. Here, a good nation is not a

110. See, e.g., Pss 6:4; 13:5[6]; 17:7; 21:7; 25:7.

defeated nation; it is a grateful nation, thankful for God's ever-expanding "benevolence" in the world.

Justice for the World

Speaking of world, the creator God does not limit justice to individuals or the oppressed or a people, or even all the nations. God's justice ultimately includes the world.

YHWH sits enthroned forever;
he assumes his throne for the sake of justice [*mišpāṭ*].
Indeed, he establishes justice in the world with righteousness [*ṣedeq*];
he judges the people with equity [*mêšārîm*]. (9:7-8[8-9])

But what does God's justice "in the world" look like? Why does the earth need justice?

Psalm 96: Sing a New Song of Justice

As vividly conveyed in the following enthronement psalm, the scope of divine justice includes all of creation.

Sing to YHWH a new song!
Sing to YHWH, all the earth!
Sing to YHWH! Bless his name!
Proclaim his salvation from day to day!
Declare his glory among the nations,
among all the peoples his wondrous works,
for great is YHWH, and most worthy of praise,
fearfully revered beyond all gods,
for all the people's gods are worthless idols,
but it is YHWH who created the heavens.
Majesty and splendor are before him;
strength and beauty are in his sanctuary. (96:1-6)

Give to YHWH, O clans of the peoples!
    Give to YHWH glory and strength!
        Give to YHWH the glory of his name!
Offer gift[s] and enter his courts!
Bow down to YHWH in holy splendor!
    Tremble before him, all the earth!
        Declare among the nations, "YHWH reigns!"
For sure, the world is firmly established;
    it will not be shaken.
He will judge the peoples with equity. (96:7-10)

Celebrating YHWH's unrivaled sovereignty, Psalm 96 proclaims YHWH's justice for all the world. The earth responds with "trembling" (96:9b). At first glance, the expression "all the earth" seems to refer only to all the peoples of the earth (see 96:7a). But following the summons is the affirmation that the world remains "firmly established," not to be "shaken," as God judges "the peoples with equity" (96:10). With the world firmly established, so justice is established. The result is an eruption of creation's praise.

Let the heavens be glad and the earth rejoice;
    let the sea roar and everything in it.
Let the field exult and all therein;
    then so all the trees of the forest will rejoice aloud, before YHWH,
    for he is coming, for he is coming to establish justice for the earth.
He will establish justice for the world with righteousness
    and the people with his faithfulness. (96:11-13)

As the earth is populated by the peoples, it is also populated by its natural elements: the sea (and all therein), the lands, and the trees, all of which respond with the raucous "roar" of praise (96:11-12). Like the theophany passages discussed above, YHWH's impending presence is matched by creation's upheaval. But in this case, it is not creation's convulsions but creation's acclamations that erupt.

Psalm 97: A Theophany of Justice

In Psalm 97, creation's convulsions are more vividly described in the face of theophany:

> YHWH reigns! Let the earth rejoice!
> Let the many isles be glad!
> Cloud and thick darkness [are] around him!
> Righteousness and justice [are] the foundation of his throne!
> Fire goes forth before him,
> incinerating his enemies all around.
> His lightnings light up the world;
> the earth sees and trembles.
> The mountains melt like wax before YHWH,
> before the Lord of all the earth.
> The heavens proclaim his righteousness,
> and all the peoples behold his glory. (97:1-6)

The scene contains elements of cosmic upheaval that highlight the formidable might of the divine warrior, cast as a storm deity. Throughout biblical tradition, theophanic language underscores YHWH's overwhelming presence in a variety of contexts: setting the stage for the giving of the law on Mount Sinai (Exod 19:16-20), delivering the Israelites from Egypt (Ps 77:16-19[17-20]), commissioning a prophet (Isa 6:1-7), restoring God's "heritage" (Ps 68:7-11[8-12]); saving YHWH's "people" and "anointed" (Hab 3:2-15), manifesting God's presence to an exiled people (Ezek 1), and rescuing the king on the battlefield (Ps 18:7-15[8-16]). In Psalm 97, however, theophanic storm imagery is pressed in another direction: to establish justice.

Picking up from the end of Psalm 96, Psalm 97 gives the theophanic trope a judicial twist. Embedded within the fray of cosmic travail are affirmations of God's "righteousness and justice" (97:2b, 6a). As the earth "trembles" (97:4b), the heavens "proclaim his righteousness" (97:6a). Such is creation's response. Theophany is wedded to doxology ("Let the earth rejoice!" [97:1a]), and justice finds a home even within the arena of theophany.

Psalm 98: Just Praise

How the earth "rejoices" is described even more vividly in the next enthronement psalm.

Sing to YHWH a new song,
  for he has done wonders.
    His right hand, his holy arm, has won him victory.
YHWH has made known his salvation;
  before the eyes of the nations he has revealed his righteousness.
He remembers his faithful benevolence to the house of Israel.
  All the ends of the earth have seen the salvation of our God. (98:1-3)

Raise a shout to YHWH, all the earth!
  Burst forth and rejoice aloud and sing praises!
Sing praises to YHWH with the lyre,
  with the lyre and the sound of music.
With trumpets and the blast of the horn,
  shout for joy before the king, YHWH! (98:4-6)

Let the sea thunder and all that fills it, the world and its inhabitants.
  Let the rivers clap their hands,
and the mountains together rejoice aloud, before YHWH,
  for he is coming to establish justice for the earth;
he will establish justice for the world with righteousness
  and the peoples with equity. (98:7-9)

The psalm opens with an exuberant call to "sing . . . a new song." What is "new" about this song, as in other psalms,[111] points to what YHWH has done, namely "wonders" (*niplāʾôt* [98:1]). God's "wonders" often denote works of victory performed on behalf of Israel, followed by international acclaim.[112] But they also include God's works in creation.[113] YHWH's "wonders" are both cosmic and historical. Reference in Psalm

111. Pss 33:3; 40:3; 96:1; 98:1; 144:9; 149:1.

112. E.g., Josh 3:5; Mic 7:15; Pss 9:1[2]; 78:1, 32; 105:5; 106:22.

113. E.g., Pss 136:4; cf. 119:18; Job 5:9; 37:5, 14.

98 to YHWH's "right hand" and "holy arm" indicate that YHWH's works of salvation are indeed works of "victory" (√*yšʿ*).[114] While YHWH is profiled as the divine warrior who fights for Israel,[115] the psalm indicates in its conclusion an additional, perhaps even more fundamental, role: YHWH as cosmic judge (98:9).

The call to praise at the beginning spills into the final strophe, which expands the worshipping community to include various elements, or better agents, of the natural world: sea, rivers, and mountains, as well as the world and all its inhabitants. The imperatives of praise in the previous strophes correspond to the jussives of praise in the final one ("let . . ."), as the circle of praise expands to include nonhuman agents (cf. Gen 1:9, 11, 20, 24). The roll call alternates between water-based ("seas" and "rivers") and land-based domains ("world" and "mountains"). As in Ps 96:11, the seas are called to roar thunderously (√*rʿm*) in praise. More often, however, the grammatical subject of the verb "roar" is the deity in the context of theophany.[116] Here, the seas mimic YHWH's thunderous voice, while elsewhere the sea's "roaring" (e.g., *šĕʾōn*) is considered chaotic and threatening, and therefore must be suppressed.[117] Not so in Psalm 98: the seas are given full, unmuzzled voice. The lively imagery of "clapping hands" describing the rivers' praise is applied metaphorically only elsewhere to trees, conferring hospitable joy for the returning exiles (Isa 55:12). In the psalm, the rivers join in praise with their thunderous rapids.

Land and sea, rivers and mountains, all join together in praise, each in their own way, to welcome the One who is coming to establish justice for the earth, just as in 96:11-13. The language of theophanic "coming" is pressed not toward military victory on the battlefield or toward vanquishing the forces of chaos but toward justice in and for creation. In Psalm 98, YHWH, the divine sovereign, is welcomed by the "rivers" and "the

114. See Exod 15:16; Pss 20:6[7]; 78:53-55; 44:3[4]; 71:18; 89:10[11].

115. Tremper Longman III, "Psalm 98: A Divine Warrior Victory Song," *JETS* 27 (1984): 267–74.

116. E.g., Pss 18:13[14]; 29:3; 77:19; 104:7.

117. Pss 33:7; 65:7[8]; 74:13; 89:9[10]; 107:29.

mountains" as they render praise (v. 8). YHWH's theophanic "coming" throws creation not into convulsions but into rejoicing, testifying to the cosmic scope of divine justice on creation's behalf. And what is the nature of such justice? It remains unspecified but presupposed at the very least is peace among all nations, unified in praise, and peace throughout all creation, united in song.

In these enthronement psalms, YHWH's coming to establish justice is an event celebrated by the very elements and realms of creation. Justice is conferred not only on "the peoples" but also to the world as a whole. By means of YHWH's justice, the "sea" and the "torrents" roar and rejoice rather than are contained or conquered. From the psalmist's perspective, there is no praise without justice! Indeed, the sound of creation's praise *is* the sound of justice, including the sound of cascading waters and ever-flowing streams (Amos 5:24).

A Wicked Conclusion

The nature and scope of justice are pressing issues in the Bible, as we have seen in Pentateuchal *tôrâ* (see chapter 6) and in certain prophets surveyed above. While the Pentateuch folds issues of "justice" into *tôrâ*,[118] the prophets speak of justice from God's oracular pronouncements ("Thus says YHWH"). In the Psalms, however, the concern for justice is strikingly absent in the Torah psalms, and it is not a prominent topic of divine discourse in the Psalms, certain exceptions notwithstanding, as discussed above. One could contend, however, that Psalm 82 outperforms all the prophets' pronouncements of justice with its singularly dramatic glimpse of the divine assembly in judicial session. In Psalm 82, the psalmist is more stenographer than spokesperson. Nevertheless, justice in the Psalms is most frequently addressed in the form of petition, protest, and praise. Justice pleaded in petition is justice demanded from God. Justice celebrated in praise acknowledges justice realized in action.

118. E.g., Exod 23:2-6; Deut 4:8; 10:17-19; 16:19-20; 24:17.

What the prophets and the psalmists share in common are the embodied "barometers" of justice: the orphan, the widow, the immigrant, and the oppressed. How they fare in society is a measure of how just society is.[119] Justice is demanded exclusively for them. But the Psalms insist on adding one more barometer by which to judge a community: the "righteous."[120] Psalm 146, for example, renders a near comprehensive picture of the vulnerable in ancient society:

> How happy is the one whose help[121] is the God of Jacob,
> whose hope is in YHWH, his God,
> the one who made heaven and earth,
> the sea and all that is in them,
> who remains ever faithful.
> who renders justice for the oppressed,
> who gives food to the hungry.
> YHWH breaks the prisoners free.
> YHWH opens [the eyes] of the blind;
> YHWH raises up those who are bowed down.
> YHWH loves the righteous.
> YHWH protects immigrants; supports the orphan and the widow,
> but ruins the way of the wicked. (146:5-9)

In this psalm of declarative praise, we find a taxonomy of the disadvantaged that includes the "righteous" (146:8b). They are counted along with the oppressed, the prisoner, and the hungry, as well as the orphan, the widow, and the immigrant. In Psalm 94, the "righteous" are persecuted as much as the widow, the immigrant, and the orphan are victimized (94:6, 15, 21). The "righteous" are equally deserving of divine justice because they are counted among the oppressed.

God's justice for the oppressed, the Psalms profess, is grounded in God's "benevolence" (*ḥesed*), the most prominent mark of divine character

119. See, e.g., Isa 1:17; 9:17; 61:1; Jer 7:6; 22:3; Ezek 22:7.

120. Oppression of the "righteous" is not a major concern among the prophets as it is in the Psalms: see only Amos 2:6; 5:12; Hab 2:4; Isa 57:1.

121. Read *ʿezrô* for MT *bĕʿezrô* ("in whose help"), due to dittography (so LXX).

in the Psalms, signifying God's initiative of care and solidarity, a "tenacious solidarity"[122] realized in deliverance from oppression and vindication in the face of false accusation. God's justice is not punishment for punishment's sake but restoration for freedom's sake, freedom from the "hand" of the wicked. The Psalms recognize that such freedom is never freely given. Something has to give, and it is the wicked. Many psalms, thus, see an inverse relationship between the wicked and the oppressed, since one is defined antithetically in relation to the other. The wicked are wicked because their "hand" (or power) is set against the oppressed. The wicked, thus, must be forced to give up their "hand," while the "afflicted" are raised up by God's hand.

Such an inverse relationship prompts a question. For all the harsh language leveled against the "wicked," is there any mercy for them in the Psalms? It is admittedly hard to find, unless one discerns the voice of the wicked in those psalms that plead to God for forgiveness, such as in Psalms 32, 38, 51, 130, and 143. Psalm 143 acknowledges that "no one living is righteous before you," effectively blurring the boundary between the "righteous" and the "wicked" (143:2b). The Davidic speaker in Psalm 51 admits to having been "born guilty" (146:5[6]). Such "guilt" from birth may not necessarily mean universal guilt but rather imply the guilt of being born into social dominance, in which one's status reflects complicity in systemic oppression, the guilt of supremacy.

Lamentably, nowhere in such psalms of confession are any specific sins delineated. There is, for example, no admission of having persecuted the vulnerable or the righteous. By contrast, Job's profession of innocence in 31:13-40 features the "impoverished," the "widow," the "orphan," and the "stranger." Instead, psalmic confession conveys only the effects such sins have upon the petitioner, from bodily dis-ease to social isolation. The very fact that confessed sins remain undefined in the psalms makes such psalms usable by the righteous and the wicked alike. They provide the option for the wicked to confess and receive mercy, assuming that they "turn from their wickedness," to borrow from Ezekiel (see 33:11, 19).

122. Walter Brueggemann, "The Psalms: Tenacious Solidarity," in Walter Brueggemann, *Tenacious Solidarity: Biblical Provocations on Race, Religion, Climate, and the Economy*, ed. Davis Hankins (Minneapolis: Fortress, 2018), 354–55.

As for the nations, justice takes on different forms. In some cases, justice is meted out *against* the nations, particularly those that have been instrumental in Israel's national trauma. In others, justice is established as an act of divine "benevolence" *for* the nations, as an extension of what God has done for Israel. In such cases, justice is established not at the nations' expense but for their praise and thanksgiving.

Finally, God's justice includes all of creation. As judge, YHWH "comes" to establish justice wreaking cosmic havoc. In the enthronement psalms, however, divine theophany elicits not creation's fearful "trembling" but raucous praise, even from the one domain most often associated with chaos and evil, the sea. Justice for creation is justice that ensures the flourishing of all creation, human and nonhuman, animate and even "inanimate."[123] The "roaring" of the seas in praise invites one to imagine praise coming even from the "wicked," the purveyor of social chaos, whose "ways" have perished (Ps 1:6) but not necessarily themselves. Psalmic praise is transformative, and creation's inclusion into the chorus of praise not only presupposes justice, it establishes justice. Call it "just praise."

123. See Mari Joerstad, *The Hebrew Bible and Environmental Ethics: Humans, Nonhumans, and the Living Landscape* (Cambridge: Cambridge University Press, 2019).

Part III
WRITINGS

CHAPTER 9

WISDOM'S WORKS: SAPIENTIAL AND PSALMIC

The fear of the LORD is the beginning of wisdom,

and the knowledge of the Holy One is insight.

—Proverbs 9:10 (NRSV)

We are drowning in information, while starving for wisdom.

—E. O. Wilson[1]

The so-called wisdom literature (i.e., Proverbs, Job, and Ecclesiastes) enjoys a prominent place among the Writings (*Ketubim*), as does the Psalms. They are all, in fact, canonical neighbors. In the Protestant Bible, the Psalter is bracketed by Job and Proverbs, with Ecclesiastes immediately following. In the Jewish Bible, Psalms is followed by Proverbs and Job, while Ecclesiastes is set aside, not too far off, as a member of the *Megillot*.[2] In either case, such canonical proximity is rife with dialogical potential, even across their considerable theological and literary differences. While

1. Edward O. Wilson, *Consilience: The Unity of Knowledge* (New York: Vintage Books, 1999), 294.

2. Song of Solomon, Ruth, Lamentations, Ecclesiastes, and Esther.

psalmic discourse is largely oriented toward God, the wisdom literature is primarily directed toward the community. Except for certain parts of Job and one case in Proverbs, addressing God in prayer and praise is not a major feature in the wisdom corpus.[3] Neither is Israel's collective history, to which the Psalms make frequent reference.[4]

Nevertheless, despite these distinctions, the Psalms and the wisdom corpus teem with dialogical engagement. This chapter explores how certain psalms, as well as the Psalter as a whole, engage the wisdom literature dialogically. But before doing so, one must first address a fundamental matter: what actually is biblical wisdom? Easier said than done.

Wisdom in the Wisdom Literature

The wisdom corpus of the Hebrew Bible is as eclectic in content as it is diverse in its rhetoric, which is why the notion of biblical wisdom is so hard to pin down, let alone define. Given the sheer diversity of the literature, there is no one-size-fits-all definition. Indeed, it is even questionable whether "wisdom" constitutes its own tradition in the Bible,[5] let alone its own genre and worldview.[6] Still, it remains useful to group Proverbs, Job, and Ecclesiastes together for comparative purposes to highlight

3. No prayer is featured in Ecclesiastes, and only one is found in Proverbs (30:7-9). Job's discourse, however, is occasionally interspersed with prayers: 7:12-21; 9:27-31; 10:2-22; 13:20-28; 14:13-22; 30:20-23; cf. 42:9. This is not to say that the sages were uninterested in cultic matters (e.g., Prov 3:9-10; 15:8, 29; 21:3, 27; 28:9; Eccl 5:1). See the foundational analyses of Leo G. Perdue, *Wisdom and Cult: A Critical Analysis of the Views of Cult in the Wisdom Literature of Israel and the Ancient Near East*, SBLDS 30 (Missoula, MT: Scholars Press, 1977); and, more recently, Katharine J. Dell, "'I Will Solve My Riddle to the Music of the Lyre' (Psalm XLIX 4[5]): A Cultic Setting for Wisdom Psalms?" *VT* 54, no. 4 (2004): 445–58.

4. E.g., Pss 44, 74, 78, 79, 80, 81, 105, 106, 114, 135, 136. In the wisdom literature, Solomon and Hezekiah are merely objects of literary attribution (Prov 1:1; 10:1; 25:1; and perhaps Eccl 1:1, 12; cf. the superscriptions of Pss 72 and 127), whereas David and Moses (sometimes with Aaron), as well as Samuel and other characters, are given historical significance in the Psalms (e.g., 18:50[51]; 77:20[21]; 78:70; 89:3[4]; 99:6; 103:7; 105:27; 106:16, 23, 32).

5. Mark Sneed, "Is the 'Wisdom Tradition' a Tradition?" *CBQ* 73 (2011): 50–71.

6. The categorization has been artificially constructed by scholars that has limited the ways in which these three books have been interpreted, specifically limiting their intertextual or dialogical partners. See Will Kynes, *An Obituary for "Wisdom Literature": The Birth, Death, and Intertextual Reintegration of a Biblical Corpus* (New York: Oxford University Press, 2019).

their dialogical differences. Broadly speaking, whereas Proverbs forges a bond between human act and consequence on the anvil of character formation, the book of Job severs the connection, and Ecclesiastes leaves it all to chance (Eccl 9:11). Where Proverbs sees cosmic order, Job discerns profound disorder, and Ecclesiastes perceives only inscrutable mystery. Throughout this corpus, biblical wisdom covers the epistemological spectrum from confident certainty to unsettling uncertainty. One reason these wisdom books are so diverse is because much of biblical wisdom is grounded in human experience and inquiry. If anything, wisdom is fluid.

While defining biblical wisdom in terms of a common outlook is impossible, one can nevertheless say something about its general features, first by enumerating what wisdom is *not*. The wisdom literature in the Hebrew Bible is nonhistoriographical, nonprophetic, and largely (though not entirely) noncultic in orientation. In the place of national history, creation captures the sages' focus. Instead of Zion's temple, we find the home, the marketplace, the city gates, and the royal court shaping much of wisdom's landscape. In the broadest of terms, wisdom's focus is on human understanding and conduct.

One can also identify certain "salient features" within the wisdom corpus,[7] from concrete guidance for success and moral instruction to reflection on the vicissitudes of daily life and the inscrutable wonders of God and creation.[8] But underlying all of wisdom's features is a fundamental dynamic that can be encapsulated as follows: wisdom imparts wisdom. Though seemingly tautological, such a claim highlights two important aspects of wisdom: (1) wisdom's dynamic nature and (2) wisdom's telos. First, by its very nature wisdom is something to be shared. It is to be given and received. Wisdom kept to itself is hardly wisdom; it is simply a secret destined to die with its keeper. Wisdom is wisdom when it is imparted. From the tiniest maxim to the mightiest rebuke, wisdom never sits still, as it continues to be passed on to those who have hearts to receive and ears to hear, as well as minds to test. Wisdom is meant to be not only received

7. See, e.g., Simon Chi-chung Cheung, *Wisdom Intoned: A Reappraisal of the Genre "Wisdom Psalms,"* LHB/OTS 613 (London: Bloomsbury T&T Clark, 2015), 22–52.

8. For discussion of the latter, see William P. Brown, *Wisdom's Wonder: Character, Creation, and Crisis in the Bible's Wisdom Literature* (Grand Rapids: Eerdmans, 2014), 24–27.

but critically assessed (cf. Job 12:11-12). Second, wisdom is wisdom when it is deemed *worthy* of sharing, worthy of providing some benefit to the receiver, including the basic benefit of understanding. At its core, wisdom is edifying.[9]

One definitive aspect of biblical wisdom is its power to cultivate a critical consciousness, as demonstrated by the collected sayings in Proverbs. Far from being "dead,"[10] a collected proverb is a dialogically engaged proverb. A proverb on its own imparts a certain insight or encourages a particular course of action, but when it is placed in the company of other proverbs, it enters into the dialogical imagination of the reader, who must adjudicate between proverbs to decide which one applies best in a given context. In doing so, the reader fosters a critical consciousness. Take, for example, the well-discussed "dueling" sayings of Proverbs 26:4-5, which were singled out by the rabbis as a point of controversy (*b Shabbath* 30b):

> Do not answer a fool according to his folly,
> or you yourself will be just like him.
> Answer a fool according to his folly,
> or he will be wise in his own eyes. (Prov 26:4-5)

Two contradictory proverbs set side by side mandate two opposing courses of action, accompanied by different motivating reasons. So what are readers (who are presumably not "fools") to do? Instead of being paralyzed by indecision, readers must discern for themselves which course of action to take by weighing the pros and cons of responding to "fools" in a given situation. Discerning, deciding, and acting with informed judgment, as well as suffering the consequences, all make for moral growth. By their sheer number and diversity, proverbs set within

9. Edifying specifically for building human agency and shaping character. For a recent defense of the use of character ethics for exploring the coherence and diversity of the wisdom corpus, see William P. Brown, "Virtue and Its Limits in the Wisdom Corpus: Character Formation, Disruption, and Transformation," in *The Oxford Handbook of Wisdom and the Bible,* ed. Will Kynes (New York: Oxford University Press, 2020), 45–64.

10. Contra Wolfgang Mieder, who claimed that "the proverb in a collection is dead" (Carol R. Fontaine, *Traditional Sayings in the Old Testament,* BLS 5 [Sheffield, UK: Almond, 1982], 54).

their various collections cultivate critical discernment by deploying a wide variety of rhetorical means, from their poetic power and semantic polyvalence to their dialogical tensions and pedagogical strategies.[11] The same can generally be said of the wisdom literature as a whole.

A Brief Overview

With such sapiential complexities in view, an all-too-brief overview of the Hebrew wisdom books, conducted dialogically, is needed before exploring how the Psalms engage them dialogically.

Proverbs

The book of Proverbs features various instructions and extended admonitions (1:8–9:18; 31:1-31), on the one hand, and collections of short sayings, on the other (10:1–30:33), all prefaced by a prologue designed to orient the reader to the book as a whole (1:2-7). Although the book is attributed to Solomon (1:1), the titles or superscriptions of its various sections and collections indicate a more diverse origin. "Agur, son of Jakeh," for example, is an otherwise unknown sage and a non-Israelite from northern Arabia (30:1). So also Lemuel, "king of Massa" (31:1). Moreover, Proverbs 22:17–24:22 is directly dependent upon a much older corpus of Egyptian wisdom, the *Instruction of Amenemope*.[12] While Proverbs is eclectic in content as well as international in its scope, its editors attributed the book to Solomon, Israel's second dynastic king who was

11. For extended studies on this topic, see William P. Brown, "The Pedagogy of Proverbs 10:1–31:9," in *Character and Scripture: Moral Formation, Community, and Biblical Interpretation,* ed. William P. Brown (Grand Rapids: Eerdmans, 2002), 150–82; Christine Roy Yoder, "Forming 'Fearers of Yahweh': Repetition and Contradiction as Pedagogy in Proverbs," in *Seeking Out the Wisdom of the Ancients: Essays Offered to Honor Michael V. Fox on the Occasion of His Sixty-Fifth Birthday,* ed. Ronald L. Troxel, Kelvin G. Friebel, and Dennis R. Magary (Winona Lake, IN: Eisenbrauns, 2005), 167–83; Peter T. H. Hatton, *Contradiction in the Book of Proverbs: The Deep Waters of Counsel* (Farnham, UK: Ashgate, 2008); and most recently Suzanna R. Millar, *Genre and Openness in Proverbs 10:1–22:16,* Ancient Israel and Its Literature 39 (Atlanta: SBL Press, 2020), esp. 73–88, 191–220.

12. On the mechanism of such dependency, see Bernd U. Schipper, *Proverbs 1–15: A Commentary,* Hermeneia (Minneapolis: Fortress, 2019), 17–18.

remembered as quintessentially wise,[13] despite his religious failings (1 Kgs 11:1-13).

The book of Proverbs opens with a prologue featuring a collage of values and virtues: shrewdness, prudence, discretion, skill, instruction, insight, wisdom, and "fear" or reverence of YHWH (1:2-7). While certain virtues ensure success in one's endeavors (e.g., shrewdness and discretion), others are distinctly moral in orientation, such as three found in 1:3b: "righteousness, justice, and equity." In all cases, however, every virtue in Proverbs' storehouse is considered consequential; it can shape, no less, a person's sphere of destiny (see 2:10-12). Much (but not all) of Proverbs assumes an unbreakable bond between human act and consequence.[14]

The prologue highlights the importance of cultivating such values for the young or inexperienced (1:4). It is no coincidence, then, that much of the following material is cast as a father's address to his son, in which the father also defers to the mother and her "teaching" (*tôrâ*).[15] Wisdom begins in the home. Nevertheless, wisdom is not just for the young: "Let the wise also hear and gain in learning, and the discerning acquire skill" (1:5). Wisdom is for all ages, and no one, regardless of experience, can exhaust it.

The last verse in the prologue establishes the book's theological framework. Often called the "motto" of Proverbs, 1:7 situates wisdom in the context of reverence: "The fear of YHWH is the beginning of knowledge" (see also 9:10; Ps 111:10). Such godly "fear" is meant not to terrorize but to elicit a sense of religious reverence and humility that compels one to move toward gaining wisdom by first acknowledging wisdom's divine source. "The fear of YHWH is the beginning" of one's growth in wisdom. In view of the book's "motto," one could describe wisdom in Proverbs as "fear seeking understanding" (with apologies to St. Anselm).

In addition to being grounded in reverence, wisdom is also a matter of acquisition, as the father instructs his son to "get wisdom" and "esteem

13. See 1 Kgs 3:1-28; 4:29-34; 10:1-13.

14. For a comparative discussion, see Samuel L. Adams, *Wisdom in Transition: Act and Consequence in Second Temple Instructions,* SJSJ 125 (Boston: Brill, 2008), esp. 53–100.

15. See 1:8; 2:1; 3:1, 11; 4:1; 5:1, 7; 6:1; 7:1.

her highly" (4:7-8). The "beginning of wisdom," thus, is a twofold matter: revering God and seeking wisdom. It requires a posture of humility, on the one hand, and an initiative to search for wisdom, on the other. Regarding the latter, wisdom is a possession to be sought as priceless treasure (4:5; 8:35-36). Wisdom requires a quest; "she" is both the destination and the pathway (4:11-13).

The metaphor of the "way" refers to one's conduct in life, straight or crooked, moral or corrupt. These two paths shape the moral landscape of Proverbs: there is the path of wisdom, which includes the ways of righteousness, justice, and peace (3:17; 4:11; 8:20), the path that is "like the light of dawn, which shines brighter and brighter until full day" (4:18). And there is the path of the wicked, crooked and dark, leading to death (2:15; 4:14, 19). Proverbs lays out both paths in order to take readers to the crossroads and point them toward the right way.

Also at the crossroads stand two formidable figures. One is the figure of Wisdom. That she is personified as female is no accident. Her gendering suggests that the book of Proverbs was intended primarily for a male audience. Wisdom both cajoles and woos her listeners and readers to accept her wise teachings. Her profile is matched by another female figure, a femme fatale, who is seductively described in 7:6-27 as the adulterous "Stranger" (*zārâ/nokrîyâ*), against whom the "son" is repeatedly warned (2:16; 5:3; 7:5; 22:14). As the hypersexualized "other," she represents folly whose ways lead to "Sheol" (7:27). Although opposing figures, both Wisdom and the Stranger share the same public space (1:20-22; 7:12), albeit at different times. They also issue similar invitations, even as their messages could not be more different (9:4, 16). Whereas Wisdom stresses marital fidelity and joy, honor, prosperity, and life, the Stranger offers illicit sex, broken relationships, disgrace, and death. Such stereotyped polarity is a product of patriarchal convention; it is Proverbs' antecedent to the "Madonna and the Whore."

As a central text, Proverbs 8:22-31 establishes Wisdom's preeminent place in creation and with God. Indeed, her account is not so much about creation per se as about the one who describes it. Birthed by God, Wisdom claims her preexistence before all things and witnesses God's work in creation. The poem is her soliloquy of self-praise, or aretalogy,[16] infused with a distinctly rhetorical purpose: to claim her inestimable worth and authority vis-à-vis humanity. At the same time, Wisdom depicts herself playing with God and the world (8:30-31). By claiming such an intimate and lively association with both the creator and creation, Wisdom seeks to gain the (male) reader's allegiance.

So also at the end of Proverbs: the acrostic poem casts embodied Wisdom as the matriarch of a flourishing family (31:10-31). She is designated a "woman of strength" (*'ēšet-ḥayil*) who manages a prosperous household, conducts real estate transactions, and engages in international trade.[17] The silent "son" at the beginning of Proverbs finds his place also at the end: he has grown up to become the grateful and honored spouse and father who speaks in praise of his partner (31:29-31). He has chosen the right path in marriage. Such is the "metanarrative" of Proverbs: the journey of cosmic Wisdom into domesticity and the journey of the son into adulthood. Their respective journeys find a common destination in the household.

Job

Job begins where Proverbs ends, with the scene of an affluent household. But in Job the attention shifts from the matriarch to the patriarch, and with a very different outcome. The story's upstanding protagonist is demoralized in a parody of divine providence. In two fell swoops, Job, a man of unassailable moral rectitude (1:1, 3), is stripped of security, prosperity, and health, all the while his character is dismantled by his friends in the name of "comfort" and retributive justice (2:11; 22:4-11). From Job's perspective, the efficacy of virtue is thrown out the window. As such, the prosaic prologue of Job (1:1–2:13) paints a "perversion of moral

16. Proverbs 8:22-31 is often identified generically and comparatively as an "aretalogy," a form of self-praise associated with the goddess Isis. For the Egyptian background, see Schipper, *Proverbs 1–15*, 292–94.

17. For the socioeconomic context of this woman, see Christine Roy Yoder, *Wisdom as a Woman of Substance: A Socioeconomic Reading of Proverbs 1–9 and 31:10-31*, BZAW 304 (Berlin: de Gruyter, 2001).

causality."[18] It is Job's "integrity,"[19] after all, that invites his suffering from the beginning (1:8; 2:3). Being "blameless and upright" is rendered meaningless in the face of such calamity. With Job's world turned upside down at all levels, wisdom is deemed ultimately inaccessible (28:12-22). Job has every reason to lapse into bitter lament, and he does so with gusto. Job models a defiant faith.

It may be best to think of the book of Job more as a parable than as a straightforward narrative, a story that aims to raise more questions than answers about the shape of human integrity, divine purpose, and how the world works. Job questions why the wicked prosper and, in turn, the righteous suffer, with Job offering himself as exhibit A.[20] Indeed, the story of Job prompts various questions: What is piety if it has nothing to do with blessing? What is righteousness if it only invites disaster? What if God were no protector of the righteous? What if the world does not bend toward justice? What does human integrity look like in the face of horrific suffering? What is the "fear" of God within the crucible of suffering?

Such questions begin with the question posed by Job's wife (2:9) and continue throughout the torturous "dialogues" between Job and his friends, who attempt to make sense of Job's predicament, providing wisdom for Job's benefit, but fail to move Job from lament to consolation. Indeed, Job 28 delivers a negative judgment on all their discourse, including Job's. The quest to find wisdom fails because Wisdom remains ever beyond human reach. Instead, the "fear of the Lord," echoing 1:1, is all that matters. The full statement, "the fear of the Lord, that is wisdom" (28:28), reduces wisdom to "fear" or sheer awe. There is no "beginning" of wisdom and knowledge (cf. Prov 1:7); thus, there is no quest or pathway to follow, as in Proverbs. "Fear" is both the beginning and the end of wisdom.

While YHWH's appearance in the "whirlwind" marks the climax of the book, it does not resolve the issue of suffering as posed by Job. Indeed, YHWH's "answers" are themselves full of questions that challenge Job to

18. Thanks to ethicist Frederick Simmons for articulating this so pointedly (personal communication).

19. Hebrew *tummâ*; 2:3, 9; 27:5; 31:6.

20. Job 21:7-16, 29-33; 10:15; 30:25-26.

put him in his place within the greater cosmos. YHWH presses Job on his limited knowledge of the world, from the heights and depths of creation to the creatures that populate the wilderness, both land and sea. YHWH opens Job's eyes to the wonders, terrors, and mysteries of creation. And Job's response is also mysterious: is he penitent or not (42:6)? While Job's final words have generated a great variety of interpretations, it does seem that Job has at least found resolution, if not comfort, in YHWH's answer.[21] In the end, YHWH demonstrates to Job a sovereign care for creation that includes Job, and he is restored.

Matching the prosaic style of the prologue (Job 1–2), the epilogue depicts Job's restoration (42:7-17), which seems to be a mere recapitulation of the beginning: Job once again assumes his lofty and wealthy position as patriarch of a new family. But things have changed: Job, rather than his friends, is vindicated by God for having spoken "what is right" (42:7). Job gratefully receives restorative help from his family and community (42:11). He treats his children differently by giving his daughters a share of the inheritance (42:15). Job himself has changed. Even at its prosaic conclusion, Job's story is full of ironic twists and surprising outcomes. As a result, the book of Job prompts searching questions and challenging reflections about life in a complex, messy, awful and awe-filled world, one that does not operate retributively, contrary to what is typically claimed in proverbial wisdom. The book of Job, in short, is a dramatic testimony to the limitations of human wisdom.

Ecclesiastes

The same can be said of Ecclesiastes, a book with its fair share of contradictions, paradoxes, and ambiguities. Attributed to "the son of David" (1:1), Ecclesiastes is the Bible's strangest book. Yet for all its interpretive challenges, the book has an uncanny ability to "tell it like it is."

21. For detailed discussion, see William P. Brown, "Job and the 'Comforting Chaos,'" in *Seeking Wisdom's Depths and Torah's Heights: Essays in Honor of Samuel E. Balentine,* ed. Barry R. Huff and Patricia Vesely (Macon, GA: Smyth & Helwys, 2020), 247–66.

The main character of the book calls himself Qoheleth (NRSV "the Teacher"), but his historical identity remains shrouded in mystery. His allegedly royal pedigree (1:1, 12) fades after the first two chapters. His name, or better self-title, means "assembler." Like an auditor, this sage takes an inventory of life by collecting the "data" of experience, both individual (his own) and collective (tradition). And like a teacher, an "assembler" of students, Qoheleth candidly shares the results of his work in the language of personal observation and testimony.

Qoheleth aims to investigate everything by means of observation and critical assessment in order to discover ultimate purpose in the world, both human and divine. Some regard Qoheleth as the Bible's true empiricist. But for all his efforts, this ancient sage fails to find what he desires. Wisdom, he discovers, lies utterly beyond him, while enjoyment and toil yield no lasting gain. All that goes on in the world yields no direction, let alone any progress (1:4-11; 3:1-8). The "same fate," death, befalls everyone, the fool and the wise, human and animal alike (2:14; 3:19). Death casts an all-encompasssing shadow in Ecclesiastes.

Unlike Job, Qoheleth is not privy to divine revelation. His verdict on all that he has seen and studied is "vanity," or better "futility" or "pointlessness" (*hebel*; 1:2; 12:8), the book's single-word thesis. The word itself conjures the image of vapor, something ephemeral and ungraspable, like wind (1:14; 2:11). But in view of life's frailty and futility, Qoheleth does not counsel despair but instead commends joy, seven times no less.[22] Through his failure to find all-encompassing wisdom, the elder sage nevertheless comes to certain understandings: the value of a "nonprofit" existence, the redemptive import of enjoyment, a life of simplicity, the pointlessness of super righteousness (7:16), God's inscrutability, the tenuousness of life, the pervasiveness of chance, and perhaps most profound of all: "a living dog is better than a dead lion" (9:4). In the face of death, life is stripped of all illusions of grandeur and ultimate purpose and yet is still worth living, when one's expectations are reoriented toward the simple gifts of enjoyment. In the face of *hebel*, wisdom is divested of Wisdom's promises of security and prosperity (cf. Prov 3:16) yet remains

22. Eccl 2:24-26; 3:12-13, 22; 5:18-20; 8:15; 9:7-9; 11:7-10.

worthwhile in mitigating life's maelstroms. Qoheleth's "wisdom" is forged in a world that resists control and comprehension.

The wisdom literature is an eclectic mix of observations and teachings, queries and convictions, some theological, some practical, all poised for dialogical engagement. If there is one broad development in the corpus, from Proverbs to Ecclesiastes, it is the increasing recognition of wisdom's limitations. Whereas Proverbs conveys confidence in wisdom's power and accessibility, Job and Ecclesiastes find wisdom elusive. Whereas virtue has its efficacy in Proverbs, it loses it in Job and Ecclesiastes. YHWH's climactic answer to Job, which vividly portrays creation's generative "chaos," clashes with Wisdom's aretalogy in Proverbs 8, which highlights creation's order and stability. For Qoheleth, wisdom cannot be apprehended, God remains ever inscrutable, and life and death lie beyond anyone's control. The limits of wisdom, the purpose of human living, God's providence, and the value of virtue, are just a few of the many dialogical "talking points" among these books. If only we could listen in on more of the sages' table talk! But now it is time to invite the psalmists to the table.

Wisdom in the Psalms[23]

Like the sages, certain psalmists aim to impart their wisdom. Psalm 1, for example, commends the study of YHWH's "instruction" (*tôrâ*). Psalms 32 and 34 indicate the importance of teaching (32:8-9; 34:11[12]). Psalm 49 imparts "wisdom" and "understanding" in the form of a "proverb" and a "riddle" (49:3-4[4-5]; cf. 78:1-2). Psalms such as these are often categorized as "wisdom psalms" (depending on the criteria employed), distinct from the prayers and praises that populate much of the Psalter. Hymnbook, prayerbook, textbook: such are the three dimensions of psalmic discourse. It is the last dimension that is our focus, eliciting the following questions, among others: What kinds of wisdom do the Psalms impart in comparison to wisdom profiled in the wisdom corpus? Is wisdom to be acquired or received as a gift? How is wisdom mediated? What are the

23. This section builds on my more detailed essay, William P. Brown, "Psalms," in *The Wiley Blackwell Companion to Wisdom Literature,* ed. Samuel L. Adams and Matthew Goff (Hoboken, NJ: John Wiley & Sons, 2020), 67–86.

sources of wisdom? What is the way of "righteousness" in the Psalms in comparison to Proverbs? What is wisdom's place within the liturgical or cultic life of the Psalms? What are wisdom's limitations?

There has always been ambivalence about identifying wisdom psalms among scholars, since such psalms do not share common form. But this has not prevented various attempts at classifying them. The trouble is that no one's list is the same.[24] With various criteria employed, differing identifications are the inevitable result. The details need not concern us. But one thing is obvious. The psalms most often identified as wisdom psalms comprise a diverse grouping, just like the wisdom corpus! In order to group these psalms together, content and style must be considered.[25] But by whatever criteria, I prefer to think of the wisdom psalms as points of dialogical contact between Psalms and the wisdom corpus, snapshots of a larger dialogue over what it means to live with understanding. The following discussion explores such psalms with the aim of exploring not just their similarities to the wisdom books but also their dialogical differences.

Psalm 1: Whose Torah Is It?

Unlike most psalms, the first psalm of the Psalter does not address God. Instead, it commends the righteous individual over and against the wicked. Psalm 1 paints a binary world, but it does so not by enumerating the moral qualities of the righteous and, in turn, the immoral characteristics of the wicked, as found in Proverbs.[26] The actual "ways" of the righteous and the wicked remain undefined in Psalm 1. The first verse, an *'ašrê* saying ("How happy are"), only makes the claim that the righteous and the wicked are mutually exclusive characters. The wicked will not endure while the righteous will prevail. How so? Not so much by force of human character or consequential conduct (à la Proverbs) as by divine protection (1:6).

24. For a comparison of lists, see Brown, "Psalms," 69–71.

25. See J. Kenneth Kuntz, "Reclaiming Biblical Wisdom Psalms: A Response to Crenshaw," *Currents in Biblical Research* 1, no. 2 (2003): 151.

26. E.g., Prov 8:20; 10:31-32; 11:28; 12:5, 10; 13:5; 15:28; 21:15, 26; 24:15-16; 29:7; 31:9.

While righteousness in Psalm 1 remains largely undefined in terms of conduct, there is one specific mode of practice that the psalm highlights as central, one that is unprecedented in the wisdom corpus. The righteous individual is one who engages YHWH's *tôrâ* ("instruction" or "teaching") with both alacrity and due diligence (1:2). As the source of both delight and moral direction, *tôrâ* is central to the psalm, as it is in other psalms (e.g., Pss 19; 37; 119). But what precisely is *tôrâ* in Psalm 1? Whatever it is, YHWH is undeniably its source. *Tôrâ* is quintessentially *divine* instruction, worthy of constant "deliberation."[27]

There is no comparable use of *tôrâ* in the wisdom literature except perhaps in Job 22:22, in which Eliphaz exhorts Job to return to God and "receive *tôrâ* from [God's] mouth." Job himself avoids reference to *tôrâ* altogether. In the first nine chapters of Proverbs, *tôrâ* is associated not with God but with parents: "Listen, my son, to your father's discipline [*mûsār*] and do not forsake your mother's *tôrâ*" (1:8).[28] Proverbs 13:4, moreover, refers to the "*tôrâ* of the wise" (cf. 31:26). Three sayings in Proverb 28 are more ambiguous (28:4, 7, 9), with v. 4 most closely resembling Psalm 1:

> Those who forsake *tôrâ* praise the wicked,
> but those who keep tôrâ strive against them. (Prov 28:4)

As in Psalm 1, the wicked are cast as opponents. But in Proverbs *tôrâ* is not explicitly associated with God. Psalm 1 rectifies that: righteousness comes from diligently engaging YHWH's *tôrâ*. Parental and, indeed, human mediation is not required. *Tôrâ* itself is the teacher. That Psalm 1 makes no mention of "wisdom" (*ḥokmâ*) is also significant (cf. 111:10), a silence made deafening in the bold claim made in Psalm 119:

> O how I love your *tôrâ*!
> It is my deliberation all day long!
> Your commandment[29] makes me wiser than my enemies,

27. For further discussion, see chapter 6.

28. Cf. Prov 3:1; 4:2; 6:20; 7:2.

29. Read singular (*miṣwotkā),* requiring only a slight consonantal change.

for it is always mine.
I have greater insight than all my teachers,
for your decrees are my deliberation.
I have more understanding than the elders,
for I guard your precepts. (119:97-100)

As for gaining "insight" and "understanding," the speaker disparages human mediation. Wisdom rests solely and exclusively on YHWH's "commandment," "decrees," and "precepts"—the constituents of *tôrâ*. The joy of *lex* in Psalm 1, or the love of law in Psalm 119, is claimed to be more efficacious than human wisdom, or even personified Wisdom (cf. Prov 1:20-33; 8:1-36).

Regarding the nature and cultivation of righteousness, Psalm 1 and Proverbs provide two different perspectives. While Psalm 1 stresses the destiny of the righteous (and the demise of the wicked) rather than the moral qualities that make for righteousness, there is one defining mode of activity that the psalmist considers indispensable: diligent engagement with YHWH's *tôrâ* as an alternative to seeking wisdom. Such a central emphasis is nowhere to be found in the wisdom texts. In Proverbs, estimable character is cultivated through the appropriation of parental *tôrâ*, or familial teaching, and more broadly through the *tôrâ* of the wise (13:14). With its emphasis on *divine tôrâ*, Psalm 1 addresses a perceived deficiency in Proverbs, namely a theocentric framing of instruction that is weightier than Proverbs' little "motto." The psalm, in effect, replaces human wisdom with divinely wrought *tôrâ* as the center and source of right human conduct. The psalmist prefers YHWH's *revealed* instruction over wisdom grounded in experience or mediated by others, including Wisdom herself. *Tôrâ* does not need wisdom to be efficacious; it comes from God after all.

Psalm 34: Wisdom as Testimony of Salvation

Often considered a "wisdom psalm," Psalm 34 is form-critically an acrostic thanksgiving psalm, one that opens with words of praise (34:1-3) yet concludes, as in Psalm 1, with contrasting portrayals of the righteous and the wicked (34:15-22). We begin with the psalm's central sections.

I sought YHWH, and he answered me;
  From all my fears he delivered me.
Look[30] to him and be radiant,[31]
  and your faces[32] will not be ashamed.
Here is an afflicted person who cried out, and YHWH heard,
  and he saved him from all his troubles.
YHWH's messenger encamps around those who fear him,
  delivering them. (34:4-7)

Taste and see how good YHWH is!
How happy is the one who takes refuge in him!
Fear YHWH, you holy ones of his;
  for those who fear him suffer no lack.
Even young lions suffer want and hunger,
  but those who seek YHWH lack no good thing. (34:8-10)

Come, children, and listen to me;
  let me teach you the fear of YHWH.
Which of you desires life,
  and longs for days of enjoyment?
Guard your tongue from evil,
  and your lips from duplicitous speech!
Turn away from evil and do good!
  Seek shalom, indeed pursue it! (34:11-14)

The moral admonition of 34:11-14 imbues the entire psalm with didactic intent; it also renders a strikingly complex profile of the speaking voice. The one who teaches (34:11-12) is also the "afflicted" one who is "saved from every trouble" (34:6). This teacher, moreover, is counted among "the broken of heart" (34:18a), "the crushed in spirit" (34:18b),

30. Read *habbîṭû,* along with various versions, for MT *hibbîṭû* ("they looked").

31. Read the imperative form *ûnĕhārû* for MT *wĕnāhārû* ("they became radiant"), as with LXX.

32. Read *ûpĕnêkem* for MT *ûpĕnêhem* ("their faces"). Cf. LXX.

and "the humble" (34:2b), as well as among "the righteous" (34:15) and YHWH's "servants" (34:22). The speaker provides testimonial credence to the claim that YHWH delivers the righteous. Deliverance by God forms an integral part of the psalmist's teaching. In Psalm 34, teaching is testimony (and vice versa). The speaker's testimony of salvation provides the basis for both thanksgiving and moral admonition. Moral instruction, in other words, is an expression of gratitude, deemed foundational to "fearing" YHWH.

The admonition to "fear YHWH" summarizes the psalm's prescriptive force, as it also constitutes the motto of sapiential teaching in Proverbs. Divine reverence is the expressed object and objective of the psalmist's teaching (34:9, 11), but in contrast to Proverbs it is not so much the object of understanding and knowledge[33] as it is the subject of personal testimony and holy orientation. Such fear is life-giving (34:12)[34] and sufficient for all needs (34:9b).[35] To "fear YHWH" is to "seek YHWH" (34:10) and to reflect YHWH's holy effulgence (34:5). Reverential fear casts out "all . . . fears" (34:4). Such reverence has its home in "refuge," which confers happiness (34:8b) and security (see 34:7). The fear of YHWH is charged with salvific significance in the psalm (34:22; cf. 52:8) as much as such fear is infused with sapiential import in Proverbs.

While psalmic teaching and sapiential instruction find common ground in the motif of divine reverence, they part ways regarding the function of such fear. In the psalm, reverence establishes refuge from evildoers. It is apotropaic or evil-averting. In Proverbs, the fear of YHWH provides insight and cultivates integrity; it is the beginning point of knowledge and wisdom (Prov 1:7; 9:10). Fear in Proverbs is sapiential; in Psalm 34 it is salvific.

33. Cf. Prov 1:7, 29; 2:5; 9:10; 15:33.

34. See Prov 10:27; 14:27; 19:23.

35. Parallels in older wisdom material include Prov 10:27; 14:26–27; 19:23.

Psalm 37: Does Righteousness Save?

Thoroughly admonitory in tone, Psalm 37 profiles the righteous and the wicked in sharply contrasting ways, as in Proverbs (and in Ps 1). The psalm's central theme is indicated in the opening verse, paralleled nicely in Proverbs 24:19, and effectively summarized in one verse:

> Be still before YHWH,
> and wait fervently[36] before him.
> Do not get worked up about the one who makes his way prosperous,
> about the one who carries out evil schemes. (37:7)

Characteristic of the psalm as a whole, this verse is balanced by positive and negative commands. The positive imperatives profile a particular posture before YHWH (37:7a), namely that of patient longing, whereas the negative command does the same vis-à-vis the wealthy wicked (37:7b). The juxtaposition results in a striking irony: a posture of restraint is commanded before both the wicked and the deity! This paradox of God and the wicked sharing the same syntactic stage, however, stops here. While the commands in 37:1, 7b, 8 exhort an attitude of restraint vis-à-vis the wicked, much more is enjoined regarding one's orientation toward YHWH, as indicated in the positive commands: "Trust in YHWH" (37:3a; cf. 37:5b); "Take delight in YHWH" (37:4); "Commit your way to YHWH" (37:5a); and "Wait for YHWH, and keep to his way" (37:34). Such things are not said of the wicked, obviously. Most explicit in 37:7a, the temptation toward anger against the wicked is transformed into fervent longing for God (cf. Ps 73:25-26).

The problem of the wicked and their attendant success is resolved in a series of assurances of their imminent destruction[37] and, in turn, the vindication of the righteous.[38] The present condition of disparity will be reversed: "The meek shall inherit the land and delight themselves in

36. The verb *hitḥôlēl* can suggest writhing (Job 15:20), as in the case of giving birth (Isa 51:2), dancing (Judg 21:21), and suffering anxiety (Est 4:4).

37. Verses 2, 9, 10, 13, 15, 17a, 20, 28, 36, 38.

38. Verses 11, 17b, 18-19, 23-24, 25-26, 28, 29, 33, 34b, 37b, 39-40.

abundant riches" (37:11; cf. 37:9, 22). In the meantime, the righteous are to be content with their meager resources ("little" [37:16]). To "wait for YHWH" is, in part, to wait with assurance for the passing of the wicked "yet in a little while" (37:10).

This wisdom psalm bears certain rhetorical similarities to Proverbs, while exhibiting its own distinctive emphases. Both Psalm 37 and Proverbs affirm the connection between human act and consequence, or put more broadly (and simply): character determines destiny (37:3, 14-15, 27). However, the psalmist also gives equal, if not more, weight to YHWH's intervention to ensure that the righteous are saved.[39]

> Salvation of the righteous is from YHWH,
> their refuge in the time of distress.
> YHWH helps them and delivers them;
> he delivers them from the wicked and saves them,
> because they take refuge in him. (37:39-40)

Such statements about the righteous testify to God's saving work, a theme not well represented in the wisdom corpus. In Proverbs, righteousness wields its *own* salvific power: it "delivers from death" (Prov 10:2; 11:4), saves (11:6), and guards (13:6). Take Proverbs 14:32.

> The wicked are overthrown by their evildoing,
> but the righteous find refuge in their integrity.[40]

Proverbs 11:6 puts it more pointedly:

> The righteousness of the upright saves them,
> but by (their own) desires the treacherous are caught.

39. I.e., vv. 4, 5, 13, 17, 23, 24, 28, 33, 34.

40. Read *bĕtûmmô* ("in their integrity") in place of MT's *bĕmôtô* ("in his death"), which likely arose through metathesis of the *taw* and *mem*. See Michael V. Fox, *Proverbs 10–31*, AYB 18B (New Haven, CT: Yale University Press, 2009), 585–86.

Such a "salvific" view of *human* righteousness, one in which God is placed out of the equation, is unprecedented in the Psalms, including even in the wisdom psalms.

Comparing Psalm 37 and Proverbs points to another significant difference. Although the players remain the same (i.e., the righteous, the wicked, and the testimonial voice of experience), Psalm 37, like Psalm 1, places proportionally greater emphasis on the destiny and condition of the wicked and the righteous than on the nature of their conduct. The conduct of the wicked is an issue only in so far as it impacts the welfare of the righteous (37:12, 14, 21, 32, 35). Only peripherally are the wicked indicted specifically for their unethical behavior *apart from* their persecution of the righteous. Conversely, the righteous are distinguished primarily by the protective favor they receive from God. The wicked are destined by God for destruction; the righteous, for prosperity in the land. Akin to wisdom's laughter over the imminent destruction of scoffers (Prov 1:26-27), "YHWH laughs at the wicked, for he sees that their day is coming" (Ps 37:13), and on that day the righteous shall "inherit the land" (37:9, 22, 29, 34).[41]

In the meantime, the righteous assume a distinctively unsapiential profile: they are both vulnerable and victimized; they have "little" (37:16).[42] They are the "afflicted" and the "impoverished" (37:11, 14), designations referenced in only four passages in Proverbs, and in no instance identified with the righteous (Prov 14:31; 30:14; 31:9, 20). It is the righteous in Proverbs who are consistently in the position of *helping* the impoverished (cf. 31:9, 20; see also 29:7). The vulnerability of the righteous receives little attention in Proverbs. As in Psalm 34, what is at stake in Psalm 37 is their vindication (37:6), not their moral integrity per se. Only at one point in the psalm are the righteous morally defined.

41. The expression is not found in the wisdom corpus.

42. Several psalms identify the righteous person or speaking voice in the psalms with the "afflicted" and "deprived" (e.g., Pss 40:17[18]; 70:5[6]; 86:1; 109:22). For a general description of the vulnerable righteous in the Psalter, see J. Clinton McCann Jr., "'The Way of the Righteous' in the Psalms: Character Formation and Cultural Crisis," in *Character and Scripture,* ed. William P. Brown (Grand Rapids: Eerdmans, 2002), 141–42.

The mouths of the righteous utter wisdom,
 and their tongues speak justice.
The teaching [*tôrâ*] of their God is in their hearts;
 their steps do not slip. (37:30-31)

While wisdom and justice come from the mouth of the righteous, an inner source is also identified that makes it possible, namely God's *tôrâ* lodged in the "heart," the seat of volition. In Proverbs, it is wisdom that is implanted in the heart (e.g., Prov 2:2, 10; 14:33). In Psalm 37, it is *tôrâ*.

Finally, the frequent metaphor of the "way" winds through this psalm, as it does through much of Proverbs. In the psalm, there is YHWH's "way" (37:34a), as enjoined by the speaker, and there is the "way" of the righteous, whose "steps" are "made firm by YHWH" (37:23-24, 31). The way of the wicked, so prevalent in Proverbs, is scarcely mentioned in the psalm (only obliquely in 37:7). Indeed, like Proverbs 1–9, two distinct ways are mapped in Psalm 37. But unlike in Proverbs, the two ways in the psalm are not diametrically opposed:

Commit your way to YHWH;
 trust in him, and he will act. (37:5)

Wait for YHWH and keep to his way,
 and he will exalt you to inherit the land. (37:34a)

To "commit [one's] way to YHWH" is to "keep to [YHWH's] way." Compared to Proverbs, reference to the *via Dei* is distinctive in Psalm 37, but it is quite common throughout the Psalter.[43] The two ways in Proverbs are those of the righteous and the wicked,[44] but explicit reference to the *deity's* way is practically nonexistent.[45]

43. See Pss 44:18[19]; 77:13[14], 19-20[20-21]; 85:13[14]; 119:3, 27, 32, 33, 35, 37.

44. For the way of the wicked, see Prov 1:15, 31; 2:12, 18; 4:14, 19; 7:27; 8:13; 12:15 ("fools"), 26; 13:15; 15:19 ("lazy"). For the way of the righteous, see 2:8, 20; 3:23; 4:11 ("wisdom"); 5:8; 6:23 ("way of life"); 8:26; 9:6 ("insight"); 13:6.

45. Only Prov 10:29 ("The way of YHWH is a stronghold for the upright").

Telling is the comparison of the injunction in Psalm 37:5, cited above, with its sapiential parallel in Proverbs 16:3a:

> Commit your work to YHWH,
> and your plans will be established.

Note the different outcomes in response to dedicating one's way or "work" to YHWH: the psalm is focused on divine action on behalf of the addressee ("he will act"), whereas the saying in Proverbs is focused entirely on the human result: human "plans" are "established." Moreover, the force of the injunction in Psalm 37:5b ("trust") bears far less rhetorical weight in Proverbs.[46] Indeed, the motif of waiting for God is virtually absent in Proverbs.[47] Thus, the psalmist's call for restraint bears a distinctly theocentric cast, with God playing a decisive role in the outcome. Such is the dialogue hosted by Psalm 37 and Proverbs regarding the source and efficacy of righteousness, the consequential nature of human conduct (way), and the role of God in the mix.

Psalm 49: You Can't Take It with You

This remarkable psalm opens with a call to attention featuring a range of sapiential terminology:

> Hear this, all you peoples!
> Give ear, all you inhabitants of the world,
> people of every status,[48]
> rich and poor alike!

46. Only Prov 3:5; 16:20; 22:19.

47. Only Prov 20:22 provides a parallel.

48. Literally, "sons of humankind [*bĕnê ʾādām*] and sons of a man [*bĕnê-ʾîš*]." Given the parallelism with the second colon, the pairing could be a merismus, indicating opposing distinctions of status (so NRSV, NIV, KJV). Or it could be taken as equivalent terms (so CEB, NJPS). See the parallel in Ps 69:10 (cf. 4:3). I opt for the latter, since *ʾādām* and *ʾîš* are used elsewhere in the psalm without opposing nuance (vv. 8a and 13a).

My mouth will proclaim wisdom;
  the deliberation of my heart [will yield][49] insights.
I will incline my ear to a proverb;
  I will expound my riddle on the lyre. (49:1-4[2-5])

The terms *wisdom, insights, proverb,* and *riddle* give the psalm a sapiential hue (cf. Prov 1:2-5). But unlike a typical sapiential summons in Proverbs (e.g., Prov 1:8; 2:1; 23:15), the psalmist's call carries a broad, international scope, not unlike what is found in various psalms of praise.[50]

Following the psalmic-sapiential summons, the speaker highlights the universal nature of death, a message that resonates with certain observations featured in Ecclesiastes: the wise and the fool die together (49:10a[11a]; Eccl 2:15–16). Wealth is left for others in death (49: 10b[11b], 12a, 17; Eccl 5:15–16). Humans die like animals (49:12b[13b], 14[15]; Eccl 3:19-21). The admonition not to "fear" the rich (49:16) stems from a felt sense of unfairness that the wealthy are somehow able to retain their wealth even unto death. Not so, claims the psalmist.

Do not be afraid when a man becomes so rich
  that his house swells to glorious proportions.
For upon his death he will not take any of it;
  his glory will not descend after him.
Even though he counts himself blessed during his lifetime,
  and gives you thanks[51] when you deal well with him,[52]
    he shall go to the generation of his ancestors,
      who will never again see light.
As for human beings with [their] wealth, they do not understand;
  they are like the animals, which perish. (49:16-20[17-21])

49. The second line is elliptical, whose gap is filled verbally by the first.

50. E.g., Pss 33:8; 47:1[2]; 96:3; 99:2; 117:1. Nowhere in the wisdom corpus is such language deployed. The object of sapiential address is typically much more limited. See, e.g., Prov 4:1; 5:7; 7:24; 8:6, all of which begin with the plural command (*šim'û*; "listen").

51. Read *wĕyôdĕkā* with LXX and Peshitta for MT *wĕyôdukā* ("they will thank you").

52. Read *lô* with a few Hebrew manuscripts, LXX and Peshitta, for MT *lāk* ("for yourself"). The MT reads the line "and they laud you when you do well for yourself."

Riches cannot accompany the rich in their descent to Sheol along with the rich. All the wealth in the world, let alone the amassed wealth of one person, cannot ransom one's life from death (49:8-10[9-11]).

Yes, both Qoheleth and the psalmist highlight the indiscriminate nature of death, but they do so for different reasons. Qoheleth's emphasis on death demonstrates the utter "vanity" or futility (*hebel*) of life and, in turn, highlights the importance of enjoying momentary pleasures (e.g., Eccl 2:24-25; 8:15). The psalmist, in contrast, stresses the all-encompassing scope of death in order to bolster trust in God, in opposition to trust in wealth. Immortality is not for sale. Such trust reaches its apotheosis in a startling statement:

> Even so, God will ransom my soul from Sheol's power,
> for he shall take me. (49:15[16])

Only God, not wealth, has the power to ransom the speaker from death. Such a statement finds no warrant in Ecclesiastes; Qoheleth grants no exceptions, including himself. Whether or not Psalm 49 espouses immortality is not the presenting issue.[53] Either way, the statement represents a culmination of the psalmist's trust in God. Trust in God's power to "ransom" or "redeem" one from dire straits is the frequent subject of prayer and testimony in the Psalms.[54]

The psalmist, in sum, presses a Qohelethian view of death toward a very un-Qohelethian conclusion, yet espouses an entirely psalmic point of view pressed to its logical, if surprising, conclusion. Only God can redeem from death. The psalmist's testimony of trust undercuts Qoheleth's argument by positing an exception from death, an exception cast in a very unsapiential way: a confession of trust in God's saving power *coram morte.* Psalm 49 critically engages the wisdom of Ecclesiastes from a distinctly

53. For further discussion that leans toward affirming an afterlife, see Philip S. Johnston, *Shades of Sheol: Death and Afterlife in the Old Testament* (Downers Grove: IVP Academic, 2002), 202–4.

54. E.g., 25:22; 26:11; 31:5[6]; 33:18-19; 34:22[23]; 44:27; 55:18[19]; 69:19; 119:34; 130:8.

psalmic perspective, from an expression of radical trust in a God that proves not to be so inscrutable as Qoheleth claims.

Psalm 73: Sanctuary Reckoning

In its own way, Psalm 73 is something of a hybrid. It resembles both a confessional psalm minus the appeal to God for forgiveness and a song of thanksgiving without the testimony of deliverance (cf. 73:23-25). It is a personal confession not of guilt but of ignorance, resulting in the speaker's testimony of gaining new understanding. The opening verse makes a thesis-like claim about divine favor: "Truly God is good to Israel, to the pure in heart." But then the psalm launches into recounting a time in which the speaker severely doubted such a claim—a near "stumbling" (73:2). The speaker calls into question the psalm's opening thesis by bearing witness to the prosperity of the wicked (73:3b-5), a prosperity that slides into self-pride (73:6) and sin (73:7), including oppression (73:8) and defiance of God (73:9, 11)—from prosperity to impunity. The speaker finds the wealth of the wicked to be offensively perplexing.

The speaker returns to self-reflection in 73:13, calling into question the efficacy of one's own "pure" conduct. Two interrelated issues come to the fore: (1) Why do the wicked prosper? and (2) Why should one lead an "upright" life? Such cognitive dissonance (73:16) leads to ethical crisis (73:13). But suddenly and decisively this crisis of dissonance is resolved in a way that only the Psalms can do: a cultic-based revelation.

> And when I pondered how to understand this,
> it was toilsome in my eyes,
> until I entered the sanctuary of God,
> and discerned their end. (73:16-17)

This whiplash moment of revelation, not unlike the movement from protest to praise in other psalms, identifies the sanctuary as the *setting* of resolution. It is there that the speaker envisions the demise of the wicked, vividly described in 73:18-20. As a result, the psalm pivots from confessional lament to unwavering trust. As the locus of revelation, the sanctuary serves, one could say, as the "temple of doom" for the wicked, as it is the "temple of trust" for the speaker.

Psalm 73 offers not so much a theodicy as an anthropodicy. The central question is this: How should one respond to the swelling prosperity and flagrant impunity of the wicked? The answer is trust in God, in the God who will destroy the wicked, sooner or later. The "sanctuary of God" serves as both a demonstration and a confirmation of such trust. It is a "refuge," a place in which one can "recount all of [God's] works," including God's works against the wicked. The sanctuary is a place for reckoning with the wicked in view of God's reckoning for the wicked.

It is often noted that Psalm 73 and Job share in common the vexing issue of the prosperity of the wicked.[55] Less acknowledged, however, is that both press the issue in quite different ways. While Psalm 73 presents the issue as an anthropodicy, Job (the character) casts the issue as a matter of theodicy. More contrastive still, YHWH's answer in Job minimizes all sense of divine retribution at work in creation. Whatever qualities Psalm 73 and the book of Job share in common, their resemblance comes down to addressing a common problem, even as their respective solutions are worlds apart.

Psalm 78: History Matters

Like Psalm 49, Psalm 78 identifies itself as a psalm of instruction, and it does so in similar fashion to the opening prologue of Proverbs. I highlight their overlapping terminology.

---

55. Compare, e.g., Job 21:13-14 and Ps 73:11. For a discussion of the intertextual correspondences, see Will Kynes, *My Psalm Has Turned into Weeping: Job's Dialogue with the Psalms*, BZAW 473 (Berlin: de Gruyter, 2012), 161–79, who argues that the Joban poet commented on the psalm.

Psalm 78	**Proverbs 1**
1 Give ear, my people, to my teaching; incline your ear to the words of my mouth. 2 I will open my mouth with a proverb; I will declare enigmas from of old, 3 which we have heard and known, which our ancestors have told us. 4 We will not conceal [them] from their descendants, declaring to the next generation the praiseworthy deeds of YHWH and his might, the wonders he has wrought.	2 For learning about wisdom and instruction, for understanding words of insight, 3 for gaining instruction in wise dealing, righteousness, justice, and equity; 4 to teach shrewdness to the simple, knowledge and prudence to the young. 5 Let the wise also hear and gain in learning, and the discerning acquire skill, 6 to understand a ***proverb*** and a figure, the ***words*** of the wise and their ***enigmas***. 7 The fear of YHWH is the beginning of knowledge; fools despise wisdom and instruction.

Words, *proverb*, and *enigmas*: such terms are shared by both prologues. Psalm 78 indicates at the outset that it is all about the speaker's "teaching" or *tôrâ* (78:1). Although Proverbs favors another didactic term, "instruction" (*mûsār*), in its opening verse, it also references *tôrâ* repeatedly, as we have seen.

While instructional terminology is more extensive in Proverbs, as one would expect, the prologue of Psalm 78 suggests that what follows is something akin to what is offered in Proverbs, namely instruction for living, beginning with the family. Proverbs follows its prologue with instruction passed on from a father to his son (1:8-19). In Psalm 78, reference to the "ancestors" (or "fathers") suggests wisdom passed on from one generation to the next, as one finds in Proverbs 4:4-5. But "getting wisdom" based on familial advice is not the psalmist's concern. While both prologues conclude with reference to YHWH (Ps 78:4b; Prov 1:7a), they do so in strikingly different ways. Whereas divine reverence ("fear") holds the theological key to proverbial instruction, the psalm signals its focus on YHWH's "praiseworthy deeds." What follows is a historical review of the "works of God," but not without a word of warning:

He set up a decree in Jacob,
and established a law in Israel,
which he commanded our ancestors
to make known to their children,
so that the next generation will know, children yet to be born,
and[56] rise up and tell their children,
placing their confidence in God,
not forgetting God's deeds,
but keeping his commandments,
not becoming like their ancestors,
an obstinate and contentious generation,
a generation whose heart was not resolute,
and whose spirit was not faithful to God. (78:5-8)

Whereas the parents, both father and mother, are the source of wisdom in much of Proverbs, the ancestors in Psalm 78 hold an ambivalent position: while they are the source of "decreed" knowledge passed on to subsequent generations, they are by no means exemplars of it. The past generation is discredited for failing to remember "God's deeds" and to "keep his commandments" (78:7), even as they are to pass on such "teaching." Psalm 78 passes on the turbulent history of Israel and God, from the exodus, through the wilderness, and concluding with the rise of the Davidic kingdom. The lesson? Israel should not forget God's miraculous deeds and its own failures of the past (78:10-11, 17-19, 32, 36-37, 40-42, 56-58).

Under the guise of wisdom, Psalm 78 does what the wisdom literature never does, namely treat matters of national history as subjects of sapiential reflection. The psalmist finds the lessons of history more critical than, say, observations about creation. Yes, the ancestors have their wisdom to share, but they are an obstinate brood; they cannot be trusted entirely. Do not follow what they did, the psalmist warns, but accept what they say. Follow God's "commandments" and remember God's "wonders" (78:32). It is in history, the psalmist claims, that Israel learns of God's salvific power, compassionate forbearance, and punishing judgment. It is also in history that

56. Reading with LXX and Peshitta, suggesting haplography in the MT.

Israel is given the law and the commandments to follow. History matters to the psalmist; it too is a source of wisdom. Psalm 78 is both a dialogical corrective and complement to wisdom's instructional ethos.

Psalms 111–112: A Godly Man and a Manly God

Opening with a call to praise and an *ʾašrê* saying, Psalm 112 presents a paradigmatic profile of the righteous man (*ʾîš*), a fitting counterpart to the acrostic poem of Proverbs 31:10-31, featuring the wise matriarch.[57] Curiously, "righteousness" is not a quality attributed to the "woman of strength" as it is with the righteous man, suggesting that righteousness here is a specifically androcentric virtue. Nevertheless, they share much in common. Both the righteous man and the resourceful woman are generous, industrious, steadfast, and therefore prosperous characters. So also their respective households (Ps 112:3; Prov 31:11, 18).

But that is where the similarity ends. While Psalm 112 could easily find a home in Proverbs[58] or serve as an appropriate description of Job in his prime (cf. Job 29:1-25), it finds its psalmic home by virtue of its "twin psalm," Psalm 111. In Psalm 111, YHWH is profiled as righteous, gracious, and merciful—identical terms for how the righteous person is described in Psalm 112 (111:3-4; 112:3-4). The theocentric focus of Psalm 111 perfectly complements the androcentric orientation of Psalm 112. The righteous man is made in the image of the righteous God, and vice versa. Wedded together, the two psalms fill out a profile of righteousness in which YHWH "himself" has an active hand. Human righteousness is modeled after divine righteousness, but with Psalm 111 placed before Psalm 112 the claim is made that the relationship is causal: the righteousness of the righteous is derived and patterned from the righteousness of God. That is to say, God comes first in the cultivation of righteousness. Whereas Psalm 112 itself could easily find a home in Proverbs, its

57. Beth LaNeel Tanner, *The Book of Psalms through the Lens of Intertextuality*, Studies in Biblical Literature 26 (New York: Peter Lang, 2001), 141–57.

58. It could describe, for example, the mature adult version of the silent "son" in Proverbs, the companion to the "woman of strength."

compositional link with Psalm 111 cannot be severed. They are both cut from the same cloth.

While the topic of righteousness is one bridge that unites these two psalms, so also is wisdom. Psalm 111 concludes with a sapiential statement that weds these two psalms:

> The beginning of wisdom is the fear of YHWH;
> all who perform them[59] gain a good understanding.
> His praise stands forever. (111:10)

The first line aligns itself with comparable wisdom "mottos" found in Proverbs 1:7; 9:10. But whereas "wisdom" (*ḥokmâ*) in Proverbs is something to be sought and possessed,[60] wisdom in Psalm 111 is something to be "performed" (√*ʿśh*). But what is to be performed exactly? YHWH's "precepts," which are modeled after "truth," "justice," and "uprightness":

> The works of [YHWH's] hands are truth[61] and justice;
> trustworthy are all his precepts,
> Upheld forever and ever,
> to be performed with truth and uprightness.[62] (111:7-8)

The final verse of the psalm reduces the sapiential to the morally prescriptive.[63] The fear of YHWH in Psalm 111, moreover, is not so much a posture as it is a practice. As an *act* of holy reverence, "performing" YHWH's "precepts" results in "good understanding" (*śēkel ṭôb*) or wisdom. With this modified sapiential motto concluding Psalm 111, Psalm 112 fills out what the profile of wisdom looks like for a man, wisdom that begins

59. The masculine plural suffix in the MT is a crux. LXX and Peshitta read a feminine singular suffix, whose subject is "wisdom." MT, however, bears the more difficult reading, whose antecedent is "precepts" in v. 7b.

60. E.g., Prov 2:1-4; 4:5-8; 7:4; 8:10-12; 14:6; 16:16.

61. Hebrew *ʾĕmet,* which also connotes a sense of steadfastness and faithfulness.

62. Perhaps read *wāyōšer* (n.), along with the versions, for MT's *wĕyāšār* (adj.). While the adjective could be considered abstract, it would be the only case for *yāšār*.

63. Wisdom's scope in Proverbs includes both instrumental and moral virtues (e.g., Prov 1:2-6).

in reverence: one who "delights greatly in [YHWH's] commandments" (112:1b; cf. Ps 1:2), "lends freely" (112:5a), practices "justice" (112:5b), and "distributes freely to those in need" (112:9). Such are the ways of justice and righteousness, according to Psalm 112. Such are the ways of wisdom, according to Psalm 111.

Nowhere in Proverbs is wisdom or reverence of God referred to as something specifically performed. Wisdom, rather, is primarily *found* and *possessed*; sapiential reverence ("the fear of YHWH") is *chosen* and *understood*.[64] They are primarily objects of attainment in Proverbs. The psalmist, however, offers a different nuance: wisdom and reverence are matters of practice. Wisdom is found in *fulfilling* the divine commandments (cf. Deut 4:5-6), and it includes the practice of giving thanks and praise, with which the psalm opens (Ps 111:1). The psalm concludes with the claim that "[YHWH's] praise stands forever," immediately following the sapiential motto (112:10b). To fear YHWH is ultimately to give due thanks and praise—an eminently wise thing to do. So central to the Psalter's ethos, praise and thanksgiving to God never fall within the sapiential orbit of Proverbs.

Conclusion

If measured by purity of form, there are no "wisdom psalms" in the Psalter. But if measured by their potential to "interact" with the wisdom corpus, then certain psalms rise up to don the mantle of wisdom, but a mantle of their own fashioning. Each wisdom psalm imparts wisdom that distinguishes itself from the wisdom corpus of the Hebrew Bible. Overall God is given a more prominent role in psalmic wisdom. Righteousness bears a more explicit theocentric cast. Trust in God takes precedence over specific modes of conduct. The destiny of the righteous receives greater emphasis, in part because the righteous suffer more in the Psalms than they do in Proverbs. But then there's Job, who suffers the most "because"

64. The "fear of YHWH" is chosen (*bḥr*, Prov. 1:29) and understood (*byn*, 2:5); a person is "in" reverence of God (14:26; 23:17). "Wisdom," similarly, is something chosen, received, found, bought, loved, and possessed or appropriated (e.g., 2:2a, 10; 3:13; 4:5, 7; 10:13; 16:16; 19:20; 23:23; 29:3), as well as understood and communicated (2:2b; 10:31).

of his integrity. In the Psalms, history and *tôrâ* are valued over parental instruction and empirical observation. An existential conundrum regarding the wicked receives a distinctly cultic resolution. In the Torah Psalms, wisdom is the consequence of *tôrâ*, received from God rather than sought out among the sages or by observation. For the psalmists, the fear of YHWH is not only the beginning of wisdom, it is also its endpoint and goal. In view of its limitations, wisdom in the Psalms finds its grounding in God and its attainment in practice.

Reading Psalms Sapientially[65]

Having explored particular psalms and their potential for dialogue with the wisdom literature, we can press further by asking a broader question: How might the Psalms be understood from a sapiential perspective and, say, Proverbs from a psalmic perspective? How do they engage dialogically on a more general basis? To explore how the psalmist and the sage keep canonical company requires a framing that extends beyond the study of particular "wisdom" psalms. What would it mean, in other words, to read Psalms "proverbially" and Proverbs "psalmically"?

The Case of the Rebuke

Amid all their discursive dissimilarities, Psalms and Proverbs share a certain rhetorical affinity, albeit pressed in different directions. Cast in second-person address, both books are filled with admonitory discourse. The psalmic speaker is never reluctant to admonish God for neglect or abandonment and tell God what to do about it through the imperative of petition. Such examples are often called "complaints." Earlier we discussed the possibility of calling them "protests" (see chapter 1). But from a sapiential perspective, such discourse finds particular resonance with the sapiential rhetoric of "rebuke" (*tôkaḥat*).

65. The following discussion draws from my more detailed essay, "Rebuke, Complaint, Lament, and Praise: Reading Proverbs and Psalms Together," in *Reading Proverbs Intertextually*, ed. Katharine Dell and Will Kynes, LHB/OTS 629 (London: T & T Clark, 2019), 65–76.

In Proverbs, the "rebuke" is a discursive form of correction. Those on the receiving end include the wicked (24:25) and the scoffer (15:12; 9:7), as well as the wise or "intelligent" (9:8b; 19:25b), who have "a listening ear" (25:12). Rebuke is the harshest form of counsel.

> Do not rebuke [*'al-tôkāḥ*] a scoffer; otherwise, he will hate you;
> rebuke a wise man, and he will love you [*wĕye'ĕhābekkā*].
> Instruct the wise, and they will become wiser;
> teach the righteous, and they will gain insight. (Prov 9:8-9)

This admonition discourages rebuking the "scoffer" and the "wicked" (cf. Prov 26:5) but commends it for the wise. What distinguishes the wise from the wicked is that the wise respond to rebuke with appreciation. The value of rebuke is frequently highlighted in Proverbs:

> Better is open rebuke than hidden love. (Prov 27:5)

> A rebuke strikes deeper into a discerning person
> than a hundred blows into a fool. (Prov 17:10)

> Whoever rebukes a person will afterward find more favor
> than one who flatters with the tongue. (Prov 28:23)

The most extended rebuke in Proverbs comes from Wisdom herself, who opens her first discourse with the following words:

> How long [*'ad-mātay*], O simple ones, will you love being simple?
> How long will scoffers delight in their scoffing
> and fools despise knowledge?
> Turn to my rebuke [*tôkaḥtî*];
> I will pour out my thoughts to you;
> I will make my words known to you. (Prov 1:22-23)

What follows is a blistering critique that both condemns and corrects her audience (Prov 1:24-33), and it all begins with a complaint cast as a question ("how long?"). Compare Wisdom's rebuke with that of Psalm 4.

How long [*'ad-meh*], you people, will my honor be an object of shame?
[How long] will you lust for what is worthless and seek after lies?
Selah
But know that YHWH has especially favored the faithful for himself;
YHWH hears whenever I call to him.
So tremble and do not sin!
Ponder [it] in your hearts upon your bed and be silent! *Selah*
Offer proper sacrifices, and trust in YHWH. (Ps 4:2-5[3-6])

As in Wisdom's address, the speaker in Psalm 4 harshly chastises his audience (4:2[3]) and then offers counsel (4:5-6[4-5]). We find a similar, even more urgent, rebuke in Psalm 62:3[4]:

How long [*'ad-'ānāh*] will you assault someone [*'îš*],
to take him down, all of you,
as though he were a toppled wall or a caved-in stone shelter?[66]

But rebukes in the Psalms are not limited to fellow human beings as they are in Proverbs. We find them operating within the divine realm as well, specifically Psalm 82:2, in which the gods are addressed and sentenced by God: "How long [*'ad-mātay*] will you judge unjustly." Most typically, the accusing question "how long?" in the Psalms is directed toward God.

How long [*'ad-'ānâ*], YHWH, will you forget me? Forever?
How long [*'ad-'ānâ*] will you conceal your face from me?
How long [*'ad-'ānâ*] must I bear counsels in my soul,
sorrow in my heart? Daily?
How long [*'ad-'ānâ*] must my enemy rise up against me?
(13:1-2[2-3]; cf. 79:5)

How long [*'ad-mātay*], O God, will the adversary scoff?
Will the enemy revile your name forever? (74:10)

YHWH God of hosts,
how long [*'ad-mātay*] will you be angry with your people's prayers?

66. Read *gĕdērāh dĕḥûyāh*. MT has ungrammatically divided the phrase.

You have fed them with the bread of tears,
 and given them tears to drink in full measure. (80:4-5[5-6])

Turn, YHWH! How long [*'ad-mātay*]?
 Be moved to pity for your servants!
Satisfy us in the morning with your faithful love,
 that we may rejoice and be glad throughout all our days. (90:13-14)

Particularly vivid is Psalm 35.

How long [*kammâ*], O Lord, will you look on?
Rescue me from their ravages,
 my only life from the lions!
Then I will give you thanks in the great congregation;
 among the mighty people I will praise you. . . .
You have seen, YHWH; do not be silent!
 O Lord, do not be far from me! Wake up!
Rouse yourself for my defense, for my cause,
 my God and my Lord! (35:17-18, 22-23)

Such impassioned addresses "rebuke" God for negligence, injustice, lack of compassion, unrestrained anger, and rejection. The list goes on. Rhetorically equivalent to the question "how long?" is the frequently posed question "why?" in the Psalms,[67] as perhaps most famously in Psalm 22:

My God, my God, why have you abandoned me?
 Why are you so far from helping me,
  from the words of my groaning? (22:1[2])[68]

It is not difficult to view the psalmic "complaint" or protest as a way of teaching God "a thing or two" about the speaker's plight and what should be done about it. Treating the psalmic complaint as a rebuke underscores

67. The question marker "why" (*lmh*) is found in Prov 5:20; 17:16; 22:27, the first one serving as a rebuke. Examples abound in Job (7:20-21; 13:24; 18:3; 19:22; 27:12; 33:13).

68. See also 10:102; 43:2; 44:23-24[24-26]; 88:14[15].

the speaker's boldness in correcting God. As a rebuke, every psalmic complaint serves as an accusation, and every plea is a call to accountability. One intriguing question is this: If the rebuke in Proverbs elicits favor from the wise, does it likewise do so from God? Does God accept protests as much as the wise gratefully receive rebukes? Does God welcome complaints and protests as much as praise and thanksgiving? The psalmists seem convinced that God fully accepts rebukes and would be moved by them, because God is the consummate "listening ear" and witness, this God of "benevolence" (*ḥesed*).[69] As the wise demand corrective rebuke, so God expects honest complaint or protest, so the psalmists assume.

To press the matter further, does God "learn" from complaints as the wise gain in learning from rebukes? This could be where the analogy breaks down. Nevertheless, from the psalmist's perspective the complaint does serve to point out certain matters to God out of concern that they would be left unaddressed. Complaints in the Psalms, in other words, serve as correctives as much as rebukes do in Proverbs. Regardless of whether such a comparison transgresses the rhetorical and generic boundaries of Psalms and Proverbs, it is easy to see the psalmic complaint and the sapiential rebuke as rhetorical counterparts within the discourse of accountability, both human and divine.

Sapiential Lament and Praise[70]

If the sapiential rebuke finds its psalmic counterpart in the complaint/petition, do lament and praise find any resonance in Proverbs? In contrast to the Psalms, there is little room for complaint to God in Proverbs: the conditions of persecution, disease, grief, and deprivation, to name a few examples of psalmic distress, are simply not registered in Proverbs, while they are heavily featured in Job. The only petition to be found in Prov-

69. See, e.g., Pss 6:4[5]; 25:6-7; 31:16[17]; 51:1[3]; 69:16[17]; 85:7[8].

70. The following draws from my more detailed essay, "Reading Psalms Sapientially in the Writings," in *The Oxford Handbook of The Writings of the Hebrew Bible,* ed. Donn F. Morgan (Oxford: Oxford University Press, 2019), 151–68.

erbs is the prayer that seeks from God a moderation of provision, not too much and not too little, a balance that avoids prideful delusion (30:7-9). No such prayer can be found in the Psalms, a prayer that seeks some "golden mean" of sufficiency. Psalmic prayers are never golden.

There is, nevertheless, one clear example of lament in Proverbs, strategically placed near the end of the book: the opening words of Agur, which offer self-deprecating testimony to the insurmountable limits of human knowledge.[71]

> *The words of Agur son of Jakeh, the oracle, the utterance of the man:*
> I am weary, O God, I am weary, O God,
>   wasting away,[72]
> for I am too beastly stupid[73] to be human,
>   and have not human understanding.
> I have not learned wisdom,
>   nor have I knowledge of the Holy One.
> Who has ascended to heaven and come down?
>   Who has gathered the wind in his cupped hands?
> Who has wrapped the waters in [his] garment?
>   Who has established all the ends of the earth?
> What is his name,
>   and what is the name of his son?
> Surely you know! (Prov 30:1-4)

Agur's opening discourse is a confession of ignorance in the face of questions comparable to those that issue forth from the whirlwind theophany

71. See also Prov 5:12-14, where the speaker laments having rejected "discipline" and "rebuke."

72. The opening verse of ch. 30, particularly the second half, is fraught with textual and interpretive challenges. The translation above involves only slight emendation (from the verbs *l'h* and *klh* [so Fox, *Proverbs 10–31*, 854]: *lāʾîtî ʾēl lāʾîtî ʾēl wĕʾēkel*), a translation preferable to taking the words as proper names.

73. The term for "stupid" (*baʿar*) is a denominative of *bĕʿîr* ("cattle, livestock"), as also the verbal form *bʿr* II ("graze").

in Job (38:2-4).[74] Agur's confession is a self-rebuke cast as a lament, a confession of failure to attain knowledge/wisdom. His words bespeak humility to the point of self-debasement.

It is significant that Agur's sayings are placed near the end of Proverbs, casting a long shadow over everything that precedes it, from proverbs to lectures. If the objective of Proverbs is the appropriation of wisdom (1:2-7), then Agur's confession effectively hits the reset button. Agur exhibits a profound awareness of limitation that undercuts all claims of sapiential advancement. But as lament rarely has the last word in any given psalm, so Agur's lament begins, rather than concludes, the collection attributed to him in 30:1-33, a revelry of insight and awe.[75]

As a whole, Agur's discourse moves from ignorance to insight, in modest parallel to the psalmic move from lament to praise. Ignorance, in fact, is confessed both in the sage's opening statement (30:2-3) and in the numerical list of wonders in 30:18-19 ("Three things are too wonderful for me; four I do not understand"). But whereas the former passage is cast as a self-deprecation, the latter gives testimony to the marvelous. The rhetorical movement of Agur's words suggests that self-abasing humility yields to new perception, indeed new orientation, all to suggest that only in humility is one able to see the world afresh with wonder and, thus, with new wisdom. If the "fear of YHWH is the beginning of knowledge" (Prov 1:7a), then sapiential impotence, according to Agur, is the beginning of wonder.

Sapiential impotence, however, is not given functional primacy in Proverbs any more than lament or complaint ("rebuke") marks the overarching aim of Psalms. As indicated in the Psalter's title (*tĕhillîm*), the

74. Job's final words indicate an internalization of YHWH's rebuke (see Job 42:3a, 4). For similarities between Agur and Job, see James L. Crenshaw, "Clanging Symbols," in James L. Crenshaw, *Urgent Advice and Probing Questions: Collected Writings on Old Testament Wisdom* (Macon, GA: Mercer University Press, 1995), 376–78. The questions are cast rhetorically: "no human being" or "God" is the answer. The answer regarding the "name of his son" (v. 4), however, is possibly Agur himself, since "son" can designate the student of wisdom in Proverbs. So Christine Roy Yoder, "On the Threshold of Kingship: A Study of Agur (Proverbs 30)," *Int* 63, no. 3 (2009): 261.

75. Due to the lack of superscriptions within the chapter and any literary markers signaling a change in speaker, I take all of chapter 30 to be attributed to Agur.

Psalms collectively point toward praise. With few exceptions, even the complaint/protest psalms conclude on a note of trust or praise. Moreover, the book of Psalms concludes on a climactic five-note chord of praise (Pss 146–150). As the Psalter identifies praise as its end goal, so Proverbs acknowledges "gaining instruction" is its objective (Prov 1:3a).

Throughout the first nine chapters of Proverbs, the reader is repeatedly exhorted to appropriate wise counsel and discipline.[76] As for Wisdom herself, such appropriation verges on the erotic,[77] a rhetorical feature entirely lacking in the Psalms. Nevertheless, the Psalms are replete with the language of desire, specifically the desire for God's personal presence. As Wisdom in Proverbs is lover and intimate friend who enables her partner to navigate life's complexities, so God in the Psalms is the object of deepest yearning, the transcendent deity who saves, protects, bestows blessing, and teaches *tôrâ*. In sum, *praise* of God in Psalms is matched by *assent* to Wisdom in Proverbs. Viewed sapientially, praise of God necessarily involves assent to God's authority and guidance. And what is praise if not assent suffused with joy and hope?

The language of praise is, in fact, not alien to wisdom. Proverbs, like Psalms, ends with praise, albeit not praise of God:

> Her children rise up and declare her happy;
> her husband also [rises up], and praises her:
> "Many woman have done well,
> but you surpass them all."
> Charm is deceitful, and beauty is fleeting,
> but a woman who fears YHWH is to be praised.
> Give her a share in the fruit of her hands,
> and let her works praise her in the city gates. (Prov 31:28-31)

76. E.g., Prov 1:8a; 2:1, 2; 4:1a; 5:1; 7:1, 2, 24; 8:32-33; 9:4-6.

77. Prov 4:6-8; 8:34-36; cf. 5:15-19. For more on the language of desire in Proverbs, see Anne W. Stewart, *Poetic Ethics in Proverbs: Wisdom Literature and the Shaping of the Moral Self* (Cambridge: Cambridge University Press, 2016), 130–69; Christine Roy Yoder, "The Shaping of Erotic Desire in Proverbs 1–9," in *Saving Desire: The Seduction of Christian Theology*, ed. J. Henriksen and L. Shults (Grand Rapids: Eerdmans, 2011), 148–62.

As God is to be praised in "the assembly of the faithful" (Ps 149:1b), so the "woman of strength," the flesh and blood embodiment of Wisdom in the household, is to be praised in the city gates. As these verses conclude the book of Proverbs on a note of praise (Prov 31:31), so too the book of Psalms (Pss 146–50). Perhaps, then, with precedence from the Psalms, the book of Proverbs could be retitled "Praises (of Wisdom)."

Conclusion

With all these points of contact between Psalms and Proverbs, as well as the larger wisdom corpus, kept in mind, where at the table might one imagine the psalmist and the sage sitting to host such dialogues? At opposite ends (shouting), or next to each other (commiserating), or somewhere in between? Put another way, where does each corpus have its home in relation to the other within the larger landscape of ancient Israel's life?

We begin with the most obvious. While the wisdom literature contains a trove of instructional material spanning centuries of ethical and theological reflection, the Psalter provides a wide sampling of Israel's rich cultic life, whether in centralized worship or in more informal, small-scale settings in which God is invoked in various ways.[78] As most psalms have their home in worship in some form or another, whether public or private, wisdom in Proverbs operates within the familial home, as well as in the court, the city gate, and the marketplace—those places that are by and large not cultically based (Prov 1:20-21; 8:2-3). Nowhere in Proverbs does personified Wisdom gain full entrance into the temple (cf. Sir 24:8-11). Neither does Wisdom play a determinative role in Israel's national history (cf. Wis 10:1-21). History and worship are not her primary domains. Rather, it is in the hubs of day-to-day living, as well as in creation, that the sages found Wisdom to be most theologically active. Where she "stands" is outside the sanctuary of praise and prayer.

78. Psalm 91 in particular carries the widest variety of referents for God of any psalm: *ʿelyôn* ("Most High"), *šadday* ("Almighty"), *yhwh* (YHWH), *ʾĕlōhay* ("my God"), reflecting the cultic reality of ancestral religion (see chapter 3).

While Wisdom's reach extends beyond the realm of worship, the God of the Psalms reaches beyond the realm of the everyday by claiming the temple as well as places of peril and distress. From the battlefield and the prison house to the wilderness and the raging sea,[79] the Psalms address crisis and cult, life *in extremis* joined to life in worship. Both of these domains—the center and the periphery, one might say—affirm radical dependence on God. Wisdom, on the other hand, fills the gap by staking her claim wherever life is more a matter of navigation and negotiation, of mediation and balancing, wherever self-reliance through the cultivation of virtue becomes critical. Whereas the Psalms deal with life at the extremes, Proverbs covers life in the middle, beginning with the home.

For all their differences, is there common ground for wisdom and Psalms in light of their respective goals? There are certainly overlaps. One could read the book of Job, for example, as the result of a dramatic clash between the edifying wisdom of Proverbs and the "protest psalms" of the Psalter, with the result of propelling wisdom beyond the realm of human attainment (Job 28) or making it primarily a matter of divine revelation (Job 38–41). Such an outcome would have been complete if Job the protagonist had launched into praise at the end of his discourse in 42:6. But he did not. Instead, he testified in the end to his shift in understanding, more a sapiential than psalmic move. But perhaps the psalmist would encourage readers to imagine Job at some point composing or performing the hymn of Psalm 104, some of whose animals are featured in YHWH's answer, including lions and Leviathan.

Despite their theological divergences, the psalmist and the sage are canonically engaged in constructive dialogue over what constitutes a true vision of life *coram Deo*. It is perhaps no accident, for example, that the accolade "How happy is . . ." (*'ašrê*) concludes Proverbs (Prov 31:28) and opens the Psalter (Ps 1:1), a designation that commends the kind of person who seeks what is good and righteous, including God.[80] From Psalms 1:1 to 146:5, numerous commendations are made that might lead one to regard the Psalter itself as a "manual of happiness," or to be more

79. Cf. the four scenarios of distress in Psalm 107.

80. E.g., Pss 2:12; 34:8[9]; 41:1[2]; 106:3; 119:1-2

generically appropriate, a hymnbook for happiness.[81] Something comparable could be said of Proverbs. The commendation "How happy are those who find wisdom" (Prov 3:13; cf. 3:18b; 8:34) is matched with "How happy are all who take refuge in [YHWH]" (Pss 2:12b; cf. 34:8b[9b]; 146:5). But the road to such happiness, whether psalmic or sapiential, is a rugged one. The path to praise is marked by complaint and plea, protest and petition. The path to wisdom turns on rebuke and admonition. But both paths run parallel.

The canonical conjoining of Proverbs and Psalms, of the resourceful woman in Proverbs 31:10-31 and the righteous man in Psalm 112, of the battleground and the farmer's field, of the household and the sanctuary, of the public square and sacred space, of Wisdom and *tôrâ*, covers much of ancient Israel's life in its various contexts. Throughout the city, God is more distant while Wisdom roams the streets and inhabits households. Within the sanctuary, God's presence is front and center, while Wisdom lingers at the threshold. As for living wisely, the Psalms raise up history, God's voice in *tôrâ*, and creation for consideration, while Proverbs lifts up Wisdom's voice, parental *tôrâ*, and creation as well. In the end, their distinctive domains, as well as their overlaps, reflect more a division of influence than a competition for allegiance, as the psalmist and the sage continue their dialogue directly across from each other at the table over a good meal (Eccl 2:24-25). The sage would defer to the psalmist to say a blessing after the meal, while the psalmist would have listened intently to the daily news and reflections from the sage during the course of the meal. But who would have the last word when it comes time to retire might be a source of contention.

81. Although the Psalter is more than a hymnbook. For a detailed examination of the *'ašrê* sayings in the Psalms, see my "Happiness and Its Discontents in the Psalms," in *The Bible and the Pursuit of Happiness: What the Old and New Testaments Teach Us about the Good Life*, ed. Brent A. Strawn (New York/Oxford: Oxford University Press, 2012), 95–115.

CHAPTER 10
PSALMS AT THE TABLE: TALKING TWO BY TWO

Come now, let us reason together, saith the Lord.

—Isaiah 1:18 (KJV)

Thus far we have discussed various points of dialogue between the Psalms and the larger biblical corpus, the "little Bible" vis-à-vis the larger Bible. In this chapter, we turn inward to sample a few dialogues hosted among the psalms themselves. Since the Psalms assume such a prominent place in the Writings, here is as good a place as any to explore what the psalms of the Psalter have to say to each other.

What happens when two psalms are "seated" next to each other within the larger literary arrangement of the Hebrew Psalter? They start "talking," of course! The German scholar Walther Zimmerli identified at least two pairs of psalms that he considered intentionally juxtaposed, sharing linguistic and thematic connections.[1] He called them *Zwillingspsalmen* or "twin psalms," although this was not a new designation. While many adjacent psalms share a catchword or two,[2] only two pairs of psalms according to Zimmerli can best be called genuine "twins," namely Psalms 105–106

1. Walther Zimmerli, "Zwillingspsalmen," in Wort, Lied und Gottesspruch, *Beiträge zu Psalmen und Propheten: Festschrift für Joseph Ziegler,* ed. Josef Schreiner, Forschung zur Bibel 12 (Würzburg: Echter Verlag: Katholisches Bibelwerk, 1972), 105–13.

2. E.g., Pss 1–2; 38–39; 39–40; 69–70; 73–74; 127–128.

and 111–112. Other scholars, however, have added to the list by employing various criteria. Raymon Paul Hanson identifies four bona fide sets of twin psalms (Pss 56–57, 103–104, 105–106, and 111–112) by employing seven criteria: they must (1) be adjacent, (2) feature similar "introductory statements," (3) be of approximately the same length, (4) exhibit similar form, (5) feature reoccurring words and/or themes, (6) indicate similar or contrasting thoughts, and (7) be theologically interrelated.[3] Such criteria serve, in Hanson's words, to "stitch the psalms together." However, I would add that some psalms may be actually "cut from the same cloth," that is, compositionally related from the outset. In any case, one can imagine such psalms "genetically" aligned, as it were, to face each in dialogue, even as their attention is directed to God.

But we need not limit ourselves to these few twin psalms to appreciate the Psalms' dialogical dynamics. The two most identical psalms in the Psalter are not adjacent at all, not even close. For all their similarities, Psalms 14 and 53 distinguish themselves in their "dialogue" over the appropriate punishment of "evildoers" (14:5-6 and 53:6[7]). Either Psalm 53 would find Psalm 14 insufficiently weak, or Psalm 14 would consider Psalm 53 too brutal. Similarly, Psalms 57 and 108 share nearly identical expressions of praise and divine exaltation (57:7-11[8-12]; 108:1-5[2-6]). Psalm 57 concludes with praise in response to personal deliverance from devouring enemies (vv. 5[6], 7[8]). In contrast, Psalm 108 opens with such praise as the occasion for the divine oracle that follows in 108:7-13[8-14], the same oracle featured in 60:6-12[8-14] in a more dire context.

No two psalms, including twin psalms, are alike, despite their shared language. Each psalm is unique at least in terms of emphasis, if not message. But we are looking for more substantive conversations over, for example, the roles of God and Israel in history, the human condition, including the place of sin, and the relationship between *tôrâ* and king. We

3. Raymon Paul Hanson, "A Socio-rhetorical Examination of Twin Psalm 111–112" (PhD diss., Luther Seminary, 2013), 40.

begin by discussing two out of the four twin psalms identified by Hanson[4] and then broaden our scope to other psalms that can be paired for dialogical purposes.

Psalms 105–106: Who Is the God of Israel's History? Who Is Israel in God's History?

These two historical psalms cover roughly the same periods of history, but from different vantage points. Together, they complement as much as they diverge from each other. They are natural dialogical partners, in part because they open with praise and thanksgiving.

> Give thanks to YHWH!
> Call upon his name!
>   Proclaim his deeds among the peoples!
> Sing to him!
>   Sing praises to him!
>   Ponder all his wonders! (105:1-2)

> Praise YH!
> Give thanks to YHWH, for he is good;
>   indeed, his benevolence endures forever.
> Who can recount the mighty acts of YHWH,
>   [or] proclaim all his praise? (106:1-2)

By comparing the opening verses of both psalms, a subtle difference emerges. While both call forth praise and thanksgiving, Psalm 105 commands recitation ("proclaim" and "ponder") of YHWH's "wonders"

4. Psalms 111 and 112 are dialogically explored in chapter 9. As for Psalms 56 and 57, a full discussion is not warranted except to note that whereas Psalm 56 praises God's "word" (vv. 4[5], 11[12]), Psalm 57 acknowledges God's "benevolence" and "faithfulness" (v. 3[4]), which match God's glory in cosmic proportion (vv. 10[11]). In Psalm 56, God's "word" is the agent of deliverance. In Psalm 57, God sends forth "benevolence and faithfulness" to accomplish deliverance. Salvation of even one individual, according to Psalm 57, is an act of divine self-exaltation. God's glory, more than God's dispatched "word," is at stake in a person's deliverance, so claims Psalm 57.

(*niplāʾôt*), and Psalm 106 asks rhetorically who can do so. The answer is no one: God's "mighty acts" (*gibûrôt*) can never be fully recounted; they are beyond human understanding. And so these twin psalms of praise begin to embark on their separate ways.

Psalm 106:3 continues with an *ʾašrê* saying,[5] signaling further the split in perspectives: whereas Psalm 105 recounts Israel's story strictly from the side of the *magnalia Dei*, Psalm 106 counters with Israel's miserable failures, the *defectis Israël.* In contrast to those who uphold justice and righteousness, those who are deemed "happy" or fortunate, Psalm 106 proceeds to show how those who failed to do so in Israel's history were not so fortunate. While Psalm 105 revels in God's *Heilsgeschichte* ("history of salvation"), Psalm 106 exposes Israel's *Sündesgeschichte* ("history of sin").

In both psalms, the act of "remembrance" is called forth in strikingly different ways. Whereas Psalm 105:5 commands the community to "remember" YHWH's "wonders," Psalm 106 commands YHWH to "remember" who is speaking:

> Remember me, YHWH, with the favor [granted] your people!
> Visit me with your salvation,
>   so that I may behold the benefit[s] of your chosen ones.
> Rejoice in the joy of your nation,
>   and exult with your heritage. (106:4-5)

Petition, in fact, frames Psalm 106 in its entirety, highlighting another distinction: the praise of Psalm 105 is matched by petition in Psalm 106, both individual (106:4-5) and corporate:

> Save us, YHWH our God!
> Gather us from the nations,
>   to give thanks to your holy name
>   and to revel boldly in your praise! (106:47)

5. "How happy are those who uphold justice, who practice righteousness at all times."

In Psalm 106, petition and confession converge, indicating the deepest divide between the two psalms: Psalm 106 matches its predecessor's praise with a self-admonishing confession.

The historical review featured in Psalm 105 begins with Abraham, not because of anything that Abraham specifically did (105:6-11) but because of what YHWH did, in keeping with the psalm's prominent theocentric focus. YHWH makes a covenantal promise to "give the land of Canaan" to Israel as its "inherited portion" (105:9-11). It is precisely this promise of the land that drives the poetic narrative to its victorious conclusion.

> He opened the rock and out gushed water,
> flowing as a river through dry lands.
> For he remembered his sacred promise [to] Abraham his servant.
> He brought his people out in joy,
> his chosen ones with peals of jubilation.
> He gave them the lands of nations;
> they inherited the wealth of the peoples,[6]
> so that they may keep his statutes,
> and observe his laws. (105:41-45)

As the psalm begins with a call to remember YHWH's wondrous deeds (105:5), beginning with the Abrahamic covenant, so it concludes with testimony of YHWH "remembering" the ancient covenant, resulting in Israel's constitution as a people possessing the land.

In between such remembrances, Psalm 105 recounts Israel's small beginnings, as the people wander from nation to nation (105:12-13), accompanied by YHWH's protection and guidance (105:14-15). Then came famine, and Joseph is sent to Egypt (105:16-22) to pave the way for Israel to settle in Egypt (105:23-25). Because of their oppression, YHWH sends Moses and Aaron (105:26-27), followed by the miraculous plagues (105:28-36). Israel is brought out of Egypt enriched (105:37-38), receives sustenance in the wilderness (105:39-41), and comes to possess the land (105:43-44). Throughout these events, YHWH is the active agent, while Israel remains passive: its leaders are "sent," not elected by the people

6. Literally, "the labors of peoples," that is, the fruits of their labors.

(105:17, 26). While Moses and Aaron "perform the words of [YHWH's] signs and marvels" as messengers to Pharaoh (105:27), YHWH remains the acting agent enacting them, beginning with "sending darkness" (105:28). Israel's history in Psalm 105 is driven largely by a series of divine "sendings" and words (105:8, 11, 15, 19, 27, 31, 34). Even the conquest of the land minimizes human agency; it is merely a matter of YHWH assigning the land (105:44; cf. Josh 6–12).[7]

In Psalm 106, Israel's "history" is messy. The petition in 106:4-5 is followed by a confession of sin that is inclusive of Israel's "ancestors" (106:6). Their sin? Not "considering" YHWH's "wonders" and "benevolent acts" (106:7), precisely what Psalm 105 commanded the people to do (105:5). Such is Israel's foundational failure behind all the sins that punctuate Israel's history from the exodus to captivity (106:7, 46). They serve as exhibits A through G, as it were: rebellion (106:7b, 43), forgetting (106:13, 21-22), conflict over leadership (106:16-17), apostasy (106:19-20, 28, 36-39), rejecting YHWH's promise of the land (106:24-25), disobedience (106:25, 34), and provoking YHWH's wrath (106:32).

But Psalm 106 is not all negative in its assessment of Israel. At one point, the people "believed" [YHWH's] "words" and "sang his praise" (106:12), albeit momentarily (106:13-14). Phinehas stands out for his "righteousness" after having "interceded" to stop the plague during the Ba'al of Peor incident (106:28-31 [cf. Num 25:4-13]). In fact, Phinehas is the only leader in Psalm 106 endowed with righteousness, just like Abram in Genesis 15:6, and thus the only one to exemplify the *ʾašrê* saying in 106:3. Not even Moses, the most fearless of intercessors (106:23), receives such commendation. Moses, instead, is faulted for speaking "rashly" at Meribah (106:32-33). Psalm 106 does not leave much to commend Israel's conduct. The psalmist details Israel's sins for a purpose: to bind together the "ancestors" and the present generation, to link the present with the past (106:6), all to show that Israel's sins are, one could say, "original" sins, at least from the exodus onward.

7. See David Emanuel, "The Elevation of God in Psalm 105," in *Inner Biblical Allusion in the Poetry of Wisdom and Psalms*, ed. Mark J. Boda, Kevin Chau, and Beth LaNeel Tanner, LHB/OTS 659 (London: T & T Clark, 2019), 63.

While YHWH takes credit for Israel's history in Psalm 105, Israel takes some of the credit in Psalm 106. As Israel's agency is highlighted in Psalm 106, so also are Israel's tragedies, yielding a more problematic identity for YHWH's "heritage." YHWH's agency, in turn, is also given additional definition. Yes, YHWH's deeds are "mighty" (106:2), "wondrous," and "awesome" (106:7a, 22), as in Psalm 105. But there is something more in Psalm 106 regarding YHWH's agency, something that grounds all of YHWH's acts: "benevolence" (*ḥesed*), identified at the outset (106:1b) and employed as parallel reference to YHWH's "wonders" (106:7). "Benevolence" also finds prominence in the penultimate passage of the psalm:

> Many times [YHWH] would deliver them,
> but they remained deliberately rebellious,[8]
> sinking low[9] in their iniquity.
> Nevertheless, he regarded their distress,
> when he heard their loud cries.
> He remembered his covenant for their sake,
> and was remorseful on account of his abundant benevolence.
> He allowed them to receive compassion,[10] from all their captors.
> (106:43-46)

Here, divine "benevolence" (entirely lacking in Ps 105) is the motivating force that turns YHWH's wrath into compassion, suffused with remorse. It is benevolence that presses YHWH's forbearance in Psalm 106 in the face of Israel's rebellions. What Psalm 106 adds to the poetic history of Psalm 105 is not only the theme of Israel's proclivity to rebel, even in the face of YHWH's deliverance, but also that of YHWH's long-suffering forbearance—forbearance by virtue of benevolence. While the psalm does reference various divine punishments (106:15b, 17-18, 29, 32, 40-42), they are limited, the psalmist points out. At one point, YHWH's resolve to destroy the people is thwarted by Moses standing "in the breach"

8. Literally, "rebellious in their counsels."

9. From the verb *mkk.* MT makes perfect sense as it stands (contra *BHS*).

10. Literally, "turned them into compassion." For the syntax, see 1 Kgs 8:50; Dan 1:9; Neh 1:11.

(106:23a). Similarly, Phinehas's intercession stops the plague (106:30). The implied disjunctive force of the *waw* consecutive in 106:44 ("nevertheless") illustrates YHWH's willingness to turn away from wrath despite Israel's persistent intransigence. What does it take on YHWH's part to be so willing to change course? It is, according to Psalm 106, benevolence, the one underlying constancy of divine character that manifests itself in the changeability of YHWH's action toward a people. Benevolence facilitates YHWH's shift from anger to compassion. Can God change God's mind? Yes, consistently so.

These starkly different portrayals of Israel's history reflect the distinctive rhetorical intents of each psalm. In recalling YHWH's salvific acts from the Abrahamic covenant to the possession of the land, Psalm 105 commands praise and remembrance and nothing more. Like Psalm 105, Psalm 106 begins in praise but proceeds to individual petition (106:4-5) and concludes with corporate petition (106:47). The breadth of its historical review, moreover, extends beyond that of Psalm 105 to conclude with the displacement of a people from the land (106:47), presupposing the exile and beyond (106:46). As Moses and Phinehas interceded to move YHWH toward preserving a people, so Psalm 106 intercedes through petition and confession for a people in the diaspora. When it comes to historical reviews, different genres and implied contexts necessitate different pasts. Two different histories, in other words, match two different genres.

Does Psalm 106, then, trump Psalm 105 dialogically? No. Psalm 105 stands on its own as an exquisitely rendered recitation of divine action on behalf of a people. Such is the historical review of praise, focused singularly upon YHWH, the God of signs and wonders. But if YHWH's "benevolence" is to be introduced into the historical fray, as Psalm 106 does, then one must include YHWH's forbearance in the face of Israel's intransigence. On the other hand, Psalm 105 would remind Psalm 106 that praise, in addition to confession and petition, remains an integral part of the dialogue. With its rigorous theocentric focus, Psalm 105 makes claim that it is God who resides at the beginning of Israel's history (not Moses, not even Abraham), and it is God who remains at the end, regardless of outcome. Indeed, it is the end of Psalm 105 that sets the stage for Psalm

106. From the promise to Abraham to the fulfillment of that promise (105:8-11, 44), YHWH establishes a telos for Israel: to fulfill YHWH's "statutes" and "laws" (105:45). The promise of the land was "confirmed to Jacob as a statute" (105:10b); now it is extended to Israel in the land as *tôrâ*. The gift of the land is bound up with Israel's obedience in the land. Such is the link that binds the two psalms together: Israel's obedience, and lack thereof. Here, success and failure find their common ground.

Psalms 103–104: The Benefits of Benevolence

The genetic affinity of Psalms 103 and 104 is indicated by the identical imperative expression that opens and concludes each psalm: "Bless YHWH, my whole being!" Both psalms revel in giving praise to YHWH in the form of "blessing" YHWH. Unlike Psalms 105 and 106, their differences are governed not by genre but strictly by content, making them amenable dialogue partners.

Psalm 103 celebrates the "benefits" (*gĕmûlîm*) that YHWH grants human beings, which are enumerated in near taxonomic fashion. A summary of such benefits opens the psalm.

> Bless YHWH, my whole being!
> Everything inside me, [bless] his holy name!
> Bless YHWH, my whole being!
> Do not forget all his benefits—
> the one who forgives all your iniquity,
> who heals all your diseases,
> who redeems your life from the Pit,
> who crowns you with benevolence and compassion,
> who satisfies you with good things, sufficiently so,[11]
> such that your youth will be renewed like the eagle's. (103:1-5)

11. MT *'edyēk* apparently derives from *'ădî*, meaning "ornamentation" or "jewelry," which makes little sense here. I read, as proposed by *BHS*, a haplography derived from an original *'ad dayyēkî* ("until your sufficiency").

Forgiveness, healing, rescue from death, satisfaction, and renewal are all identified as reasons for praise. In the following verse, "righteousness" and "justice" for the "oppressed" also find their way on the list (103:6). They all find common ground in the two most prominent divine dispositions featured in the psalm: YHWH's "benevolence" and "compassion":

Compassionate and merciful is YHWH,
 slow to anger and abounding in benevolence. (103:8)

The language recalls YHWH's self-confession in Exodus 34:6: "YHWH passed before him and proclaimed, 'YHWH, YHWH, a God compassionate and merciful, slow to anger, and abounding in benevolence and faithfulness.'"

Such are the constituents of YHWH's "glory" set in this credal-like revelation of divine character. Psalm 103 features four out of the five attributes listed in the Exodus version: "compassionate" (*raḥûm*), "merciful" (*ḥannûn*), "slow to anger" (*'erek 'appayim*) or patience, and "abounding in benevolence" (*rab-ḥesed*) or extravagant love. This taxonomy of divine character is dispersed throughout the Hebrew Bible in variant forms.[12] Psalm 86:15, for example, features the complete list as motivation for salvific action. In Psalm 103:7, these defining marks of YHWH's character recall YHWH's ways in the past, beginning with Moses.

In the next strophe, forgiveness is deemed a natural outcome of YHWH's benevolence.

[YHWH] does not contend relentlessly,
 or keep his anger interminably.
He does not deal with us according to our sins,
 or repay us according to our iniquities.
For as the heavens are high above the earth,
 so superior[13] is his benevolence to those who fear him.
As far as the east is from the west,
 so far has he removed our sins from us.

12. Num 14:18; Neh 9:17; Pss 86:15; 145:8; Joel 2:13; Jon 4:2; Nah 1:3.

13. MT establishes an ingenious wordplay between *gbr* and *gbh*.

As a father has compassion for [his] children,
  so YHWH has compassion for those who fear him. (103:9-13)

In these verses YHWH's self-attributions in 103:8 are elaborated in greater detail: the first two are cast negatively, and the following three are evoked analogically. YHWH does not get angry enough to "repay" (√*gml*) according to sin (103:9-10). Instead, YHWH's ways are salutary, grounded in benevolence, forgiveness, and compassion (103:11-13). The poet casts these qualities with evocative analogies. YHWH's "benevolence" is as "superior" (*gābar*) as the heavens are "high" (*gĕbōah*), a clever wordplay in Hebrew (103:11). YHWH "removes" (√*rḥq*) the community's "sins" as far as the opposite horizons. YHWH is as "compassionate" (*raḥûm*) as a "father" is to his children.

Why is YHWH so compassionate? The answer is given an anthropological twist:

Because he knows how we are formed,
  he is mindful that we are dust.
As for humans, their days are like grass;
  like a wildflower, they bloom.
Yet when a wind passes over it, it is no more,
  and its place knows it no longer.
But to those who fear him, YHWH's benevolence is
  from everlasting to everlasting,
and his righteousness to [their] children's children,
    to those who keep his covenant,
      to those who remember to follow his precepts. (103:14-18)

YHWH's tender compassion is not simply self-motivated; it is prompted by humanity's frail condition as "dust" and "grass." Who else would know humanity's condition better than humanity's creator? "Dust" refers to the "dust of death,"[14] the originating substance out of which the first human was fashioned and to which all humanity returns (Gen 2:7; 3:19). As complement to "dust," withering "grass" stresses the transient

14. See Pss 22:15[16]; 30:5; 104:29.

nature of human life.[15] Psalm 103 refers to the "wind" (*rûaḥ*) that passes over the grass, causing it to disappear. Similarly, the Isaianic prophet of the exile speaks of YHWH's "breath" (also *rûaḥ*) blowing upon the grass, causing it to wither (Isa 40:6-8). In both cases, humanity as "grass" sets up a contrast to God's "word" in Isaiah's case and to YHWH's "benevolence" and "righteousness" in Psalm 103. YHWH's "benevolence" is everlasting, extending across generations (103:17-18). The psalm concludes with a cosmic call for blessing, from top to bottom and back to the individual (103:20-22), coming full circle.

Continuing such praise, Psalm 104 opens with a call to blessing from below and proceeds to expand the scope of praise cosmically. While Psalm 103 celebrates YHWH's "benefits" for those who keep YHWH's "covenants" and "commandments" (103:18), Psalm 104 explores how such "benefits" are shared by all life, acclaiming YHWH's handiwork in creation, from the earth's foundations to life's sheer diversity.

> How numerous are your works, YHWH!
> With wisdom you have made them all.
> The earth is full of your creations![16] (104:24)

In dialogue with Psalm 103, Psalm 104 poses the question, What does YHWH's benevolence look like for all of creation? It looks like springs "gushing forth in the valleys," providing sustenance for wild animals (104:10-11). It looks like birds singing in the foliage (104:12). It looks like the fertile land providing grass for "cattle" as well as food and wine for humanity's sustenance and enjoyment (104:14-15). YHWH's benevolence is reflected in the natural habitats where each animal thrives, from the stork to the coney (104:17-18). Such benevolence preserves the "cedars of Lebanon," planted by the divine gardener (104:16).

In short, the scope of YHWH's providential care turns creational in Psalm 104, evident in the provision for all life:

---

15. See also Pss 37:2; 90:5; 102:11; cf. Isa 40:6-7.

16. The term, amended to the plural in light of various Hebrew manuscripts, refers to possessions, as in the case of livestock (Gen 31:18; 34:23; Josh 14:4), but here including everything, from domains to creatures.

All of them wait for you,
to provide their food on time.
You give to them, and they gather it up;
you open your hand, and they are well filled.
But when you hide your face, they are terrified;
when you gather up their breath, they expire,
returning to their dust.
[But] when you send forth your breath, they are created,
and you renew the face of the earth. (104:27-30)

In Psalm 104, divine compassion seems indiscriminate. However, while YHWH's hand is open to provide, YHWH's "face" or life-giving presence is not guaranteed, as in the event of death (104:29). But the psalmist is quick to see the turnaround: as breath can be taken away, it can (and will) be "sent forth" to "renew the face of the earth." In Psalm 103, the only thing "renewed" is one's "youth" (103:5b). Psalm 104 takes up the language of "satisfaction" and "renewal" and applies it to all creation: "the earth is fully satisfied with the fruit of your works" (104:13b). Psalm 104, in other words, applies a creational hermeneutic to Psalm 103, whose emphasis on YHWH's benefits of benevolence extends only to those who fear YHWH. Here is where Psalm 104 exposes the previous psalm's provincial purview, even exposing an inner contradiction. In Psalm 103, YHWH's compassion is grounded in the fact that human beings are "like grass" and "dust" (103:14-15), a distinction that applies to all humanity. But the psalm also claims that YHWH's compassion is limited only to those who fear YHWH and keep covenant (103:11b, 13b, 17-18). Psalm 104 erases this disjunction by expanding YHWH's compassion to include not only human beings but all life in the form of life-sustaining provision.

Does YHWH's compassion have any limits? Psalm 104 seems to say no. Even Leviathan, the consummate creature of chaos, is not targeted for annihilation (104:25-26), as we have seen (see chapter 3). The psalmist has taken a symbol of monstrous chaos and turned it into an object of playful wonder. In the poet's hands, Leviathan, the monster of the deep, becomes Leviathan, God's partner in play, stripped of all its trappings of terror.

But inquiring minds want to know: How does YHWH's play with Leviathan fit into the deity's daily schedule? In the Talmud *Avodah Zarah* 3b, it is said that God's workday consists of twelve hours. The first three hours are devoted to matters of Torah, the second three hours with sitting in judgment of the world, the third with exercising mercy, including feeding the world. But the final three hours are devoted to playing with Leviathan. By including YHWH's play with Leviathan as part of YHWH's providential care in creation, the psalmist adds another dimension to divine benevolence: a sense of levity! There is a playful side to YHWH's benevolence, a delight that YHWH derives from creation's manifold nature. Among all of God's creatures great and small, it is Leviathan that most fully exercises God's indiscriminate "joy to the world."

Nevertheless, Psalm 103 offers a rejoinder by noting that there are some things about YHWH's benevolence and compassion that only human beings can appreciate, such as forgiveness (see 103:3a, 9-12). Does it make sense for coneys and mountain goats to be "forgiven," since the language of "iniquity" does not apply to them? The anthropocentric focus in Psalm 103 cannot be widened cosmically without diluting the benefits of benevolence for humanity, one could argue. In any case, both psalms cover the multidimensional nature of divine benevolence, both universal and particular. There is the generality of YHWH's providential care for all life, and there is the particularity of YHWH's forgiveness and vindication for those who "fear him." But regardless of scale and context, it is all benevolence, from the vindication of the oppressed (103:6) to provision for all creatures (104:10-30).

Nevertheless, there's one boundary that even Psalm 104 will not transgress in extending divine compassion and forgiveness. As much as Psalm 104 expands YHWH's benevolence to include all of life, there is a limit, as reflected in the final verse: "Let sinners vanish from the earth" (104:35). Perhaps in deference to Psalm 103, Psalm 104 finds no chance for the wicked to receive divine compassion. Extermination, rather, is called for. The wicked in Psalm 103 do not "fear" YHWH, let alone keep YHWH's "covenant" and "commandments" (103:17-18). In Psalm 104, the wicked constitute a threat to creation and YHWH's joy, no less. For all its efforts to bring all creation into the orbit of YHWH's cosmic compassion, Psalm 104 comes up short with regard to the wicked. So also Psalm 103. Such is their one point of contact amid their differing perspectives. For the eco-psalmist, the wicked is the one glitch in creation that requires correction (i.e., eradication) in order for creation to be made whole. To borrow from Psalm 103, the wicked in Psalm 104 need to be removed "as far as the east is from the west" (103:12). Psalm 103, however, prefers to talk of "iniquities" and "sins" over people as the objects of divine removal. The dialogue continues.

Psalms 38 and 39: The Sin of Silence and the Silence of Sin

As for iniquity and sin, Psalms 38–39 have much to say dialogically. If Psalms 38–39 are not twin psalms, they are at least close cousins, united by their common focus on sin and its effects. Both psalms offer pleas for forgiveness, but in strikingly different ways. Psalm 38 opens with a call to YHWH for the speaker to be spared from divine wrath.

> YHWH, rebuke me not in your anger,
>   or discipline me in your wrath.
> For your arrows have pierced me;
>   your hand has pressed down upon me.
> There is no wholeness in my flesh because of your outrage,
>   no health in my bones because of my sin.
> For my iniquities have gone way over my head;
>   like a burden they weigh too heavily on me. (38:1-4[2-5])

Here, confession and complaint find their convergence. The speaker acknowledges his "iniquities" (38:3b-4a[4b-5a]) yet pleads that YHWH exercise restraint in acting out of "wrath" (38:1[2]). Indeed, the speaker, like Job, complains of being set up as target practice by the divine archer (38:2[3]; cf. Job 6:4). The result is bodily affliction. The speaker acknowledges a body-mind unity with regard to sin and well-being. Also acknowledged is a human-divine unity: the speaker's misery is attributed to both YHWH's "outrage" and the speaker's "sin" (38:3[4]; see also 38:5[6]). Divine wrath and human iniquity are poetically paralleled in the psalm's confession. The speaker's "iniquities" weigh heavily on the speaker, so also YHWH's wrath.

The speaker provides greater detail about his ill health: festering "wounds" (38:5[6]), inflamed "loins" (38:7a[8a]), and near death (38:10a[11a]). At the same time, he affirms his "groaning"/"roaring" as unavoidable (38:8b-9[9b-10]). The speaker does not opt for silence. Quite the opposite: "I roar more than the roaring of the lion" (38:8b[9b]),[17] and for good reason: the speaker complains bitterly of social isolation and persecution.

> My friends and companions stand back from my affliction;
>   my neighbors stand far off.
> Those who seek my life set traps,
>   and those who seek me harm utter threats,
>   muttering lies all day long.
> But I myself am like the deaf; I cannot hear,
>   like the mute, who cannot open his mouth.
> I have become like one who cannot hear,
>   in whose mouth there are no rejoinders. (38:11-14[12-15])

The speaker sees himself as untouchable on account of his ruined health. Isolation gives way to persecution: by "setting traps" and "seeking harm," the speaker's acquaintances are no different from the wicked in their persecution of the righteous (38:12[13]; cf. 140:4-5[5-6]). The result is a subject who is rendered silent, incapacitated, unable to respond to attacks from friends and neighbors (38:13[14]). The speaker cannot "hear" or speak in response. He now suffers in silence, a form of social death.

But the speaker is not silent toward YHWH (38:16[17]). In pain, the speaker "confesses" his "iniquity" and appeals to YHWH for not letting

17. MT literally reads, "I roar from the groaning of my heart." With minimal emendation, *HALOT* suggests reading *lābîʾ* ("lion") for MT *libbî* ("my heart"), a likely case of haplography with the following word and with the *min* prefixed preposition functioning comparatively (676). For comparable imagery, see Ps 22:1[2], 13[14].

his enemies "rejoice" over him, who "repay evil for good" (38:17-20[18-21]). The speaker wants to have it both ways: admission of guilt and defense of innocence. He acknowledges his guilt before God but insists on his innocence before his enemies. It is the speaker's conviction that the treatment received from his "mortal enemies" is far from warranted by any guilt of his. The deliverance he seeks is both bodily and social, a sociosomatic salvation.

Psalm 39, however, favors silence over "roaring" for fear of sinning. But to no avail.

> I promised that I would keep my ways from sinning with my tongue,
> that I would keep a muzzle on my mouth
> so long as the wicked one was before me.
> So I became quiet, completely silent;[18]
> I kept quiet, [but] for no good:
> my pain flared up.
> My heart grew hot within me;
> in my pondering a fire burned,
> so I spoke with my tongue:
> "Reveal to me, YHWH, my end!
> Regarding the measure of my days, what is it?
> I want to know how fleeting my life is."
> Look, you have made my days just handbreadths long;
> my lifespan is as nothing before you;
> indeed, all humankind stands as mere vapor. *Selah*
> Indeed, everyone walks around like a shadow;[19]
> likewise, any abundance[20] a person heaps up is also vapor,
> not knowing who will gather it up. (39:1-6[2-7])

Despite the speaker's self-imposed silence, pain from within only intensifies (39:2-3[3-4]). In response, the speaker launches into speech, seeking

18. Literally, "silence" (*dûmîyâ*).

19. The term *ṣelem* is likely derived from *ṣlm* II, connoting darkness, rather than from the more common "image."

20. Read *hāmôn* for MT *yehĕmôyûn*. See Ps 37:16 for a similar use of the term.

from YHWH some indication of her end (39:4[5]), while complaining of how fleeting human life is, "mere vapor" (39:5-6a[6-7a]).

The heart of Psalm 38 is found in its appeal to YHWH for deliverance (38:7-11[8-12]).

And now, my Lord, what should I wait for?
    My hope is in you.
Deliver me from all my transgressors!
    Do not make me the scorn of fools!
I am silent; I will not open my mouth,
    for you have made it so.
Remove your plague from me!
    I am perishing from the battle blow[s][21] of your hand.
With reproofs you chasten a person for iniquity,
    and like a moth you dissipate one's objects of desire.
        Indeed, all humanity is mere breath. *Selah* (38:7-11[8-12])

The speaker pleads for deliverance from "transgressors" and "fools" (38:8[9]), as well as from YHWH's "plague" and the "battle blows of [YHWH's] hand" (38:10[11]), all the while professing "silence" (38:9[10]), as earlier (38:2[3]). But there is a difference: now the speaker's silence is imposed by God. YHWH has silenced the speaker: "you have made it so" (38:9b[10b]), consonant with having made humanity as "mere breath" (38:11b[12b]).

The speaker concludes the psalm with a plea that *YHWH* not "keep silent," in contrast to his own silence.

Hear my prayer, YHWH!
    Give ear to my cry!
Do not keep silent concerning my tears,
    for I am just an alien before you,
        an immigrant like all my ancestors.

21. Meaning uncertain. The possible verbal root (*grh*), as attested in biblical Hebrew, means to "stir up strife" or "battle" (e.g., Deut 2:9, 19; Prov 15:18; 28:25; 29:22). Targum Onkelos suggests the translation above. LXX renders "force," reading perhaps a different word (*miggĕbûrat*?). Peshitta reads "plague." See *HALOT*, 1687–88.

Look away[22] from me,
so that I may smile again before I depart and am no more!
(38:12-13[13-14])

The speaker self-identifies as an "alien" (*gēr*) and "immigrant" (*tôšāb*), just like his wandering ancestors (38:12b[13b]). And just like all humanity ("mere breath"), the speaker is consigned to a fading life. His final plea is that YHWH "look away" (38:13a[14a]).

While Psalms 38 and 39 share the language of sin, they part company with respect to how sin should be resolved. While the speaker in Psalm 38 fully acknowledges his own sin, the speaker in Psalm 39 does not do so but instead complains of the fragile state of the human condition, including her own. While Psalm 38 affirms the necessity of speaking out to God, "roaring" in fact, Psalm 39 acknowledges the role of silence in two ways: (1) self-imposed silence as a guard against sinning, and (2) silence as a testimony against God, given that it is divinely imposed. In Psalm 39, silence, instead of roaring, is the speaker's protest.

In Psalm 38, the speaker complains that the burden of his sin is itself too much to bear (38:4[5]), as if to say there is no need for YHWH to compound the burden with "wrath" and "indignation" (38:1-3[2-3]). Deliverance, thus, comes from forgiveness, on the one hand, and brings about the restoration of relationships, on the other, including the demise of enemies. In Psalm 39, deliverance on behalf of the speaker is also deliverance from "transgressors" and "fools" (39:8[9]). But persecution by enemies is not the problem, as it is in the previous psalm. The problem is primarily YHWH. The speaker in Psalm 39 would rather speak of YHWH "removing" "plagues" and "battle-blows" from her, rather than "removing" her "transgressions" (so Ps 38). Indeed, for Psalm 39 sin is not the fundamental problem; it is the human condition, frail and transient, created by God. What the speaker wants most is for YHWH to look away as her life passes away. YHWH, not sin, is the speaker's greatest burden. In comparison with its predecessor, Psalm 39 is more a protest than a confession. Its ending point shares similarity with Job's complaint:

22. The Hiphil form derives from *šʿh* ("gaze"), which functions emphatically here.

What are human beings, that you magnify them,
  that you give them your attention,
visiting them each morning,
  testing them every moment?
Why not look away from me,
  or let me alone until I swallow my spittle?
If I have sinned, what have I done to you, you watcher of humanity?
  Why have you made me your target? (Job 7:17-20a)

While Job's complaint pushes Psalm 39 further, it is certainly not where Psalm 38 wants to go. For Psalm 38, confession is part of the solution, whereas protest is key for Psalm 39. In Psalm 39, as in Job, God is more of the problem than sin.

But Psalm 38 nearly has the last word, even when the two psalms are read sequentially. It has to do with how one reads Psalm 39:8(9):

Deliver me from all my transgressors!
  Do not make me the scorn of fools!

Poetically, "transgressors" (*pōšĕʿay*) makes the best sense, given the parallelism in the second line of the verse, whereas the MT vocalizes the word as "transgressions" (*pĕšāʿay*). The consonantal text can be read either way. Dialogically, one can discern a two-way conversation in which both sides give some ground: Psalm 39 admits of the speaker's own sin with the Masoretic reading in 39:8a(9b) (cf. 39:11[12]), consonant with 38:18(19), while Psalm 38 acknowledges the afflictive consequences of divine wrath (38:2[3a], 3a[4a]), in addition to the burden of one's own sins (38:4b[5b]). The "battle blows" of YHWH near the end of Psalm 39 recall the "arrows" of YHWH, with which Psalm 38 begins. In the end, the relationship between human sin and divine punishment is a matter of proportion. Depending on how one is weighted in relation to the other determines how one petitions God and, in so doing, how one identifies the reason for such petition: is it God or sin that is most to blame? Together, Psalms 38–39 cover the bases by virtue of their dialogical divergences.

Psalms 89 and 90: Looking Backward to Move Forward, but to Whom?

These two psalms form the literary "seam" between books 3 (73–89) and 4 (90–106), hence one might think that they would share little in common. Not so. They turn out to be close dialogue partners. As discussed earlier, Psalm 89 is the one psalm in the Psalter that most thoroughly deconstructs itself. As David's kingdom lies in ruins in Psalm 89, Psalm 90, attributed to Moses, picks up the pieces. But it does so not to reconstruct David's kingdom in hope for its restoration but to build something else, which, according to Psalm 90, had been there all along. So begins the dialogue, one that actually begins *within* Psalm 89.

To review briefly (see chapter 7), Psalm 89 praises YHWH for having established David and his kingdom with a solemn covenant (89:28-34[29-35]). The absolute sovereign, enthroned in the heavens, bestows upon the earthly sovereign, David, an enduring lineage ("seed") and an everlasting kingdom ("throne"). Such a glorious promise includes YHWH's declaration of David's sonship as "firstborn" (89:26-27[27-28]), comparable to Psalm 2:6-7. The resulting picture is that of divine sovereign power mirrored in human imperial power.

The psalmist declares that both heaven and earth belong to YHWH, established by vanquishing the chaos monster Rahab and all other enemies, as well as by stilling the waves of the "raging sea" (89:9-11[10-12]). In parallel, YHWH empowers David to hold sway over the "sea" and the "rivers" (89:25[26]). YHWH's "benevolence" (*ḥesed*) and "faithfulness" (*'ĕmûnâ*) are the two pillars upon which David's kingdom stands.[23] YHWH promises to neither "remove benevolence" from David nor "betray faithfulness" (89:34[35]). "I will not lie to David," so says YHWH (89:35b[36b]).

But in light of all that follows in Psalm 89, it appears that YHWH did lie to David. Everything crumbles in the psalm's second half: YHWH has rejected David, repudiated the covenant, destroyed his "strongholds," raised up his enemies, and "hurled his throne to the ground" (89:39-44[40-45]). Everything that YHWH had done for David and his

23. Verses 2-3[3-4], 6[7], 9[10], 15[16], 25[26], 34[35].

kingdom is now undone, down to the last detail. Psalm 89 concludes with the accusatory question:

> Where are your benevolent acts of old, my Lord,
> which you swore to David by your faithfulness? (89:49[50])

Did YHWH's "benevolent acts" simply vanish? If they did, what does that say about YHWH? By losing "benevolence," YHWH has lost integrity. But the psalmist does not give up hope:

> Remember, my Lord, the abuses [suffered by] your servant![24]
> [Remember] how I bear in my bosom all the peoples' discords,[25]
> with which your enemies defy, YHWH,
> with which they defy the footsteps of your anointed.
> (89:50-51[51-52])

The psalm calls YHWH to "remember" David's hardships in the face of betrayal. Here, memory leads to hope, but only in the slightest measure.

What could possibly come after the destruction of the Davidic kingdom? Enter Psalm 90 with a countertestimony to its predecessor's own counter testimony. It opens not with David; indeed, David is nowhere mentioned in the psalm—a deafening silence that confirms the kingdom's obituary. Rather, it opens with God:

> *A Prayer of Moses, the Man of God:*
> O Lord, you have been our dwelling place
> throughout generation after generation.
> Before the mountains were born,
> and [before] you birthed[26] the earth, the inhabited world,
> from everlasting to everlasting you have been God. (90:1-2)

---

24. Read *'abdekā*, along with many Hebrew manuscripts against MT ("servants").

25. Read *ribîm* (with enclitic *mem*) for MT *rabbîm* ("many").

26. Hebrew *wattĕḥôlēl* (√*ḥwl*). For use of this term with God as subject, see Deut 32:18; cf. Prov 8:23-26.

From the very first verse, Psalm 90 establishes a stark contrast with Psalm 89. God is now claimed as the people's "dwelling place" (*mā'ôn*), in contradistinction to "strongholds" now lying in ruins in 89:40[41], or the city of David that once was. This "dwelling place," however, remains divinely intact, preexistent to all creation, a "dwelling place" not made by human hands or royal appointment. It connotes both human "refuge" (91:9) and God's holy residence (26:8; 68:6). "Dwelling place" suggests cohabitation, divine and human.

But no utopian vision of safety and security follows in Psalm 90. Instead, the psalm fully acknowledges the ravages of divine wrath, the same wrath that led to the kingdom's destruction.

> Indeed, we waste away by your wrath;
>   by your rage we are paralyzed.
> You set our iniquities before you,
>   our hidden [iniquities] into the light of your face.
> Indeed, all our days dwindle away because of your rage;
>   we finish[27] our years with a whimper. (90:7-9)

Divine "rage" is manifest in the "dwindling" of human life, concluded "with a whimper." But such rage, the psalmist admits, is not entirely arbitrary, unlike in Psalm 89. It is based on hidden "iniquities" exposed by the light of God's effulgent presence ("face"). The language of sin, in fact, is entirely absent in Psalm 89, since blame is cast exclusively upon YHWH. Not so in Psalm 90: the community shoulders the responsibility of God's wrath and rage.

Nevertheless, Psalms 89 and 90 do share one thing in common. While not acknowledging the people's sin as a justification for God's anger, Psalm 89 acknowledges human transience as a manifestation of divine wrath.

> You have diminished the days of his prime;
>   you have wrapped him up with shame. *Selah*
> How long, YHWH, will you hide yourself? Forever?

27. LXX reads *kālînû* ("[our years] come to an end") for MT *killînû*, which requires no consonantal change and establishes better poetic parallelism.

> [How long] will your wrath burn like fire?
> Remember how transient[28] I am!
> For what futile aim have you created all mortals?
> Who can live and never see death?
> Who can escape from the power of Sheol? *Selah* (89:45-48[46-49]

By its poetic movement, Psalm 89 connects the "diminishing" of David's life with the futility that afflicts "mortals" in general, all due to YHWH's burning "wrath." The question "How long?" accuses YHWH of eternal abandonment, in keeping with what YHWH has already done by destroying the kingdom. Either this section, specifically 89:47-48[48-49], is an editorial addition inspired by Psalm 90, or Psalm 90 picks up this thread of human transience to develop further.[29] In either case, it could be taken as a dialogical exchange. Psalm 90 takes up this snippet of an individual lament from Psalm 89 and expands it corporately.

> You turn humans back to dust,
> decreeing, "Turn back, O mortals!"
> For a thousand years in your sight
> are like yesterday when it is past,
> or a watch in the night.
> You overwhelm them [with] sleep.
> In the morning they are like grass that is renewed.
> In the morning it flourishes and is renewed,
> but toward evening it withers and dries up. (90:3-6)

Human transience ("dust") is divinely commanded and divinely fulfilled, echoing the judgment given in Genesis 3:19. The poet also conjures

28. Read *ḥādēl* for MT *ḥeled* ("duration" or "lifespan"), an emendation supported by two Hebrew manuscripts. See the partial parallel in Ps 39:5[4].

29. See the full discussion in Jerome F. D. Creach, "The Mortality of the King in Psalm 89," in *Constituting the Community: Studies on the Polity of Ancient Israel in Honor of S. Dean McBride*, ed. John T. Strong and Steven S. Tuell (Winona Lake, IN: Eisenbrauns, 2005), 237–50.

"sleep" and withering grass to stress the power of death over human life. But even if one were to live long, life is by no means pleasant.

> As for the days of our years—their height[30] is seventy years,
> or if [endowed] with vitality, eighty years.
> But their duration abounds[31] with toil and trouble.
> Indeed, it passes[32] quickly, and then we fly away.
> Who knows the power of your anger?
> As is your fear, so is your wrath.
> So teach [us] how to count our days,
> so that we may gain a wise heart. (90:10-12)

It all sounds quite like Ecclesiastes: the fleeting nature of life filled with "toil and trouble,"[33] except for one major difference: the psalmist attributes the tragedy of human transience to the "power of [God's] anger" (90:11a). For Qoheleth, the fleeting nature of life remains a mystery lodged in God's inscrutable ways. The lesson? For the psalmist of Psalm 90, it is to "count our days" and find wisdom in doing so (90:12). For Qoheleth, it is to enjoy the simple pleasures of life while they last.[34] Perhaps there is something in common here. But in Psalm 89, there is no moral lesson to be learned—only dismay over YHWH's violation of the covenant (89:39[40]), concluding with the dire question, "Where are your benevolent acts of old?" (89:50[51]).

It may seem, then, that Psalm 90, in contrast to Psalm 89, simply accepts the fate of human transience and makes the best of it. The psalm takes up the theological atrocity of David's ruination and applies it to all of humanity, while at the same time finding some measure of

30. Read *gobhām* for MT *bāhem* ("in them"), which is poetically redundant. The omitted *gimel* is likely a case of haplography due to graphic confusion with the preceding *waw*.

31. MT *rohbām* is a hapax legomenon, likely meaning "their pride." *BHS* proposes *rubbām* ("quantity"), which is adopted here in light of the versions (e.g., LXX *pleion*).

32. The subject, singular in the MT, is "their duration."

33. Cf. Eccl 1:3; 2:3, 17-18, 22; 3:19; 4:2.

34. E.g., Eccl 2:24-25; 3:13; 5:18; 9:7.

justification for it. In so doing, the catastrophe suffered by "David" is made communal, and its seemingly arbitrary nature is resolved, at least halfway. Nevertheless, the psalmist is not satisfied with resolution alone, given the conclusion of Psalm 90, which, like that of Psalm 89, packs its own petitionary punch:

> Turn, YHWH! How long?
>   Change your mind[35] regarding your servants!
> Satisfy us in the morning with your benevolence,
>   that we may rejoice and be glad throughout all our days.
> Gladden us according to the days that you have afflicted us,
>   the years that we have seen such trouble.
> Let your work be seen by your servants,
>   and your majesty by their children.
> May the exquisite kindness of the Lord, our God, be upon us.
>   Establish for us the work of our hands!
>   Establish the work of our hands! (90:13-17)

As if echoing the desperate plea of its predecessor (minus the Davidic focus), Psalm 90 commands YHWH to reverse course, to "turn" and have a "change" of heart (90:13). Such language matches the psalm's attribution to Moses in the superscription, for only Moses is known for demanding God to repent with such language: "Turn [√*šwb*] from your fierce anger; change your mind [√*nḥm*] and do not bring disaster on your people" (Exod 32:12). Even the accusatory question ("How long?") finds its way into the petition, as it does in 89:46[47]).

Psalm 90, moreover, does not give up on divine "benevolence" (90:14a), the theological foundation of the Davidic covenant in Psalm 89 that was never to be "removed" (89:33[34]). Psalm 90, in fact, demands "benevolence" from God, come morning, when the chaos of the night is passed and salvation dawns (cf. 46:5[6]; 59:16[17]). For the speaker, the shape of such benevolence is retributive: the time for restoration and

35. Hebrew *nḥm*, which can also mean "be sorry" or "have regret." The parallel with Exod 32:12 is unmistakable.

joy should match the period of past affliction, day by day, year by year (90:15). As "an eye for an eye" (Exod 21:24), so a joy for an affliction. Such is the psalmist's demand: a *lex talionis* in reverse, the poetic justice of opposite equivalents. YHWH owes the people nothing less.

Psalm 90 concludes with a plea to "establish [√*kwn*] the work of our hands" (90:17). As YHWH established David and his throne in Psalm 89, only to dismantle it, so YHWH in Psalm 90 is to establish the work of rebuilding the community. The people are ready to get to work. With native kingship terminated, the work of the community begins, God willing. The "benevolence" that YHWH once promised David for the sake of the kingdom is to be bestowed upon all YHWH's "servants" (90:13b-14a).

Psalms 89 and 90 host an earnest dialogue over the future of God's people. Even in the wake of destruction, Psalm 89 pleads for restoration on David's behalf. For the psalm's finale, the speaker identifies himself as David(ic), as YHWH's "servant" now turned suffering servant. Psalm 89 culminates with this final question: "Where are your benevolent acts [*ḥăsādêkā*] of old?" (89:49a[50a]). The question is not raised as a matter of curiosity; it is a protest and a plea. The "benevolent acts" of the past were meant to continue into the present by virtue of David's legacy. The promise of David's dynasty was for eternity, because, as the speaker reminds YHWH, such promises were sworn in "faithfulness," now betrayed (89:49b[50b]). So remembrance is once again called for, but this time remembrance of the abuses suffered by YHWH's servant. Remembrance on God's part, it is hoped, will lead to restoration.

Psalm 90 offers an alternative vision, one not for YHWH's anointed servant, but for YHWH's many "servants" (90:13). YHWH's benevolence is not limited to its royal manifestation in David; it is for the whole community: "Satisfy *us* in the morning with your benevolence" (90:14a). What was once the work of David is now the work of the whole community, wrought by "our hands" (90:17), for David's "hand" is no longer in play (89:26[27]). As a vision for moving forward, Psalm 90 looks backward before David to the time of Moses. The cry, "Turn, YHWH! How long? // Change your mind!" (90:13) takes up Moses's cry at a moment of deep despair when YHWH was set to destroy the people in the wilderness (Exod

32:12). Moses's cry is now taken up communally. While the future of the community remains in God's hands, two psalms aim to urge God to move forward, but in two different directions: Davidic and Mosaic. If David's restoration is not in the offing, then how about a restoration of Moses? To press the matter, the psalms seem to ask, Whose leadership suffered the most from conflict and abuse? Whose "bosom" took in the "people's discords" (89:50[51]; cf. Num 11:12)? Psalm 89 assumes David; Psalm 90 chooses Moses. Either way, in the wake of exile, both psalms propose reaching back in history to move forward in the face of unimaginable disruption.

Psalms 137 and 138: To Sing or Not to Sing

Far from being twins, let alone distant cousins, these two psalms share little in common. Yet they are bound together by their adjacency, forcing a dialogue that is as uncomfortable as it is profound. By itself, Psalm 137 is one of the most anguished protests in the Psalter. Paired with its successor, Psalm 137 initiates a dialogue about how to respond to national trauma.

Psalm 137 begins by lamenting the displacement of the community in Babylonian exile.

> By the rivers of Babylon, there we sat weeping, as we remembered Zion.
> Upon the poplars[36] there,[37] we hung up our lyres,
> for there our captors asked us for words of a song,
> our abductors[38] [asked] for mirth:[39]

36. Or "willows" (cf. Lev 23:40; Isa 44:4; Job 40:2).

37. Hebrew "in its midst" (i.e., within the city of Babylon).

38. Specifically, "those who forcibly lead us." Hebrew *tôlāl* is a hapax legomenon whose meaning is disputed. One possibility is to derive the word from *hll* III ("make a mockery") as a Poel (so *HALOT*, 1700–1701). LXX, Vulgate, and Peshitta read: "those who take us away"; Symmachus: "those who boast"; Targum: "our plunderers," which all appear to be guesses. *BHS* proposes the root *yll* ("howl, lament"). Alfred Guillaume proposes the root *tll*, whose cognate can be found in the Arabic *talla*: "to carry off by force" ("The Meaning of *twll* in Psalm 137:3," *JBL* 75, no. 2 [1956]: 143–44). This plausible meaning is adopted here.

39. Or "with mirth." The absence of a preposition leaves both possibilities open.

"Sing to us from the songs[40] of Zion!"
    But how shall we sing YHWH's song on foreign soil? (137:1-4)

The scene is set next to the Babylonian canals, the lifeblood of Mesopotamian agriculture. Canals were vital for irrigation throughout Lower Mesopotamia, requiring ongoing supervision. They had to be cleared of vegetation and salt, as well as dredged of silt.[41] Canals were dug and dredged on a continual basis. The first verse of Psalm 137 speaks from the perspective of deported Judeans likely tasked with canal building and upkeep.

The speakers are identified as musicians who refuse their captors' demand to sing. The middle verse poetically escalates what is demanded: "words of a song" to "the songs of Zion." A "song of Zion" celebrates Zion's invincibility grounded in God's protective presence (e.g., Pss 46, 48, 122, 125). Indeed, Psalm 137 may very well have something akin to Psalm 46 in mind:

There is a river whose channels gladden the city of God,
    the holiest dwelling of the Most High.
God is in its midst; it shall not be shaken;
    God will help it at daybreak. (137:4-5[5-6])

The river and its channels serve as signs of God's commitment to the city's security—Jerusalem. The opening scene of Psalm 137, however, features the antitype of Jerusalem and its river, namely Babylon and its canals. Babylonian canals are no "channels" of joy for the exiled Judeans, but joy ("delight") is precisely what their captors want in their taunting demands (137:3aβ). A song of Zion is a song of joy. But to manufacture such joy amid displacement and servitude is traumatizing. While to sing a song of victory in the wake of utter defeat is insane, to be *forced* to sing a song of victory is insanely humiliating. Such is the goal of their captors:

40. The versions read plural, taking the singular as collective or perhaps as a collection of songs.

41. See John J. Ahn, "Psalm 137: Complex Communal Laments," *JBL* 127, no. 2 (2008): 277–78.

more than just rubbing the exiles' noses in defeat, their overlords want to sustain their trauma in the most cognitively disruptive way.

But Psalm 137 registers resistance through the noncompliance of silence. How can such a song be sung? It cannot. The opening scene serves to set up the question and to provide its own answer: no, not in Babylon can YHWH's song be sung. The question is turned into a lament: lyres are hung, and mouths remain closed. But that does not mean forgetting Zion.

> If I forget you, O Jerusalem,
>   then may my righthand become paralyzed.[42]
> May my tongue stick to my gums if I do not remember you,
>   if I do not raise Jerusalem above my chief joy. (137:5-6)

Cast as a self-oath, the individual speaker utters self-debilitating consequences in the case Jerusalem is forgotten and considered less than one's supreme joy. The consequences have to do with both "hand" and "tongue," both essential for musical performance. The self-imprecatory oath exhibits its own logic: to forget Jerusalem would be to lose the ability to celebrate Jerusalem. The hand and the tongue stand for two defining human abilities: action and communication. For both to be incapacitated is tantamount to death.

For all its dire consequences, the self-curse invites its positive converse: to *choose* not to sing at the whim of one's tormentors, to refuse to give into their demands, is to resist forgetting Zion. The refusal to sing YHWH's song of Zion in Babylon does not diminish the memory of Jerusalem/ Zion. To the contrary, it honors and sustains the memory. But such refusal requires steely resolve, hence the necessity of the oath with its dire consequences. If Zion's song cannot be sung, the memory of Jerusalem, nevertheless, can be sustained even "on foreign soil."

42. MT (*tiškaḥ*) reads "forget," identical to the first verb, which could be taken elliptically as indicated in the Peshitta ("forget me"). LXX renders "be forgotten," reading the form as a Niphal. Some read *tikḥaš* or *tĕkaḥēš* ("fail, grow lean"), proposing scribal metathesis, or similarly *tikšaḥ* ("become paralyzed"), from the Arabic *kasiḥa* (so *HALOT*, 502). The parallel with the tongue cleaving to the palate suggests the hand becoming incapacitated. Thus, the latter suggestion (*tikšaḥ*) seems most plausible.

The final strophe is most troublesome for modern readers. But as the psalm's shattering conclusion, critical to its subversive logic, it cannot be avoided. There is nothing to prevent one from imagining this final strophe voiced by an enraged mother, which begins by shifting the focus from the earlier speaker's memory of Jerusalem to YHWH's.

> Remember, YHWH, the Edomites on the day of Jerusalem.
> How they shouted, "Tear it down, tear it down to its foundations!"[43]
> O daughter Babylon, you devastated one,[44]
> how happy is the one who pays you back in kind
> with what you have done to us!
> how happy is the one who seizes and shatters
> your infants against the rock! (137:7-9)

The opening command prompts YHWH to "remember" the "day of Jerusalem." Whereas the Zion psalms celebrate Jerusalem's invincibility,[45] Psalm 137 recalls the event of Jerusalem's destruction, particularly two aspects of it: the role of the Edomites and that of the Babylonians. The speaker vividly highlights the complicity of the Edomites as demonstrated in their call to raze the city to "its foundations." The repeated imperative conveys the sense of extreme violation, indeed sexual violation, as the verb √*'rh* ("lay bare, make naked") suggests.[46] A literal rendering of the Edomites' shout would be: "Strip [her], strip [her] down to her foundations!"

The psalmist follows with an urgent call for justice against Babylon, as expressed in two macarisms or beatitudes (*'ašrê* sayings) that conclude the psalm (137:8-9). Babylon is addressed as "daughter" (*bat*), comparable to the title of endearment "daughter Zion"[47] or "daughter Jerusalem."[48] Casting cities as feminine, whether as daughters, mothers, or wives, was

43. The Hebrew presupposes the feminine personification of Jerusalem ("her").

44. So MT (*haššĕdudâ*). Many, however, read *haššôdĕdâ* ("devastator"), which admittedly makes more sense in the immediate moment. The MT reading is proleptic or anticipatory.

45. E.g., Pss 46:4-5[5-6]; 48:11-14[12-15].

46. Lev 20:18-19; Isa 3:17; cf. Lam 4:21.

47. E.g., 2 Kgs 19:21a; Ps 9:14[15]; Isa 1:8; 10:32; 62:11.

48. E.g., 2 Kgs 19:21b; Lam 2:13, 15; Mic 4:8; Zeph 3:14; Zech 9:9.

conventional in ancient Near Eastern political discourse. In Babylon's case, reference to "daughter" is a fitting correspondence to "daughter Zion/Jerusalem" assumed in the previous verse, underlining the horrific sense of violation that Babylon is to suffer, justified in the eyes of the psalmist. However, the punishment called upon is not rape (as called for by the Edomites against Jerusalem) but maternal loss: Babylon shifts from "daughter" to mother in the final verse.

Verse 8 clarifies the shocking conclusion in 137:9. The killing of infants called forth at the end is considered the fitting fulfillment of talion-oriented justice, infanticide as payback. As daughter/mother Zion suffered the violent deaths of "her" children, recalling the horrors of Babylonian invasion, so shall daughter/mother Babylon. The practice of war in antiquity was well known for its extreme violence: the raping of women, ripping of pregnant women, and murder of old people and young children.[49] The endorsement of infanticide in Psalm 137 is a direct response to the infanticide suffered by Judeans at the hands of the Babylonians.

Cast as a macarism, the agent of such vengeance is left open. Normally, an *'ašrê* saying has a person or community in mind.[50] The only exception is found in Ecclesiastes 10:17, where the "land" (*'ereṣ*) is deemed "happy." It would be unprecedented if God were the subject of an *'ašrê* saying, but it is rhetorically possible as a way of commending God to take such action. The psalm is most likely open to any agent who would be in a position of power to inflict such suffering upon the Babylonian empire. It establishes a placeholder for anyone (divine or human) who could exact vengeance against the Babylonians. Perhaps only God would qualify, but a Persian king would do just as well.

In any case, the speaker of the psalm would not qualify. She does not consider herself or her fellow victims to be in such a position. The commendation to kill Babylonian babies comes from a people disempowered and traumatized by the murder of their own children, as also reflected in the oracle against Babylon in Isaiah 13:14-19, in which the prophesied

49. E.g., Deut 32:25; 2 Kgs 8:12; Isa 13:15-18; Jer 51:20-23; Hos 14:1; Nah 3:10.

50. E.g., Deut 33:29; Job 5:17; Pss 1:1; 2:12; 33:12; 106:3; 144:15.

horror of infanticide committed against Babylon is attributed to the collaborative work of human and divine agency: God will "stir up the Medes" to destroy Babylon once and for all. The empire's children will not be spared, just as Israel's were not. The oppressors asked for "mirth," but what they get in Psalm 137 is a violent curse.[51]

Psalm 137 stands out among the surrounding psalms for its raw pathos, introducing a dramatic counterbalance to the confident testimony of God's work in history expressed in Psalm 136 and the enthused spirit of gratitude conveyed in Psalm 138. It appears that Psalm 137 was intentionally placed in between these two psalms as an interruption. The result is a rending of the seamless connection of thanksgiving that connects these two psalms, creating an exilic disruption, one of trauma, resistance, and anticipated justice.

For all its testimonial confidence, Psalm 136 serves to introduce Psalm 137 with its concluding testimony of the God

> who remembered us in our low estate,
>   for his benevolence is everlasting,
>   and has snatched us from our foes,
>   for his benevolence is everlasting. (136:23-24)

Psalm 137 beseeches God to remember "the day of Jerusalem" (137:7), the time of Judah's lowest "estate." Psalm 136 tells of God having "killed famous kings," such as Sihon and Og (137:18-20). Such testimony may tip the scales toward God being the subject of the *'ašrê* sayings in Psalm 137—the God who both rescues and destroys.

However, our primary focus is on what follows. Psalm 138, given its adjacency, serves as a response to Psalm 137. As James Chatham aptly points out, the Psalter's editors could have followed Psalm 137 with Psalm 37 and its admonition to refrain from anger (37:8-9).[52] But they

51. For further discussion on the subversively clever nature of Psalm 137, see Rodney M. Sadler, "Singing a Subversive Song: Psalm 137 and 'Colored Pompey,'" in *The Oxford Handbook of the Psalms*, ed. William P. Brown (New York: Oxford University Press, 2014), 447–58.

52. James O. Chatham, *Psalm Conversations: Listening In as They Talk with One Another* (Collegeville, MN: Liturgical Press, 2018), 64.

did not, thereby preserving the freedom in Psalm 137 to express bitter grievance unhindered, without pushback. Instead, Psalm 137 is followed by a thanksgiving psalm, one that presupposes deliverance from Babylon's brutality and the temple's restoration (138:2a).

I give you thanks with my whole heart;
 before the gods I sing your praises.
I bow down toward your holy temple;
 I give thanks to your name for your benevolence and faithfulness,
  for you have exalted your name [and] your word above all.[53]
On the day I cried out, you answered me;
 you emboldened me[54] with strength to the core of my being. (138:1-3)

May all the kings of the earth give you thanks, YHWH,
 when they hear the words of your mouth.
May they sing of YHWH's ways,
 for great is YHWH's glory.
Though YHWH is high, he looks favorably upon the lowly,
 but the lofty he recognizes[55] [only] from afar. (138:4-6)

Though I walk amid distress, you preserve my life;
 you stretch out your hand against the anger of my enemies;
  you save me with your right hand.
YHWH accomplishes [this] in my behalf.
 YHWH, your benevolence is everlasting;
  [so] do not let go of the works of your hand! (138:7-8)

Psalm 138 offers personal thanksgiving to YHWH for having answered and sustained the speaker "amid distress." As the speaker gives thanks to YHWH, so also should the "kings of the earth" (138:3). The psalm affirms that even in divinely enthroned supremacy, YHWH regards the "lowly"

53. MT makes little sense as it stands. Read *'al kōl* ("above all/everything") for MT's *'al kol*.

54. The meaning of the verb *rhb* is disputed. Its basic meaning is "storm against, assault, confuse" (Isa 3:5; Song 6:5). Perhaps its meaning here should be drawn from the nominal cognate *rōhab*, meaning "pride" (Ps 90:10).

55. Read *yêdā'* for the mispointing in MT.

with favor (138:4), including the speaker, who credits YHWH with her salvation. The speaker testifies that YHWH saves her by the "hand" (138:7). Nevertheless, the psalm concludes with a plea for YHWH to "not let go" of YHWH's handiwork (138:8b).

Psalm 138 answers Psalm 137 with a look back at Babylon's demise, now that it, like Jerusalem's "day" of destruction, is an event of the past (c. 538 BCE). Now the "holy temple" is restored (138:2a). Now YHWH's "benevolence" and "faithfulness" have been confirmed (138:2b). Now YHWH has "handled" the "anger" of the speaker's "enemies" (138:7a; cf. 137:7b). The speaker gives thanks for having been "emboldened" (138:3b), in addition to being saved, perhaps a nod toward the bold language of Psalm 137. Only someone who is emboldened to overcome the silencing power of trauma could ever pray such a prayer to its bitter end as Psalm 137.

Another connecting element between the two psalms is the reference to the anger or fury of the speaker's enemies, so vividly exemplified by the Edomites' call for Jerusalem's destruction in Psalm 137. By following Psalm 137, Psalm 138 provides both a testimonial response to the trauma of exile and a fulfillment of the *'ašrê* sayings at the end of Psalm 137, but not a direct fulfillment: no babies were harmed in the composition of Psalm 138. While the historical response to Jerusalem's destruction was Persia's victory over Babylon,[56] the psalmic response is testimony of YHWH's benevolence (138:8a). Beyond the imaginative scope of the singer who could not "sing YHWH's song" is the anticipation that even the kings of the earth "shall sing of the ways of YHWH" (138:5a). Now that would be a new song of Zion!

Nevertheless, the psalm ends with a commanding plea to God to never "let go of the works of your hand" (138:8b; cf. Isa 43:1a). The exile was a spectacularly horrific example of divine abandonment, and the speaker beseeches God to not let it be repeated. While the speaker hands it to God for having come through, God is not left off the hook. Once was enough under the poplar with lyres hung. Never again.

56. Noted for its lack of violence, according to Persian propaganda (lines 16-19 of "The Cyrus Cylinder" [539 BCE]).

Psalms 8 and 144

Two very different psalms positioned on almost opposite ends of the Psalter answer a nearly identical question. Call them distant cousins.

Psalm 8	Psalm 144
What are human beings that you call them to mind [√*zkr*], mortals that you attend to them [√*pkd*]? (8:4[5]) You have made them slightly less than divine; with glory and majesty you have crowned them. (8:5[6])	YHWH, what are humans that you acknowledge them [√*ydh*], or mortals that you consider them [√*ḥšb*]? (144:3) Humans are like a breath; their days are like a passing shadow. (144:4)

Both questions address the issue of human identity with slightly different terminology. The verbs, though not identical, share a common subject: God cast in direct address. Moreover, they share similar semantic sense. If there is any difference between the two questions, it is that the one in Psalm 8 presupposes a bit more investment on the part of God. Psalm 8 acknowledges that God is "mindful" of human beings, whereas Psalm 144 wonders how God would even "acknowledge" or "consider" them at all. Nevertheless, the difference is slight. Both psalms ponder the sheer contingency of God's attention toward human beings. Neither expected nor necessary, God's consideration of humanity is cast as a surprise, an amazement, no less.

Equally surprising are the respective answers they give to their similar questions.

You have made them slightly less than divine; with glory and majesty you have crowned them. (8:5[6])	Humans are like a breath; their days are like a passing shadow. (144:4)

In Psalm 8, humanity is "crowned" with "glory and majesty" and deemed nearly divine. In Psalm 144, humans are regarded as mere "breath" (*hebel*) and a "passing shadow" (*ṣēl ʿōbēr*). Psalm 8 describes humanity's "dominion" over all of God's handiwork, including domestic and wild animals, avian and sea creatures, all "put . . . under their feet" (8:6-8[7-9]). Psalm 144 says little of human supremacy, given its primary focus on YHWH. The query in Psalm 144, in fact, prefaces a desperate plea for help from God.

> YHWH, bend down your heavens and come down!
> Strike the mountains so that they smoke!
> Flash forth lightning and scatter them!
> Send forth your arrows and rout them!
> Stretch out your hands from on high!
> Rescue me and deliver me from the mighty waters,
> from the hand of foreigners,
> whose mouths speak lies,
> and whose right hand is the right hand of deception! (144:5-8)

The speaker calls for nothing short of a theophany, one that dramatically intervenes on behalf of a speaker who finds himself overcome, "drowning," as it were, from the verbal assaults ("mighty waters") of "foreigners." The specifics of the setting need not concern us, but notable is how Psalm 144 begins, immediately preceding the common query of human identity.

> Blessed be YHWH, my rock,
> who trains my hands for battle,
> my fingers for war.
> My stronghold[57] and my fortress;
> my secured height and my deliverer,
> my shield, in whom I take refuge,
> who subdues [√*rdd*] peoples[58] under me. (144:1-2)

Psalm 144 acknowledges God as the "stronghold" and "fortress," one who "subdues" the speaker's enemies ("under me"). Here is the one instance of "dominion" acknowledged in Psalm 144, in consort with Psalm 8.

57. Read *ḥosnî* for MT *ḥasdî* ("my benevolence") due to graphic confusion.

58. Read *ʿammîm* instead of MT *ʿammî* ("my people").

You grant them dominion over the works of your hands;
you have put everything under their feet. (8:6[7])

Such dominion is God-given. But whereas Psalm 8 expounds on human dominion over all creation, Psalm 144 limits dominion to one person, a king, over the "peoples," and only in passing. Otherwise, the focus in Psalm 144 is on YHWH's power to rescue the king and defeat his enemies (144:11-14). As for domestic animals ("flocks" and "cattle"), Psalm 144 does not revel in exercising dominion over them, as in Psalm 8, but rather expresses hope for their flourishing for the community's benefit (8:14). Flourishing families and flocks, abundant produce, and lasting security ("no breach, no exile") are the necessary conditions for a vital community, all being the outcome of the speaker's deliverance by God.

Such are the backgrounds for the two nearly identical questions and their widely divergent responses. As a plea for deliverance, Psalm 144 stresses the inability of "mortals" to do anything for themselves, let alone save themselves in battle. They are tantamount to nothing. The answer given to the question in Psalm 144 is an answer fit for a desperate petition. Only God can help. Inefficacy is the human condition, setting in stark relief God's power.

Divine power is also lauded in Psalm 8, particularly at the beginning. But the psalm is no desperate plea; it is a hymn of praise to YHWH's majesty (8:1-2[2-3]).[59] While both psalms describe God as refuge (8:2a[3a]; 144:2b), Psalm 144 does so in contrast to human inefficacy. Psalm 8, however, finds divine and human power comfortably coexistent. In Psalm 8, God grants dominion to human beings. In Psalm 144, God grants salvation to an embattled king.

The common question along with their divergent answers reflects contrasting views of one's posture before God. Psalm 8 conjures a cosmic setting for the question:

When I observe your heavens, the works of your fingers—
the moon and the stars that you have established—

59. See translation in chapter 2.

> "What are human beings that you call them to mind,
> mortals that you care for them?" (8:3-4[4-5])

The speaker scans the night sky, observing the moon and the constellations, all bona fide creations of God. The celestial bodies evoke a sense of cosmic vastness, an overwhelming perspective that invariably diminishes one's sense of self, individually or corporately. Such an experience is what psychologists call the "small self."[60] Just ask Job (see 40:4).

The irony of Psalm 8 is that the psalmist does not follow through as Psalm 144 does. The more natural response to beholding the heavens' glory would have been the answer given in Psalm 144: "Humans are like a breath" (144:4a). Or a mere speck on a "pale blue dot." While a provisional sense of the small self is implied in Psalm 8, the psalmist leaps immediately to pondering humanity's "big self" on earth. To go from the vastness of the cosmos to the vastness of the human species requires a significant shift in scale, and it is signaled by a shift from the celestial to the earthly. On earth humanity is big, but before the cosmos humanity will always be small. But in either case, a sense of wonder is shared: the wonder of the heavens' glory and the wonder of humanity's dominion. In Psalm 8, the link between the speaker's small self and big self is YHWH's mindful attention, and perhaps that is the greatest wonder of all.

So which is it? Are humans "crowned with glory" or are they a "passing shadow"? Psalms 8 and 144 offer their opposing perspectives, comparable to the differing anthropologies profiled in the first two creation accounts in Genesis: (1) humanity "made in God's image" to exercise dominion (Gen 1:26-28), and (2) humanity fashioned from the "dust of the ground" to "serve" the soil (Gen 2:15). It all depends on the scale or setting. Psalm 144 identifies the battlefield as the arena of human inefficacy, highlighting the need for divine intervention. Psalm 8 identifies the earth to highlight humanity's power over nonhuman creatures, but not without conveying a sense of insignificance before creation's celestial face. In Psalm 144, human inefficacy highlights divine potency. In Psalm 8, humanity's hierarchy

60. Paul Piff et al. "Awe, the Small Self, and Prosocial Behavior," *Journal of Personality and Social Psychology* 108, no. 6 (2015): 883.

on earth highlights the wonder and mystery of divine governance. In dialogue, both psalms find their way to acknowledging God's power and majesty, even as they arrive at contrasting conclusions about what it means to be human.

Psalm 1 and 2: Of *Tôrâ* and Tyranny

We conclude our listening in on the psalmic dialogues by returning to the Psalter's very first dialogue, thanks to the pairing of Psalms 1 and 2. While these two psalms could not be more different in content and setting, they serve as the dual introduction to the Psalms as a whole. Their divergence points to the Psalter's diversity; their dialogical engagement reverberates throughout the Psalms.

To review, Psalm 1 metaphorically profiles two contrasting characters, the wicked and the righteous. The righteous one is like a flourishing tree; the wicked, by contrast, are like blown chaff. The righteous one "deliberates" on YHWH's instruction (*tôrâ*); the wicked fail to measure up. As the source of delight and direction for the righteous, *tôrâ* stands front and center in Psalm 1, denoting divine instruction but left unspecified (see chapter 6). As a result, the psalm sets the reader on a quest to discover YHWH's *tôrâ* throughout the Psalms, including divine admonitions and judgments as well as promises of salvation.[61]

But at the outset of this search for *tôrâ* in the Psalms, the reader suddenly enters a whole other world, no longer the "meditative" world of the righteous delighting in *tôrâ* but the noisy realm of a king quelling rebellious nations.

Why do the nations rant,
    and the peoples rave in vain?
[Why do] the kings of the earth take their stand,

61. Pss 46, 50, 60//108, 75, 81, 82, 90, 95, 105. In a special class are those psalms that feature covenantal promises, both conditional and unconditional, made by God to David or the Davidic king: Pss 2, 89, 110, 132. For further discussion, see my "The Law and the Psalmists: Seeking *Tôrâ* among the Psalms," in *The Cambridge Companion to the Psalms*, ed. Joel LeMon and Brent Strawn (Cambridge: Cambridge University Press, forthcoming).

and potentates conspire together,
against YHWH and his anointed?
"Let us tear up their fetters,
and fling off their cords from us!" (2:1-3)

The One who sits enthroned in the heavens laughs;
the Lord derides them.
He then speaks to them in his anger,
terrifying them in his fury.
"I hereby establish[62] my king
upon Zion, my holy mountain." (2:4-6)

I will recount the decree that YHWH has declared to me:
"My son you are; today I hereby beget you.
Ask of me to make the nations your possession,
and the ends of the earth your property.
You will smash them with an iron rod;
like a potter's vessel you will shatter them in pieces." (2:7-9)

So now kings, wise up!
Be warned, you rulers of the earth!
Serve YHWH with fear!
Rejoice with trembling!
Kiss the son,[63] lest he become angry,
and you perish on the way,
or his wrath is quickly kindled.
How happy are all who take refuge in him! (2:10-12)

Psalm 2 plunges headlong into the savage world of international conflict. As Psalm 1 points to the Torah Psalms and divine discourse in the Psalter, Psalm 2 introduces an imperial vision that is also prevalent in the Psalms. But just between these two psalms, the righteous individual is

62. Or "install"/"appoint," a variant use of the verb (*nsk* III in *BDB*), which more typically means "pour out," but whose nominal form can mean "prince" (*nāsîk:* Ps 83:12; Josh 13:21; Ezek 32:30; Mic 5:4). The syntax reflects the so-called declarative perfect, by which an action is marked as completed at the moment of utterance.

63. So MT (Aramaic).

paired with the anointed one, and the wicked are paired with conspiring kings. Psalms 1 and 2 offer contrastive yet parallel worlds: the righteous individual "rooted" in *tôrâ* set apart from the wicked and YHWH's king established in Zion subjugating the nations. Neither psalm offers neutral space; there is no middle ground between the righteous and the wicked, or between the king and enemy nations. Moreover, the pairing of Psalms 1 and 2 forges a bond of allegiance: to be on the side of the righteous is to be on the side of YHWH's chosen king. To devote oneself to YHWH's *tôrâ* is to acknowledge the God of Zion.

Though widely divergent in content and style, Psalms 1 and 2 are bound together by two linguistic links. The righteous individual "deliberating" on *tôrâ* in 1:2 finds its counterpoint in the rebellious nations "raving" in vain (2:1b): the same verb is used (√*hgh*) but with entirely opposite meanings. An ironic link, yes, but ironic to make a point: while the proper exercise of "deliberation" is with *tôrâ*, "deliberation" left to the nations proves politically chaotic. Another connection is found in the opening word of Psalm 1 and of the last line in Psalm 2: "How happy . . ." (*'ašrê*). Bounded by these two beatitudes, Psalms 1 and 2 introduce two contexts for "happiness": refuge and righteousness—the security of divine protection on YHWH's holy mountain, Zion, and the attainment of righteousness made possible by YHWH's *tôrâ*.

One could imagine the conjoining of these two psalms reflecting an editorial compromise between two opposing parties: a *tôrâ*-based party and a royal-based (or messianic) party: the "royalists" versus the "toracists."[64] While forced to complement each other by their juxtaposition, Psalms 1 and 2 in isolation represent two divergent, if not competing, viewpoints. Together, they pose the question: Which is more important, the divinely constituted institution of kingship, or the divinely communicated corpus of instruction? Is it *tôrâ* or throne that is of ultimate value? One can imagine the question situated at a historical crossroads. The cessation of native kingship presses the question with the greatest of urgency. Should a people keep hope alive for a Davidic restoration? Or should they rely

64. Cf. Walter Brueggemann, "Twin Themes for Ecumenical Singing: The Psalms," *JP* 43, no. 4 (2020): 3–10.

singularly on YHWH's *tôrâ* for the community's (re)constitution?[65] That both psalms serve to introduce the Psalter acknowledges the need for ongoing dialogue regarding a community's future.

As for the Psalter, Psalms 1 and 2 provide the hermeneutical "spectacles" by which to read the Psalms as a whole, directing the reader's attention to various themes present therein: righteousness and refuge, *tôrâ* and Zion, judgment and protection, righteousness and kingship, divine instruction and royal dominion, pathway and refuge, individual and king. Psalms 1 and 2, in other words, train the reader's eye and the listener's ear to linger over these themes and discern how they are related throughout the Psalter. This is not to say that Psalms 1 and 2 accommodate everything in the Psalter, as if any two psalms could, but they initiate a dialogue that proves to be ongoing throughout the Psalms.

Such dialogue is hosted in various ways, as in the dramatic shift that transpires between Psalms 89 and 90, when David is superseded by Moses, to be followed by the enthronement psalms (93, 95–100), in which kingship is ascribed solely to YHWH, and culminating with the quintessential *tôrâ* psalm of the Psalter, Psalm 119. The dialogue is found also in the placement of Psalm 19, another *tôrâ* psalm, bracketed by royal psalms 18 and 20–21 (see chapter 6). The fact that Psalm 19 is placed at the center of a chiastic arrangement spanning Psalms 15–24 indicates *tôrâ*'s overriding importance in matters of royalty and temple.

The dialogue between *tôrâ* and kingship initiated by the first two psalms is not a winner-take-all debate. The fact that the Torah psalms and the royal psalms coexist in the Psalter is itself a testament to mutual acknowledgment, one that in fact extends beyond the Psalter. Deuteronomy, most significantly, binds the exercise of the royal office to *tôrâ* obedience. Chosen from the community, the king is prohibited from getting involved in commercial activity with Egypt (specifically in horses), acquiring "many wives for himself," and amassing great wealth (Deut 17:14-17). Amid these prohibitions, Deuteronomy singles out the one thing that the king ought to do.

65. Such as articulated in the "book of the law" promulgated by Ezra (Neh 8–9).

> When he sits on his royal throne, he himself must write a copy of this law on a scroll in the presence of the levitical priests. It must remain with him, and he must recite it all the days of his life, so that he learns to fear YHWH his God, diligently observing all the words of this law and these statutes, neither exalting himself above other members of the community nor turning aside from the commandment, either to the right or to the left, so that he and his descendants may reign long over his kingdom in Israel. (Deut 17:18-20)

By writing a copy of the "law" and reciting it daily, the king comes to internalize *tôrâ*. Deuteronomy specifies two outcomes: "fear of YHWH" and no self-exaltation. Here is how *tôrâ* and kingship can embrace, according to Deuteronomy. Reciting *tôrâ* day by day in Deuteronomy parallels the righteous person's unceasing "deliberation" on *tôrâ* in Psalm 1. *Tôrâ* in Deuteronomy serves, among other things, as a check on the exercise of royal power. In Psalm 2, however, there is no check on the king; his sovereignty is unapologetically imperial (2:4-7). Is this a case of royal self-exaltation? Is Psalm 1, therefore, meant to counter such imperial presumption? Or is royal exaltation given free reign when it comes to ruling *other* nations, but not so with respect to Israel? Such questions remain open.

But then another psalm enters the fray, Psalm 3, the first psalm attributed to David, adding to the Psalter's introduction.[66] It too is a willing participant in this dialogue, and it does so by highlighting the king's vulnerable status. Surrounded by enemies, the speaker professes trust in YHWH's protection and cries out (3:2-4a[3-5a]). YHWH responds "from his holy hill" (3:4b[5b]), a point that recalls the king's installation on YHWH's "holy mountain" in 2:6-7. Who are the king's enemies in Psalm 3? They are identified as "the wicked" (3:7[8]), recalling their description in 1:4-6. Who is the speaker? As Psalm 1 profiles the righteous and Psalm 2 features a potentate, Psalm 3 presents a king overwhelmed by enemies. Is he righteous? Psalm 1 would say so. Elsewhere in the Psalms, the righteous are frequently profiled as the special targets of the wicked and, thus,

66. Beat Weber has argued that Psalm 3, the first Davidic psalm, also forms part of the Psalter's introduction, in addition to Psalms 1 and 2 ("Moses, David and the Psalms: The Psalter in the Horizon of the 'Canonical' Books," *Rivista Biblica* 68, no. 2 [2020]: 190–92).

are ever in need of deliverance.[67] In contrast, Psalm 1 gives no hint of such vulnerability, expressing complete confidence that the wicked will meet their demise (1:4-6). The same goes for the king in Psalm 2: while there is rebellion among the nations, the king has no reason to worry. But in Psalm 3, the king finds himself under attack and cries out for help. In Psalms 2 and 3, the imperial king meets the embattled king.

The dialogue cuts both ways. While Psalms 1 and 2 express confidence in God's power to vanquish enemies on behalf of the righteous and the king, subsequent psalms profile desperate speakers, both royal and righteous, pleading for help. The contrast could not be greater. On the one hand, Psalms 1 and 2 instill hope and trust that God will achieve victory over the wicked and the nations. The two psalms, in effect, provide the theological bulwark for all petitions and protests that follow in the Psalms: God will come through for the righteous and for the king. On the other hand, Psalm 3 and all that follows remind the reader (and God) that God has yet to do so, that the twofold vision of Psalms 1 and 2 has yet to be fulfilled. The wicked are not yet chaff, and the righteous are not yet flourishing trees. In fact, the wicked, as it were, have taken an axe to the "transplanted tree." "Many are the afflictions of the righteous" (34:19). The plaintive cry "How long, YHWH?" counters the divine decree "Today I have begotten you" (2:7). "Today" remains tomorrow, and the questions "How long?" and "Why?" persist.[68]

Psalms 1 and 2 serve as programmatic partners that launch a dialogue to be joined by many other partners and many other dialogues. We have listened to a few of them. It would seem that the Psalter's dialogical dynamics are never contained until the end, when the book concludes with its symphony of praise in the final psalm. Unlike the orchestral praise performed before Nebuchadnezzar's golden statue in Daniel (3:5, 7, 10, 15),

67. E.g., 11:1-3; 31:18[19]; 34:17-19; 37:12-14, 32; 146:8.

68. For an engaging discussion of how these two psalms are treated in Jewish and Christian traditions, see Susan E. Gillingham, *The Journey of Two Psalms: The Reception of Psalms 1 and 2 in Jewish and Christian Tradition* (Oxford: Oxford University Press, 2013).

a "forced act of homage to a state-sponsored cult image,"[69] the symphonic praise of Psalm 150 is invitational, not coercive, issued in response to God's power to save and sustain. Such praise acknowledges God's justice and mercy, compassion and judgment, wisdom and righteousness, guidance and salvation, this God of glory and solidarity whose "benevolence endures forever." It is in praise that every living thing finds its voice and, indeed, fulfillment in God.

But questions remain. Where are the wicked in this consummation of praise? Are they vanquished or redeemed? What does it take for all creation to give praise to God? Where is the place of freedom within the imperative of praise? How is praise performed by nonhuman creatures? What is humanity's role in creation's praise? May the dialogues continue.

69. Carol A. Newsom with Brennan W. Breed, *Daniel: A Commentary,* OTL (Louisville, KY: Westminster John Knox, 2014), 108. This taxonomy of musical instruments, repeated four times in this court-conflict tale of Dan 3, serves as a parody of imperial submission.

Part IV

REFLECTIONS

CHAPTER 11
ON BIBLICAL *AUCTORITAS*: A DIALOGUE

I will deliberate on your precepts and fix my eyes on your ways.

I will delight in your statutes; I will not forget your word.

—Psalm 119:15-16

How does the Bible's dialogical diversity inform its "authority"? From the two differing accounts of creation in Genesis to the divergent Psalms to the four distinct Gospels, the Bible demonstrates its unique authority by calling forth eyes wide open in critical discernment, not by imposing blind obedience. If biblical authority is not authoritarian, then what kind of authority is it? We will explore this topic dialogically, of course! The following discussion draws from a broad spectrum of divided theological positions, but the primary focus is on what the Bible says and how it says it, authoritatively.[1]

"Authority" as a Point of Contention

The topic of biblical authority continues to be a divisive issue for Christians. For some, the term *authority* smacks of legalism and tyranny,

1. This chapter builds on my "Introduction," in *Engaging Biblical Authority: Perspectives on the Bible as Scripture*, ed. William P. Brown (Louisville, KY Westminster John Knox, 2007), ix–xvi.

as reflected in the painful history of the church's abuse of the Bible to enslave and oppress, including the history of white supremacy in America. Others, however, regard authority as an essential feature of scripture, the very "Word of God," no less. Biblical authority means different things to different people from different contexts, even among people of faith, for whom the language of authority is inescapable, if not fundamental. For most Christians, but not all, the authority of scripture is a given, but its import and implications in the life of faith are a matter of serious debate.

The roots of such debate run deep. The formation of the Christian canon was met with its detractors from the outset, including the gnostic Marcion of Pontus of the second century CE, who considered the Old Testament and some of the New Testament scriptures to be theologically and morally objectionable. Around the same time, the pagan philosopher Celsus wrote extensively on the Bible's internal contradictions and dependency on popular myths. Propelled by advancements in scientific and historical inquiry, the Enlightenment of seventeenth-century Europe challenged the veracity of biblical revelation while, at the same time, setting the stage for the "scientific" study of the Bible. A mixed blessing by any measure, the rise of rationalism in Western thought resulted, as coined by Hans Frei, in the "eclipse of biblical narrative."[2]

More recently, the claim of biblical authority has had to confront both the rise of biblical illiteracy within the church and the emergence of postmodernism with its deconstruction of monolithic "truth." And, again, there is the undeniable history of oppression and exploitation committed in the name of God, such as the horrors of Western colonialism, including the "Doctrine of Discovery," manifest destiny, and the displacement of indigenous peoples, all examples of "biblical supremacy" at work.[3] In the face of such realities, some have found the very language of authority to be an impediment for engaging scripture for guidance and transformation.

---

2. Hans W. Frei, *The Eclipse of Biblical Narrative: A Study of Eighteenth and Nineteenth Century Hermeneutics* (New Haven, CT: Yale University Press, 1974).

3. See the trenchant analysis in Jeannine Hill Fletcher, *The Sin of White Supremacy: Christianity, Racism, and Religious Diversity in America* (Maryknoll, NY: Orbis, 2017), esp. 1–44.

Authority from the Bottom Up

To explore the nature of biblical authority, we do not begin with a top-down approach to the topic, which is how biblical authority is often cast: the Bible is the "Word of God"; therefore, it is authoritative. I ponder whether there is a way to come to such a claim by way of conclusion rather than premise, which only begs the question. If the claim is made that the Bible is uniquely authoritative as God's Word, we first need to know what the Bible is and what it does. We also need to know what happens when the Bible is read and interpreted. In other words, exploring biblical authority means entering into the hermeneutical fray of biblical interpretation.

Defining Authority: Constrictive and Creative

First, however, we need to know what "authority" is. Below are two dictionary definitions:

> the power and a right to command, act, enforce obedience, or make final decisions; jurisdiction . . . authorization . . . the power derived from opinion, respect or esteem; influence of character or office.[4]

> power to influence or command thought, opinion, or behavior . . . freedom granted . . . convincing force . . . grounds, warrant.[5]

Common to both definitions is the element of power. Authority wields power, from enforcing "obedience" to exercising "influence" and persuading "opinion." Etymologically, "authority" spans an even wider range. The Latin root bears a distinctly creative nuance: *auctoritas*, meaning "origination," from which the word "author" derives. The word is also related to the verb *auctorare*, "to bind." There is, thus, a tension within the word itself: on the one hand, authority has to do with creative generativity

4. *Webster's New Universal Unabridged Dictionary*, 2nd ed. (New York: Simon & Schuster, 1983).

5. *Webster's Seventh New College Dictionary* (Springfield, MA: G. & C. Merriam Co., 1969).

that leads to "authoring" or "authorizing" something. On the other hand, authority has the power to "bind," as in "binding the conscience," a phrase often used to describe the primary function of the Bible's authority. The semantic tension, however, is depleted in contemporary discourse, which tends to side exclusively with the sense of binding. In the judicial domain, for example, an authoritative precedent or reason is often sought that results in a binding decision.

The Question of Domain

To what domain(s) does the Bible's authority pertain? Does it apply to scientific and legal matters as much as it does to matters of faith and moral conduct? That may be easy to answer, but what about murkier matters such as sexuality, climate change, abortion, and stem-cell research, where theological reflection needs to engage the natural and social sciences? To complicate matters further, whereas the recourse to authority frequently involves seeking a specific decision or answer for a specific issue, how does one seek such things from court narratives and lament poetry? How does one derive authority from the Song of Solomon? Or is only the instructional material of the Bible (e.g., *tôrâ*) to be deemed authoritative? Given its diversity, the Bible is an altogether uniquely authoritative source of guidance, quite different from things we usually regard as authoritative, such as legal texts and scientific reports.

One place to begin is to acknowledge first and foremost that scripture is authoritative primarily with respect to its theological subject, God, who lies beyond scientific investigation and historical inquiry yet is active in creation and history.[6] Nevertheless, because God is the creator of all things, scriptural authority also requires respect for authorities outside its primary purview, such as science and medicine. The Bible, in other words, does not cover everything about the irreducibly complex world that we inhabit, and what it does reveal can be misleading if taken scientifically.

6. For the simple reason that neither science nor historical investigation can prove or disprove God's existence. Yet for people of faith, much of God's handiwork can be discerned by science and historical inquiry. Moreover, the incarnation is testimony that God has entered into the fray of history in Jesus Christ (John 1:1-14).

Is infertility a sign of divine disfavor or affliction?[7] Must we adopt a geocentric worldview because the sun "stood still" at Gibeon when Joshua defeated the Amorites (Josh 10:12)? The sky-dome model of creation (Gen 1:6-8) finds little correspondence with the structure of the cosmos as we know it. The Bible acknowledges that there are many aspects about our world that can be understood through observation and that there are realities that will always remain inexplicable. Such is the premise of much of the wisdom corpus, whose diversity is itself testimony to the lively dialogues of the sages over such matters.

Authority and Interpretation

Authority as it pertains to the Bible takes on a different nuance from its normal usage in everyday discourse. For example, Solomon's decree to cut the infant in half was not in itself the right *legal* decision (1 Kgs 3:25). Indeed, it would have been horrifically wrong had it been *literally* carried out! Rather, it served to provoke a response from the contesting parties to resolve a conflict. The Bible's authority, thus, is more at home with the generative sense of the term (*auctoritas*), one that creatively elicits (or "authors") responses from its readers. For Christians, the Bible is ultimately authored by God, but through human authors complete with their varying personalities embedded within their ancient cultures. However the mystery of biblical inspiration is to be explained (and it can't be), it did not cancel the personal, cultural, and historical particularities of each author and tradition behind the words of scripture.

Any doctrine of the Bible's authority must grapple with the nature of what the Bible is and what it does. The Bible is no monolith. It comprises a diverse array of genres conveying a host of various perspectives, all brought together within the overarching claim that God is fundamentally benevolent, this God of *ḥesed* (see below). The Bible's diversity has been described in various ways. Employing the metaphor of the lawcourt, Walter Brueggemann identifies "testimonies" and "counter testimonies"

7. Cf. Gen 20:17-18; 29:31; Exod 23:25-26; Deut 7:14.

canonically bound together.[8] Others apply the framework of logic to highlight the Bible's "contradictions."[9] Doing so treats scripture as either a treatise or a court case. From a dialogical perspective, however, such differences constitute "disagreements" that invite deep listening, critical reflection, and continuing dialogue. Through dialogical engagement, the books and authors of the Bible can "agree to disagree," offering ample opportunity for ongoing dialogue and resisting the urge to treat the Bible as an echo chamber.

Biblical authority rests on biblical interpretation, and biblical interpretation is by nature dialogical. Dialogue unfolds not only between texts in scripture but also between scripture and its readers. Meaning is not something unlocked, as if the biblical text were a heavy safe waiting for the right key to be inserted.[10] Meaning emerges from a reader's encounter with a text, which is authorized by its author(s). Meaning is evoked within the interactive space between reader and text. Meaning is relational and active. So also is truth, for truth rests on meaning. It is simply a hermeneutical fact that a reader is required for a text to be meaningful, including meaningfully true. The same goes for the Bible. By itself, a text contains merely marks on a page or pixels on a screen. It does not exist as meaningful without its readers, past and present. It comes alive, as it were, when it is read or recited, whenever it is communicated or interpreted. In the encounter, the text becomes a partner in the construction of meaning. On the one hand, the text's meaning grasps the reader as an experience outside of the reader's own context. On the other hand, the reader has some leeway in deciding how a text is to be communicated and interpreted, like a musician playing from a score. Not unlike musical notations regarding tempo, phrasing, and volume, setting the parameters and constraints of every performance, there are textual signs and rhetorical conventions that cue the reader in interpreting a biblical text. Nevertheless, readers invest

8. Walter Brueggemann, *Theology of the Old Testament: Testimony, Dispute, Advocacy* (Minneapolis: Fortress, 2005), esp. 317–32.

9. E.g., Peter T. H. Hatton, *Contradiction in the Book of Proverbs: The Deep Waters of Counsel* (Aldershot, UK: Ashgate, 2008).

10. I explore this more deeply in *A Handbook to Old Testament Exegesis* (Louisville, KY: Westminster John Knox, 2017), esp. 3–8.

something of themselves in every act of interpretation, situated as they are in a certain time and place. In the process of interpretation, the reader interrogates the text, and the text interrogates the reader. The result is dialogue in search of meaningful truth.

A Dialogue with the Westminster Confession of Faith

As for truth, the Westminster Confession of Faith (1646),[11] influential among Reformed churches worldwide, as well as many evangelical churches, finds convergence between the Bible's "infallible truth" and its "divine authority," worked out by the "inward work of the Holy Spirit bearing witness by and with the Word in our hearts" (1.5). The Bible's "truth," in other words, may not be self-evident, because such truth is mediated by God's Spirit, which in practice involves interpretation.

> The infallible rule of interpretation of Scripture is the Scripture itself: and therefore, when there is a question about the true and full sense of any Scripture (which is not manifold, but one), it must be searched and known by other places that speak more clearly. (1.9)

In other words, scripture interprets scripture, in part because not all passages are equal in clarity.

> All things in Scripture are not alike plain in themselves, nor alike clear unto all: yet those things which are necessary to be known, believed, and observed for salvation, are so clearly propounded and opened in some place of Scripture or other, that not only the learned, but the unlearned, in a due use of the ordinary means, may attain unto a sufficient understanding of them. (1.7)

Precisely. "Searching" scripture means exploring the dialogical dynamics that unfold among the diverse texts of scripture and adjudicating them in terms of clarity and significance. This involves both discerning the dialogue among texts and engaging in dialogue with them.

11. Drawn up for the purpose of reforming the Church of England during the English Civil War (1642–49) along the lines of Calvinism, the Westminster Confession of Faith remains the "subordinate standard" of doctrine in the Church of Scotland.

The interpretive process is dialogically charged through and through, beginning with the text and a reader, leading to a community of readers—the more diverse, the livelier the dialogue! When a biblical text meets differently situated readers, it is hard to predict what will happen. Any notion of biblical authority must acknowledge both the dialogical nature of scripture and the dialogical nature of interpretation. By its diversity, the Bible generates dialogue. By its authority, the Bible enlists its readers to listen deeply as it initiates the kinds of dialogue that form vital communities of discernment. Such is the Bible's formative, "authorizing" power. As much as biblical truth is the result of the "energetic interplay of the Spirit of God working in and through human authors,"[12] it is also the result of interaction among readers and God's Spirit. Such interaction "in front of the text" is also "energetic interplay," or lively dialogue.

Edifying Authority

One of the few places in which the Bible speaks about itself is found in 2 Timothy 3:16-17.

> Every scripture is inspired by God and is useful for teaching, for showing mistakes, for correcting, and for training character, so that the person who belongs to God can be equipped to do everything that is good. (CEB)

On the face of it, this passage makes a rather modest claim. Simply put, scripture is a gift from God that serves to teach and equip the community of faith. Its inspiration is paralleled by what it can do for the body of Christ. For something to be useful, it must prove its usefulness. Timothy's claim is that the Bible's authority is demonstrated by its capacity to edify and sustain, to teach and equip people for the life of faith. The Bible's authority, like psalmic *tôrâ*, is lodged in its efficacy.

According to this brief epistle, the Bible's authority is a functional or formative authority. What makes the Bible the "Word of God" does

12. Peter Enns, "'God Is Truth': The First Summary Statement of CSBI, Part 2," in *The Biologos Forum: Science and Faith in Dialogue* (June 21, 2011): 6. Accessed at http://wp.production.patheos.com/blogs/peterenns/files/2014/08/Science-Faith-and-the-Chicago-Statement-on-Biblical-Inerrancy-Enns-Edited-no-watermark.pdf.

not depend upon any particular theory of inspiration, which remains a mystery. Rather, the Bible's authority depends on the testimony of what the Bible can do for equipping communities to do "everything that is good." To talk about the Bible as a normative document is to say a lot about what is formative about the Bible. Scripture's authority denotes the Bible's capacity to shape and transform people into mature communities of faith, to command as well as to edify, to charge as well as to bless. Biblical authority is demonstrated in practice as it is lived out by the Bible's readers. Such authority is not something that adheres to the printed words of the text, such as font size or the color of its letters (even if it is red). Rather, it is lived out in one's engagement with the text: in making sense of the text, interpreting the text, and embodying the result in "faith, hope, and love" (1 Cor 13:13).

Authority Dialogically Framed

The difference between "authoritative" and "authoritarian" is deep. For one thing, the Bible allows for questions that prompt answers.[13] Such dialogical exchanges are "*quite unauthoritarian* but utterly *authoritative*."[14] Biblical authority does not mean biblical supremacy. The Bible gives reasons and warrants for its claims, indicating that proper authority is to be freely acknowledged; it rests not on coercion but on persuasion and pathos, as conveyed in its compelling stories and cogent wisdom, on the power of its vision for abundant life, on the breadth of its diversity. Featuring both human and divine discourse, the Bible is complex and, as such, so is its authority. The Bible is not a systematic book of definitions and diagnoses, complete with a handy index. It is a corpus filled with polity and piety, epistles and stories, songs of praise and protest, not to mention love poetry. The literature spans over a millennium of history, punctuated by national disruptions and crises. The Bible was not dropped from heaven on gold plates. It was not transmitted to an illiterate prophet. The Bible,

13. Such as the catechetical exchanges in Exod 13:14; Deut 6:20-21; Josh 4:6, 21.

14. Walter Brueggemann, *The Creative Word: Canon as Model for Biblical Education*, 2nd ed. (Minneapolis: Fortress, 2015), 22 (italics original).

rather, reflects centuries upon centuries of communal struggle and theological discernment. It speaks in many voices, some harmonious, some dissonant. The Bible is the product of inspired dialogues that inspires dialogues, and so much more.

Discerning the many voices of scripture, cast in various rhetorical forms and rooted in diverse historical contexts, is part of the challenging task of interpretation. For people of faith, the Bible's authority is realized in its interpretation, and interpretation gives concrete expression to the Bible's authority. Because scripture interprets itself as earlier traditions or perspectives are recast and revised for new contexts, scripture counters and corrects itself.[15] In so doing, scripture "reauthorizes" itself. Certain Jewish interpreters have a pointed way of describing this: the Bible *debates* itself![16] "Do not answer fools according to their folly, or you will be a fool yourself" is an admonition in Proverbs that is followed immediately by opposite counsel: "Answer fools according to their folly, or they will be wise in their own eyes" (Prov 26:4-5). To respond or not to respond, that is the question with regard to fools, and there is no one mind on the issue. Or take the example of John the Baptist's declaration, recast from Isaiah: "The voice of one crying out in the wilderness: 'Prepare the way of the Lord, make his paths straight'" (Matt 3:3). Ecclesiastes, however, observes, "Consider the work of God; who can make straight what [God] has made crooked?" (Eccl 7:13). Qoheleth laments that "there is nothing new under the sun" (Eccl 1:9), while the prophet of the exile declares on God's behalf, "I am about to do a new thing; now it springs forth, do you not perceive it?" (Isa 43:19a). Truth in these cases emerges from dialogically engaging divergent voices, truth that is specific for one's context, which is to say that the Bible conveys not only *timeless* truths but also *timely* truths, truths that address specific contexts.

15. We have seen this, for example, in Deuteronomy's revision of the Covenant Code (chapter 6). One can also cite the reversal of the "act-consequence connection" in Job, in contrast to Proverbs. One clear case of corrective canceling is Jesus's overturning the dietary restrictions in Mark 7:18-19. See also Matt 4:6-7.

16. See Marc Zvi Brettler, "Biblical Authority: A Jewish Pluralistic View," in *Engaging Biblical Authority: Perspectives on the Bible as Scripture*, ed. William P. Brown (Louisville, KY: Westminster John Knox, 2007), 1–9.

The dialogical, self-interpretive nature of scripture complexifies the issue of biblical authority, for the task of interpretation requires the reader to find ways to navigate and mediate the contesting claims about God and God's ways in the world. Nevertheless, is there a theological center or focal point to the Bible, an overarching coherence or framework to be privileged above everything else? That too is a matter of dialogue. What about the voices and perspectives muted by scripture that cry out for a hearing, such as the voice of the immigrant, the cry of the Canaanite, the cries of Hagar and other women marginalized in the patriarchal household, the groanings of the enslaved *within* the Israelite household? Every interpreter must engage dialogically with the plethora of voices that make up the great extended family called scripture, both dominant and suppressed. The Bible has them all, if one looks hard enough.

How does one adjudicate such competing voices? To do so dialogically requires care and patience, for true dialogue involves listening attentively and striving toward critical understanding. But often a choice must be made in the end, one that either favors one text or tradition over others or finds a creative way of integrating diverse perspectives without resorting to harmonization. What criteria are available? How does one decide? Here, the Bible itself offers help, but it revolves around a question that every reader/interpreter must decide: What does scripture consider most central about God?

One possibility is to follow the lead of the psalmists, who repeat God's "self-confession," in variant ways,[17] given in response to Moses's request to see God's "glory" in Exodus 34:6.

> YHWH passed before him and proclaimed, "YHWH, YHWH, a God compassionate and merciful, slow to anger, and abounding in benevolence and faithfulness."

This creed-like statement of YHWH's character, positioned at the chiastic center of the entire Hexateuch (Genesis to Joshua),[18] suggests its

17. Pss 85:15; 103:8; 145:8. See also Num 14:18; Neh 9:17; Joel 2:13; Jon 4:2; Nah 1:3.

18. See Jacob Milgrom, *The JPS Torah Commentary: Numbers*, JPS Torah Commentary (Philadelphia: Jewish Publication Society, 1990), xviii.

theological centrality or primacy in the Hebrew scriptures. The divine dispositions identified in this self-confession fundamentally underwrite both YHWH's "ways" and "deeds," from the creation of the cosmos and the liberation of the enslaved to the constitution of a community at Sinai and the blessing of all the families of the earth. Any text that falls short of acknowledging God's abundant "benevolence and faithfulness,"[19] any message that diminishes the God who is "compassionate and merciful," the same mercy and kindness incarnated in Christ, falls short of full authority:

> We ourselves were once foolish, disobedient, deceived, and slaves to various passions and pleasures, passing our days in malice and jealousy. We were despicable, hating one another. But when the goodness and loving kindness of God our Savior appeared, he saved us, not because of any righteous works we had done, but according to his mercy, through the water of rebirth and renewal by the Holy Spirit. (Titus 3:3-5)

Such is the theological high bar for all of scripture, transforming malice, hatred, and division into kindness, mercy, and renewal.

So what is the Bible's authority framed dialogically? It is reflected first and foremost in the church's commitment to read and consult scripture, every time, all the time. In the life of the church, scripture is to be always held front and center as its "founding document." Such is biblical authority manifested in practice. Dialogically, biblical authority is manifest in reading scripture as a chorus of voices crossing the divide of time and cultures to direct our attention. It is demonstrated in readers being captured and captivated by their voices and listening in on how they engage each other. The Bible does not invite its readers to enter blindly but beckons readers with eyes to see and ears to hear, receptively and critically. While the Bible's authority, weighty as it is, pulls its readers into its gravitational orbit, beckoning receptive hearts and minds, it is the Bible's diversity that invites its readers to exercise critical discernment, manifest in dialogue. Such is how the Bible earns its authority.

---

19. Indeed, God's "benevolence" (*ḥesed*) is so central in the Psalms that many petitions appeal to God's "benevolence" for a response, even reminding God of God's own benevolent character. See, e.g., 25:6-7; 33:22; 40:11[12]; 77:8[9]; 86:5; 89:49[50]; 98:3; 143:8.

God's Creative Word

What does it mean, then, to claim the Bible as God's Word dialogically? As scripture is "authored" by God, much like creation fashioned by God in complex ways, the Bible is first and foremost God's creative, generative Word.[20] As God's words launched creation into being "in the beginning" (Gen 1), resulting in a manifold creation (Ps 104:24), so God's Word in scripture has a hand in fashioning diverse communities of discernment, communities that seek, question, wonder, and strive to embody scripture, each true to its own setting and context. To claim the Bible as God's Word is to claim scripture as the fertile field for cultivating the life of faith, for nurturing lives of faith in community. It is to claim the transformative power that comes from wrestling with the Word, like Jacob at the Jabbok, whose change of identity did not come without concerted effort. It is to claim the work and play of God's Spirit when scripture is read and interpreted, the same Spirit or divine breath (*rûaḥ*) that "hovered" over the waters of creation, poised to create (Gen 1:2).

In the end, biblical authority rests on trust. It is the Bible's trustworthiness that makes the Bible authoritative. As the God who is trustworthy seeks our prayers and praise, as well as our laments and protests, so the Bible earns and elicits our respect and our questions, our hopes and our doubts, all offered in trust that in the end wisdom will be gained, faith strengthened, hope sustained, and renewal made real (Rev 21:5). This, too, is the work of God's Spirit. In short, the Bible's authority both "binds the conscience" and expands it. As Christ is God's Word "made flesh" (John 1:14), so the Bible is God's written Word made fresh by God's Spirit with each new question, with each new issue, for each new generation.

20. I draw from Brueggemann, *The Creative Word*, for such language.

CHAPTER 12
CONCLUSION: PERSONAL AND PEDAGOGICAL REFLECTIONS

If I do not love the world—if I do not love life—

if I do not love people—I cannot enter into dialogue.

—Paulo Freire[1]

If God can speak through an ass,

then surely God can speak through someone with whom you disagree.

—Mark Douglas[2]

It is one thing to write a book on the dialogical dynamics of the Psalms; it is another thing to teach about it, and online no less. My sabbatical project involved not only writing about dialogical diversity in the Bible but also teaching about it in a way that was itself dialogical. The course, titled "Breaking the Impasse: Dialogue, Diversity, and Transformation in the Old Testament," extended beyond the Psalms to incorporate much of the Hebrew Bible. Its objective was twofold: to explore the dialogical

1. Paulo Freire, *The Pedagogy of the Oppressed, Fiftieth Anniversary Edition* (New York: Bloomsbury Academic, 2018), 89.

2. It is what my colleague Mark Douglas calls "Balaam's law"(personal communication).

dynamics of scripture and to model genuine dialogue in our interactions with each other.

While not a case study of my class, this concluding chapter shares a few anecdotes on how the class furthered my own understanding of dialogue in the Bible and how it yielded insights on how to practice dialogue in the classroom. The class was diverse: Africans and Black Americans, gay and straight, women and men, white and Korean. With only thirteen participants, including myself, we were able to engage each other deeply. Through online prompts, participants were invited to read the biblical material dialogically and to engage each other in the same manner.

The class was an entirely new venture for me. I found myself playing a different pedagogical role from what I was accustomed to, one that better suited the student-centered ethos of online learning. For the sake of the class (and my own), I had to come down from my pedagogical "throne," relinquish my professorial privilege, and enter into the fray of posted discussions as an equal participant, a colleague among colleagues. In other words, I had to resign myself from having the final word in our discussions. All I had was the first question to launch the dialogue, which took its unpredictable turns. Otherwise, I was another participant sharing thoughts and asking questions. There were times when I saw my well-articulated insights "plop" as participants found greater value in the postings of their peers than in my own. It was easy to see why: many of their posts were more insightful and relevant than anything I offered in response to *my own* questions. This new format of teaching exposed my pedagogical bias for wielding control by giving authoritative lectures. But I got over it. I realized that even though I had some background information to share from my work as a biblical scholar, my opinions held the same weight as everyone else's. It was both humbling and liberating.

Our liveliest discussions revolved around questions that connected the biblical dialogues with what class participants considered worthy of dialogue within their own contexts. Would you vote for David as president? How is the biblical notion of law different from "law and order" in American political discourse? How does Israel's experience in the wilderness connect with your own experience of navigating the pandemic "wilderness"? But I begin with a topic that touched on the nature of dialogue itself by way of negative example.

Job and the Dialogue Debacle

We discovered that the one formal example of sapiential dialogue in the Bible proved to be a disaster. Spanning three cycles (Job 3–27), the so-called dialogues between Job and his friends turned out to be an exercise in futility. No common ground between Job and his friends was reached, no level of mutual understanding achieved, no wisdom gained. Instead, the "dialogues" degenerated into condemnation, a perfect model of how *not* to conduct a dialogue by any modern standards. True dialogue aims for mutual understanding and the building of relationships,[3] marked by humility, an openness to learning, and a "sense of wonder about others."[4] And it all begins with "creating safe space."[5]

Job sitting on an ash heap surrounded by his three "friends" was perhaps not the safest place to hold a dialogue (Job 2:8, 11-12). Nevertheless, the "friends" begin on a promising note by sitting together in silence for a week. Job breaks the silence by cursing his birthday (3:1-26). Eliphaz is the first to respond by offering advice: "Seek God," he implores Job, and you will be blessed with peace and prosperity (5:8, 19-26). At the same time, he admonishes Job for being "impatient" and lacking the confidence he once had (4:5-6). And so begin the judgments. As the friends condemn Job, one after the other, for not accepting their advice to confess his alleged iniquities, Job condemns them for being "treacherous" "companions" (6:15), breaking him "in pieces with words" (19:2), being "miserable comforters" (16:2), and offering him "empty nothings" (21:34). Job protests against being cast as "inferior" to his friends (13:2); he too, Job insists, has "understanding" on par with theirs (13:3).

3. Lisa Schirch and David Campt, *The Little Book of Dialogue for Difficult Subjects: A Practical, Hands-On Guide*, The Little Books of Justice & Peacebuilding (New York: Good Books, 2007), 5–7.

4. Schirch and Campt, *The Little Book of Dialogue*, 10.

5. Schirch and Campt, *The Little Book of Dialogue*, 37.

So what did Job want from his friends? They came to "console and comfort" him (2:11), and Job hoped for his pain to be assuaged by their honest words (6:25; 16:5). But instead, he is attacked with false accusations, forcing him to defend his innocence in lieu of his suffering (9:15, 20, 28; 27:6; 34:5). Perhaps the most damning criticism is found in Job's question, "Why do you, like God, pursue me?" (19:22). God does not come off looking good either, this God who set Job up for target practice (6:4; 16:9, 12-13), who hunted him like a lion (10:16). No wonder Job wishes only to be left alone by God (7:16) and for his friends to "keep silent" (13:5). As a last resort, Job appeals to a "witness in heaven" to hear his case (16:19; cf. 9:33; 19:25).

So what went wrong dialogically? To be sure, the friends came with their own preconceptions about Job, derived from their unyielding sense of moral retribution and meritocracy, to which Job himself was not immune (Job 29–30). But what went wrong that turned this well-intended comfort session into a fight for vindication (e.g., 11:2)? I asked participants to imagine themselves as facilitators.[6] All agreed that certain ground rules had to be established at the outset, such as the following: listen for understanding, avoid accusations, use "I" language, ask honest questions, acknowledge connections, and be open to seeing things in a new way.[7] It all sounds quite idealistic, if not anachronistic, to expect such respectful conduct among these ancient discussants. But there is one "on ramp" in ancient sapiential rhetoric that might have salvaged the dialogical debacle: the reciprocal nature of "rebuke," as encouraged in Proverbs 9:8-9 (see chapter 9). Although harsh in tone, the sagacious rebuke was meant to elicit gratitude, even love, by the one rebuked. Recognized as a discursive form of wisdom, such rebukes were welcomed by the sages. Moreover, the rebuke was an equal opportunity right, hence its reciprocity. "Iron sharpens iron" (Prov 27:17a). One would think that the reciprocal nature of rebuke would instill not only gratitude but also humility among Job and his friends.

6. A requirement for deep, constructive dialogue (Schirch and Campt, *The Little Book of Dialogue*, 35).

7. See Schirch and Campt, *The Little Book of Dialogue*, 40–41.

But no. To be sure, Job and his friends issued their fair share of rebukes, but it was clear from the outset that a hierarchy of discourse was quickly and rigidly established: the friends cast themselves as teachers and Job as the student, which at one point Job sarcastically internalizes (6:24; see 21:22; 27:11; 33:33). The friends were interested more in "sage-splaining" than in understanding Job's condition and offering comfort. Call it the "pedagogy of the oppressor," which in Job's case was meant first to silence and then to compel him to confess and repent, in short, to prove him wrong. If, however, the dialogue had been set in which all parties could have seen themselves as equals, if, as two students suggested, the friends had lifted Job up from the ashes to a safer space, then perhaps the proceedings might have gone differently. Sitting on the ground with Job in silence was a commendable act of mutual mourning, but finding another venue before the words started flying like barbs might have sustained that solidarity. In any case, with the friends physically or figuratively standing over Job as they hurled their condemnations, no wisdom could ever be gained, and no comfort offered.[8]

David for President?

Another question that prompted lively dialogue was "Would you vote for David as president?" It was posed as the culminating question in our comparative work on the character of David as treated in 1 Samuel 16–1 Kings 2, 1 Chronicles 10–29, and various psalms, complemented with Steve McKenzie's chapter on "royal propaganda" in his biography on David (see chapter 7). Not coincidentally, our study of David occurred the week prior to the 2020 presidential election. Emotions and anxieties were running high. The class was split with a few abstaining. On the one hand, David was chosen by God to succeed in establishing a unified nation through God's help. On the other hand, David would have become a national headliner in the #MeToo movement, as one student pointed out. Another observed that David was no worse than other candidates and

8. Note William Blake's engraving of "Job Rebuked by His Friends" (1825), which depicts the friends half sitting and standing with their fingers all pointed to the kneeling Job.

most politicians in general, so why bother voting? One said he would vote for David, but only if he could "discharge [his] duty as 'Nathan' without fear or favor."

The class seemed quite divided until one student posed another question, taking the dialogue in a new direction: "*Which* David?" By acknowledging the differing ways David is depicted in the Bible, the question shifted the focus to identifying which David was most electable. Complementing that question was another: What are the marks of good political leadership? "Killing men to have their wives is not the mark of a good leader," one student stated without any pushback.[9] Another argued that the presidency today requires not so much a warrior as a negotiator and diplomat. Required in a leader is humility as well as courage and compassion for the vulnerable, as in the case of Mephibosheth (although this could be argued otherwise, as another student noted). There is the humble David crying out to God in trust in the Psalms, and there is the conquering and cunning David with all his baggage in DtrH. Such spirited discussions made us wonder whether the Bible's scribes (or "spin doctors") had similar discussions on how to preserve David's legacy for future generations.

The Pandemic Wilderness

Another topic that elicited lively dialogue was Israel in the wilderness. After comparing the accounts in Exodus and Numbers with the historical psalms, we addressed the question, "How might the 'wilderness' from ancient Israel's perspectives serve as an apt metaphor for the pandemic?" It seemed like a fair question to ask, one that immediately established common ground among us: Who has not felt the debilitating effects of the pandemic, albeit in varying degrees? The wilderness was a place and a time of testing, of hardship amid newly found freedom. It was a place not for settlement but for learning, a place of formation. All agreed that the pandemic was a "place" one wished to pass through as quickly as possible. Some reflected back in the spring when it was clear that Easter 2020 was

9. Jacqueline Turner, "David for President?" (Moodle Forum Post, October 29, 2020).

not going to be celebrated in places of worship, but hope was alive that by Pentecost, at least, public worship would return.

Nope. Summer, fall, and winter, the worst yet. Will the vaccine prove to be the "promised land"? The COVID-19 "wilderness" lasted much longer than anyone anticipated, so also the wilderness for the wandering Israelites, forty years no less. We saw other parallels: the hardships of deprivation, such as food insecurity, combined with "pestilence." One student noted that Moses wore a mask (a "veil") to alleviate the people's fear (Exod 34:33-35). Another noticed the parallel between the people's "rush" to take the promised land, a failure of patience that resulted in devastating defeat (Num 14:35-49), and the strident demands of many to reopen nonessential businesses even as the virus continued its deadly scourge. As the wilderness exposed the Israelites' stubborn resistance to becoming God's people, so COVID-19 exposed the stubborn realities of racism, economic disparity, and climate change. "Is the Lord among us or not?" (Exod 17:7) is both the cry of the Israelites and the lament of many Christians.

Nevertheless, as one student noted, the "liminal space" of the pandemic, like that of the wilderness, has also been transformative.

> Like the Israelites of the wilderness who sought out Moses to teach them "the statutes and instructions of God" (Exod 18:16), so we too can seek out wilderness leaders, those of the Black Lives Matter movement, public health professionals, fair and equal voting organizations, pastors, to teach us "the way [we] are to go and the things [we] are to do" (v. 20).[10]

The wilderness was a test of leadership, in which Moses both failed and succeeded. The same could be said of the pandemic "wilderness" of 2020–2021: a testing of governance informed by science, of sufficient preparation for disaster, and of genuine care for the well-being of the nation, particularly for the most vulnerable.

I would also add technological innovation to the list of wilderness-inspired changes. What would we have done without Zoom and other

10. Candace Rowell, "Wilderness as Metaphor Today" (Moodle Forum Post, October 6, 2020).

online pathways for keeping connected? Public meetings and gatherings would not have been possible without such resources. For churches, connecting online has given birth to new and creative forms of worship, decentralized from a common physical space and extending into the security of people's homes. Is there a parallel in Israel's wandering in the wilderness? Indeed, there is, as we discovered: the tabernacle, itself a technological achievement, a community "techno-art project" designed to facilitate God's presence with a people on the move, a decentralized form of divine presence that facilitated God's accompaniment of the people in their sojourns, in contrast to the centralized temple. As one participant proposed, the tabernacle was God's "mobile device" for Israel.

We discovered that the pandemic and the biblical wilderness exposed something fundamentally in common: the nostalgic desire to return to "normalcy," to go back to how things once were, no matter how bad. While we identified the good things we yearned for, such as being physically in touch with our loved ones and at our places of worship, there were other matters the pandemic exposed that should be left behind, such as America's "business as usual" in exercising white supremacy over Black and brown bodies and human supremacy over the environment. The desire to go back to "Egypt" must be resisted. From clear blue skies over Los Angeles to protests in the streets of Minneapolis, Atlanta, and Louisville, the pandemic opened up space for self-examination in how we ought to live our lives forward rather than backward. The pandemic wilderness gave opportunity to shed those idolatries and ideologies that have prevented communities, and American society as a whole, from embodying the ideals of the "beloved community."[11] Given its liminality, the wilderness proved to be richly (trans)formative as much as it was harrowingly disruptive.

11. First coined by American philosopher Josiah Royce (1855–1916), who defined it as "a spiritual or divine community capable of achieving the highest good as well as the common good" (Kelly A. Parker, "Josiah Royce," *The Stanford Encyclopedia of Philosophy* [Spring 2020 edition], ed. Edward N. Zalta. Accessed at https://plato.stanford.edu/archives/spr2020/entries/royce/. The "Beloved Community" came to be championed by Martin Luther King Jr., who emphasized its foundation on agapic love. For the connection, see Gary Herstein, "The Roycean Roots of the Beloved Community," *The Pluralist* 4, no. 2 (2009): 91–107.

By way of conclusion, I include a spoken-word poem composed by Natarsha Sanders, a doctoral student and Christian educator. She recited it to the class via Zoom and has given permission to publish it here.

From one unknown wilderness to this uncultivated space,
  no one wants to live forsaken.
Have we been forsaken in this dry, barren place,
  where my uncertain soul is awakened?
Awakened, O yes, to the opportunity to survive,
  while my spirit is in between.
Awakened to conflict and challenge,
  indeed, separation and challenge, O yes.
The climate changed a long time ago,
  and Black Lives matter in this nation
    like the people of Israel mattered to Pharaoh.
      Is that not an abomination?
So while we interpret this deadly pandemic,
  we must reshape our trust in God.
Our trust in God has been transformed,
  and perhaps we have learned things we cannot unlearn.
But we are called to form a community
  in which we may grow and thrive.
We cannot neglect the testing, the trials, the hopelessness,
  our need to survive,
the selfishness and violence, the burnout and the overwhelm,
  the chaos that screams,
    and Peace practices her right to remain silent.
No doubt the wilderness is dangerous; it is!
  But the "go back to normal" ain't it!
We serve a God who dwells in both Israel and Egypt,
  and we've built a community that's craving and thirsty,
    and too lost to call it quits.
So we will move forward through this wilderness,
  through this station that seeks transformation,
    knowing that the grace of God will guide us,
      from this station to that station,
        like the God above the nations.

We pray to this God; we need this God.
  This God is our reason to survive.
And so we build a community that we call "beloved,"
  so that we may love and thrive.

Moving Forward to "Grow and Thrive"

Forged from national and social disruption, the Bible's hallmark is its dialogical diversity. Such uniqueness among sacred texts need not be treated as a liability but cherished as an asset and opportunity, particularly now. Appreciating the Bible's dialogical diversity, I am convinced, can foster dialogical engagement across the differences that divide us.

This class was living proof. Taught at the height of polarizing divisiveness in American politics and amid global disruptions brought on by the pandemic and environmental catastrophes, this class encouraged participants to be both empathetic and fearless in their engagement with others different from themselves. And it began by appreciating how dialogically diverse scripture is. As one participant put it,

> Perhaps a Bible that makes room for tension between divergent perspectives, a Bible that models a brave refusal to delete the voices that disagree, a Bible that is comfortable with leaving questions open and unanswered, a Bible that invites dialogue, a Bible that compels us to take an active role in wrestling with its ideas in our own hearts and in community with other people who interpret it differently than we do, is precisely the kind of Bible that God intended for us to have.[12]

If the Bible can "make room" for "divergent perspectives," then so can its readers. We discovered that the Bible's diversity, on the one hand, gave us freedom to differ among ourselves and, on the other hand, invited us to interrogate our differences more deeply so as to break new ground, if not common ground, in mutual understanding.

The class, diverse as it was, turned into a community, whose members both supported and challenged each other in dialogue. We came to appreciate each other's differences in background, identity,

12. Katherine S. Johnson, "Reflection Paper 3" (September 20, 2020).

and perspective. Stereotypes crumbled, and paradoxes emerged: some participants I had pegged as conservative acted as liberals and vice versa, depending on the issue. We came to see each other as complex, always evolving subjects embodying multiple identities and perspectives. We allowed ourselves to change our minds. "There is no shame in change" could have been our mantra, in addition to "difference does not mean defective." We found, moreover, that "at the table of dialogue, there is no competition,"[13] and "when people engage in dialogue, they can reap a 'new thing,'"[14] so observed our Kenyan colleague in the spirit of Isaiah 43:19. While reaching common ground may not be the outcome (or even goal) of all dialogues, breaking new ground is inevitable.

Our class was by no means a complete microcosm of American society. There were no QAnon supporters or neo-Nazis among us. We were self-selected for such a course, having recognized the dire need for dialogue, some of us having been victims or perpetrators of division. We were a rather tame group, but we were by no means like-minded. We learned how to respectfully disagree and did so not by digging in but by asking questions of each other out of curiosity and for clarification with the aim of understanding each other more fully and, in so doing, better understanding ourselves. Those most adept at dialogue would express appreciation of another person's viewpoint and ask questions for further articulation, while also relating something personal in their own lives to provide further background for their own position. The best kind of dialogue, we discovered, is invitational, and accepting the invitation proves beneficial for all involved.

Can such success be replicated in the larger public arena? I don't know, but some are trying. One is David Campt, the principal of the Dialogue Company (https://thedialoguecompany.com), who works with organizations on matters of inclusion and equity, conflict resolution, and dialogue. He asks whether a truly inclusive narrative of American history can be created, one that celebrates America's successes and ideals and at the same time admits to its failings and atrocities. "Maybe, but we certainly can't as

13. Lucas Mburu, "Reflection Paper 3" (September 25, 2020).

14. Lucas Mburu, "A New Thing: Reflection Paper 4" (October 1, 2020).

long as we see each other as enemies whose views are despicable, ignorant, or otherwise worthy of scorn. But if we start actually talking to each other about our personal experiences of learning and relating to history, perhaps something new can emerge."[15]

Campt proposes three steps: (1) "shift our intention" from trying to prove the other person wrong to focusing on finding mutual connections; (2) "share personal experiences" that have formed our beliefs rather than arguing for our beliefs; and (3) listen and try "to see the issue from the standpoint of the other person." In so doing, Campt hopes that Americans may be able to "replace the fear and loathing in our hearts for each other with the curiosity and compassion that are the heart of dialogue."[16]

Campt's vision is powerful; it is also idealistic, perhaps naively so. I wonder how I could ever engage someone who belongs to a "hate group."[17] There are certain ideologies and attitudes that simply leave no room for dialogue and, instead, call for resistance. For many Black participants, I have discovered, to engage in dialogue with those who are staunchly committed to their racist beliefs is pointless if the result only elicits more trauma. "Do not answer fools" is sage advice (Prov 26:4). Perhaps a "contrite heart" (Ps 51:17) should be a requirement to sit at the table.[18] Or at least a willing heart. As a white, civil-minded, naturally conflict-averse Christian, I do need to remind myself that dialogue does not mean playing nice. Taking my cue from the Psalms, I have come to regard protest and resistance, confronting and contesting, as parts of a larger, collective dialogue that strives for justice (see chapter 1). On the other hand, I am always interested in knowing how one comes to hold racist beliefs and

---

15. David Campt, "The Road Ahead for Us Americans" (Opinion in *Atlanta Journal-Constitution*, November, 10, 2020) at https://www.ajc.com/opinion/opinion-the-road-ahead-for-us-americans/ULVMM6DWMBB7HFPL7KXV4O2HW4/.

16. Campt, "The Road Ahead for Us Americans."

17. "Hate groups" are those groups whose "beliefs or practices . . . attack or malign an entire class of people, typically for their immutable characteristics." See the searchable "hate map" devised by the Southern Poverty Law Center at https://www.splcenter.org/hate-map.

18. I recommend the steps that Nibs Stroupe outlines for "recovering racists": recognition, repentance, resistance, resilience, reparations, reconciliation, and recovery in Catherine Meeks and Nibs Stroupe, *Passionate for Justice: Ida B. Wells as Prophet for Our Time* (New York: Church Publishing, 2019), 98–133.

biases, to know what is it in their experience that brought them to the point of blinding themselves to the dignity of others, of looking at others only with suspicion and loathing. Such curiosity about others is, I confess, more than simple curiosity; it is a necessity for my own self-examination.

I am reminded of what Andrew Sung Park says about the categorical difference between *seeing* and *watching*. "Seeing implies a warm intention, yielding constructive transformation," whereas "watching involves a biased look, engendering harmful consequences."[19] Whereas seeing allows for sensing the wonder of the other, watching smacks of suspicion and prejudice. "Seeing stands for visual dialogue and understanding, arousing sympathy; watching [stands] for a visual monologue, yielding an unpleasant staring, cold look."[20] Put another way, to behold another in wonder, as made in God's image, made "slightly less than divinity," is to be beholden to the other. By contrast, "watching" alienates and kills, as the history of racism in America attests time and again.[21] Park goes on to say, "[The] courage to have constructive images of others constitutes the strength of seeing."[22] Such courage resists fear and hatred. It is the courage to enter into dialogue.

> Then victory won't lie in the blade,
> but in all the bridges we've made.
>
> —Amanda Gorman[23]

19. Andrew Sung Park, "A Theology of Transmutation," in *A Dream Unfinished: Theological Reflections on America from the Margins,* ed. Eleazar S. Fernandez (Maryknoll, NY: Orbis, 2001), 158.

20. Park, "A Theology of Transmutation," 158.

21. As, for example, in the shooting of Trayvon Martin, a seventeen-year-old unarmed African American high school student in Sanford, Florida (2/12/2012), and the slaying of Ahmaud Arbery, an unarmed African American jogging in the Brunswick area of Georgia (2/23/2020). Both were "watched" and stalked before being killed.

22. Park, "A Theology of Transmutation," 159.

23. Amanda Gorman, "The Hill We Climb," poem given at the US presidential inauguration (January 20, 2021) at https://www.cnn.com/videos/style/2021/01/20/amanda-gorman-youth-poet-laureate-full-poem-biden-capitol-inauguration-vpx.cnn/video/playlists/cnn-style/.

BIBLIOGRAPHY

Adams, Samuel L. *Wisdom in Transition: Act and Consequence in Second Temple Instructions*. SJSJ 125. Boston, MA: Brill, 2008.

Adichie, Chimamanda Ngozi. "The Danger of a Single Story." *Ted Talk* (October 7, 2009) at https://www.youtube.com/watch?v=D9Ihs241zeg&t=47s.

Ahn, John J. "Psalm 137: Complex Communal Laments." *JBL* 127, no. 2 (2008): 267–89.

Albertz, Rainer. *Israel in Exile: The History and Literature of the Sixth Century B.C.E.* Translated by David Green. Studies in Biblical Literature 3. Atlanta, GA: SBL Press, 2003.

Allen, Danielle S. *Talking to Strangers: Anxieties of Citizenship since Brown v. Board of Education*. Chicago, IL: The University of Chicago Press, 2004.

Allender, Dan B., and Tremper Longman III. *The Cry of the Soul: How Our Emotions Reveal Our Deepest Questions about God.* Colorado Springs, CO: NavPress, 2015.

Alt, Albrecht. "The God of the Fathers." In *Essays on Old Testament History and Religion*, by Albrecht Alt. Translated by R. A. Wilson. Oxford: Blackwell, 1966 [1929], 3–77.

Ariarajah, S. Wesley. "Creation of a 'Culture of Dialogue' in a Multicultural and Pluralist Society." In *Communication and Reconciliation: Challenges Facing the 21st Century*, edited by Philip Lee, 1–9. Geneva: WCC Publications, 2001.

Bakhtin, Mikhail M. *Problems of Dostoevsky's Poetics*. Edited and translated by Caryl Emerson. Theory and History of Literature 8. Minneapolis, MN: University of Minnesota Press, 1984.

Balentine, Samuel E. *Prayer in the Hebrew Bible: The Drama of Divine-Human Dialogue.* OBT. Minneapolis, MN: Augsburg Fortress, 1993.

Boase, Elizabeth, and Christopher G. Frechette, ed. *The Bible through the Lens of Trauma*. Semeia Studies 86. Atlanta, GA: SBL Press, 2016.

Bohm, David. *On Dialogue*. London: Routledge Classics, 2004.

Bolyki, János. *Jesu Tischgemeinschaften*. WUNT 96. Tübingen: Mohr Siebeck, 1998.

Borgman, Paul. *David, Saul, and God: Rediscovering an Ancient Story*. New York: Oxford University Press, 2008.

Braude, William G. *The Midrash on Psalms*. Vol. 1. Yale Judaica Series 13. New Haven, CT: Yale University Press, 1952.

Brettler, Marc Zvi. "Biblical Authority: A Jewish Pluralistic View." In *Engaging Biblical Authority: Perspectives on the Bible as Scripture*, edited by William P. Brown, 1–9. Louisville, KY: Westminster John Knox, 2007.

Brown, William P. *A Handbook to Old Testament Exegesis*. Louisville, KY: Westminster John Knox, 2017.

———. "Happiness and Its Discontents in the Psalms." In *The Bible and the Pursuit of Happiness: What the Old and New Testaments Teach Us about the Good Life*, edited by Brent A. Strawn, 95–115. New York: Oxford University Press, 2012.

———. "Introduction." In *Engaging Biblical Authority: Perspectives on the Bible as Scripture*, edited by William P. Brown, ix–xvi. Louisville, KY: Westminster John Knox, 2007.

———. "Job and the 'Comforting Chaos.'" In *Seeking Wisdom's Depths and Torah's Heights: Essays in Honor of Samuel E. Balentine*, edited by Barry R. Huff and Patricia Vesely, 247–66. Macon, GA: Smyth & Helwys, 2020.

———. "The Law and the Sages: A Reexamination of *Tôrâ* in the Book of Proverbs." In *Constituting the Community: Studies on the Polity of Ancient Israel in Honor of S. Dean McBride Jr*, edited by John T. Strong and Steven S. Tuell, 251–80. Winona Lake, IN: Eisenbrauns, 2005.

———. "The Pedagogy of Proverbs 10:1–31:9." In *Character and Scripture: Moral Formation, Community, and Biblical Interpretation*, edited by William P. Brown, 150–82. Grand Rapids, MI: Eerdmans, 2002.

———. *Psalms*. IBT. Nashville, TN: Abingdon, 2010.

———. "Psalms." In *The Wiley Blackwell Companion to Wisdom Literature*, edited by Samuel L. Adams and Matthew Goff, 67–86. Hoboken, NJ: John Wiley & Sons, 2020.

———. "Reading Psalms Sapientially in the Writings." In *The Oxford Handbook of The Writings of the Hebrew Bible*, edited by Donn F. Morgan, 151–68. Oxford: Oxford University Press, 2019.

———. "Rebuke, Complaint, Lament, and Praise: Reading Proverbs and Psalms Together." In *Reading Proverbs Intertextually*, edited by Katharine J. Dell and Will Kynes, 65–76. LHB/OTS 629. London: T & T Clark, 2019.

———. *Seeing the Psalms: A Theology of Metaphor*. Louisville, KY: Westminster John Knox, 2002.

———. *The Seven Pillars of Creation: The Bible, Science, and the Ecology of Wonder*. New York: Oxford University Press, 2010.

———. "Virtue and Its Limits in the Wisdom Corpus: Character Formation, Disruption, and Transformation." In *The Oxford Handbook of Wisdom and the Bible*, edited by Will Kynes, 45–64. New York: Oxford University Press, 2020.

———. *Wisdom's Wonder: Character, Creation, and Crisis in the Bible's Wisdom Literature*. Grand Rapids, MI: Eerdmans, 2014.

Brueggemann, Walter. "The Costly Loss of Lament." In Walter Brueggemann, *The Psalms and the Life of Faith*, edited by Patrick D. Miller, 98–111. Minneapolis, MN: Augsburg Fortress, 1995.

———. *The Creative Word: Canon as Model for Biblical Education*. 2nd ed. Minneapolis, MN: Fortress, 2015.

———. "From Hurt to Joy, from Death to Life." In Walter Brueggemann, *The Psalms and the Life of Faith*, edited by Patrick D. Miller, 67–83. Minneapolis, MN: Fortress, 1995.

———. "Of the Same Flesh and Bone [Gen 2,23a]." *CBQ* 32 (1970): 532–42.

———. "The Psalms: Tenacious Solidarity." In Walter Brueggemann, *Tenacious Solidarity: Biblical Provocations on Race, Religion, Climate, and the Economy*, edited and introduced by Davis Hankins, 353–75. Minneapolis, MN: Fortress, 2018.

———. *Theology of the Old Testament: Testimony, Dispute, Advocacy*. Minneapolis, MN: Fortress, 2005.

———. "Twin Themes for Ecumenical Singing: The Psalms." *Journal for Preachers* 43, no. 4 (2020): 3–10.

Campt, David. "The Road Ahead for Us Americans." Opinion, *Atlanta Journal-Constitution* (November 10, 2020). At https://www.ajc.com/opinion/opinion-the-road-ahead-for-us-americans/ULVMM6DWMBB7HFPL7KXV4O2HW4/.

Carey, Greg. "Originalism in Bible and Law." *Church Anew* (October 15, 2020). At https://churchanew.org/blog/posts/greg-carey-originalism-in-bible-and-in-law.

Carr, David M. *Holy Resilience: The Bible's Traumatic Origins*. New Haven, CT: Yale University Press, 2014.

Case, Anne, and Angus Deaton. "Rising Morbidity and Mortality in Midlife among White Non-Hispanic Americans in the 21st Century." *Proceedings of the National Academy of Sciences* 112, no. 49 (December 8, 2015): 15078–83.

Chatham, James O. *Psalm Conversations: Listening In as They Talk with One Another*. Collegeville, MN: Liturgical Press, 2018.

Cheung, Simon Chi-chung. *Wisdom Intoned: A Reappraisal of the Genre "Wisdom Psalms."* LHB/OTS 613. London: Bloomsbury T&T Clark, 2015.

Childs, Brevard S. *Introduction to the Old Testament as Scripture*. Philadelphia, PA: Fortress, 1979.

Chua, Amy. *Political Tribes: Group Instinct and the Fate of Nations*. New York: Penguin, 2018.

Clarke, Clifton R. "Shalom Justice." *Fuller Magazine* 9 (2017): 60–65.

Cohn, D'Vera. "It's Official: Minority Babies Are the Majority among the Nation's Infants, but Only Just." *Pew Research Center* (June 23, 2016). At https://www.pewresearch.org/fact-tank/2016/06/23/its-official-minority-babies-are-the-majority-among-the-nations-infants-but-only-just/.

Cone, James. "Whose Earth Is It Anyway?" *Cross Currents* 50 (Spring/Summer 2000): 36–46.

Cooper, Alan. "Creation, Philosophy and Spirituality: Aspects of Jewish Interpretation of Psalm 19." In *Pursuing the Text: Studies in Honor of Ben Zion Wacholder on the Occasion of His Seventieth Birthday*, edited by John Reeves and John Kampen, 15–33. JSOTSup 184. Sheffield, UK: Sheffield Academic Press, 1994.

Creach, Jerome F. D. *The Destiny of the Righteous in the Psalms*. St. Louis, MO: Chalice Press, 2008.

———. *Discovering the Psalms: Content, Interpretation, Reception*. Grand Rapids, MI: SPCK/Eerdmans, 2020.

———. "Like a Tree Planted by the Temple Stream: The Portrait of the Righteous in Psalm 1:3." *CBQ* 61, no. 1 (1999): 34–46.

———. "The Mortality of the King in Psalm 89." In *Constituting the Community: Studies on the Polity of Ancient Israel in Honor of S. Dean McBride*, edited by John T. Strong and Steven S. Tuell, 237–50. Winona Lake, IN: Eisenbrauns, 2005.

Crenshaw, James L. "Clanging Symbols." In James L. Crenshaw, *Urgent Advice and Probing Questions: Collected Writings on Old Testament Wisdom*. Macon, GA: Mercer University Press, 1995, 371–82.

Crossan, John Dominic. *The Birth of Christianity: Discovering What Happened in the Years Immediately after the Execution of Jesus*. San Francisco, CA: HarperSanFrancisco, 1998.

Dalley, Stephanie. *Myths from Mesopotamia: Creation, the Flood, Gilgamesh and Others*. World's Classics. Oxford: Oxford University Press, 1991.

Davis, James Calvin. *In Defense of Civility: How Religion Can Unite America on Seven Moral Issues That Divide Us*. Louisville, KY: Westminster John Knox, 2010.

———. *Forbearance: A Theological Ethic for a Disagreeable Church*. Grand Rapids, MI: Eerdmans, 2017.

Dedyo, Morgan Day. In NextGen Voices. "Defining Events: 2020 in Hindsight." *Science* 371, no. 6524 (January 1, 2020): 22–24.

Dell, Katharine J. "'I Will Solve My Riddle to the Music of the Lyre' (Psalm XLIX 4[5]): A Cultic Setting for Wisdom Psalms?" *VT* 54, no. 4 (2004): 445–58.

Dever, William G. *Did God Have a Wife? Archaeology and Folk Religion in Ancient Israel*. Grand Rapids, MI: Eerdmans, 2005.

Dvorjetski, Esteē. "From Ugarit to Madaba: Philological and Historical Functions of the *marzēaḥ*." *Journal of Semitic Studies* 61, no. 1 (2016): 17–39.

Ellison, Gregory C., II. *Fearless Dialogues: A New Movement for Justice*. Louisville, KY: Westminster John Knox, 2017.

Emanuel, David. "The Elevation of God in Psalm 105." In *Inner Biblical Allusion in the Poetry of Wisdom and Psalms*, edited by Mark J. Boda, Kevin Chau, and Beth LaNeel Tanner, 49–64. LHB/OTS 659. London: T & T Clark, 2019.

Enns, Peter. "'God Is Truth': The First Summary Statement of CSBI, Part 2." In *The Biologos Forum: Science and Faith in Dialogue* (June 21, 2011): 5–7. Accessed at http://wp.production.patheos.com/blogs/peterenns/files/2014/08/Science-Faith-and-the-Chicago-Statement-on-Biblical-Inerrancy-Enns-Edited-no-watermark.pdf.

Fackenheim, Emil L. *God's Presence in History: Jewish Affirmations and Philosophical Reflections*. New York: Harper & Row, 1972.

Finsterbusch, Karin. "Yahweh's Torah and the Praying 'I' in Psalm 119." In *Wisdom and Torah: The Reception of 'Torah' in the Wisdom Literature of the Second Temple Period*, edited by Bernd U. Schipper and D. Andrew Teeter, 119–36. SJSJ 163. Boston, MA: Brill, 2013.

Fletcher, Jeannine Hill. *The Sin of White Supremacy: Christianity, Racism, and Religious Diversity in America*. Maryknoll, NY: Orbis, 2017.

Fontaine, Carol R. *Traditional Sayings in the Old Testament*. BLS 5. Sheffield, UK: Almond, 1982.

Fox, Michael V. *Proverbs 1–9*. AB 18A. Garden City, NY: Doubleday, 2000.

———. *Proverbs 10–31*. AYB 18B. New Haven, CT: Yale University Press, 2009.

Freedman, David Noel. *Psalm 119: The Exaltation of Torah*. Biblical and Judaic Studies 6. Winona Lake, IN: Eisenbrauns, 1999.

Frei, Hans W. *The Eclipse of Biblical Narrative: A Study of Eighteenth and Nineteenth Century Hermeneutics*. New Haven, CT: Yale University Press, 1974.

Freire, Paulo. *The Pedagogy of the Oppressed, Fiftieth Anniversary Edition*. New York: Bloomsbury Academic, 2018.

Fretheim, Terence E. "Nature's Praise of God in the Psalms." *Ex Auditu* 3 (1987): 16–30.

Gafney, Wilda C. *Womanist Midrash: A Reintroduction to the Women of the Torah and the Throne*. Louisville, KY: Westminster John Knox, 2017.

Gillingham, Susan E. *The Journey of Two Psalms: The Reception of Psalms 1 and 2 in Jewish and Christian Tradition*. Oxford: Oxford University Press, 2013.

Gottwald, Norman K. *The Hebrew Bible: A Socio-literary Introduction*. Philadelphia, PA: Fortress, 1985.

Green, Barbara. *How Are the Mighty Fallen? A Dialogical Study of King Saul in 1 Samuel*. JSOTSup 365. London: Sheffield Academic Press, 2003.

———. *Mikhail Bakhtin and Biblical Scholarship: An Introduction*. Semeia Studies 38. Atlanta, GA: SBL Press, 2000.

Guillaume, Alfred. "The Meaning of *twll* in Psalm 137:3." *JBL* 75, no. 2 (1956): 143–44.

Gurganus, Allan. "At Last, the South Loses Well." Opinion, *New York Times* (December 8, 1996). At https://www.nytimes.com/1996/12/08/opinion/at-last-the-south-loses-well.html.

Hanson, Raymon Paul. "A Socio-rhetorical Examination of Twin Psalm 111–112." PhD diss., Luther Seminary, 2013.

Hare, Brian, and Vanessa Woods. *Survival of the Friendliest: Understanding Our Origins and Rediscovering Our Common Humanity*. New York: Random House, 2020.

Hatton, Peter T. H. *Contradiction in the Book of Proverbs: The Deep Waters of Counsel*. Aldershot, UK: Ashgate, 2008.

Herstein, Gary. "The Roycean Roots of the Beloved Community." *The Pluralist* 4, no. 2 (2009): 91–107.

Hiebert, Theodore. *The Beginning of Difference: Discovering Identity in God's Diverse World*. Nashville, TN: Abingdon Press, 2019.

———. *The Yahwist's Landscape: Nature and Religion in Early Israel*. New York: Oxford University Press, 1996.

Hundley, Michael B. "Sacred Spaces, Objects, Offerings, and People in the Priestly Texts: A Reappraisal." *JBL* 132, no. 4 (2013): 749–67.

Jacobson, Rolf A. "Christian Theology of the Psalms." In *The Oxford Handbook of the Psalms*, edited by William P. Brown, 499–514. New York: Oxford University Press, 2014.

Janowski, Bernd. *Arguing with God: A Theological Anthropology of the Psalms*. Louisville, KY: Westminster John Knox, 2013.

Janzen, Gerald J. "Another Look at Psalm XII 6." *VT* 54, no. 2 (2004): 157–64.

Japhet, Sara. *I and II Chronicles: A Commentary*. OTL. Louisville, KY: Westminster John Knox, 1993.

Jennings, Willie James. "Can White People Be Saved?" in *Can "White" People Be Saved?: Triangulating Race, Theology, and Mission*, edited by Love L. Sechrest, Johnny Ramírez-Johnson, Amos Yong, 27–43. Missiological Engagements 12. Downers Grove, IL: IVP Academic, 2018.

Jenson, Philip P. *Graded Holiness: A Key to the Priestly Conception of the World*. JSOTSup 106. Sheffield, UK: JSOT Press, 1992.

Joerstad, Mari. *The Hebrew Bible and Environmental Ethics: Humans, Nonhumans, and the Living Landscape*. Cambridge: Cambridge University Press, 2019.

Johnson, Vivian L. *David in Distress: His Portrait through the Historical Psalms*. LHB/OTS 505. New York: T&T Clark, 2009.

Johnston, Philip S. *Shades of Sheol: Death and Afterlife in the Old Testament*. Downers Grove, IL: IVP Academic, 2002.

Jones, Scott C. "Psalm 1 and the Hermeneutics of Torah." *Biblica* 97, no. 4 (2016): 537–51.

———. "Who Can Narrate El's Wonders? The Reception of Psalm 19 in Ben Sira and the Qumran Hodayot." In *Fromme und Frevler: Studien zu Psalmen und Weisheit. Festschrift für Hermann Spieckermann zum 70. Geburtstag*, edited by Corinna Körting and Reinhard Gregor Kratz, 31–40. Tübingen: Mohr Siebeck, 2020.

Khan-Cullors, Patrisse, and Asha Bandele. *When They Call You a Terrorist: A Black Lives Matter Memoir*. New York: St. Martin's Press, 2018.

Klein, Anja. "Half Way between Psalm 119 and Ben Sira: Wisdom and Torah in Psalm 19." In *Wisdom and Torah: The Reception of 'Torah' in the Wisdom Literature of the Second Temple Period*, edited by Bernd U. Schipper and D. Andrew Teeter, 137–56. SJSJ 163. Boston, MA: Brill, 2013.

Klein, Ezra. "White Threat in a Browning America: How Demographic Change Is Fracturing Our Politics." *Vox* (July 30, 2018). At https://www.vox.com/policy-and-politics/2018/7/30/17505406/trump-obama-race-politics-immigration.

———. *Why We're Polarized*. New York: Avid Reader Press, 2020.

Kuntz, J. Kenneth. "Reclaiming Biblical Wisdom Psalms: A Response to Crenshaw." *Currents in Biblical Research* 1, no. 2 (2003): 145–54.

Kynes, Will. *My Psalm Has Turned into Weeping: Job's Dialogue with the Psalms*. BZAW 473. Berlin: de Gruyter, 2012.

———. *An Obituary for "Wisdom Literature": The Birth, Death, and Intertextual Reintegration of a Biblical Corpus*. New York: Oxford University Press, 2019.

LeFebvre, Michael. *Collections, Codes, and Torah: The Re-characterization of Israel's Written Law.* LHB/OTS 451. New York: T&T Clark, 2016.

———. "'On His Law He Meditates': What Is Psalm 1 Introducing?" *JSOT* 40, no. 4 (2016): 439–50.

Levenson, Jon D. *Creation and the Persistence of Evil: The Jewish Drama of Divine Omnipotence.* San Francisco, CA: Harper & Row, 1988.

———. "The Sources of Torah: Psalm 19 and the Modes of Revelation." In *Ancient Israelite Religion*, edited by Patrick D. Miller, Paul D. Hanson, and S. Dean McBride, 559–74. Minneapolis, MN: Fortress, 1987.

Levine, Herbert J. *Sing unto God a New Song: A Contemporary Reading of the Psalms.* Bloomington, IN: Indiana University Press, 1995.

Levinson, Bernard M. *Deuteronomy and the Hermeneutics of Legal Innovation*. New York: Oxford University Press, 1997.

Long, V. Philips. *The Reign and Rejection of King Saul: A Case for Literary and Theological Coherence*. SBLDS 118. Atlanta: Scholars Press, 1989.

Longman, Tremper, III. *The Bible and the Ballot: Using Scripture in Political Decisions.* Grand Rapids, MI: Eerdmans, 2020.

———. "Psalm 98: A Divine Warrior Victory Song." *JETS* 27 (1984): 267–74.

Lustgarten, Abraham. "The Great Climate Migration: Climate Change Will Force a New American Migration." *ProPublica* (September 15, 2020). At https://www.propublica.org/article/climate-change-will-force-a-new-american-migration.

Luther, Martin. "Preface to the Psalter" (1545 [1528]). In *Luther's Works Volume 35: Word and Sacrament*, edited by E. Theodore Bachmann, 253–55. Philadelphia, PA: Muhlenberg, 1960.

Machinist, Peter. "How Gods Die, Biblically and Otherwise: A Problem of Cosmic Restructuring." In *Reconsidering the Concept of Revolutionary Monotheism*, edited by Beate Pongratz-Leisten, 189–240. Winona Lake, IN: Eisenbrauns, 2011.

Mandolfo, Carleen. *God in the Dock: Dialogic Tension in the Psalms of Lament*. JSOT 357. London: Sheffield Academic Press, 2002.

———. "Language of Lament in the Psalms." In *The Oxford Handbook of the Psalms*, edited by William P. Brown, 114–30. New York: Oxford University Press, 2014.

Mays, James Luther. "The David of the Psalms." *Int* 40, no. 2 (1986): 143–55.

———. *The Lord Reigns: A Theological Handbook to the Psalms*. Louisville, KY: Westminster John Knox, 1990.

———. "The Place of the Torah-Psalms in the Psalter." *JBL* 106, no. 1 (1987): 3–12.

———. *Psalms*. IBC. Louisville, KY: Westminster John Knox, 1994.

McBride, S. Dean, Jr. "Divine Protocol: Genesis 1:1–2:3 as Prologue to the Pentateuch." In *God Who Creates: Essays in Honor of W. Sibley Towner*, edited by William P. Brown and S. Dean McBride Jr., 3–41. Grand Rapids, MI: Eerdmans, 2000.

———. "Polity of the Covenant People: The Book of Deuteronomy." *Interpretation* 41 (1987): 229–44. Reprinted in *Constituting the Community: Studies on the Polity of Ancient Israel in Honor of S. Dean McBride Jr.*, edited by John T. Strong and Steven S. Tuell, 17–33. Winona Lake, IN: Eisenbrauns, 2005.

McCann, J. Clinton, Jr. "The Single Most Important Text in the Entire Bible: Toward a Theology of the Psalms." In *Soundings in the Theology of the Psalms: Perspectives and Methods in Contemporary Scholarship*, edited by Rolf A. Jacobson, 63–75. Minneapolis, MN: Fortress, 2011.

———. "'The Way of the Righteous' in the Psalms: Character Formation and Cultural Crisis." In *Character and Scripture*, edited by William P. Brown, 135–49. Grand Rapids, MI: Eerdmans, 2002.

McKenzie, Steven L. *King David: A Biography*. New York: Oxford University Press, 2000.

Meeks, Catherine, and Nibs Stroupe. *Passionate for Justice: Ida B. Wells as Prophet for Our Time*. New York: Church Publishing, 2019.

Middleton, J. Richard. *The Liberating Image: The* Imago Dei *in Genesis 1*. Grand Rapids, MI: Brazos, 2005.

Milgrom, Jacob. *The JPS Torah Commentary: Numbers*. JPS Torah Commentary. Philadelphia, PA: Jewish Publication Society, 1990.

Millar, Suzanna R. *Genre and Openness in Proverbs 10:1–22:16*. Ancient Israel and Its Literature 39. Atlanta, GA: SBL Press, 2020.

Miller, Patrick D. "Constitution or Instruction? The Purpose of Deuteronomy." In *Constituting the Community: Studies on the Polity of Ancient Israel in Honor of*

S. Dean McBride Jr., edited by John T. Strong and Steven S. Tuell, 125–41. Winona Lake, IN: Eisenbrauns, 2005.

———. "Deuteronomy and the Psalms: Evoking a Biblical Conversation." *JBL* 118, no. 1 (1999): 3–18.

———. "Syntax and Theology of Genesis 12:3a." *VT* 34, no. 4 (1984): 472–76.

———. *They Cried to the Lord: The Form and Theology of Biblical Prayer.* Minneapolis, MN: Fortress, 1994.

———. "The Wilderness Journey in Deuteronomy: Style, Structure, and Theology in Deuteronomy 1–3." In *To Hear and Obey: Essays in Honor of Frederick Carlson Holmgren*, edited by Bradley J. Bergfalk and Paul E. Koptak, 50–68. Chicago: Covenant Publications, 1997. Reprinted in Patrick D. Miller, *Israelite Religion and Biblical Theology: Collected Essays*, 572–92. JSOTSup 267. Sheffield, UK: Sheffield Academic Press, 2000.

———. "*Yāpîaḥ* in Psalm XII, 6." *VT* 28, no. 4 (1978): 495–500.

Moberly, R. W. L. *The Old Testament of the Old Testament: Patriarchal Narratives and Mosaic Yahwism.* OBT. Minneapolis, MN: Augsburg Fortress, 1992.

Nadella, Raj. *Dialogue Not Dogma: Many Voices in the Gospel of Luke.* LNTS 413. New York: Bloomsbury T&T Clark, 2011.

Newsom, Carol A. *The Book of Job: A Contest of Moral Imaginations.* New York: Oxford University Press, 2003.

Newsom, Carol A., with Brennan W. Breed. *Daniel: A Commentary.* OTL. Louisville, KY: Westminster John Knox, 2014.

O'Connor, Kathleen M. *Jeremiah: Pain and Promise.* Minneapolis, MN: Fortress, 2011.

———. *Lamentations and the Tears of the World.* Maryknoll, NY: Orbis, 2002.

———. "Let All the Peoples Praise You: Biblical Studies and a Hermeneutics of Hunger." *CBQ* 72, no. 1 (2010): 1–14.

Olson, Dennis T. *Deuteronomy and the Death of Moses: A Theological Reading.* OBT. Minneapolis, MN: Fortress, 1994.

———. *Numbers: A Bible Commentary for Teaching and Preaching.* IBC. Louisville, KY: Westminster John Knox, 1996.

Pardee, Dennis. "*ypḥ* 'Witness' in Hebrew and Ugaritic." *VT 28* (1978): 204–13.

Park, Andrew Sung. "A Theology of Transmutation." In *A Dream Unfinished: Theological Reflections on America from the Margins*, edited by Eleazar S. Fernandez, 152–66. Maryknoll, NY: Orbis, 2001.

Parker, Kelly A. "Josiah Royce." In *The Stanford Encyclopedia of Philosophy* (Spring 2020 edition), edited by Edward N. Zalta. At https://plato.stanford.edu/archives/spr2020/entries/royce/.

Perdue, Leo G. *Wisdom and Cult: A Critical Analysis of the Views of Cult in the Wisdom Literature of Israel and the Ancient Near East.* SBLDS 30. Missoula, MT: Scholars Press, 1977.

Petersen, David. "Genesis and Family Values." *JBL* 124, no.1 (2005): 5–23.

Piff, Paul et al. "Awe, the Small Self, and Prosocial Behavior." *Journal of Personality and Social Psychology* 108, no. 6 (2015): 883–99.

Ponti, Crystal. "America's History of Slavery Began Long before Jamestown." *History* (August 26, 2019). At https://www.history.com/news/american-slavery-before-jamestown-1619.

Reed, Walter L. *Dialogues of the Word: The Bible as Literature according to Bakhtin.* New York: Oxford University Press, 1993.

Reynolds, Kent A. *Torah as Teacher: The Exemplary Torah Student in Psalm 119.* VTSup 137. Boston, MA: Brill, 2010.

Rochberg, Francesca. *The Heavenly Writing: Divination, Horoscopy, and Astronomy in Mesopotamian Culture.* Cambridge: Cambridge University Press, 2004.

Sadler, Rodney M. "Singing a Subversive Song: Psalm 137 and 'Colored Pompey.'" In *The Oxford Handbook of the Psalms,* edited by William P. Brown, 447–58. New York: Oxford University Press, 2014.

Sanders, Seth L. "What If There Aren't Any Empirical Models for Pentateuchal Criticism?" In *Contextualizing Israel's Sacred Writings: Ancient Literacy, Orality, and Literary Production,* edited by Brian B. Schmidt, 281–304. Ancient Israel and Its Literature 22. Atlanta, GA: SBL Press, 2015.

Sanders, Symone D. *No, You Shut Up: Speaking Truth to Power and Reclaiming America.* New York: HarperCollins, 2020.

Savran, George W. "Contrasting Voices in Psalm 95." *RB* 110, no. 1 (2003): 17–32.

Schipper, Bernd U. *Proverbs 1–15: A Commentary.* Hermeneia. Minneapolis, MN: Fortress, 2019.

Schirch, Lisa, and David Campt. *The Little Book of Dialogue for Difficult Subjects: A Practical, Hands-On Guide.* The Little Books of Justice & Peacebuilding. New York: Good Books, 2007.

Scholz, Suzanne. *Sacred Witness: Rape in the Hebrew Bible.* Minneapolis, MN: Fortress, 2010.

Schüle, Andreas. "Made in the 'Image of God': The Concepts of Divine Images in Gen 1–3." *ZAW* 117, no. 1 (2005): 1–20.

Smith, J. M. P. "The Character of King David." *JBL* 52, no. 1 (1933): 1–11.

Smith, Mark S. *The Early History of God: Yahweh and Other Deities in Ancient Israel.* 2nd ed. Grand Rapids, MI: Eerdmans, 2002.

———. "Psalm 8:2b-3: New Proposals for Old Problems." *CBQ* 59, no. 4 (1997): 637–41.

Smith, Warren Cole. "We're All 'Moviegoers' Now: Fifty Years Ago Walker Percy's *The Moviegoer* Launched an Unlikely Literary Career." *World Magazine* (July 14, 2012). At https://world.wng.org/2012/06/were_all_moviegoers_now.

Smith-Christopher, Daniel L. *A Biblical Theology of Exile.* OBT. Minneapolis, MN: Fortress, 2002.

Sommer, Benjamin D. "Nature, Revelation, and Grace in Psalm 19: Towards a Theological Reading of Scripture." *HTR* 108, no. 3 (2015): 376–401.

Spieckermann, Hermann. "What Is the Place of Wisdom and Torah in the Psalter?" In *"When the Morning Stars Sang": Essays in Honor of Choong Leong Seow on the Occasion of His Sixty-Fifth Birthday*, edited by Scott C. Jones and Christine Roy Yoder, 287–316. BZAW 500. Boston, MA: De Gruyter, 2018.

Steussy, Marti J. *David: Biblical Portraits of Power.* Studies on Personalities of the Old Testament. Columbia, SC: University of South Carolina Press, 1999.

Stewart, Anne W. *Poetic Ethics in Proverbs: Wisdom Literature and the Shaping of the Moral Self.* Cambridge: Cambridge University Press, 2016.

Strawn, Brent A. "The Poetics of Psalm 82: Three Critical Notes Along with a Plea for the Poetic." *RB* 121, no. 1 (2014): 21–46.

Tanner, Beth LaNeel. *The Book of Psalms through the Lens of Intertextuality.* Studies in Biblical Literature 26. New York: Peter Lang, 2001.

Walton, John H. *The Lost World of Genesis One: Ancient Cosmology and the Origins Debate.* Downers Grove, IL: InterVarsity, 2009.

Wazwaz, Noor. "It's Official: The U.S. Is Becoming a Minority-Majority Nation." *US News and World Report* (July 6, 2015). At http://www.usnews.com/news/articles/2015/07/06/its-official-the-us-is-becoming-a-minority-majority-nation.

Weber, Beat. "Moses, David and the Psalms: The Psalter in the Horizon of the 'Canonical' Books." *Rivista Biblica* 68, no. 2 (2020): 187–212.

White, Lynn T., Jr. "The Historical Roots of Our Ecological Crisis." *Science* 144 (March 10, 1967): 1203–7.

Willgren, David. *Like a Garden of Flowers: A Study of the Formation of the "Book" of Psalms.* Lund, Sweden: Lund University, 2016.

Wilkerson, Isabel. *Caste: The Origins of Our Discontents*. New York: Random House, 2020.

Wilson, Edward O. *Consilience: The Unity of Knowledge*. New York: Vintage Books, 1999.

Wilson, Gerald H. *The Editing of the Hebrew Psalter*. SBLDS 76. Chico, CA: Scholars Press, 1985.

Wolff, Hans Walter. *Anthropology of the Old Testament*, trans. Margaret Kohl. Philadelphia, PA: Fortress, 1974.

Wright, David P. *Inventing God's Law: How the Covenant Code of the Bible Used and Revised the Laws of Hammurabi*. Oxford: Oxford University Press, 2009.

Yoder, Christine Roy. "Forming 'Fearers of Yahweh': Repetition and Contradiction as Pedagogy in Proverbs." In *Seeking Out the Wisdom of the Ancients: Essays Offered to Honor Michael V. Fox on the Occasion of His Sixty-fifth Birthday*, edited by Ronald L. Troxel, Kelvin G. Friebel, and Dennis R. Magary, 167–83. Winona Lake, IN: Eisenbrauns, 2005.

———. "On the Threshold of Kingship: A Study of Agur (Proverbs 30)." *Int* 63, no. 3 (2009): 254–63.

———. *Proverbs*. AOTC. Nashville, TN: Abingdon Press, 2009.

———. "The Shaping of Erotic Desire in Proverbs 1–9." In *Saving Desire: The Seduction of Christian Theology*, edited by J. Henriksen and L. Shults, 148–62. Grand Rapids, MI: Eerdmans, 2011.

———. *Wisdom as a Woman of Substance: A Socioeconomic Reading of Proverbs 1–9 and 31:10-31*. BZAW 304. Berlin: de Gruyter, 2001.

Zimmerli, Walther. "Zwillingspsalmen." In *Wort, Lied und Gottesspruch, Beiträge zu Psalmen und Propheten: Festschrift für Joseph Ziegler*, edited by Josef Schreiner, 105–13. Forschung zur Bibel 12. Würzburg: Echter Verlag: Katholisches Bibelwerk, 1972.

PSALMS INDEX

NAME INDEX

CPSIA information can be obtained
at www.ICGtesting.com
Printed in the USA
BVHW052113280921
617659BV00007B/147

9 781501 858956